TRADIVOX

VOLUME XVI

TRADIVOX

CATHOLIC CATECHISM INDEX

VOLUME XVI

Baltimore

Edited by
Aaron Seng

SOPHIA INSTITUTE PRESS
MANCHESTER, NEW HAMPSHIRE

This book is an original derivative work comprised of newly typeset and reformatted editions of the following Catholic catechisms, once issued with ecclesiastical approval and now found in the public domain:

Bishops of the United States. *A Catechism of Christian Doctrine*. New York: The Catholic Publication Society Co., 1885.

Kinkead, Thomas. *An Explanation of the Baltimore Catechism*. New York: Benziger Brothers, 1891.

Scripture references follow the Douay-Rheims Bible, per the imprint of John Murphy Company (Baltimore, 1899).

Cover and interior design by Perceptions Design Studio.
Unless otherwise noted, all illustrations are in the public domain.

Sophia Institute Press
Box 5284, Manchester, NH 03108
1-800-888-9344

www.SophiaInstitute.com

Sophia Institute Press® is a registered trademark of Sophia Institute.

ISBN 978-1-64413-380-4
LCCN 2023935332

First printing

Dedicated with love and deepest respect
to all the English Martyrs and Confessors.
Orate pro nobis.

CONTENTS

CONTENTS

ACKNOWLEDGMENTS

THE publication of this series is due primarily to the generosity of countless volunteers and donors from several countries. Special thanks are owed to Mr. and Mrs. Phil Seng, Mr. and Mrs. Michael Over, Mr. and Mrs. Jim McElwee, Mr. and Mrs. John Brouillette, Mr. and Mrs. Thomas Scheibelhut, Mr. and Mrs. Kyle Barriger, as well the visionary priests and faithful of St. Stanislaus Bishop and Martyr parish in South Bend, Indiana, and St. Patrick's Oratory in Green Bay, Wisconsin. May God richly reward their commitment to handing on the Catholic faith.

FOREWORD

The Catholic faith remains always the same throughout the centuries and millennia until the coming of our Lord at the end of the time, likewise "Jesus Christ is the same yesterday, today and forever" (Heb 13:8). The Catholic faith is "the faith, which was once delivered unto the saints" (Jude 1:3). The Magisterium of the Church teaches us solemnly the same truth in the following words of the First Vatican Council: "The doctrine of the faith which God has revealed, is put forward not as some philosophical discovery capable of being perfected by human intelligence, but as a divine deposit committed to the spouse of Christ to be faithfully protected and infallibly promulgated. Hence, too, that meaning of the sacred dogmas is ever to be maintained, which has once been declared by holy mother Church, and there must never be any abandonment of this sense under the pretext or in the name of a more profound understanding. May understanding, knowledge and wisdom increase as ages and centuries roll along, and greatly and vigorously flourish, in each and all, in the individual and the whole Church: but this only in its own proper kind, that is to say, in the same doctrine, the same sense, and the same understanding (cf. Vincentius Lerinensis, *Commonitorium*, 28)."[1]

An authentically Catholic catechism has the function of learning and teaching the unchanging Catholic faith throughout all generations. The Roman Pontiffs indeed, taught: "There is nothing more effective than catechetical instruction to spread the glory of God and to secure the salvation of souls."[2] Saint Pius X said, that "the great loss of souls is due to ignorance

[1] Vatican I, Dogmatic Constitution *Dei Filius de fide catholica*, Ch. 4

[2] Pope Benedict XIV, Apostolic Constitution *Etsi minime*, n. 13

of divine things."[3] Therefore, the traditional catechisms have enduring value in our own day and age, which is marked by an enormous doctrinal confusion, which reigns in the life of the Church in the past six decades, and which reaches its peak in our days.

I welcome and bless the great project of the "Tradivox" in cataloguing and preserving the hundreds of long-lost Catholic catechisms issued with episcopal approval over the last millennium. This project will convincingly show the essentially unchanging nature of the apostolic doctrine across time and space, and so I invite the faithful of the entire world to support this historic effort, as we seek to restore the perennial catechism of the Church. The project of a catechism restoration on behalf of "Tradivox" will surely be of great benefit not only to many confused and disoriented Catholic faithful, but also to all people who are sincerely seeking the ultimate and authentic truth about God and man, which one can find only in the Catholic and apostolic faith, and which is the only religion and faith willed by God and to which God calls all men.

+Athanasius Schneider, O.R.C.,
Titular Bishop of Celerina
Auxiliary Bishop of the Archdiocese of Saint Mary in Astana

[3] Cf. Pope St. Pius X, Encyclical *Acerbo nimis*, n. 27

SERIES EDITOR'S

PREFACE

SOME are surprised to find that when a given Catholic is asked to "look something up in the catechism," he may well respond: "Which one?" The history of the Catholic Church across the last millennium is in fact filled with the publication of numerous catechisms, issued in every major language on earth; and for centuries, these concise "guidebooks" to Catholic doctrine have served countless men and women seeking a clear and concise presentation of that faith forever entrusted by Jesus Christ to his one, holy, Catholic, and apostolic Church.

Taken together, the many catechisms issued with episcopal approval can offer a kind of "window" on to the universal ordinary magisterium—a glimpse of those truths which have been held and taught in the Church *everywhere, always, and by all.* For, as St. Paul reminds us, the tenets of this Faith do not change from age to age: "Jesus Christ yesterday and today and the same for ever. Be not led away with various and strange doctrines" (Heb 13:8-9).

The catechisms included in our *Tradivox Catholic Catechism Index* are selected for their orthodoxy and historical significance, in the interest of demonstrating to contemporary readers the remarkable continuity of Catholic doctrine across time and space. Long regarded as reliable summaries of Church teaching on matters of faith and morals, we are proud to reproduce these works of centuries past, composed and endorsed by countless priests, bishops, and popes devoted to "giving voice to tradition."

In This Volume

It may be defensibly maintained that, in the United States of America, no single catechism has had a more expansive impact on Catholic religious education than *A Catechism of Christian Doctrine, Prepared and Enjoined by Order of the Third Plenary Council of Baltimore*, most commonly known as "the Baltimore Catechism," or even more simply, "the Baltimore."

The work of many hands over several years, the Baltimore Catechism has shaped the religious education of American Catholics in countless schools, parishes, and mission societies across the continent, and continues to do so today. This volume of the Tradivox collection includes the two most influential iterations of that text: the original catechism itself, unaltered as it came off the press in 1885, and Fr. Thomas Kinkead's expanded version, published six years later "for the use of Sunday-school teachers and advanced classes."

The three Plenary Councils of Baltimore—held in 1852, 1866, and 1884—represented the first gatherings of the bishops in North America apart from Canada. The councils spanned a critical juncture in the history of the fledgling nation; not least of which being the bloody war for Southern independence, which ended just months before the opening of Baltimore II. In this period, the growing desire for an American catechism was generally felt, as evidenced by the remarkable efforts of Bishop John McGill of Richmond, who published his own catechism in 1865 within "the District Court of the Confederate States of America," and acknowledged:

> It is not only desirable, but even most necessary, that we should have some books of religious instruction for our people. … [Thus] I have been induced, in view of our manifest need, to write and publish this volume, notwithstanding the difficulties attending such an enterprise in our present circumstances.[1]

This need would only increase with the explosive immigration to the continent between Baltimore II and III, when the Catholic population of America more than doubled in size in less than twenty years.

[1] John McGill, *Faith, the Victory* (Richmond: J. W. Randolph, 1865), v.

The desire for a uniform catechism was met by the decrees of Baltimore III, which placed Catholic religious education among the principal issues of concern, in the face of a growing materialism in the culture and widespread opposition to Catholic schooling in public policy. In meeting these challenges, the Baltimore Catechism—especially the expanded edition by Fr. Kinkead—gives remarkable testimony to the kind of conflicted self-perception prevalent among American Catholics of the time. Intent on being an obedient citizen (largely in order to avoid the kind of continued persecution made famous by the Know-Nothing party), the American Catholic is bidden in the Baltimore Catechism to hail "the wise makers of the Constitution," and yet to regard the Roman pontiff's actions as done "with the authority of our Lord himself"—a disposition which, albeit somewhat exaggerated with regard to the doctrine of papal infallibility, must leave him ill at ease with his own national government, as Pope Pius IX's *Syllabus of Errors* (1864) had recently condemned several tenets that remain central to the American Constitution.

While the original text of the Baltimore Catechism has been reproduced in this volume with no change, we have made a few minor adjustments to Kinkead's expanded edition that warrant exact description. First, we have clarified the author's anachronistic use of "viz." and "Maji," opting for consistency. Second, we removed the author's system of asterisk marks, which referenced a different contemporary edition that would have been confusing to include in this series. Third, we have withheld the "complete index of subjects" mentioned in the author's preface, the better to accord with the full series index found in Volume XX of the Tradivox collection. Finally, we added a few simple subheadings within some of the lengthier explanations, and clarified the wording of review question 798. We can confidently say that these minimal and cautious adjustments leave the reader in possession of the two most influential early editions of the Baltimore Catechism, as well as a helpful measure of historical insight for understanding the situation of American Catholics today.

Editorial Note

Our *Catholic Catechism Index* series generally retains only the doctrinal content of those catechisms it seeks to reproduce, as well as that front matter most essential to establishing the credibility of each work as an authentic expression of the Church's common doctrine, e.g., any episcopal endorsement, *nihil obstat*, or *imprimatur*. However, it should be noted that especially prior to the eighteenth century, a number of catechisms were so immediately and universally received as reliably orthodox texts (often simply by the reputation of the author or publisher), that they received no such "official" approval; or if they did, it was often years later and in subsequent editions. We therefore include both the original printing date in our Table of Contents, and further edition information in the Preface above.

Our primary goal has been to bring these historical texts back into publication in readable English copy. Due to the wide range of time periods, cultures, and unique author styles represented in this series, we have made a number of editorial adjustments to allow for a less fatiguing read, more rapid cross-reference throughout the series, and greater research potential for the future. While not affecting the original content, these adjustments have included adopting a cleaner typesetting and simpler standard for capitalization and annotation, as well as remedying certain anachronisms in spelling or grammar.

Woodcut depicting an early method used in the production of Catholic catechisms, circa 1568.

At the same time, in deepest respect for the venerable age and subject matter of these works, we have been at pains to adhere as closely as possible to the original text: retaining archaisms such as "doth" and "hallowed," and avoiding any alterations that might affect the doctrinal content or authorial voice. We have painstakingly restored original artwork wherever possible, and where the rare explanatory note has been deemed necessary, it is not made in the text itself, but only in a marginal note. In some cases, our editorial refusal to "modernize" the content of these classical works may require a higher degree of attention from today's reader, who we trust will be richly rewarded by the effort.

We pray that our work continues to yield highly readable, faithful reproductions of these time-honored monuments to Catholic religious instruction: catechisms once penned, promulgated, and praised by bishops across the globe. May these texts that once served to guide and shape the faith and lives of millions now do so again; and may the scholars and saints once involved in their first publication now intercede for all who take them up anew. *Tolle lege!*

Sincerely in Christ,
Aaron Seng

TRADIVOX

VOLUME XVI

A CATECHISM OF CHRISTIAN DOCTRINE.

PREPARED AND ENJOINED
BY ORDER OF THE
THIRD PLENARY COUNCIL OF BALTIMORE.

Published by Ecclesiastical Authority.

NEW YORK:
THE CATHOLIC PUBLICATION SOCIETY CO.,
9 BARCLAY STREET.

A CATECHISM OF CHRISTIAN DOCTRINE.

PREPARED AND ENJOINED
BY ORDER OF THE
THIRD PLENARY COUNCIL OF BALTIMORE.

Published by Ecclesiastical Authority.

NEW YORK:
THE CATHOLIC PUBLICATION SOCIETY CO.,
9 BARCLAY STREET.

Imprimatur:
JOHN CARDINAL McCLOSKEY,
Archbishop of New York.

NEW YORK, April 6, 1885.

The catechism ordered by the Third Plenary Council of Baltimore, having been diligently compiled and examined, is hereby approved.

+ JAMES GIBBONS,
Archbishop of Baltimore,
Apostolic Delegate.

BALTIMORE, April 6, 1885.

Catechism of Christian Doctrine

PRAYERS

The Lord's Prayer

Our Father, who art in heaven, hallowed be thy name, thy kingdom come, thy will be done on earth as it is in heaven. Give us this day our daily bread, and forgive us our trespasses as we forgive those who trespass against us, and lead us not into temptation, but deliver us from evil. Amen.

The Angelical Salutation

Hail Mary, full of grace! the Lord is with thee: blessed art thou amongst women, and blessed is the fruit of thy womb, Jesus. Holy Mary, Mother of God, pray for us sinners, now and at the hour of our death. Amen.

The Apostles' Creed

I believe in God, the Father Almighty, Creator of heaven and earth; and in Jesus Christ, his only Son, our Lord, who was conceived by the Holy Ghost, born of the Virgin Mary, suffered under Pontius Pilate, was crucified, died, and was buried. He descended into hell; the third day he arose again from the dead. He ascended into heaven, and sitteth at the right hand of God, the Father Almighty; from thence he shall come to judge the living and the dead. I believe in the Holy Ghost, the holy Catholic Church, the communion of saints, the forgiveness of sins, the resurrection of the body, and the life everlasting. Amen.

The Confiteor

I confess to Almighty God, to Blessed Mary, ever Virgin, to blessed Michael the archangel, to blessed John the Baptist, to the holy apostles Peter and Paul, and to all the saints, that I have sinned exceedingly in thought, word, and deed, through my fault, through my fault, through my most grievous fault. Therefore, I beseech the Blessed Mary, ever Virgin, the blessed Michael the archangel, the blessed John the Baptist, the holy apostles Peter and Paul, and all the saints, to pray to the Lord our God for me.

May the Almighty God have mercy on me, and forgive me my sins, and bring me to everlasting life. Amen.

May the Almighty and merciful Lord grant me pardon, absolution, and remission of all my sins. Amen.

An Act of Faith

O my God! I firmly believe that thou art one God in three divine Persons, the Father, the Son, and the Holy Ghost. I believe that the divine Son became man, and died for our sins, and that he will come to judge the living and the dead. I believe these and all the truths which the holy Catholic Church teaches, because thou hast revealed them, who canst neither deceive nor be deceived.

An Act of Hope

O my God! relying on thy infinite goodness and promises, I hope to obtain pardon of my sins, the help of thy grace, and life everlasting, through the merits of Jesus Christ, my Lord and Redeemer.

An Act of Love

O my God! I love thee above all things, with my whole heart and soul, because thou art all-good and worthy of all love. I love my neighbor as myself for the love of thee. I forgive all who have injured me, and ask pardon of all whom I have injured.

An Act of Contrition

O my God! I am heartily sorry for having offended thee, and I detest all my sins, because I dread the loss of heaven and the pains of bell, but most of all because they offend thee, my God, who art all-good and deserving of all my love. I firmly resolve, with the help of thy grace, to confess my sins, to do penance, and to amend my life.

The Manner in Which a Lay Person Is to Baptize in Case of Necessity

Pour common water on the head or face of the person to be baptized, and say while pouring it: "I baptize thee, in the name of the Father, and of the Son, and of the Holy Ghost."

Note.—Any person of either sex who has reached the use of reason can baptize in case of necessity.

Catechism

LESSON FIRST

On the End of Man

1. **Who made the world?**
God made the world.

2. **Who is God?**
God is the Creator of heaven and earth, and of all things.

3. **What is man?**
Man is a creature composed of body and soul, and made to the image and likeness of God.

4. **Is this likeness in the body or in the soul?**
This likeness is chiefly in the soul.

5. **How is the soul like to God?**
The soul is like God because it is a spirit that will never die, and has understanding and free will.

6. **Why did God make you?**
God made me to know him, to love him, and to serve him in this world, and to be happy with him forever in the next.

7. **Of which must we take more care, our soul or our body?**
We must take more care of our soul than of our body.

8. **Why must we take more care of our soul than of our body?**
We must take more care of our soul than of our body, because, in losing our soul, we lose God and everlasting happiness.

9. **What must we do to save our souls?**
To save our souls, we must worship God by faith, hope, and charity; that is, we must believe in him, hope in him, and love him with all our heart.

10. **How shall we know the things which we are to believe?**
We shall know the things which we are to believe from the Catholic Church, through which God speaks to us.

11. **Where shall we find the chief truths which the Catholic Church teaches?**
We shall find the chief truths which the Catholic Church teaches in the Apostles' Creed.

12. **Say the Apostles' Creed.**
I believe in God, the Father Almighty, Creator of heaven and earth; and in Jesus Christ, his only Son, our Lord, who was conceived by the Holy Ghost, born of the Virgin Mary, suffered under Pontius Pilate, was crucified, died, and was buried. He descended into hell; the third day he arose again from the dead. He ascended into heaven, and sitteth at the right hand of God, the Father Almighty; from thence he shall come to judge the living and the dead. I believe in the Holy Ghost, the holy Catholic Church, the communion of saints, the forgiveness of sins, the resurrection of the body, and the life everlasting. Amen.

LESSON SECOND

On God and His Perfections

13. **What is God?**
God is a Spirit infinitely perfect.

14. **Had God a beginning?**
God had no beginning; he always was and he always will be.

15. **Where is God?**
God is everywhere.

16. **If God is everywhere, why do we not see him?**
We do not see God, because he is a pure Spirit and cannot be seen with bodily eyes.

17. **Does God see us?**
God sees us and watches over us.

18. **Does God know all things?**
God knows all things, even our most secret thoughts, words, and actions.

19. **Can God do all things?**
God can do all things, and nothing is hard or impossible to him.

20. **Is God just, holy, and merciful?**
God is all-just, all-holy, all-merciful, as he is infinitely perfect.

LESSON THIRD

On the Unity and Trinity of God

21. **Is there but one God?**
Yes; there is but one God.

22. **Why can there be but one God?**
There can be but one God because God, being supreme and infinite, cannot have an equal.

23. **How many Persons are there in God?**
In God, there are three divine Persons, really distinct and equal in all things—the Father, the Son, and the Holy Ghost.

24. **Is the Father God?**
The Father is God and the first Person of the Blessed Trinity.

25. **Is the Son God?**
The Son is God and the second Person of the Blessed Trinity.

26. **Is the Holy Ghost God?**
The Holy Ghost is God and the third Person of the Blessed Trinity.

27. **What do you mean by "the Blessed Trinity"?**
By "the Blessed Trinity," I mean one God in three divine Persons.

28. **Are the three divine Persons equal in all things?**
The three divine Persons are equal in all things.

29. **Are the three divine Persons one and the same God?**
The three divine Persons are one and the same God, having one and the same divine nature and substance.

30. **Can we fully understand how the three divine Persons are one and the same God?**
We cannot fully understand how the three divine Persons are one and the same God, because this is a mystery.

31. **What is a mystery?**
A mystery is a truth which we cannot fully understand.

LESSON FOURTH

On Creation

32. **Who created heaven and earth, and all things?**
God created heaven and earth, and all things.

33. **How did God create heaven and earth?**
God created heaven and earth from nothing, by his Word only; that is, by a single act of his all-powerful will.

34. **Which are the chief creatures of God?**
The chief creatures of God are angels and men.

35. **What are angels?**
Angels are pure spirits without a body, created to adore and enjoy God in heaven.

36. **Were the angels created for any other purpose?**
The angels were also created to assist before the throne of God and to minister unto him; they have often been sent as messengers from God to man; and are also appointed our guardians.

37. **Were the angels, as God created them, good and happy?**
The angels, as God created them, were good and happy.

38. **Did all the angels remain good and happy?**
All the angels did not remain good and happy; many of them sinned and were cast into hell; and these are called "devils" or "bad angels."

LESSON FIFTH

On Our First Parents and The Fall

39. **Who were the first man and woman?**
The first man and woman were Adam and Eve.

40. **Were Adam and Eve innocent and holy when they came from the hand of God?**
Adam and Eve were innocent and holy when they came from the hand of God.

41. **Did God give any command to Adam and Eve?**
To try their obedience, God commanded Adam and Eve not to eat of a certain fruit which grew in the garden of paradise.

42. **Which were the chief blessings intended for Adam and Eve, had they remained faithful to God?**
The chief blessings intended for Adam and Eve, had they remained faithful to God, were a constant state of happiness in this life and everlasting glory in the next.

43. **Did Adam and Eve remain faithful to God?**
Adam and Eve did not remain faithful to God, but broke his command by eating the forbidden fruit.

44. **What befell Adam and Eve on account of their sin?**
Adam and Eve on account of their sin lost innocence and holiness, and were doomed to sickness and death.

45. **What evil befell us on account of the disobedience of our first parents?**
On account of the disobedience of our first parents, we all share in their sin and punishment, as we should have shared in their happiness if they had remained faithful.

46. **What other effects followed from the sin of our first parents?**
Our nature was corrupted by the sin of our first parents, which darkened our understanding, weakened our will, and left in us a strong inclination to evil.

47. **What is the sin called which we inherit from our first parents?**
The sin which we inherit from our first parents is called "original sin."

48. **Why is this sin called "original"?**
This sin is called "original," because it comes down to us from our first parents, and we are brought into the world with its guilt on our souls.

49. **Does this corruption of our nature remain in us after original sin is forgiven?**
This corruption of our nature and other punishments remain in us after original sin is forgiven.

50. **Was anyone ever preserved from original sin?**
The Blessed Virgin Mary, through the merits of her divine Son, was preserved free from the guilt of original sin, and this privilege is called her "immaculate conception."

LESSON SIXTH

On Sin and Its Kinds

51. **Is original sin the only kind of sin?**
Original sin is not the only kind of sin; there is another kind of sin which we commit ourselves, called "actual sin."

52. **What is actual sin?**
Actual sin is any willful thought, word, deed, or omission contrary to the law of God.

53. **How many kinds of actual sin are there?**
There are two kinds of actual sin—mortal and venial.

54. **What is mortal sin?**
Mortal sin is a grievous offense against the law of God.

55. **Why is this sin called "mortal"?**
This sin is called "mortal," because it deprives us of spiritual life, which is sanctifying grace, and brings everlasting death and damnation on the soul.

56. **How many things are necessary to make a sin mortal?**
To make a sin mortal, three things are necessary: a grievous matter, sufficient reflection, and full consent of the will.

57. **What is venial sin?**
Venial sin is a slight offense against the law of God in matters of less importance; or, in matters of great importance, it is an offense committed without sufficient reflection or full consent of the will.

58. **Which are the effects of venial sin?**
The effects of venial sin are the lessening of the love of God in our heart, the making us less worthy of his help, and the weakening of the power to resist mortal sin.

59. **Which are the chief sources of sin?**
The chief sources of sin are seven: pride, covetousness, lust, anger, gluttony, envy, and sloth; and they are commonly called "capital sins."

LESSON SEVENTH

On the Incarnation and Redemption

60. **Did God abandon man after he fell into sin?**
God did not abandon man after he fell into sin, but promised him a Redeemer, who was to satisfy for man's sin and reopen to him the gates of heaven.

61. **Who is the Redeemer?**
Our Blessed Lord and Savior Jesus Christ is the Redeemer of mankind.

62. **What do you believe of Jesus Christ?**
I believe that Jesus Christ is the Son of God, the second Person of the Blessed Trinity, true God and true man.

63. **Why is Jesus Christ true God?**
Jesus Christ is true God because he is the true and only Son of God the Father.

64. **Why is Jesus Christ true man?**
Jesus Christ is true man because he is the Son of the Blessed Virgin Mary, and has a body and soul like ours.

65. **How many natures are there in Jesus Christ?**
In Jesus Christ, there are two natures: the nature of God and the nature of man.

66. **Is Jesus Christ more than one Person?**
No, Jesus Christ is but one divine Person.

67. **Was Jesus Christ always God?**
Jesus Christ was always God, as he is the second Person of the Blessed Trinity, equal to his Father from all eternity.

68. **Was Jesus Christ always man?**
Jesus Christ was not always man, but became man at the time of his incarnation.

69. **What do you mean by "the incarnation"?**
By "the incarnation," I mean that the Son of God was made man.

70. **How was the Son of God made man?**
The Son of God was conceived and made man by the power of the Holy Ghost, in the womb of the Blessed Virgin Mary.

71. **Is the Blessed Virgin Mary truly the Mother of God?**
The Blessed Virgin Mary is truly the Mother of God, because the same divine Person who is the Son of God is also the Son of the Blessed Virgin Mary.

72. **Did the Son of God become man immediately after the sin of our first parents?**
The Son of God did not become man immediately after the sin of our first parents, but was promised to them as a Redeemer.

73. **How could they be saved who lived before the Son of God became man?**
They who lived before the Son of God became man could be saved by believing in a Redeemer to come, and by keeping the commandments.

74. **On what day was the Son of God conceived and made man?**
The Son of God was conceived and made man on Annunciation day, the day on which the angel Gabriel announced to the Blessed Virgin Mary that she was to be the Mother of God.

75. **On what day was Christ born?**
Christ was born on Christmas day, in a stable at Bethlehem, nearly nineteen hundred years ago.

76. **How long did Christ live on earth?**
Christ lived on earth about thirty-three years, and led a most holy life in poverty and suffering.

77. **Why did Christ live so long on earth?**
Christ lived so long on earth to show us the way to heaven by his teachings and example.

LESSON EIGHTH

On Our Lord's Passion, Death, Resurrection, and Ascension

78. **What did Jesus Christ suffer?**
Jesus Christ suffered a bloody sweat, a cruel scourging, was crowned with thorns, and was crucified.

79. **On what day did Christ die?**
Christ died on Good Friday.

80. **Why do you call that day "good" on which Christ died so sorrowful a death?**
We call that day "good" on which Christ died, because by his death he showed his great love for man, and purchased for him every blessing.

81. **Where did Christ die?**
Christ died on Mount Calvary.

82. **How did Christ die?**
Christ was nailed to the cross and died on it, between two thieves.

83. **Why did Christ suffer and die?**
Christ suffered and died for our sins.

84. **What lessons do we learn from the sufferings and death of Christ?**
From the sufferings and death of Christ, we learn the great evil of sin, the hatred God bears to it, and the necessity of satisfying for it.

85. **Whither did Christ's soul go after his death?**
After Christ's death, his soul descended into hell.

86. **Did Christ's soul descend into the hell of the damned?**
The hell into which Christ's soul descended was not the hell of the damned, but a place or state of rest called "limbo," where the souls of the just were waiting for him.

87. **Why did Christ descend into limbo?**
Christ descended into limbo to preach to the souls who were in prison—that is, to announce to them the joyful tidings of their redemption.

88. **Where was Christ's body while his soul was in limbo?**
While Christ's soul was in limbo, his body was in the holy sepulchre.

89. **On what day did Christ rise from the dead?**
Christ rose from the dead, glorious and immortal, on Easter Sunday, the third day after his death.

90. **How long did Christ stay on earth after his resurrection?**
Christ stayed on earth forty days after his resurrection, to show that he was truly risen from the dead, and to instruct his apostles.

91. **After Christ had remained forty days on earth, whither did he go?**
After forty days, Christ ascended into heaven, and the day on which he ascended into heaven is called "Ascension day."

92. **Where is Christ in heaven?**
In heaven, Christ sits at the right hand of God the Father Almighty.

93. **What do you mean by saying that Christ sits at the right hand of God?**
When I say that Christ sits at the right hand of God, I mean that Christ as God is equal to his Father in all things, and that as man he is in the highest place in heaven next to God.

LESSON NINTH

On the Holy Ghost and His Descent upon the Apostles

94. **Who is the Holy Ghost?**
The Holy Ghost is the third Person of the Blessed Trinity.

95. **From whom does the Holy Ghost proceed?**
The Holy Ghost proceeds from the Father and the Son.

96. **Is the Holy Ghost equal to the Father and the Son?**
The Holy Ghost is equal to the Father and the Son, being the same Lord and God as they are.

97. **On what day did the Holy Ghost come down upon the apostles?**
The Holy Ghost came down upon the apostles ten days after the ascension of our Lord; and the day on which he came down upon the apostles is called "Whitsunday" or "Pentecost."

98. **How did the Holy Ghost come down upon the apostles?**
The Holy Ghost came down upon the apostles in the form of tongues of fire.

99. **Who sent the Holy Ghost upon the apostles?**
Our Lord Jesus Christ sent the Holy Ghost upon the apostles.

100. **Why did Christ send the Holy Ghost?**
Christ sent the Holy Ghost to sanctify his Church, to enlighten and strengthen the apostles, and to enable them to preach the gospel.

101. **Will the Holy Ghost abide with the Church forever?**
The Holy Ghost will abide with the Church forever, and guide it in the way of holiness and truth.

LESSON TENTH

On the Effects of the Redemption

102. **Which are the chief effects of the redemption?**
The chief effects of the redemption are two: the satisfaction of God's justice by Christ's sufferings and death, and the gaining of grace for men.

103. **What do you mean by "grace"?**
By "grace," I mean a supernatural gift of God bestowed on us, through the merits of Jesus Christ, for our salvation.

104. **How many kinds of grace are there?**
There are two kinds of grace—sanctifying grace and actual grace.

105. **What is sanctifying grace?**
Sanctifying grace is that grace which makes the soul holy and pleasing to God.

106. **What do you call those graces or gifts of God by which we believe in him, hope in him, and love him?**
Those graces or gifts of God by which we believe in him, and hope in him, and love him, are called the "divine virtues" of faith, hope, and charity.

107. **What is faith?**
Faith is a divine virtue by which we firmly believe the truths which God has revealed.

108. **What is hope?**

Hope is a divine virtue by which we firmly trust that God will give us eternal life and the means to obtain it.

109. **What is charity?**

Charity is a divine virtue by which we love God above all things for his own sake, and our neighbor as ourselves for the love of God.

110. **What is actual grace?**

Actual grace is that help of God which enlightens our mind and moves our will to shun evil and do good.

111. **Is grace necessary to salvation?**

Grace is necessary to salvation, because without grace we can do nothing to merit heaven.

112. **Can we resist the grace of God?**

We can and unfortunately often do resist the grace of God.

113. **What is the grace of perseverance?**

The grace of perseverance is a particular gift of God which enables us to continue in the state of grace till death.

LESSON ELEVENTH

On the Church

114. **Which are the means instituted by our Lord to enable men at all times to share in the fruits of the redemption?**

The means instituted by our Lord to enable men at all times to share in the fruits of his redemption are the Church and the sacraments.

115. **What is the Church?**

The Church is the congregation of all those who profess the faith of Christ, partake of the same sacraments, and are governed by their lawful pastors under one visible head.

116. **Who is the invisible head of the Church?**

Jesus Christ is the invisible head of the Church.

117. **Who is the visible head of the Church?**

Our holy father the pope, the bishop of Rome, is the vicar of Christ on earth and the visible head of the Church.

118. **Why is the pope, the bishop of Rome, the visible head of the Church?**

The pope, the bishop of Rome, is the visible head of the Church, because he is the successor of St. Peter, whom Christ made the chief of the apostles and the visible head of the Church.

119. **Who are the successors of the other apostles?**

The successors of the other apostles are the bishops of the holy Catholic Church.

120. **Why did Christ found the Church?**

Christ founded the Church to teach, govern, sanctify, and save all men.

121. **Are all bound to belong to the Church?**

All are bound to belong to the Church, and he who knows the Church to be the true Church and remains out of it cannot be saved.

LESSON TWELFTH

On the Attributes and Marks of the Church

122. **Which are the attributes of the Church?**

The attributes of the Church are three: authority, infallibility, and indefectibility.

123. **What do you mean by "the authority of the Church"?**

By "the authority of the Church," I mean the right and power which the pope and the bishops, as the successors of the apostles, have to teach and to govern the faithful.

124. **What do you mean by "the infallibility of the Church"?**

By "the infallibility of the Church," I mean that the Church cannot err when it teaches a doctrine of faith or morals.

125. **When does the Church teach infallibly?**

The Church teaches infallibly when it speaks through the pope and bishops united in general council, or through the pope alone when he proclaims to all the faithful a doctrine of faith or morals.

126. **What do you mean by "the indefectibility of the Church"?**

By "the indefectibility of the Church," I mean that the Church, as Christ founded it, will last till the end of time.

127. **In whom are these attributes found in their fullness?**

These attributes are found in their fullness in the pope, the visible head of the Church, whose infallible authority to teach bishops, priests, and people in matters of faith or morals will last to the end of the world.

128. **Has the Church any marks by which it may be known?**

The Church has four marks by which it may be known: it is one; it is holy; it is catholic; it is apostolic.

129. **How is the Church one?**

The Church is one because all its members agree in one faith, are all in one communion, and are all under one head.

130. **How is the Church holy?**

The Church is holy because its founder, Jesus Christ, is holy; because it teaches a holy doctrine, invites all to a holy life, and because of the eminent holiness of so many thousands of its children.

131. **How is the Church catholic or universal?**

The Church is catholic or universal because it subsists in all ages, teaches all nations, and maintains all truth.

132. **How is the Church apostolic?**

The Church is apostolic because it was founded by Christ on his apostles and is governed by their lawful successors, and because it has never ceased, and never will cease, to teach their doctrine.

133. **In which church are these attributes and marks found?**

These attributes and marks are found in the holy Roman Catholic Church alone.

134. **From whom does the Church derive its undying life and infallible authority?**

The Church derives its undying life and infallible authority from the Holy Ghost, the Spirit of truth, who abides with it forever.

135. **By whom is the Church made and kept one, holy, and catholic?**

The Church is made and kept one, holy, and catholic by the Holy Ghost, the Spirit of love and holiness, who unites and sanctifies its members throughout the world.

LESSON THIRTEENTH

On the Sacraments in General

136. **What is a sacrament?**

A sacrament is an outward sign instituted by Christ to give grace.

137. **How many sacraments are there?**

There are seven sacraments: baptism, confirmation, Holy Eucharist, penance, extreme unction, holy orders, and matrimony.

138. **Whence have the sacraments the power of giving grace?**

The sacraments have the power of giving grace from the merits of Jesus Christ.

139. **What grace do the sacraments give?**

Some of the sacraments give sanctifying grace, and others increase it in our souls.

140. **Which are the sacraments that give sanctifying grace?**

The sacraments that give sanctifying grace are baptism and penance; and they are called "sacraments of the dead."

141. **Why are baptism and penance called "sacraments of the dead"?**

Baptism and penance are called "sacraments of the dead," because they take away sin, which is the death of the soul, and give grace, which is its life.

142. **Which are the sacraments that increase sanctifying grace in our soul?**

The sacraments that increase sanctifying grace in our soul are: confirmation, Holy Eucharist, extreme unction, holy orders, and matrimony; and they are called "sacraments of the living."

143. **Why are confirmation, Holy Eucharist, extreme unction, holy orders, and matrimony called "sacraments of the living"?**
Confirmation, Holy Eucharist, extreme unction, holy orders, and matrimony are called "sacraments of the living," because those who receive them worthily are already living the life of grace.

144. **What sin does he commit who receives the sacraments of the living in mortal sin?**
He who receives the sacraments of the living in mortal sin commits a sacrilege, which is a great sin, because it is an abuse of a sacred thing.

145. **Besides sanctifying grace, do the sacraments give any other grace?**
Besides sanctifying grace, the sacraments give another grace, called "sacramental."

146. **What is sacramental grace?**
Sacramental grace is a special help which God gives to attain the end for which he instituted each sacrament.

147. **Do the sacraments always give grace?**
The sacraments always give grace, if we receive them with the right dispositions.

148. **Can we receive the sacraments more than once?**
We can receive the sacraments more than once, except baptism, confirmation, and holy orders.

149. **Why can we not receive baptism, confirmation, and holy orders more than once?**
We cannot receive baptism, confirmation, and holy orders more than once, because they imprint a character in the soul.

150. **What is the character which these sacraments imprint in the soul?**
The character which these sacraments imprint in the soul is a spiritual mark which remains forever.

151. **Does this character remain in the soul even after death?**
This character remains in the soul even after death: for the honor and glory of those who are saved; for the shame and punishment of those who are lost.

LESSON FOURTEENTH

On Baptism

152. **What is baptism?**
Baptism is a sacrament which cleanses us from original sin, makes us Christians, children of God, and heirs of heaven.

153. **Are actual sins ever remitted by baptism?**
Actual sins and all the punishment due to them are remitted by baptism, if the person baptized be guilty of any.

154. **Is baptism necessary to salvation?**
Baptism is necessary to salvation, because without it we cannot enter into the kingdom of heaven.

155. **Who can administer baptism?**
The priest is the ordinary minister of baptism; but in case of necessity, anyone who has the use of reason may baptize.

156. **How is baptism given?**
Whoever baptizes should pour water on the head of the person to be baptized, and say, while pouring the water: "I baptize thee in the name of the Father, and of the Son, and of the Holy Ghost."

157. **How many kinds of baptism are there?**
There are three kinds of baptism: baptism of water, of desire, and of blood.

158. **What is baptism of water?**
Baptism of water is that which is given by pouring water on the head of the person to be baptized, and saying at the same time: "I baptize thee in the name of the Father, and of the Son, and of the Holy Ghost."

159. **What is baptism of desire?**
Baptism of desire is an ardent wish to receive baptism, and to do all that God has ordained for our salvation.

160. **What is baptism of blood?**
Baptism of blood is the shedding of one's blood for the faith of Christ.

161. **Is baptism of desire or of blood sufficient to produce the effects of baptism of water?**
Baptism of desire or of blood is sufficient to produce the effects of the baptism of water, if it is impossible to receive the baptism of water.

162. **What do we promise in baptism?**
In baptism, we promise to renounce the devil with all his works and pomps.

163. **Why is the name of a saint given in baptism?**
The name of a saint is given in baptism in order that the person baptized may imitate his virtues and have him for a protector.

164. **Why are godfathers and godmothers given in baptism?**
Godfathers and godmothers are given in baptism in order that they may promise in the name of the child what the child itself would promise if it had the use of reason.

165. **What is the obligation of a godfather and a godmother?**
The obligation of a godfather and a godmother is to instruct the child in its religious duties if the parents neglect to do so or die.

LESSON FIFTEENTH

On Confirmation

166. **What is confirmation?**
Confirmation is a sacrament through which we receive the Holy Ghost to make us strong and perfect Christians and soldiers of Jesus Christ.

167. **Who administers confirmation?**
The bishop is the ordinary minister of confirmation.

168. **How does the bishop give confirmation?**
The bishop extends his hands over those who are to be confirmed, prays that they may receive the Holy Ghost, and anoints the forehead of each with holy chrism in the form of a cross.

169. **What is holy chrism?**
Holy chrism is a mixture of olive oil and balm, consecrated by the bishop.

170. **What does the bishop say in anointing the person he confirms?**
In anointing the person he confirms, the bishop says: "I sign thee with the sign of the cross, and I confirm thee with the chrism of salvation, in the name of the Father, and of the Son, and of the Holy Ghost."

171. **What is meant by anointing the forehead with chrism in the form of a cross?**
By anointing the forehead with chrism in the form of a cross is meant that the Christian who is confirmed must openly profess and practice his faith, never be ashamed of it, and rather die than deny it.

172. **Why does the bishop give the person he confirms a slight blow on the cheek?**
The bishop gives the person he confirms a slight blow on the cheek to put him in mind that he must be ready to suffer everything, even death, for the sake of Christ.

173. **To receive confirmation worthily, is it necessary to be in the state of grace?**
To receive confirmation worthily, it is necessary to be in the state of grace.

174. **What special preparation should be made to receive confirmation?**
Persons of an age to learn should know the chief mysteries of faith and the duties of a Christian, and be instructed in the nature and effects of this sacrament.

175. **Is it a sin to neglect confirmation?**
It is a sin to neglect confirmation, especially in these evil days when faith and morals are exposed to so many and such violent temptations.

LESSON SIXTEENTH

On the Gifts and Fruits of the Holy Ghost

176. **What are the effects of confirmation?**
The effects of confirmation are an increase of sanctifying grace, the strengthening of our faith, and the gifts of the Holy Ghost.

177. **Which are the gifts of the Holy Ghost?**
The gifts of the Holy Ghost are wisdom, understanding, counsel, fortitude, knowledge, piety, and fear of the Lord.

178. **Why do we receive the gift of fear of the Lord?**
We receive the gift of fear of the Lord to fill us with a dread of sin.

179. **Why do we receive the gift of piety?**

We receive the gift of piety to make us love God as a Father, and obey him because we love him.

180. **Why do we receive the gift of knowledge?**

We receive the gift of knowledge to enable us to discover the will of God in all things.

181. **Why do we receive the gift of fortitude?**

We receive the gift of fortitude to strengthen us to do the will of God in all things.

182. **Why do we receive the gift of counsel?**

We receive the gift of counsel to warn us of the deceits of the devil, and of the dangers to salvation.

183. **Why do we receive the gift of understanding?**

We receive the gift of understanding to enable us to know more clearly the mysteries of faith.

184. **Why do we receive the gift of wisdom?**

We receive the gift of wisdom to give us a relish for the things of God and to direct our whole life and all our actions to his honor and glory.

185. **Which are the beatitudes?**

The beatitudes are:

1. Blessed are the poor in spirit, for theirs is the kingdom of heaven.
2. Blessed are the meek, for they shall possess the land.
3. Blessed are they that mourn, for they shall be comforted.
4. Blessed are they that hunger and thirst after justice, for they shall be filled.
5. Blessed are the merciful, for they shall obtain mercy.
6. Blessed are the clean of heart, for they shall see God.
7. Blessed are the peacemakers, for they shall be called the children of God.

8. Blessed are they that suffer persecution for justice' sake, for theirs is the kingdom of heaven.

186. **Which are the twelve fruits of the Holy Ghost?**
The twelve fruits of the Holy Ghost are charity, joy, peace, patience, benignity, goodness, long-suffering, mildness, faith, modesty, continency, and chastity.

LESSON SEVENTEENTH

On the Sacrament of Penance

187. **What is the sacrament of penance?**
Penance is a sacrament in which the sins committed after baptism are forgiven.

188. **How does the sacrament of penance remit sin and restore to the soul the friendship of God?**
The sacrament of penance remits sin and restores the friendship of God to the soul by means of the absolution of the priest.

189. **How do you know that the priest has the power of absolving from the sins committed after baptism?**
I know that the priest has the power of absolving from the sins committed after baptism, because Jesus Christ granted that power to the priests of his Church when he said: "Receive ye the Holy Ghost. Whose sins you shall forgive, they are forgiven them; whose sins you shall retain, they are retained."[1]

[1] Jn 20:22-23

190. **How do the priests of the Church exercise the power of forgiving sins?**
The priests of the Church exercise the power of forgiving sins by hearing the confession of sins, and granting pardon for them as ministers of God and in his name.

191. **What must we do to receive the sacrament of penance worthily?**
To receive the sacrament of penance worthily, we must do five things:
1. We must examine our conscience.
2. We must have sorrow for our sins.
3. We must make a firm resolution never more to offend God.
4. We must confess our sins to the priest.
5. We must accept the penance which the priest gives us.

192. **What is the examination of conscience?**
The examination of conscience is an earnest effort to recall to mind all the sins we have committed since our last worthy confession.

193. **How can we make a good examination of conscience?**
We can make a good examination of conscience by calling to memory the commandments of God, the precepts of the Church, the seven capital sins, and the particular duties of our state in life, to find out the sins we have committed.

194. **What should we do before beginning the examination of conscience?**
Before beginning the examination of conscience, we should pray to God to give us light to know our sins and grace to detest them.

LESSON EIGHTEENTH

On Contrition

195. **What is contrition or sorrow for sin?**
Contrition or sorrow for sin is a hatred of sin and a true grief of the soul for having offended God, with a firm purpose of sinning no more.

196. **What kind of sorrow should we have for our sins?**
The sorrow we should have for our sins should be interior, supernatural, universal, and sovereign.

197. **What do you mean by saying that our sorrow should be interior?**
When I say that our sorrow should be interior, I mean that it should come from the heart, and not merely from the lips.

198. **What do you mean by saying that our sorrow should be supernatural?**
When I say that our sorrow should be supernatural, I mean that it should be prompted by the grace of God, and excited by motives which spring from faith, and not by merely natural motives.

199. **What do you mean by saying that our sorrow should be universal?**
When I say that our sorrow should be universal, I mean that we should be sorry for all our mortal sins without exception.

200. **What do you mean when you say that our sorrow should be sovereign?**
When I say that our sorrow should be sovereign, I mean that we should grieve more for having offended God than for any other evil that can befall us.

201. **Why should we be sorry for our sins?**
We should be sorry for our sins, because sin is the greatest of evils and an offense against God our Creator, Preserver, and Redeemer, and because it shuts us out of heaven and condemns us to the eternal pains of hell.

202. **How many kinds of contrition are there?**
There are two kinds of contrition: perfect contrition and imperfect contrition.

203. **What is perfect contrition?**

Perfect contrition is that which fills us with sorrow and hatred for sin, because it offends God, who is infinitely good in himself and worthy of all love.

204. **What is imperfect contrition?**

Imperfect contrition is that by which we hate what offends God, because by it we lose heaven and deserve hell; or because sin is so hateful in itself.

205. **Is imperfect contrition sufficient for a worthy confession?**

Imperfect contrition is sufficient for a worthy confession, but we should endeavor to have perfect contrition.

206. **What do you mean by "a firm purpose of sinning no more"?**

By "a firm purpose of sinning no more," I mean a fixed resolve not only to avoid all mortal sin, but also its near occasions.

207. **What do you mean by "the near occasions of sin"?**

By "the near occasions of sin," I mean all the persons, places, and things that may easily lead us into sin.

LESSON NINETEENTH

On Confession

208. **What is confession?**

Confession is the telling of our sins to a duly authorized priest, for the purpose of obtaining forgiveness.

209. **What sins are we bound to confess?**

We are bound to confess all our mortal sins, but it is well also to confess our venial sins.

210. **What are the chief qualities of a good confession?**

The chief qualities of a good confession are three: it must be humble, sincere, and entire.

211. **When is our confession humble?**

Our confession is humble when we accuse ourselves of our sins, with a deep sense of shame and sorrow for having offended God.

212. **When is our confession sincere?**

Our confession is sincere when we tell our sins honestly and truthfully, neither exaggerating nor excusing them.

213. **When is our confession entire?**

Our confession is entire when we tell the number and kinds of our sins and the circumstances which change their nature.

214. **What should we do if we cannot remember the number of our sins?**

If we cannot remember the number of our sins, we should tell the number as nearly as possible, and say how often we may have sinned in a day, a week, or a month, and how long the habit or practice has lasted.

215. **Is our confession worthy if, without our fault, we forget to confess a mortal sin?**

If without our fault we forget to confess a mortal sin, our confession is worthy, and the sin is forgiven; but it must be told in confession if it again comes to our mind.

216. **Is it a grievous offense willfully to conceal a mortal sin in confession?**

It is a grievous offense willfully to conceal a mortal sin in confession, because we thereby tell a lie to the Holy Ghost, and make our confession worthless.

217. **What must he do who has willfully concealed a mortal sin in confession?**
He who has willfully concealed a mortal sin in confession must not only confess it, but must also repeat all the sins he has committed since his last worthy confession.

218. **Why does the priest give us a penance after confession?**
The priest gives us a penance after confession that we may satisfy God for the temporal punishment due to our sins.

219. **Does not the sacrament of penance remit all punishment due to sin?**
The sacrament of penance remits the eternal punishment due to sin, but it does not always remit the temporal punishment which God requires as satisfaction for our sins.

220. **Why does God require a temporal punishment as a satisfaction for sin?**
God requires a temporal punishment as a satisfaction for sin to teach us the great evil of sin, and to prevent us from falling again.

221. **Which are the chief means by which we satisfy God for the temporal punishment due to sin?**
The chief means by which we satisfy God for the temporal punishment due to sin are: prayer, fasting, almsgiving, all spiritual and corporal works of mercy, and the patient suffering of the ills of life.

222. **Which are the chief spiritual works of mercy?**
The chief spiritual works of mercy are seven: to admonish the sinner, to instruct the ignorant, to counsel the doubtful, to comfort the sorrowful, to bear wrongs patiently, to forgive all injuries, and to pray for the living and the dead.

223. **Which are the chief corporal works of mercy?**
The chief corporal works of mercy are seven: to feed the hungry, to give drink to the thirsty, to clothe the naked, to ransom the captive, to harbor the harborless, to visit the sick, and to bury the dead.

LESSON TWENTIETH

On the Manner of Making a Good Confession

224. **What should we do on entering the confessional?**
On entering the confessional, we should kneel, make the sign of the cross, and say to the priest: "Bless me, Father"; then add, "I confess to Almighty God, and to you, Father, that I have sinned."

225. **Which are the first things we should tell the priest in confession?**
The first things we should tell the priest in confession are the time of our last confession and whether we said the penance and went to Holy Communion.

226. **After telling the time of our last confession and Communion, what should we do?**
After telling the time of our last confession and Communion, we should confess all the mortal sins we have since committed, and all the venial sins we may wish to mention.

227. **What must we do when the confessor asks us questions?**
When the confessor asks us questions, we must answer them truthfully and clearly.

228. **What should we do after telling our sins?**
After telling our sins, we should listen with attention to the advice which the confessor may think proper to give.

229. **How should we end our confession?**
We should end our confession by saying, "I also accuse myself of all the sins of my past life," telling, if we choose, one or several of our past sins.

230. **What should we do while the priest is giving us absolution?**

While the priest is giving us absolution, we should from our heart renew the act of contrition.

LESSON TWENTY-FIRST

On Indulgences

231. **What is an indulgence?**

An indulgence is the remission, in whole or in part, of the temporal punishment due to sin.

232. **Is an indulgence a pardon of sin, or a license to commit sin?**

An indulgence is not a pardon of sin, nor a license to commit sin, and one who is in a state of mortal sin cannot gain an indulgence.

233. **How many kinds of indulgences are there?**

There are two kinds of indulgences—plenary and partial.

234. **What is a plenary indulgence?**

A plenary indulgence is the full remission of the temporal punishment due to sin.

235. **What is a partial indulgence?**

A partial indulgence is the remission of a part of the temporal punishment due to sin.

236. **How does the Church by means of indulgences remit the temporal punishment due to sins?**

The Church by means of indulgences remits the temporal punishment due to sin by applying to us the merits of Jesus Christ, and the superabundant satisfactions of the Blessed Virgin Mary and of the saints, which merits and satisfactions are its spiritual treasury.

237. **What must we do to gain an indulgence?**
To gain an indulgence, we must be in a state of grace and perform the works enjoined.

LESSON TWENTY-SECOND

On the Holy Eucharist

238. **What is the Holy Eucharist?**
The Holy Eucharist is the sacrament which contains the body and blood, soul and divinity of our Lord Jesus Christ under the appearances of bread and wine.

239. **When did Christ institute the Holy Eucharist?**
Christ instituted the Holy Eucharist at the last supper, the night before he died.

240. **Who were present when our Lord instituted the Holy Eucharist?**
When our Lord instituted the Holy Eucharist, the twelve apostles were present.

241. **How did our Lord institute the Holy Eucharist?**
Our Lord instituted the Holy Eucharist by taking bread, blessing, breaking, and giving to his apostles, saying: "Take ye and eat. This is my body";[2] and then, by taking the cup of wine, blessing and giving it, saying to them: "Drink ye all of this. This is my blood which shall be shed for the remission of sins. Do this for a commemoration of me."[3]

[2] Mt 26:26; 1 Cor 11:24
[3] Cf. Mt 26:27-28; 1 Cor 11:25

242. **What happened when our Lord said, "This is my body; this is my blood"?**
When our Lord said, "This is my body," the substance of the bread was changed into the substance of his body. When he said, "This is my blood," the substance of the wine was changed into the substance of his blood.

243. **Is Jesus Christ whole and entire both under the form of bread and under the form of wine?**
Jesus Christ is whole and entire both under the form of bread and under the form of wine.

244. **Did anything remain of the bread and wine after their substance had been changed into the substance of the body and blood of our Lord?**
After the substance of the bread and wine had been changed into the substance of the body and blood of our Lord, there remained only the appearances of bread and wine.

245. **What do you mean by "the appearances of bread and wine"?**
By "the appearances of bread and wine," I mean the figure, the color, the taste, and whatever appears to the senses.

246. **What is this change of the bread and wine into the body and blood of our Lord called?**
This change of the bread and wine into the body and blood of our Lord is called "transubstantiation."

247. **How was the substance of the bread and wine changed into the substance of the body and blood of Christ?**
The substance of the bread and wine was changed into the substance of the body and blood of Christ by his almighty power.

248. **Does this change of bread and wine into the body and blood of Christ continue to be made in the Church?**
This change of bread and wine into the body and blood of Christ continues to be made in the Church by Jesus Christ through the ministry of his priests.

249. **When did Christ give his priests the power to change bread and wine into his body and blood?**
Christ gave his priests the power to change bread and wine into his body and blood when he said to his apostles: "Do this in commemoration of me."[4]

250. **How do the priests exercise this power of changing bread and wine into the body and blood of Christ?**
The priests exercise this power of changing bread and wine into the body and blood of Christ through the words of consecration in the Mass, which are the words of Christ: "This is my body; this is my blood."

LESSON TWENTY-THIRD

On the Ends for Which the Holy Eucharist Was Instituted

251. **Why did Christ institute the Holy Eucharist?**
Christ instituted the Holy Eucharist:

1. To unite us to himself and to nourish our soul with his divine life.
2. To increase sanctifying grace and all virtues in our soul.
3. To lessen our evil inclinations.
4. To be a pledge of everlasting life.
5. To fit our bodies for a glorious resurrection.
6. To continue the sacrifice of the cross in his Church.

[4] Lk 22:19; Cf. 1 Cor 11:24-25

252. **How are we united to Jesus Christ in the Holy Eucharist?**
We are united to Jesus Christ in the Holy Eucharist by means of Holy Communion.

253. **What is Holy Communion?**
Holy Communion is the receiving of the body and blood of Christ.

254. **What is necessary to make a good Communion?**
To make a good Communion, it is necessary to be in the state of sanctifying grace and to be fasting from midnight.

255. **Does he who receives Communion in mortal sin receive the body and blood of Christ?**
He who receives Communion in mortal sin receives the body and blood of Christ, but does not receive his grace, and he commits a great sacrilege.

256. **Is it enough to be free from mortal sin to receive plentifully the graces of Holy Communion?**
To receive plentifully the graces of Holy Communion, it is not enough to be free from mortal sin, but we should be free from all affection to venial sin, and should make acts of lively faith, of firm hope, and ardent love.

257. **What is the fast necessary for Holy Communion?**
The fast necessary for Holy Communion is the abstaining from midnight from everything which is taken as food or drink.

258. **Is anyone ever allowed to receive Holy Communion when not fasting?**
Anyone in danger of death is allowed to receive Communion when not fasting.

259. **When are we bound to receive Holy Communion?**
We are bound to receive Holy Communion, under pain of mortal sin, during the Easter time and when in danger of death.

260. **Is it well to receive Holy Communion often?**
It is well to receive Holy Communion often, as nothing is a greater aid to a holy life than often to receive the author of all grace and the source of all good.

261. **What should we do after Holy Communion?**
After Holy Communion, we should spend some time in adoring our Lord, in thanking him for the grace we have received, and in asking him for the blessings we need.

LESSON TWENTY-FOURTH

On the Sacrifice of the Mass

262. **When and where are the bread and wine changed into the body and blood of Christ?**
The bread and wine are changed into the body and blood of Christ at the consecration in the Mass.

263. **What is the Mass?**
The Mass is the unbloody sacrifice of the body and blood of Christ.

264. **What is a sacrifice?**
A sacrifice is the offering of an object by a priest to God alone, and the consuming of it to acknowledge that he is the Creator and Lord of all things.

265. **Is the Mass the same sacrifice as that of the cross?**
The Mass is the same sacrifice as that of the cross.

266. **How is the Mass the same sacrifice as that of the cross?**
The Mass is the same sacrifice as that of the cross because the offering and the priest are the same—Christ our Blessed Lord; and the ends for which the Sacrifice of the Mass is offered are the same as those of the sacrifice of the cross.

267. **What were the ends for which the sacrifice of the cross was offered?**
The ends for which the sacrifice of the cross was offered were: first, to honor and glorify God; second, to thank him for all the graces bestowed on the whole world; third, to satisfy God's justice for the sins of men; fourth, to obtain all graces and blessings.

268. **Is there any difference between the sacrifice of the cross and the Sacrifice of the Mass?**
Yes; the manner in which the sacrifice is offered is different. On the cross, Christ really shed his blood and was really slain; in the Mass, there is no real shedding of blood nor real death, because Christ can die no more; but the Sacrifice of the Mass, through the separate consecration of the bread and the wine, represents his death on the cross.

269. **How should we assist at Mass?**
We should assist at Mass with great interior recollection and piety and with every outward mark of respect and devotion.

270. **Which is the best manner of hearing Mass?**
The best manner of hearing Mass is to offer it to God with the priest for the same purpose for which it is said, to meditate on Christ's sufferings and death, and to go to Holy Communion.

LESSON TWENTY-FIFTH

On Extreme Unction and Holy Orders

271. **What is the sacrament of extreme unction?**
Extreme unction is the sacrament which, through the anointing and prayer of the priest, gives health and strength to the soul, and sometimes to the body, when we are in danger of death from sickness.

272. **When should we receive extreme unction?**
We should receive extreme unction when we are in danger of death from sickness, or from a wound or accident.

273. **Should we wait until we are in extreme danger before we receive extreme unction?**
We should not wait until we are in extreme danger before we receive extreme unction, but if possible, we should receive it whilst we have the use of our senses.

274. **Which are the effects of the sacrament of extreme unction?**
The effects of extreme unction are: first, to comfort us in the pains of sickness and to strengthen us against temptations; second, to remit venial sins and to cleanse our soul from the remains of sin; third, when God sees fit to restore us to health.

275. **What do you mean by "the remains of sin"?**
By "the remains of sin," I mean the inclination to evil and the weakness of the will, which are the result of our sins and which remain after our sins have been forgiven.

276. **How should we receive the sacrament of extreme unction?**
We should receive the sacrament of extreme unction in the state of grace, and with lively faith and resignation to the will of God.

277. **Who is the minister of the sacrament of extreme unction?**
The priest is the minister of the sacrament of extreme unction.

278. **What is the sacrament of holy orders?**
Holy orders is a sacrament by which bishops, priests, and other ministers of the Church are ordained and receive the power and grace to perform their sacred duties.

279. **What is necessary to receive holy orders worthily?**
To receive holy orders worthily, it is necessary to be in the state of grace, to have the necessary knowledge, and a divine call to this sacred office.

280. **How should Christians look upon the priests of the Church?**
Christians should look upon the priests of the Church as the messengers of God and the dispensers of his mysteries.

281. **Who can confer the sacrament of holy orders?**
Bishops can confer the sacrament of holy orders.

LESSON TWENTY-SIXTH

On Matrimony

282. **What is the sacrament of matrimony?**
The sacrament of matrimony is the sacrament which unites a Christian man and woman in lawful marriage.

283. **Can a Christian man and woman be united in lawful marriage in any other way than by the sacrament of matrimony?**
A Christian man and woman cannot be united in lawful marriage in any other way than by the sacrament of matrimony, because Christ raised marriage to the dignity of a sacrament.

284. **Can the bond of Christian marriage be dissolved by any human power?**
The bond of Christian marriage cannot be dissolved by any human power.

285. **Which are the effects of the sacrament of matrimony?**
The effects of the sacrament of matrimony are: first, to sanctify the love of husband and wife; second, to give them grace to bear with each other's weaknesses; third, to enable them to bring up their children in the fear and love of God.

286. **To receive the sacrament of matrimony worthily, is it necessary to be in the state of grace?**
To receive the sacrament of matrimony worthily, it is necessary to be in the state of grace, and it is necessary also to comply with the laws of the Church.

287. **Who has the right to make laws concerning the sacrament of marriage?**
The Church alone has the right to make laws concerning the sacrament of marriage, though the state also has the right to make laws concerning the civil effects of the marriage contract.

288. **Does the Church forbid the marriage of Catholics with persons who have a different religion or no religion at all?**
The Church does forbid the marriage of Catholics with persons who have a different religion or no religion at all.

289. **Why does the Church forbid the marriage of Catholics with persons who have a different religion or no religion at all?**
The Church forbids the marriage of Catholics with persons who have a different religion or no religion at all, because such marriages generally lead to indifference, loss of faith, and to the neglect of the religious education of the children.

290. **Why do many marriages prove unhappy?**
Many marriages prove unhappy because they are entered into hastily and without worthy motives.

291. **How should Christians prepare for a holy and happy marriage?**
Christians should prepare for a holy and happy marriage by receiving the sacraments of penance and Holy Eucharist; by begging God to grant them a pure intention and to direct their choice; and by seeking the advice of their parents and the blessing of their pastors.

LESSON TWENTY-SEVENTH

On the Sacramentals

292. **What is a sacramental?**

A sacramental is anything set apart or blessed by the Church to excite good thoughts and to increase devotion, and, through these movements of the heart, to remit venial sin.

293. **What is the difference between the sacraments and the sacramentals?**

The difference between the sacraments and the sacramentals is: first, the sacraments were instituted by Jesus Christ, and the sacramentals were instituted by the Church; second, the sacraments give grace of themselves when we place no obstacle in the way; the sacramentals excite in us pious dispositions by means of which we may obtain grace.

294. **Which is the chief sacramental used in the Church?**

The chief sacramental used in the Church is the sign of the cross.

295. **How do we make the sign of the cross?**

We make the sign of the cross by putting the right hand to the forehead, then on the breast, and then to the left and right shoulders, saying, "In the name of the Father, and of the Son, and of the Holy Ghost. Amen."

296. **Why do we make the sign of the cross?**

We make the sign of the cross to show that we are Christians and to profess our belief in the chief mysteries of our religion.

297. **How is the sign of the cross a profession of faith in the chief mysteries of our religion?**

The sign of the cross is a profession of faith in the chief mysteries of our religion, because it expresses the mysteries of the unity and trinity of God and of the incarnation and death of our Lord.

298. **How does the sign of the cross express the mystery of the unity and trinity of God?**
The words, "In the name," express the unity of God; the words that follow, "of the Father, and of the Son, and of the Holy Ghost," express the mystery of the trinity.

299. **How does the sign of the cross express the mystery of the incarnation and death of our Lord?**
The sign of the cross expresses the mystery of the incarnation by reminding us that the Son of God, having become man, suffered death on the cross.

300. **What other sacramental is in very frequent use?**
Another sacramental in very frequent use is holy water.

301. **What is holy water?**
Holy water is water blessed by the priest with solemn prayer to beg God's blessing on those who use it, and protection from the powers of darkness.

302. **Are there other sacramentals besides the sign of the cross and holy water?**
Besides the sign of the cross and holy water, there are many other sacramentals, such as blessed candles, ashes, palms, crucifixes, images of the Blessed Virgin and of the saints, rosaries, and scapulars.

LESSON TWENTY-EIGHTH

On Prayer

303. **Is there any other means of obtaining God's grace than the sacraments?**
There is another means of obtaining God's grace, and it is prayer.

304. **What is prayer?**
Prayer is the lifting up of our minds and hearts to God to adore him, to thank him for his benefits, to ask his forgiveness, and to beg of him all the graces we need whether for soul or body.

305. **Is prayer necessary to salvation?**
Prayer is necessary to salvation, and without it no one having the use of reason can be saved.

306. **At what particular times should we pray?**
We should pray particularly on Sundays and holy days, every morning and night, in all dangers, temptations, and afflictions.

307. **How should we pray?**
We should pray: first, with attention; second, with a sense of our own helplessness and dependence upon God; third, with a great desire for the graces we beg of God; fourth, with trust in God's goodness; fifth, with perseverance.

308. **Which are the prayers most recommended to us?**
The prayers most recommended to us are the Lord's Prayer, the Hail Mary, the Apostles' Creed, the *confiteor*, and the acts of faith, hope, love, and contrition.

309. **Are prayers made with distractions of any avail?**
Prayers made with willful distractions are of no avail.

LESSON TWENTY-NINTH

On the Commandments of God

310. **Is it enough to belong to God's Church in order to be saved?**
It is not enough to belong to the Church in order to be saved, but we must also keep the commandments of God and of the Church.

311. **Which are the commandments that contain the whole law of God?**
The commandments which contain the whole law of God are these two: first, thou shalt love the Lord thy God with thy whole heart, with thy

whole soul, with thy whole strength, and with thy whole mind; second, thou shalt love thy neighbor as thyself.

312. **Why do these two commandments of the love of God and of our neighbor contain the whole law of God?**
These two commandments of the love of God and of our neighbor contain the whole law of God because all the other commandments are given either to help us to keep these two, or to direct us how to shun what is opposed to them.

313. **Which are the commandments of God?**
The commandments of God are these ten:

1. I am the Lord thy God, who brought thee out of the land of Egypt, out of the house of bondage. Thou shalt not have strange gods before me. Thou shalt not make to thyself a graven thing, nor the likeness of anything that is in heaven above, or in the earth beneath, nor of those things that are in the waters under the earth. Thou shalt not adore them, nor serve them.
2. Thou shalt not take the name of the Lord thy God in vain.
3. Remember thou keep holy the sabbath day.
4. Honor thy father and thy mother.
5. Thou shalt not kill.
6. Thou shalt not commit adultery.
7. Thou shalt not steal.
8. Thou shalt not bear false witness against thy neighbor.
9. Thou shalt not covet thy neighbor's wife.
10. Thou shalt not covet thy neighbor's goods.

314. **Who gave the ten commandments?**
God himself gave the ten commandments to Moses on Mount Sinai, and Christ our Lord confirmed them.

LESSON THIRTIETH

On the First Commandment

315. **What is the first commandment?**
The first commandment is: "I am the Lord thy God, thou shalt not have strange gods before me."

316. **How does the first commandment help us to keep the great commandment of the love of God?**
The first commandment helps us to keep the great commandment of the love of God because it commands us to adore God alone.

317. **How do we adore God?**
We adore God by faith, hope, and charity, by prayer and sacrifice.

318. **How may the first commandment be broken?**
The first commandment may be broken by giving to a creature the honor which belongs to God alone; by false worship; and by attributing to a creature a perfection which belongs to God alone.

319. **Do those who make use of spells and charms, or who believe in dreams, in mediums, spiritists, fortune tellers, and the like, sin against the first commandment?**
Those who make use of spells and charms, or who believe in dreams, in mediums, spiritists, fortune tellers, and the like, sin against the first commandment, because they attribute to creatures perfections which belong to God alone.

320. **Are sins against faith, hope, and charity also sins against the first commandment?**
Sins against faith, hope, and charity are also sins against the first commandment.

321. **How does a person sin against faith?**
A person sins against faith: first, by not trying to know what God has taught; second, by refusing to believe all that God has taught; third, by neglecting to profess his belief in what God has taught.

322. **How do we fail to try to know what God has taught?**
We fail to try to know what God has taught by neglecting to learn the Christian doctrine.

323. **Who are they who do not believe all that God has taught?**
They who do not believe all that God has taught are the heretics and infidels.

324. **Who are they who neglect to profess their belief in what God has taught?**
They who neglect to profess their belief in what God has taught are all those who fail to acknowledge the true Church in which they really believe.

325. **Can they who fail to profess their faith in the true Church in which they believe expect to be saved while in that state?**
They who fail to profess their faith in the true Church in which they believe cannot expect to be saved while in that state, for Christ has said: "Whoever shall deny me before men, I will also deny him before my Father who is in heaven."[5]

326. **Are we obliged to make open profession of our faith?**
We are obliged to make open profession of our faith as often as God's honor, our neighbor's spiritual good, or our own requires it. "Whosoever," says Christ, "shall confess me before men, I will also confess him before my Father who is in heaven."[6]

[5] Mt 10:33
[6] Mt 10:32

327. **Which are the sins against hope?**
The sins against hope are presumption and despair.

328. **What is presumption?**
Presumption is a rash expectation of salvation without making proper use of the necessary means to obtain it.

329. **What is despair?**
Despair is the loss of hope in God's mercy.

330. **How do we sin against the love of God?**
We sin against the love of God by all sin, but particularly by mortal sin.

LESSON THIRTY-FIRST

The First Commandment—On the Honor and Invocation of Saints

331. **Does the first commandment forbid the honoring of the saints?**
The first commandment does not forbid the honoring of the saints, but rather approves of it; because, by honoring the saints, who are the chosen friends of God, we honor God himself.

332. **Does the first commandment forbid us to pray to the saints?**
The first commandment does not forbid us to pray to the saints.

333. **What do we mean by "praying to the saints"?**
By "praying to the saints," we mean the asking of their help and prayers.

334. **How do we know that the saints hear us?**
We know that the saints hear us because they are with God, who makes our prayers known to them.

335. **Why do we believe that the saints will help us?**

We believe that the saints will help us because both they and we are members of the same Church, and they love us as their brethren.

336. **How are the saints and we members of the same Church?**

The saints and we are members of the same Church, because the Church in heaven and the Church on earth are one and the same Church, and all its members are in communion with one another.

337. **What is the communion of the members of the Church called?**

The communion of the members of the Church is called "the communion of saints."

338. **What does "the communion of saints" mean?**

"The communion of saints" means the union which exists between the members of the Church on earth with one another and with the blessed in heaven and with the suffering souls in purgatory.

339. **What benefits are derived from the communion of saints?**

The following benefits are derived from the communion of saints: the faithful on earth assist one another by their prayers and good works, and they are aided by the intercession of the saints in heaven, while both the saints in heaven and the faithful on earth help the souls in purgatory.

340. **Does the first commandment forbid us to honor relics?**

The first commandment does not forbid us to honor relics, because relics are the bodies of the saints or objects directly connected with them or with our Lord.

341. **Does the first commandment forbid the making of images?**

The first commandment does forbid the making of images if they are made to be adored as gods, but it does not forbid the making of them to put us in mind of Jesus Christ, his Blessed Mother, and the saints.

342. **Is it right to show respect to the pictures and images of Christ and his saints?**
It is right to show respect to the pictures and images of Christ and his saints, because they are the representations and memorials of them.

343. **Is it allowed to pray to the crucifix or to the images and relics of the saints?**
It is not allowed to pray to the crucifix or images and relics of the saints, for they have no life, nor power to help us, nor sense to hear us.

344. **Why do we pray before the crucifix and the images and relics of the saints?**
We pray before the crucifix and the images and relics of the saints because they enliven our devotion by exciting pious affections and desires, and by reminding us of Christ and of the saints, that we may imitate their virtues.

LESSON THIRTY-SECOND

On the Second and Third Commandments

345. **What is the second commandment?**
The second commandment is: "Thou shalt not take the name of the Lord thy God in vain."

346. **What are we commanded by the second commandment?**
We are commanded by the second commandment to speak with reverence of God and of the saints, and of all holy things, and to keep our lawful oaths and vows.

347. **What is an oath?**
An oath is the calling upon God to witness the truth of what we say.

348. **When may we take an oath?**
We may take an oath when it is ordered by lawful authority or required for God's honor or for our own or our neighbor's good.

349. **What is necessary to make an oath lawful?**
To make an oath lawful, it is necessary that what we swear to be true, and that there be a sufficient cause for taking an oath.

350. **What is a vow?**
A vow is a deliberate promise made to God to do something that is pleasing to him.

351. **Is it a sin not to fulfill our vows?**
Not to fulfill our vows is a sin, mortal or venial, according to the nature of the vow and the intention we had in making it.

352. **What is forbidden by the second commandment?**
The second commandment forbids all false, rash, unjust, and unnecessary oaths, blasphemy, cursing, and profane words.

353. **What is the third commandment?**
The third commandment is: "Remember thou keep holy the sabbath day."

354. **What are we commanded by the third commandment?**
By the third commandment, we are commanded to keep holy the Lord's day and the holy days of obligation, on which we are to give our time to the service and worship of God.

355. **How are we to worship God on Sundays and holy days of obligation?**
We are to worship God on Sundays and holy days of obligation by hearing Mass, by prayer, and by other good works.

356. **Are the sabbath day and the Sunday the same?**
The sabbath day and the Sunday are not the same. The sabbath is the seventh day of the week, and is the day which was kept holy in the old law; the Sunday is the first day of the week, and is the day which is kept holy in the new law.

357. **Why does the Church command us to keep the Sunday holy instead of the sabbath?**
The Church commands us to keep the Sunday holy instead of the sabbath because on Sunday Christ rose from the dead, and on Sunday he sent the Holy Ghost upon the apostles.

358. **What is forbidden by the third commandment?**
The third commandment forbids all unnecessary servile work and whatever else may hinder the due observance of the Lord's day.

359. **What are servile works?**
Servile works are those which require labor rather of body than of mind.

360. **Are servile works on Sunday ever lawful?**
Servile works are lawful on Sunday when the honor of God, the good of our neighbor, or necessity requires them.

LESSON THIRTY-THIRD

On the Fourth, Fifth, and Sixth Commandments

361. **What is the fourth commandment?**
The fourth commandment is: "Honor thy father and thy mother."

362. **What are we commanded by the fourth commandment?**
We are commanded by the fourth commandment to honor, love, and obey our parents in all that is not sin.

363. **Are we bound to honor and obey others than our parents?**
We are also bound to honor and obey our bishops, pastors, magistrates, teachers, and other lawful superiors.

364. **Have parents and superiors any duties toward those who are under their charge?**
It is the duty of parents and superiors to take good care of all under their charge and give them proper direction and example.

365. **What is forbidden by the fourth commandment?**
The fourth commandment forbids all disobedience, contempt, and stubbornness toward our parents or lawful superiors.

366. **What is the fifth commandment?**
The fifth commandment is: "Thou shalt not kill."

367. **What are we commanded by the fifth commandment?**
We are commanded by the fifth commandment to live in peace and union with our neighbor, to respect his rights, to seek his spiritual and bodily welfare, and to take proper care of our own life and health.

368. **What is forbidden by the fifth commandment?**
The fifth commandment forbids all willful murder, fighting, anger, hatred, revenge, and bad example.

369. **What is the sixth commandment?**
The sixth commandment is: "Thou shalt not commit adultery."

370. **What are we commanded by the sixth commandment?**
We are commanded by the sixth commandment to be pure in thought and modest in all our looks, words, and actions.

371. **What is forbidden by the sixth commandment?**
The sixth commandment forbids all unchaste freedom with another's wife or husband: also all immodesty with ourselves or others in looks, dress, words, or actions.

372. **Does the sixth commandment forbid the reading of bad and immodest books and newspapers?**
The sixth commandment does forbid the reading of bad and immodest books and newspapers.

LESSON THIRTY-FOURTH

On the Seventh, Eighth, Ninth, and Tenth Commandments

373. **What is the seventh commandment?**
The seventh commandment is: "Thou shalt not steal."

374. **What are we commanded by the seventh commandment?**
By the seventh commandment, we are commanded to give to all men what belongs to them and to respect their property.

375. **What is forbidden by the seventh commandment?**
The seventh commandment forbids all unjust taking or keeping what belongs to another.

376. **Are we bound to restore ill-gotten goods?**
We are bound to restore ill-gotten goods, or the value of them, as far as we are able; otherwise, we cannot be forgiven.

377. **Are we obliged to repair the damage we have unjustly caused?**
We are bound to repair the damage we have unjustly caused.

378. **What is the eighth commandment?**
The eighth commandment is: "Thou shalt not bear false witness against thy neighbor."

379. **What are we commanded by the eighth commandment?**
We are commanded by the eighth commandment to speak the truth in all things, and to be careful of the honor and reputation of everyone.

380. **What is forbidden by the eighth commandment?**
The eighth commandment forbids all rash judgments, backbiting, slanders, and lies.

381. **What must they do who have lied about their neighbor and seriously injured his character?**
They who have lied about their neighbor and seriously injured his character must repair the injury done as far as they are able, otherwise they will not be forgiven.

382. **What is the ninth commandment?**
The ninth commandment is: "Thou shalt not covet thy neighbor's wife."

383. **What are we commanded by the ninth commandment?**
We are commanded by the ninth commandment to keep ourselves pure in thought and desire.

384. **What is forbidden by the ninth commandment?**
The ninth commandment forbids unchaste thoughts, desires of another's wife or husband, and all other unlawful impure thoughts and desires.

385. **Are impure thoughts and desires always sins?**
Impure thoughts and desires are always sins, unless they displease us and we try to banish them.

386. **What is the tenth commandment?**
The tenth commandment is: "Thou shalt not covet thy neighbor's goods."

387. **What are we commanded by the tenth commandment?**
By the tenth commandment, we are commanded to be content with what we have, and to rejoice in our neighbor's welfare.

388. **What is forbidden by the tenth commandment?**
The tenth commandment forbids all desires to take or keep wrongfully what belongs to another.

LESSON THIRTY-FIFTH

On the First and Second Commandments of the Church

389. **Which are the chief commandments of the Church?**
The chief commandments of the Church are six:
1. To hear Mass on Sundays and holy days of obligation.
2. To fast and abstain on the days appointed.
3. To confess at least once a year.
4. To receive the Holy Eucharist during the Easter time.
5. To contribute to the support of our pastors.
6. Not to marry persons who are not Catholics, or who are related to us within the fourth degree of kindred, nor privately without witnesses, nor to solemnize marriage at forbidden times.

390. **Is it a mortal sin not to hear Mass on a Sunday or a holy day of obligation?**
It is a mortal sin not to hear Mass on a Sunday or a holy day of obligation, unless we are excused for a serious reason. They also commit a mortal sin, who, having others under their charge, hinder them from hearing Mass without a sufficient reason.

391. **Why were holy days instituted by the Church?**
Holy days were instituted by the Church to recall to our minds the great mysteries of religion and the virtues and rewards of the saints.

392. **How should we keep the holy days of obligation?**
We should keep the holy days of obligation as we should keep the Sunday.

393. **What do you mean by "fast days"?**
By "fast days," I mean days on which we are allowed but one full meal.

394. **What do you mean by "days of abstinence"?**
By "days of abstinence," I mean days on which we are forbidden to eat flesh meat, but are allowed the usual number of meals.

395. **Why does the Church command us to fast and abstain?**
The Church commands us to fast and abstain in order that we may mortify our passions and satisfy for our sins.

396. **Why does the Church command us to abstain from flesh meat on Fridays?**
The Church commands us to abstain from flesh meat on Fridays in honor of the day on which our Savior died.

LESSON THIRTY-SIXTH

On the Third, Fourth, Fifth, and Sixth Commandments of the Church

397. **What is meant by the command of confessing at least once a year?**
By the command of confessing at least once a year is meant that we are obliged, under pain of mortal sin, to go to confession within the year.

398. **Should we confess only once a year?**
We should confess frequently, if we wish to lead a good life.

399. **Should children go to confession?**
Children should go to confession when they are old enough to commit sin, which is commonly about the age of seven years.

400. **What sin does he commit who neglects to receive Communion during the Easter time?**
He who neglects to receive Communion during the Easter time commits a mortal sin.

401. **What is the Easter time?**
The Easter time is, in this country, the time between the First Sunday of Lent and Trinity Sunday.

402. **Are we obliged to contribute to the support of our pastors?**
We are obliged to contribute to the support of our pastors, and to bear our share in the expenses of the Church and school.

403. **What is the meaning of the commandment not to marry within the fourth degree of kindred?**
The meaning of the commandment not to marry within the fourth degree of kindred is that no one is allowed to marry another within the fourth degree of blood relationship.

404. **What is the meaning of the command not to marry privately?**
The command not to marry privately means that none should marry without the blessing of God's priests or without witnesses.

405. **What is the meaning of the precept not to solemnize marriage at forbidden times?**
The meaning of the precept not to solemnize marriage at forbidden times is that, during Lent and Advent, the marriage ceremony should not be performed with pomp or a nuptial Mass.

406. **What is the nuptial Mass?**
The nuptial Mass is a Mass appointed by the Church to invoke a special blessing upon the married couple.

407. **Should Catholics be married at a nuptial Mass?**
Catholics should be married at a nuptial Mass, because they thereby show greater reverence for the holy sacrament and bring richer blessings upon their wedded life.

LESSON THIRTY-SEVENTH

On the Last Judgment and the Resurrection, Hell, Purgatory, and Heaven

408. **When will Christ judge us?**
Christ will judge us immediately after our death, and on the last day.

409. **What is the judgment called which we have to undergo immediately after death?**
The judgment we have to undergo immediately after death is called "the particular judgment."

410. **What is the judgment called which all men have to undergo on the last day?**
The judgment which all men have to undergo on the last day is called "the general judgment."

411. **Why does Christ judge men immediately after death?**
Christ judges men immediately after death to reward or punish them according to their deeds.

412. **What are the rewards or punishments appointed for men's souls after the particular judgment?**
The rewards or punishments appointed for men's souls after the particular judgment are heaven, purgatory, and hell.

413. **What is hell?**
Hell is a state to which the wicked are condemned, and in which they are deprived of the sight of God for all eternity, and are in dreadful torments.

414. **What is purgatory?**
Purgatory is the state in which those suffer for a time who die guilty of venial sins, or without having satisfied for the punishment due to their sins.

415. **Can the faithful on earth help the souls in purgatory?**
The faithful on earth can help the souls in purgatory by their prayers, fasts, almsdeeds; by indulgences, and by having Masses said for them.

416. **If everyone is judged immediately after death, what need is there of a general judgment?**
There is need of a general judgment, though everyone is judged immediately after death, that the providence of God, which, on earth, often permits the good to suffer and the wicked to prosper, may in the end appear just before all men.

417. **Will our bodies share in the reward or punishment of our souls?**
Our bodies will share in the reward or punishment of our souls, because, through the resurrection, they will again be united to them.

418. **In what state will the bodies of the just rise?**
The bodies of the just will rise glorious and immortal.

419. **Will the bodies of the damned also rise?**
The bodies of the damned will also rise, but they will be condemned to eternal punishment.

420. **What is heaven?**
Heaven is the state of everlasting life in which we see God face-to-face, are made like unto him in glory, and enjoy eternal happiness.

421. **What words should we bear always in mind?**
We should bear always in mind these words of our Lord and Savior Jesus Christ: "What doth it profit a man if he gain the whole world and suffer the loss of his own soul, or what exchange shall a man give for his soul? For the Son of Man shall come in the glory of his Father with his angels: and then will he render to every man according to his works."[7]

[7] Cf. Mk 8:36-38; Rom 2:6

AN

EXPLANATION

OF THE

Baltimore Catechism

of Christian Doctrine.

FOR THE USE OF

Sunday-School Teachers and Advanced Classes.

BY

REV. THOMAS L. KINKEAD.

NEW YORK, CINCINNATI, CHICAGO:

BENZIGER BROTHERS,

PRINTERS TO THE HOLY APOSTOLIC SEE | PUBLISHERS OF BENZIGER'S MAGAZINE

AN

EXPLANATION

OF THE

Baltimore Catechism

of Christian Doctrine.

FOR THE USE OF

Sunday-School Teachers and Advanced Classes.

BY

REV. THOMAS L. KINKEAD.

NEW YORK, CINCINNATI, CHICAGO:

BENZIGER BROTHERS.

PRINTERS TO THE HOLY APOSTOLIC SEE | PUBLISHERS OF BENZIGER'S MAGAZINE

Nihil Obstat:
D. J. McMahon,
Censor Librorum.

Imprimatur:
Michael Augustine
Archbishop of New York.

NEW YORK, September 5, 1891.

Author's Preface

It must be evident to all who have had experience in the work of our Sunday schools that much time is wasted in the classes. Many teachers do little more than mark the attendance and hear the lessons; this being done, time hangs heavily on their hands till the school is dismissed. They do not or cannot explain what they are teaching, and the children have no interest in the study.

The *Explanation of the Baltimore Catechism* is intended for their use. The explanations are full and simple. The examples are taken from holy scripture, from the parables of our Lord, from incidents in his life, and from the customs and manners of the people of his time. These are made applicable to our daily lives in reflections and exhortations.

The plan of the book makes it very simple and handy. The catechism is complete and distinct in itself, and may be used with or without the explanations. The teacher is supposed, after hearing the lesson, to read the explanation of the new lesson as far as time will allow. It may be read just as it is, or may be learned by the teacher and given to the children in substance.

The *Explanation of the Baltimore Catechism* will be found very useful also for the instruction of adults and converts. The priest on the mission is often called upon to instruct persons who can come to him but seldom, and only for a short time; and who, moreover, are incapable of using with profit such books as *The Faith of Our Fathers*, *Catholic Belief*, or works of controversy. They are simply able to use the child's catechism when explained to them. If the *Explanation of the Baltimore Catechism* is in their hands, they may read the explanations and study the catechism with pleasure.

Indeed, the book should do good in any Catholic family. The majority of our people are children as far as their religious knowledge goes. They may, it is true, have books on particular subjects, such as the *Duties of Parents to Their Children*, *The Sure Way to a Happy Marriage*, etc.; but a book that explains to them in the simplest manner all the truths of their religion, and applies the same to their daily lives, ought to be useful.

The chief aim of the book is to be practical, and to teach Catholics what they should know, and how these truths of their catechism are constantly coming up in the performance of their everyday duties. It is therefore neither a book of devotion nor of controversy, though it covers the ground of both. As in this book, the explanations are interrupted by the questions and answers of the catechism proper, it will, it is hoped, be read with more pleasure than a book giving solid page after page of instruction.

Wherever a fact is mentioned as being taken from holy scripture, it will generally be given in substance and not in the exact text; though the reference will always be given, so that those wishing may read it as it is in the holy scripture. The children are not supposed to memorize the explanation as they do the catechism itself, yet the teacher, having once read it to them, should ask questions on it. The book may be used as a textbook or catechism for the more advanced classes, and the complete list of numbered questions on the explanations given at the end will render it very serviceable for that purpose.

As the same subject often occurs in different parts of the catechism, explanations already given may sometimes be repeated. This is done either to show the connection between the different parts of the catechism, or to impress the explanation more deeply on the minds of the children, or to save the teacher the trouble of always turning back to preceding explanations. The numbering of the questions and answers throughout the catechism, and the complete index of subjects and list of questions at the end, will, it is hoped, make these comparisons and references easy, and the book itself useful.

With the hope, then, that the *Explanation of the Baltimore Catechism* may do all the good intended, I commend it to all who desire a fuller knowledge of their holy religion that they may practice it more faithfully.

Feast of St. Aloysius, 1891.

An Explanation of the Catechism of Christian Doctrine

Prayers

The Lord's Prayer

Our Father, who art in heaven, hallowed be thy name. Thy kingdom come. Thy will be done on earth as it is in heaven. Give us this day our daily bread. And forgive us our trespasses, as we forgive those who trespass against us. And lead us not into temptation, but deliver us from evil. Amen.

This is the most beautiful and best of all prayers, because our Lord himself made it.[1] One day when he was praying and explaining to his apostles the great advantages of prayer, one of them said to him: "Lord, teach us to pray." Then Jesus taught them this prayer. It contains everything we need or could ask for. We cannot see its full meaning at once. The more we think over it, the more clearly we understand it. We could write whole pages on almost every word, and still not say all that could be said about this prayer. It is called "the Lord's" because he made it, and sometimes the "Our Father" from the first words.

Our. We say, "Our," to show that we are all brethren, and that God is the Father of us all, and therefore we pray not for ourselves alone but for all God's children.

[1] Cf. Mt 6:8; Lk 11:2

Father. We say, "Father," because God really is our Father. We do not mean here by *Father* the first Person of the Blessed Trinity, but the Blessed Trinity itself—one God. What does a father do for his children? He gives them their natural existence, provides them with food and clothing, teaches, protects, and loves them, shares with them all that he has, and, when he dies, leaves them his possessions. Now, in all these ways, and in a much truer sense, God is our Father. He created us and gives us all that is necessary to sustain life. He gives light, heat, and air, without any one of which we could not live. He provides for us also food and clothing, and, long before we need or even think of these things, God is thinking of them.

Did you ever reflect upon just how much time and trouble it costs to produce for you even one potato, of which you think so little? About two years before you need that potato, God puts it into the mind of the farmer to save the seed that he may plant it the following year. In the proper season he prepares the ground with great care and plants the seed. Then God sends his sunlight and rain to make it grow, but the farmer's work is not yet ended: he must continue to keep the soil in good condition and clear away the weeds. In due time, the potato is taken from the ground, brought to the market, carried to your house, cooked and placed before you. You take it without even thinking, perhaps, of all this trouble, or thanking God for his goodness. This is only one article of food, and the same may be said of all the rest. Your clothing is provided for you long before you need it. The little lamb upon whose back the wool is growing, from which your coat is some day to be made, is even now far away on some mountain, growing stronger with the food God gives it till you need its wool. The little pieces of coal, too, that you so carelessly throw upon the fire were formed deep down in the earth hundreds of years ago.

God produces all you use, because he foresees and knows you will use it. Moreover, he protects us from danger; he teaches us by the voice of our conscience and the ministers of his Church, our priests and bishops. He loves us too, as we may learn from all that he does for us, and from the many times he forgives us our sins. He shares what he possesses with us. He has given us understanding and a free will resembling his own. He has given us immortality, i.e., when once he has created us, we shall exist as long as himself—that is, forever. When Our Lord died on the cross, he left us his many possessions—his graces and merits, the holy sacraments, and heaven itself.

It is surely, then, just and right to call God *Father*. Our natural fathers give us only what they, themselves, get from God. So even what they give us also comes from him. Before the time of our Lord, the people in prayer did not call God *Father*. They feared him more than they loved him. When he spoke to them—as he did when he gave the commandments to Moses—it was in thunder, lightning, and smoke.[2] They looked upon God as a great and terrible king who would destroy them for their sins. He sent the deluge on account of sin, and he destroyed the wicked city of Sodom with fire from heaven.[3] They called him *Jehovah*, and were afraid sometimes even to pronounce his name. But our Lord taught that God, besides being a great and powerful King—the ruler of the universe and Lord of all things—is also a kind and good Father, who wishes his children not to offend him, because they love him rather than because they fear him, and therefore he taught his disciples and all Christians to call God by the sweet name of *Father*.

Who art in heaven. The catechism says God is everywhere. Why then do we say, "who art in heaven," as if he were no place else? We say so to remind us, first, that heaven is our true home, and that this world is only a strange land in which we are staying for a while to do the work that God wishes us to do here, and then return to our own home; second, that in heaven we shall see God face-to-face and as he is; third, that heaven is the place where God will be for all eternity with the blessed.

Hallowed means "made holy or sacred." *Halloween* is the name given to the evening before the feast of All Hallows or All Saints.

Thy kingdom come. This petition contains a great deal more than we at first see in it. In it we ask that God may reign in our hearts and in the hearts of all men by his grace in this life, and that we and all men may attain our eternal salvation, and thus be brought to reign forever with God in heaven—the kingdom of his glory. As the Church on earth is frequently called "the kingdom of Christ," and as all the labors of the Church are directed to the

[2] Cf. Ex 19

[3] Cf. Gn 7; 19

salvation of souls, we pray also in this petition that the Church may be extended upon earth, that the true religion may be spread over the whole world, that all men may know and serve the true God and cheerfully obey his holy laws; that the devil may have no dominion over them. While saying this petition, we may have it in our minds to pray even for particular ways in which the true religion can be spread; for example, by praying that the missionaries may meet with success and all the missions prosper; that priests and bishops may be ordained to preach the gospel; that the Church may overcome all her enemies everywhere, and the true religion triumph.

Thy will be done on earth as it is in heaven. In heaven, all the angels and saints obey God perfectly; they never offend him; so we pray that it may be on earth as it is in heaven, all men doing God's will, observing his laws and the laws of his Church, and living without sin.

Give us this day our daily bread. In this petition *bread* means not merely bread, but everything we need for our daily lives; such as food, clothing, light, heat, air, and the like; also, food for the soul, i.e., grace. If a beggar told you that he had not tasted bread for the whole day, you would never think of asking him if he had eaten any cake, because you would understand by his word *bread* all kinds of food. We say, "daily," to teach us not to be greedy or too careful about ourselves, and not to ask for unnecessary things, but to pray for what we need for our present wants.

And forgive us our trespasses as we forgive those who trespass against us. Trespasses means here "our sins," "our offenses against God." When we trespass, we enter places we should not, or where we are forbidden to go. So, when we sin, we go where we should not go, namely, out of the path of virtue that leads to God, and into the way of vice that leads to the devil.

As we forgive them. We take this to mean: "We forgive others who have offended us, and for that reason, God, you should forgive us who have offended you." Our Lord told[4] a beautiful parable, i.e., a story by way of illustration, to explain this. A very rich man had a servant who owed him a large sum of money. One day, the master asked the servant for the money, and the poor servant had none to give. Now, the law of the country was

[4] Cf. Mt 18:23ff

that when anyone could not pay his debts, all that he had could be sold and the money given to the one to whom it was due, and if that was not sufficient, he and his wife and his children could be sold as slaves. The servant, knowing this, fell on his knees and begged his master to be patient with him, and to give him time and he would pay all. Then his master was moved to pity, granted not only what he asked, but freed him from the debt altogether. Afterward, when this servant, who had just been forgiven the large sum, was going out, he found one of his fellow servants who owed him a very small sum of money, and taking hold of him by the throat, demanded payment. Now, this poor servant, having nothing to give just then, implored his assailant to be patient with him, and he would pay all. But the hard-hearted servant—though he himself had a little while before asked and obtained the very same favor from his own master—would not listen to the request or wait longer, but went and had his fellow servant cast into prison till he should pay the debt. The other servants, seeing how unforgiving this man was who had himself been forgiven, went and told all to their master, and he, being angry at such conduct, had the unforgiving servant brought back and cast into prison.

And lead us not into temptation. Temptation means "a trial to see whether we will do a thing or not." Here it means a trial made by some person or thing—the devil, the world, or our own flesh—to see whether we will sin or not. God does not exactly lead us into temptation; but he allows us to fall into it. He allows others to tempt us. We can overcome any temptation to sin by the help or grace that God gives us. Therefore, we ask in this petition that God will always give us the grace to overcome the temptation, and that we may not consent to it. A temptation is not a sin. It becomes sin only when we are overcome by it. When we are tempted, we are like soldiers fighting a battle: if the soldiers are conquered by their enemy, they are disgraced; but if they conquer their enemy, they have great glory and great rewards. So, when we overcome temptation, God gives us a new glory and reward for every victory.

Deliver us from evil. From every kind of evil, and especially the evil of being conquered by our spiritual enemies, and thus falling into sin, and offending God by becoming his enemy ourselves. It would be a sin to seek temptation, though we have a reward for resisting it when it comes.

Amen means "be it so." May all we have asked be granted just as we have asked it.

The Angelical Salutation

Hail, Mary, full of grace! the Lord is with thee: blessed art thou amongst women, and blessed is the fruit of thy womb, Jesus. Holy Mary, Mother of God, pray for us sinners, now and at the hour of our death. Amen.

Next in beauty to the Lord's Prayer comes this prayer. It is made up of three parts.

Hail, full of grace! the Lord is with thee: blessed art thou amongst women was composed by the angel Gabriel, for these are the words he used when he came to tell the Blessed Virgin that she was selected to be the Mother of God.[5] All her people knew that the Redeemer promised from the time of Eve down to the time of the Blessed Virgin was now to be born, and many good women were anxious to be his mother, and they believed the one who would be selected the most blessed and happy of all women.

The Lord is with thee by his grace and favor, since you are the one he loves best. He is with all his creatures, but he is with you in a very special manner.

Blessed art thou amongst women, and blessed is the fruit of thy womb. After the visit of the angel, the Blessed Virgin went a good distance to visit her cousin, St. Elizabeth, who was the mother of St. John the Baptist.[6] When St. Elizabeth saw her, she, without being told by the Blessed Virgin what the angel had done, knew by the inspiration of the Holy Ghost what had taken place, and said to the Blessed Virgin: "Blessed art thou amongst women, and blessed is the fruit of thy womb." That is, *blessed* because, of all the women that have ever lived or ever shall live, you are the one selected by God to be the Mother of his Son and our Redeemer, and blessed is that

[5] Lk 1:28
[6] Cf. Lk 1:39ff

Son himself. This is the second part of the prayer. The third part, from *Holy Mary* to the end, was composed by the Church.

Hail. This was the word used by the people of that country in saluting one another when they met. We say when meeting anyone we know, "Good day," or "How do you do?" or some such familiar expression used by all in salutation. So, these people, instead of saying, "Good day," etc., said, "Hail," i.e., "I wish you health," "I greet you," etc. The angel did not say "Mary," because she was the only one present to address.

Full of grace. When anything is full, it has no room for more. God's grace and sin cannot exist in the same place. Therefore, when the Blessed Virgin was full of grace, there was no room for sin. So, she was without any sin and gifted with every virtue.

Holy Mary, because one full of grace must be holy.

Mother of God, because her Son was true God and true man in the one Person of Christ, our Lord.

Pray for us, because she has more power with her Son than all the other saints.

Sinners, and therefore we need forgiveness.

At the hour of our death especially, because that is the most important time for us. No matter how bad we have been during our lives, if God gives us the grace to die in his friendship, we shall be his friends forever. On the other hand, no matter how good we may have been for a part of our lives, if we become bad before death, and die in that state, we shall be separated from God forever, and be condemned to eternal punishment. It would be wrong, therefore, to live in sin, with a promise that we shall die well, for God may not give us the grace or opportunity to repent, and we may die in sin if we have lived in sin. Besides this, the devil knows how much depends upon the state in which we die, and so he perhaps will tempt us more at death than at any other time; for if we yield to him and die in sin, we shall be with him forever—it is his last chance to secure our souls.

The Angelus. Besides the Hail Mary, there is another beautiful prayer on the same subject, called the *Angelus*. It is a little history of the incarnation, and is said morning, noon, and evening in honor of our Lord's incarnation, death, and resurrection. It is made up of three parts. The first part tells what the angel did, namely: "The angel of the Lord declared unto Mary. And she conceived of the Holy Ghost." After saying these words, we say one Hail Mary in honor of the angel's message. The second part tells what Mary answered, namely: "Behold the handmaid of the Lord. Be it done unto me according to thy word." We say another Hail Mary in honor of Mary's consent. The third part tells how our Lord became man, namely: "And the Word was made flesh. And dwelt among us." The *Word* means here the second Person of the Blessed Trinity; and *made flesh* means "became man." Then another Hail Mary is said in honor of our Lord's goodness in humbling himself so much for our sake. After these three parts, we say: "Pray for us, O holy Mother of God! That we may be made worthy of the promises of Christ"; and, finally, we say a prayer in honor of our Lord's incarnation, passion, and resurrection. This beautiful prayer is said three times a day in all seminaries, convents, and religious houses. The time for saying it is made known by the ringing of a bell called the "Angelus bell." In many parishes, the church bell rings out the *Angelus*. In Catholic countries, the people stop wherever they are and whatever they are doing, and bowing their heads, say the *Angelus* when they hear its bell. It is a beautiful practice and one most pleasing to our Blessed Lord and his holy Mother. Good Catholics should not neglect it.

The Litany of the Blessed Virgin, and other litanies. I might mention here another kind of prayer often said in honor of our Blessed Mother. It is the litany. In this form of prayer, we call our Lady many beautiful names which we know are most dear to her, asking her after each one to pray for us. We address her first by names reminding her that she is the Mother of God and has therefore great influence with her divine Son. We say: "Mother of Christ," "Mother of our Creator," "Mother of our Redeemer," etc., "pray for us." Next, we remind her that she is a Virgin and should take pity on us who are exposed to so many temptations against holy purity. We call her "Virgin most pure," "Virgin most chaste," etc., and again ask her to pray for us. Lastly, we call her all those names that could induce her to hear us. We say: "Health of the weak," "Refuge of sinners," "Help of Christians," "pray for us."

In addition to the Litany of the Blessed Virgin, we have the Litany of the Holy Name of Jesus, the Litany of the Blessed Sacrament, the Litany of the Sacred Heart, the Litany of St. Joseph, and many others—all made up in the same form. We have also the Litany of all the Saints, in which we beg the help and prayers of the different classes of saints—the apostles, martyrs, virgins, etc.

The Apostles' Creed

I believe in God, the Father Almighty, Creator of heaven and earth; and in Jesus Christ, his only Son, our Lord, who was conceived by the Holy Ghost, born of the Virgin Mary, suffered under Pontius Pilate, was crucified, died, and was buried. He descended into hell; the third day he arose again from the dead; he ascended into heaven, sitteth at the right hand of God, the Father Almighty; from thence he shall come to judge the living and the dead. I believe in the Holy Ghost, the holy Catholic Church, the communion of saints, the forgiveness of sins, the resurrection of the body, and the life everlasting. Amen.

A creed is a definite list or summary of all the things one believes. The Apostles' Creed is therefore a list or collection of all the truths the apostles believed. The apostles were the twelve men that our Lord selected to be his first bishops. We know they were bishops because they could ordain priests and consecrate other bishops. They lived with our Lord like a little family during the three and a half years of his public life; they went with him and learned from him wherever he preached. Besides these, he had also his disciples, i.e., followers who went with him frequently but did not live with him.

Our Lord wished his doctrine to be taught to all the people of the world, and so he told his apostles that they must go over the whole world and preach in every country. During the life of our Lord and for a short time after his death, they preached in only one country, namely, Palestine—now called "the Holy Land"—in which country the Jews, up to that time God's chosen people, lived. Since the apostles were to preach to all nations, the time came when they must separate, one going to one country, and another to another. In those days there were no steamboats or railroads, no post offices, telegraph offices, telephones, or newspapers. If the apostles wished to communicate with anyone, they had either to go to the place themselves or send a messenger. By walking or riding, it might have taken them months or years in those days to make a journey that we can make now in a few days; and for an answer to a message which we can get now by telegraph in a few hours, they might have had to wait months. The apostles knew of all these inconveniences, and, before leaving the places they were in, pointed out the chief truths that all should know and believe before receiving baptism, that Christian teachers who should come after them might neglect nothing—just as we use catechisms containing all the truths of religion, for fear the teachers might forget to speak of some of them.

There are twelve articles or parts in the Apostles' Creed, and each part is meant to refute some false doctrine taught before the time of the apostles or while they lived. Thus, there were those—as the Romans—who said there were many gods; others said not God, but the devil created the earth; others taught that our Lord was not the Son of God: and so on for the rest. All these false doctrines are denied and the truth professed when we say the Apostles' Creed. Just as in the Lord's Prayer, we do not see all its meaning at first, so, in the Apostles' Creed, we find many beautiful things only after thinking carefully over every word it contains.

I believe, without the slightest doubt or suspicion that I might be wrong.

In God, by the grace that he gives me to believe and have full confidence in him.

God, to show that there is only one.

The Father, because he brought everything into existence and keeps it so.[7]

Almighty, i.e., having all might or power; because he can do whatever he wishes. He can make or destroy by merely wishing.

Creator. *To create* means "to make out of nothing." God alone can create. When a carpenter makes a table, he must have wood; when a tailor makes a coat, he must have cloth. They are only makers and not creators. God needs no material or tools. When we make anything, we make it part by part; but God makes the whole at once. He simply wills, and it is made. Thus, he said in the beginning of the world: "Let there be light; and light was made." For

[7] See explanation of the Lord's Prayer, above.

example, suppose I wanted a piano. If I could say, "Let there be a piano," and it immediately sprang up without any other effort on my part, although neither the wood, the iron, the wire, the ivory, nor anything else in it ever existed till I said, "Let there be a piano," then it could be said I created a piano. No one could do this, for God alone has such power.

Heaven and earth and everything we can see or know of.

Jesus Christ. Our Lord is called by many names, but you must not be confused by them, for they all mean the same Person, and are given only to remind us of some particular thing connected with our Lord. He is called "Jesus," which signifies "Savior," and "Christ," which means "Anointed." He is called the "second Person of the Blessed Trinity," and when we call him "our Lord," we mean the second Person of the Blessed Trinity after he became man. He is called the "Messias" and the "Son of David" to show that he is the Redeemer promised to the Jews. Also, at the end of all our litanies, he is called the "Lamb of God," because he was so meek and humble and suffered death so patiently. In the Litany of the Holy Name of Jesus we will find many other beautiful names of our Lord, all having their special signification.

His only Son, to show that God, the first Person of the Blessed Trinity, was his real Father. We are called "God's children," but we are only his created and adopted children.

Who was conceived, i.e., he began to exist by the power of the Holy Ghost in the womb of his Mother, the Blessed Virgin.

Suffered. We shall see in the explanation of the passion what he suffered.

Under means here "at the time a man named Pontius Pilate was governor." If anyone were put to death today in this country, we should say he was executed under Governor or President so-and-so.

Crucified, i.e., nailed to a cross. We say, *died,* because our Lord is the giver of life, and no one could take his life away unless he allowed it Therefore we say he died, and not that he was killed, to show that he died by his own free will and not against his will.

Was buried. This we say to show that he was really dead; because if you bury a man who is not really dead, he must die.

Hell here does not mean the place where the damned are, but a place called "limbo." You know that when our first parents sinned, heaven was closed against them and us, and no human being could be admitted into it till after the death of our Lord; for he by his death would redeem us — make amends for our fall and once more open for us heaven. Now, from the time Adam sinned till the time Christ died is about four thousand years. During that time, there were at least some good men, like Abraham, Isaac, Jacob, Moses, David, and others in the world, who tried to serve God as best they could, keeping all the divine laws known to them, and believing that the Messias would someday come to redeem them. When, therefore, they died, they could not go to heaven, because it was closed against them. They could not go to hell, because they were good men. Neither could they go to purgatory, because they would have to suffer there. Where could they go? God, in his goodness, provided a place for them — limbo — where they could stay without suffering till our Lord reopened heaven. Therefore, while our Lord's body lay in the sepulchre, his soul went down into limbo, to tell these good men that heaven was now opened for them, and that, at his ascension, he would take them there with him.

The third day. Not three full days, but the parts of three days, namely, Friday afternoon, Saturday, and Sunday morning.

He arose by his own power: and this was the greatest of all our Lord's miracles. Some others, like the prophets and apostles, have, by the power God gave them, raised the dead to life; but no dead person ever raised himself. Our Lord is the first and only one to do this, and, by so doing, showed they could not take away his life, unless he wished to give it up; for since he could always take back his life, how could they destroy it?

He ascended forty days after his resurrection.

Right hand of God. We know God is a pure Spirit having no body; and if he has no body, he can have no hands. Why then do we say, "right hand"? When the president of the United States invites anyone to dine at his house, he makes the invited guest sit at his right hand, and thus shows his respect by giving him the place of highest honor. When our Lord ascended into heaven, he went up in the human body he had upon earth, and his Father placed him as man, in his glorified body, in the place, after his [the Father's] own, the highest in heaven; but remember, only as man, because as God he is equal to his Father in all things.

From thence—that is, from the right hand of God.

To judge. To examine them, to pronounce sentence upon them; to reward them in heaven or punish them in hell.

The living and the dead. We may take this in a double sense. As the general judgment will come suddenly and when not expected, all will be going on in the world as usual—some attending to business, others taking their ease as they do now, or as they were doing when the deluge came upon them. Just when the judgment is about to take place, God will destroy the earth; and then all those living in the world will perish with its destruction and then be judged. *The dead* means, therefore, "all those who died before the destruction of the world," and *the living*, "all those who were on earth when the time of its destruction came." Or, *the living* may mean also those in a state of grace, and *the dead*, those in mortal sin; for God will judge both classes.

Holy Ghost, i.e., the third Person of the Blessed Trinity. *Ghost* is an old word meaning "spirit." When persons say that a ghost appeared, they mean that the spirit of some dead person appeared. These stories about ghosts are told generally to frighten children or timid persons. If those who thought they saw a ghost always examined what they saw, they would find that the supposed ghost was something very natural; probably a bush swayed by the wind, or a stray animal, or perhaps some person trying to frighten them. *Ghost* here does not mean the spirit of a dead person, but the Holy Spirit, which is the proper name for the third Person of the Blessed Trinity.

The communion of saints. There are three parts in the Church. We have, first, the Church militant, i.e., the fighting Church, made up of all the faithful upon earth, who are still fighting for their salvation. The holy scripture tells us our life upon earth is a warfare. We have three enemies to fight. First, the devil, who by every means wishes to keep us out of heaven—the place he once enjoyed himself. The devil knows well the happiness of heaven, and does not wish us to have what he cannot have himself; just as you sometimes see persons who, through their own fault, have lost their situation trying to keep others out of it.

Our second enemy is the world. This does not mean the earth with all its beauty and riches, but the bad people in the world with their false doctrines; some telling us there is no God, heaven, or hell; others that we should pay no attention to the teaching of the Church or the laws of God, and advising us by word and example to resist our lawful superiors in Church or state and give free indulgence to our sinful passions.

The third enemy is our own flesh. By this, we mean our concupiscence, that is, our passions, evil inclinations, and propensity to do wrong. When God first created man, the soul was always master over the body, and the body obedient to the soul. After Adam sinned, the body rebelled against the soul and tried to lead it into sin. The body is the part of our nature that makes us like the brute animals, while the soul makes us like to God and the angels.

When we sin, it is generally to satisfy the body craving for what it has not, or for that which is forbidden. Why did God leave this concupiscence in us? He left it, first, to keep us humble, by reminding us of our former sins, and, secondly, that we might overcome it and have a reward for the victory.

The second branch of the Church is called the "Church suffering." It is made up of all those who have gone through this world and are now in purgatory.

Some of them while on earth fought well, but not as well as they could have done; they yielded to some temptations, fell into some small sins, received some slight wounds from their spiritual enemies, or they have not satisfied God entirely for the temporal guilt due to their great sins; therefore, they are in purgatory till they can be completely purified from all their sins and admitted into heaven.

The last or third branch of the Church is called the "Church triumphant," and is made up of the angels and all those who have lived at one time upon earth and who are now in heaven with God, enjoying their rewards for overcoming their spiritual enemies and serving God while upon earth. They are triumphant or rejoicing because they have reached their heavenly home.

You must not think that those only are saints who have been canonized by the Church and whose names are known to us; for all in heaven are saints, as we also shall be if admitted into that happy eternity. God wishes all to be saints, for he wishes all to be saved. You know we can pray to the saints and ask their help and prayers; but how could we know that certain men or women are really in heaven? We can know it when the Church canonizes them, and thus gives proof that they were great spiritual heroes in the service of God and can be more confidently appealed to on account of their eminent sanctity and powerful intercession.

Therefore, the Church by canonization tells us for certain that such and such persons are truly in heaven. But might not the Church be deceived like ourselves?

No! for Christ has promised to be always with his Church, and the Holy Ghost is ever directing her, so that she cannot err in faith or morals. If the Church made us pray to persons who are not saints, she would fall into the worst of errors, and our Lord would have failed to keep his promise—a saying that would be blasphemous, for Christ, being God, is infinitely true and could not deceive or be deceived. To canonize, therefore, does not mean to make a saint, but to declare to the whole world that such a one was a saint while upon earth. After death, we cannot merit, so our reward in heaven will be just what we have secured up till the moment of our death; hence, holiness is acquired in the Church militant.

How does the Church canonize a saint? Let us suppose some good man dies, and all his neighbors talk about his holy life, how much he did for the poor, how he prayed, fasted, and mortified himself. All these accounts of his life are collected and sent to Rome, to the holy father or to the cardinals appointed by him to examine such statements. These accounts must show that the good man practiced virtue in a more than ordinary manner, that he either performed some miracles while he lived, or that God granted miracles after his death through his intercession.

These accounts are not examined immediately after his death, but sometimes after a lapse of fifty years or more, so that people might not exaggerate his good works because they knew him personally. When these accounts are examined, one is appointed to prevent, if he can, the canonization. He is sometimes called the "devil's advocate," because it is his business to find fault with all the accounts and miracles, and prove them false if possible. This is done to make certain that all the accounts are true and the miracles real. If everything is found as represented, then the good man is declared venerable, later beatified, i.e., called "blessed," and still later canonized, i.e., declared a saint. If he is only beatified, he can be honored publicly only in certain places or by certain persons; but if he is canonized, he can be honored throughout the whole Church by all the faithful.

Thus, we understand the three branches of the one true Church—the Church militant, i.e., all those who are on earth trying to save their souls; the Church suffering, those in purgatory, having their souls purified for heaven; and the Church triumphant, those already in heaven.

The communion of saints means that these three branches of the Church can help one another. We help the souls in purgatory by our prayers and good works, and the saints in heaven pray for us. But *communion of saints* means still more. Let us take an example. Suppose there are in a family, living together, a mother and three sons. The eldest son earns a large salary, the second son enough to support himself, and the youngest very little. They give their earnings to their mother, who from the combined amounts provides for the wants of all and draws from the large salary of the eldest to supply the needs of the youngest. Thus, he who has too little for his support is—through his mother—aided by the one who has more than he needs. Now, the Church is our mother, and some of her children—the great saints—were rich in good works and did more than was necessary to gain heaven, while others did not do enough. Then our mother, the Church, draws from the abundant satisfaction of her rich children to help those who are poor in merit and good works. The greatest treasure she has to draw from for that purpose is the more than abundant merits of our Lord and the superabundant satisfaction of the Blessed Virgin and the greatest saints. Our Lord could have redeemed us all by the least suffering, and yet he suffered dreadful torments, and even shed his blood and died for us. The Blessed Virgin never sinned, yet she performed many good works and offered many prayers. Therefore, *communion of saints* means, also, that we all share in the merits of Christ and in the superabundant satisfaction of the Blessed Virgin and of the saints; also, in the prayers and good works of the Church and of her faithful and pious children.

The forgiveness of sins, i.e., by the sacrament of penance, through the power that God gave his priests; also, by baptism.

The resurrection of the body, i.e., on the last day.[8] When on the last day, at the general judgment, God's angel sounds the great trumpet, all the dead will arise again and come to judgment, in the same bodies they had while living. But you will say: "If their bodies are reduced to ashes and mixed with the earth, or if parts of them are in one place and parts in another, how is this possible?" Very easily, with God. If he in the beginning could make all the parts out of nothing, with how much ease can he collect them scattered here and there! When God made man, he gave him a body and a soul, and wished them never to be separated. Man was to live here upon earth for a time, and then be taken up into heaven, body and soul, as our Lord is there now. But when man sinned, in punishment God commanded that he should die; i.e., that these two dear friends, the body and the soul, should be separated for a time. Death is caused by the separation of the soul from the body. The body and soul together make a man, and neither one alone can be called a man. A dead body is only part of a man. At the resurrection, every soul will come from heaven, purgatory, or hell, to seek its own body; they will then be united again as they were in life, never to be separated—to be happy together in heaven if they have been good upon earth, or miserable together in hell if they had been bad upon earth.

Life everlasting—either, as we have said, in heaven or hell. There was a time when we did not exist; but it can never be said of us again we do not exist. When once we have been created, we shall live as long as God himself, i.e., forever. When we have lived a thousand years for every drop of water in the ocean; a thousand years for every grain of sand on the seashore; a thousand years for every blade of grass and every leaf on the earth, we shall still be existing. How short a time, therefore, is a hundred years: even if we live so long—and few do—compared with all these millions of years! And yet it depends upon the time we live here, whether all these millions of years in the next world will be for us years of happiness or of misery. The whole life of a man extends through the two worlds, namely, from the moment of his creation through all eternity; and surely the little while he stays upon earth must seem very short when, after spending a

[8] Cf. Mt 24:29; Lk 21:25

million of years in the next world, he looks back to his earthly life. There is a good example to illustrate this. If you stand on a railroad, and look away down the track for about a mile, it will seem to you that the rails come nearer and nearer, till at last they touch. It seems so on account of the distance, for, where they seem to touch, they are just as far apart as where you are standing. So, also, when you look back from eternity, the day of your birth and the day of your death will seem to coincide, and your life on earth appear nothing. Then, if you are among the lost souls, you will think, "What a fool I was to make myself suffer all this long eternity for that silly bit of earthly pleasure, which is of no benefit to me now!" And this thought will serve only to make you more miserable. But, on the other hand, if you look back from a happy eternity, you will wonder at God's goodness in giving you so much happiness for so short a service upon earth.

The Confiteor

I confess to Almighty God, to Blessed Mary ever Virgin, to blessed Michael the archangel, to blessed John the Baptist, to the holy apostles Peter and Paul, and to all the saints, that I have sinned exceedingly, in thought, word, and deed, through my fault, through my fault, through my most grievous fault. Therefore, I beseech Blessed Mary ever Virgin, blessed Michael the archangel, blessed John the Baptist, the holy apostles Peter and Paul, and all the saints, to pray to the Lord our God for me.

May the Almighty God have mercy on me, forgive me my sins, and bring me to everlasting life. Amen.

May the Almighty and merciful Lord grant me pardon, absolution, and remission of all my sins. Amen.

This is another beautiful prayer. In it we can imagine that we are permitted to enter heaven. What do we see there? God, the Blessed Virgin, the thousands of angels, the apostles, all the saints, martyrs, confessors, doctors, and virgins. They cease singing God's praises, as we enter, and fix their eyes upon us. Our guardian angel conducts us before the great throne of God, and we kneel down in the presence of the whole court of heaven, to acknowledge our sins and faults, while all listen attentively. Touched by so sublime a sight and the thought of having offended a God of so much glory, we begin our accusation of ourselves. We fix our eyes first upon God, and say: *I confess*, i.e., accuse myself, *to Almighty God*. Then we look upon the rest of the blessed, and say: *to the Blessed Mary ever Virgin*, etc. Thus we call the whole court of heaven to be a witness of the fact that we *have sinned*, not lightly, but *exceedingly*, i.e., very greatly, and in three ways: *in thought*, by thinking of things sinful and forbidden; *in word*, by lies, curses, slanders, etc.; *in deed*, by every bad action that we have committed; and each of us can say: "I have done all this *through my fault*," i.e., willingly and deliberately; and it was not a small fault, but an exceeding great fault, because God was helping me by his grace to overcome temptations and avoid bad thoughts, words, and actions, and I would not accept his help, but willingly did what was wrong. What am I to do, therefore? Will God pardon all these offenses if I alone ask him, seeing that all the angels and saints know that I have thus offended him? What shall I do? I will ask them to help me by their prayers, and to beg God's pardon for me. He may grant their prayers, especially those of the Blessed Mother and of the saints, when he would not grant mine. *Therefore, I beseech the Blessed Mary ever Virgin*, etc., *to pray to the Lord our God for me.*

When we kneel down to say the *confiteor*, if we could imagine what I have just described to take place, how well we should say it! With what attention, respect, and sorrow we should ask the prayers of the saints! When we say the *confiteor*, and indeed any prayer, we say it in the presence of God, and of the whole court of heaven, though we are not in heaven and cannot see God. The angels and saints do hear us and will pray for us. When, therefore, you are saying the *confiteor*, imagine that you see all I have described, and you will never say it badly.

An Act of Faith

O my God! I firmly believe that thou art one God in three divine Persons, Father, Son, and Holy Ghost; I believe that thy divine Son became man, and died for our sins, and that he will come to judge the living and the dead. I believe these and all the truths which the holy Catholic Church teaches, because thou hast revealed them, who canst neither deceive nor be deceived.

An act, i.e., a profession, of faith. The whole substance of the act of faith is contained in this: "I believe all that God has revealed and the Catholic Church teaches." We might mention one by one all the truths God has revealed, i.e., made known to us, and all the truths the Catholic Church teaches as revealed by God. For example, we might say, "I believe in the Holy Trinity, in the incarnation of our Lord, in the Holy Eucharist, in the immaculate conception of the Blessed Virgin, in the infallibility of the pope," and so on, till we write an act of faith twenty pages long, and yet it would all be contained in the words: "I believe all God has revealed and the Catholic Church teaches." Hence, we find in prayer books and catechisms acts of faith differing in length and words, but they are all the same in substance and have the same meaning. The act of faith in our catechism gives a few of the chief truths revealed, that it may be neither too short nor too long, and that all may learn the same words.

An Act of Hope

O my God! relying on thy infinite goodness and promises, I hope to obtain pardon of my sins, the help of thy grace, and life everlasting, through the merits of Jesus Christ, my Lord and Redeemer.

The substance of this act is: "I hope for heaven and the means to obtain it." The means by which I will obtain it are the pardon of my sins by God, and the grace which he will give me in the reception of the sacraments and in prayer; by which grace I will be able to know him, love him, and serve him, and thus come to be with him forever. Here again we could make a long act by mentioning all the things we hope for; namely, a good death, a favorable judgment, a place in heaven, etc.

An Act of Love

O my God! I love thee above all things, with my whole heart and soul, because thou art all-good and worthy of all love. I love my neighbor as myself for the love of thee. I forgive all who have injured me, and ask pardon of all whom I have injured.

The substance of this act is: "I love God above all things for his own goodness, and my neighbor as myself for the sake of God." An act of love and an act of charity are the same thing with different names. We are accustomed to call such things as the giving of alms or help to the poor, the doing of some good work that we are not bound to do for another, "charity." Surely, there are many motives that may induce persons to help others in their distress; but what is the chief Christian motive, if it be not the love we bear our brotherman because he is, like ourselves, a child of God, and the desire we have to obey God, who wishes us to help the needy? The sufferings of others excite our pity, and the more we love them the more sorry are we to see them suffer. Thanks to God for all his mercies to us; he might have made us, instead of this man, poor and in suffering, but he has spared us and afflicted him; we know not why God has done so, and therefore we help him, moved by these considerations even when we feel he is not deserving of the help, because we know his unworthiness will not prevent God from rewarding our good intention. We may be charitable to our neighbor by saying nothing hurtful about him, by never telling his faults without necessity, etc. Therefore, real charity, in its widest sense, and love are just the same.

An Act of Contrition

O my God! I am heartily sorry for having offended thee, and I detest all my sins, because I dread the loss of heaven and the pains of hell, but most of all because they offend thee, my God, who art all-good and deserving of all my love. I firmly resolve, with the help of thy grace, to confess my sins, to do penance, and to amend my life.

The substance of this act is: "O my God! I am very sorry for all my sins, because by them I have offended thee, and, with thy help, I will never sin again." It is well to know what the acts contain in substance, for we can use these short forms as aspirations during the day, when we probably would not think of saying the long forms. A fuller explanation of the qualities of our contrition will be given in Lesson Eighteenth.

The Blessing before Meals

Bless us, O Lord, and these thy gifts which we are to receive from thy bounty, through Christ our Lord. Amen.

Grace after Meals

We give thee thanks for all thy benefits, O Almighty God, who livest and reignest forever. And may the souls of the faithful departed, through the mercy of God, rest in peace. Amen.

Grace means "thanks." We saw in the explanation of the Our Father how God provides us with all we need, and most frequently with food. It is the least we can do, therefore, to thank him for it, when it is just placed before us. We should thank him also after we have eaten it and found it good, pleasing, and refreshing. When God provides us with food, he thereby makes a kind of promise that he will allow us to live awhile longer and give us strength to serve him. How shameful it is, then, to turn God's gifts into a means of offending him, as some do by the sin of gluttony!

Again, it is very wrong to murmur and be dissatisfied with what God gives us. He does not owe us anything, and need not give unless he wishes. What would you think of a beggar of this kind? He comes to your door hungry, and you, instead of simply giving him some bread to appease his hunger, take him into your house and give him a good dinner, new clothing, and some money. Now, instead of being thankful, suppose he should complain because you did not give him a better dinner, finer clothing, and more money, and should look cross and dissatisfied; what would you think of him? Would you not be tempted to turn the ungrateful fellow out of your house, with an order never to come again, telling him he deserved to starve for his ingratitude? We are not quite as ungrateful as the beggar when we neglect grace at meals, because, in saying our daily prayers, we thank God for all his gifts, our food included, and hence it is not a sin to neglect grace at meals. But do we not show some ingratitude when we murmur, complain, and are dissatisfied with our food, clothing, or homes? God, even when we are ungrateful, still gives; hence his wonderful goodness and mercy to us.

The Manner in Which a Lay Person Is to Baptize in Case of Necessity

Pour common water on the head or face of the person to be baptized, and say while pouring it: "I baptize thee, in the name of the Father, and of the Son, and of the Holy Ghost."

Note.—Any person of either sex who has reached the use of reason can baptize in case of necessity.

Catechism

A catechism is any book made up in question-and-answer form, no matter what it treats of. We have catechisms of history, of geography, etc. Our catechism is a book in the same form treating of religion. It is a little compendium of the truths of our religion, of all we must believe and do. It contains, in the simplest form, all that a priest learns during his many years of study. The theology he learns is only a deeper and fuller explanation of the catechism. A whole book might be written on almost every question. For example, might we not write a book on each of the first three questions: the world, God, and man? There is consequently much meaning in the catechism, which must be made known to us by explanation. You should therefore learn the catechism by heart now, even when you do not fully understand it; because afterward, when you read books on religion or hear sermons, all these questions and answers will come back to your mind. Sermons will help you to understand the questions, or the questions will help you to understand the sermons.

LESSON FIRST

On the End of Man

The end of a thing is the purpose for which it was made. The end of a watch is to keep time. The end of a pen is to write, etc. A thing is good only in proportion to the way it fulfills the end for which it was made. A watch may be very beautifully made, a very rare ornament, but, if it will not keep time, it is useless as a watch. The same may be said of the pen, or of anything else. Now, for what purpose was man made? If we discover that, we know his end. When we look around us in the world, we see a purpose or end for everything. We see that the soil is made for the plants and trees to grow in; because if there was no need of things growing, it would be better to have a nice clean solid rock to walk upon, and then we would be spared the trouble of making roads and paving streets. But things must grow, and so we must have soil. Again, the vegetables and plants are made for animals to feed upon; while the animals themselves are made for man, that they may help him in his work or serve him for food. Thus it is evident everything in the world was made to serve something else.

What then was man made for? Was it for anything in the world? We see that all classes of beings are created for something higher than themselves. Thus plants are higher than soil, because they have life and soil has not. Animals are higher than plants, because they not only have life, but they can feel and plants cannot. Man is higher than animals, because he not only has life and can feel, but he has also reason and intelligence, and can understand, while animals cannot. Therefore, we must look for something higher than man himself; but there is nothing higher than man in this world, and so we must look beyond it to find that for which he was made. And looking beyond it and considering all things, we find that he was made for God—to know him, to love him, and to serve him both in this world and in the next. Again, we read in the Bible[9] that at the creation of the world all things were made before man, and that he was created last. Therefore, if all these things could exist without man, we cannot say he was made for them. The world existed before him and can exist after him. The world goes along without any particular man, and the same may be said of all men.

Neither was man made to stay here awhile to become rich, or learned, or powerful, because all do not become rich—some are very poor; all are not learned—some are very ignorant; all are not powerful—some are slaves. But since all men are alike and equal in this, that they have all bodies formed in the same way, and all souls that are immortal, they should all be made for the same end. For example, you could not make a pen like a watch if you want it to write. Although pens differ in size, shape, etc., they have all one general form which is essential to them. So, although men differ in many things, they are all alike in the essential thing, namely, that they are composed of body and soul, and made to the image and likeness of God. Hence, as pens are made only to write with, so all men must have only one and the same end, namely, to serve God.

[9] Cf. Gn 5

1. **Who made the world?**

God made the world.

The *world* here means more than the earth—more than is shown on a map of the world. It means everything that we can see—sun, moon, stars, etc.; even those things that we can see only with great telescopes. Everything, too, that we may be able to see in the future, either with our eyes alone, or aided by instruments, is included in the word *world*. We can call it the universe.

2. **Who is God?**

God is the Creator of heaven and earth, and of all things.

3. **What is man?**

Man is a creature composed of a body and soul, and made to the image and likeness of God.

Creature, i.e., a thing created. Man differs from anything else in creation. All things else are either entirely matter, or entirely spirit. An angel, for example, is all spirit, and a stone is all matter; but man is a combination of both spirit and matter—of soul and of body.

4. **Is this likeness in the body or in the soul?**

This likeness is chiefly in the soul.

5. **How is the soul like to God?**

The soul is like God because it is a spirit that will never die, and has understanding and free will.

My soul is like to God in four things.

1. It is *a spirit*. It really exists, but cannot be seen with the eyes of our body. Every spirit is invisible, but every invisible thing is not a spirit. We cannot see the wind. We can feel its influence, we can see its work—for example, the dust flying, trees swaying, ships sailing, etc.—but the wind itself we never see. Again, we never see electricity. We see the light or effect it produces, but we never see the electricity itself. Yet no one denies the existence of the wind or of electricity on account of their being

invisible. Why then should anyone say there are no spirits — no God, no angels, no souls — simply because they cannot be seen, when we have other proofs, stronger than the testimony of our sight, that they really and truly exist?

2. My soul will *never die*, i.e., will never cease to exist; it is immortal. This is a very wonderful thing to think of. It will last as long as God himself.

3. My soul *has understanding*, i.e., it has the gift of reason. This gift enables man to reflect upon all his actions — the reasons why he should do certain things and why he should not do them. By reason he reflects upon the past, and judges what may happen in the future. He sees the consequences of his actions. He not only knows what he does, but why he does it. This is the gift that places man high above the brute animals in the order of creation; and hence man is not merely an animal, but he is a rational animal — an animal with the gift of reason.

Brute animals have not reason, but only instinct, i.e., they follow certain impulses or feelings which God gave them at their creation. He established certain laws for each class or kind of animals, and they, without knowing it, follow these laws; and when we see them following their laws, always in the same way, we say it is their nature. Animals act at times as if they knew just why they were acting; but it is not so. It is we who reason upon their actions, and see why they do them; but they do not reason, they only follow their instinct.

If animals could reason, they ought to improve in their condition. Men become more civilized day by day. They invent many things that were unknown to their forefathers. One man can improve upon the works of another, etc. But we never see anything of this kind in the actions of animals. The same kind of birds, for instance, build the same kind of nests, generation after generation, without ever making change or improvement in them. When man teaches an animal any action, it cannot teach the same to its young. It is clear, therefore, that animals cannot reason.

Though man has the gift of reason by which he can learn a great deal, he cannot learn all through his reason; for there are many things that God himself must teach him. When God teaches, we call the truths he makes known to us "revelation." How could man ever know about the Trinity through his reason alone, when, after God has made known to him that it exists, he cannot understand it? It is the same for all the other mysteries.

4. My soul has *free will*. This is another grand gift of God, by which I am able to do or not do a thing, just as I please. I can even sin and refuse to obey God. God himself—while he leaves me my free will—could not oblige me to do anything, unless I wished to do it; neither could the devil. I am free therefore, and I may use this great gift either to benefit or injure myself. If I were not free, I would not deserve reward or punishment for my actions, for no one is or should be punished for doing what he cannot help. God would not punish us for sin if we were not free to commit or avoid it. I turn this freedom to my benefit if I do what God wishes when I could do the opposite; for he will be more pleased with my conduct, and grant a greater reward than he would bestow if I obeyed simply because obliged to do so. Animals have no free will. If, for example, they suffer from hunger and you place food before them, they will eat; but man can starve, if he wills to do so, with a feast before him. For the same reason, man can endure more fatigue than any other animal of the same bodily strength. In traveling, for instance, animals give up when exhausted, but man may be dying as he walks, and still, by his strong willpower, force his wearied limbs to move. "But," you will say, "did not the lions in the den, into which Daniel was cast because he would not act against his conscience, obey the wicked king, and offend God—as we read in holy scripture[10]—refrain from eating him, even when they were starving with hunger?" Yes; but they did not do so of themselves, but by the power of God preventing them: and that is why the delivery of Daniel from their mouths was a miracle. It is clear, because the same lions immediately tore in pieces Daniel's enemies when they were cast into the den.

6. **Why did God make you?**

God made me to know him, to love him, and to serve him in this world, and to be happy with him forever in the next.

To know him, because we must know of a thing before we can love it. A poor savage in Africa never longs to be at a game or contest going on in

[10] Cf. Dn 6:16

America, because he does not know it and therefore cannot love it. We see a person and know him; if he pleases us, we love him, and if we love him, we will try to serve him; we will not be satisfied with doing merely what he asks of us, but will do whatever we think might give him pleasure. So it is in regard to God. We must first know him—learn who he is from our catechisms and books of instruction, but especially from the teaching of God's ministers, the holy father, bishops, and priests. When we know him, we shall love him. If we knew him perfectly, we should love him perfectly; so the better we know him, the more we shall love him. And, as it is our chief duty to love him and serve him upon earth, it becomes our strict duty to learn here whatever we can of his nature, attributes, and holy laws. The saints and angels in heaven know God so well that they must love him, and cannot therefore offend him.

You have all seen some person in the world, or maybe several persons, whom you have greatly admired; still you did not love them perfectly; there was always some little thing about them in looks, manners, or disposition that could be rendered more pleasing; some defect or want you would like to see supplied; some fault or imperfection you would like to see corrected. Now, suppose you had the power to take all the good qualities you found in the persons you loved and unite them in one person, in whom there would be nothing displeasing, but everything perfect and beautiful. Do you not think you would love such a person very much indeed?

Moreover, suppose you knew that person loved you intensely. Would it not be your greatest delight to be ever with such a friend? Well, then, all the lovable qualities and beauties you see in created beings come from God and are bestowed by him; yet all the good qualities on earth and those of the angels and saints in heaven, and even of the Blessed Virgin and St. Joseph, if united in one person, would be nothing compared to the goodness and beauty of God. How good and how lovable, therefore, must he be! And what shall we say when we think that he loves us with a greater love than we could ever love him, even with our most earnest efforts? Try then first to know God and you will surely love and serve him. Do not be satisfied with the little you learn of him in the catechism, but afterward read good books, and above all hear sermons and instructions.

In this world. Because unless we do what is pleasing to him in this world, we cannot be with him in the next. Our condition in the next world depends entirely upon our conduct in this. Thus, we have discovered the answer to the great question: What is the end of man; for what was he made?

7. **Of which must we take more care, our soul or our body?**
We must take more care of our soul than of our body.

8. **Why must we take more care of our soul than of our body?**
We must take more care of our soul than of our body, because, in losing our soul, we lose God and everlasting happiness.

Every sensible person will take most care of that which is most valuable. If a girl had a hundred dollars in a ten-cent pocketbook, you would consider her a great fool if she threw away the hundred dollars for fear of spoiling the pocketbook. Now, he is a greater fool who throws away his soul in order to save his body some little inconvenience, or gratify its wicked desires or inclinations. Wherever the soul will be, there the body will be also; so, we should, in a certain way, try to forget the body and make sure of getting the soul safely into heaven. You would not think much of the wisdom of a boy who allowed his kite to be smashed in pieces by giving his whole attention to the tail of the kite. If he took care to keep the kite itself high in air and away from every danger, the tail would follow it; and even if the tail did get entangled, it would have a good chance of being freed while the kite was still flying. But of what use is it to save a worthless piece of rag, if the kite—the valuable thing—is lost? Just in the same way, of what use is our body if our soul is lost? And remember, we have only one soul. Therefore, make sure to save the soul, and the body also will be saved—that is, the whole man will be saved; for we cannot save the soul and lose the body; they will both be saved or both be lost.

9. **What must we do to save our souls?**
To save our souls, we must worship God by faith, hope, and charity; that is, we must believe in him, hope in him, and love him with all our heart.

Worship, that is, "give him divine honor." We honor persons for their worth and excellence, and since God is the most excellent, we give him the highest honors, differing from others not merely in degree but in kind—divine honors that belong to him alone. And justly so, for the vilest animal upon the earth is a thousand times more nearly our equal than the most perfect creature, man or angel, is the equal of God. In speaking of worship, theologians generally distinguish three kinds, namely: *latria*, or that supreme worship due to God alone, which cannot be transferred to any creature without committing the sin of idolatry; *dulia*, or that secondary veneration we give to saints and angels as the special friends of God; *hyperdulia*, or that higher veneration which we give to the Blessed Virgin as the most exalted of all God's creatures. It is higher than the veneration we give to the other saints, but infinitely inferior to the worship we give to God himself. We show God our special honor by never doubting anything he reveals to us, therefore by faith; by expecting with certainty whatever he promises, therefore by hope; and finally, by loving him more than anyone else in the world, therefore by charity.

But someone may say, "I think I love my parents more than God." Well, let us see. Suppose your mother should command you to commit a sinful act (a thing no good mother would do) and you have therefore to choose between offending her or Almighty God. Now, although you love your mother very much, if in this instance you prefer to displease her rather than commit the sin that offends God, you show that you love God more than her. Again, many who dearly love their parents leave them that they may consecrate their lives to the special service of God in some religious community and thus prove their greater love for him. The love we have for God is intellectual rather than sentimental; and since it is not measured by the intensity of our feelings, how are we to know that we love him best? By our determination never to offend him for any person or thing in the world, however dear to us, and by our readiness to obey and serve him before all others.

10. **How shall we know the things which we are to believe?**
We shall know the things which we are to believe from the Catholic Church, through which God speaks to us.

Catholic Church in this answer means the pope, councils, bishops, and priests who teach in the Church.

11. **Where shall we find the chief truths which the Catholic Church teaches?**

We shall find the chief truths which the Catholic Church teaches in the Apostles' Creed.

Chief, because the Apostles' Creed does not contain in an explicit manner all the truths we must believe. For example, there is nothing in the Apostles' Creed about the sacrament of the Holy Eucharist, about the immaculate conception of the Blessed Virgin, or the infallibility of the pope; and yet we must believe these and other articles of faith not in the Apostles' Creed. It contains only the chief and not all the truths.

12. **Say the Apostles' Creed.**

I believe in God, the Father Almighty, Creator of heaven and earth; and in Jesus Christ, his only Son, our Lord, who was conceived by the Holy Ghost, born of the Virgin Mary, suffered under Pontius Pilate, was crucified, died, and was buried; he descended into hell; the third day he arose again from the dead; he ascended into heaven, and sitteth at the right hand of God, the Father Almighty; from thence he shall come to judge the living and the dead. I believe in the Holy Ghost, the holy Catholic Church, the communion of saints, the forgiveness of sins, the resurrection of the body, and the life everlasting. Amen.

Descend means to go down, and *ascend* to go up.

LESSON SECOND

On God and His Perfections

A *perfection* means "a good quality." We say a thing is perfect when it has all the good qualities it should have.

13. **What is God?**

God is a Spirit infinitely perfect.

A spirit is a living, intelligent, invisible being. It really exists, though we cannot see it with the eyes of our body. It has intelligence and can therefore think, understand, etc. It is not because we cannot see it that we call it a spirit. To be invisible is only one of the qualities of a spirit. It is also indivisible, that is, it cannot be divided into parts. God is such a being. He is *infinitely perfect*, that is, he has every perfection in the highest degree. *Infinite* means "to have without limit." If there were any perfection God did not have, he would not be infinite. He is unlimited in wisdom, in power, in goodness, in beauty, etc. "But," you will tell me, "persons on earth and the angels and saints in heaven have some wisdom and power and beauty, and therefore God cannot have all, since he has not the portion with which they are endowed." I still say he is infinite, because what the angels and others have belongs to God, and he only lends it to them. *Perfect* means "to be without any defect or fault."

14. **Had God a beginning?**

God had no beginning; he always was and always will be.

Was there ever a time when we could say there was no God? There was a time when we could say there was no heaven or earth, no angels, men, or animals; but there was never a time when there was no God. We may go back in thought millions and millions of years before the creation, and God was then existing. He had no beginning and will never cease to exist. This is a mystery; and what a mystery is will be explained in the next lesson.

15. **Where is God?**

God is everywhere.

Everywhere—not spread out like a great cloud, but whole and entire in every particular place: and yet there is only one God, and not as many gods as there are places. How this can be we cannot fully understand, because this also is a mystery. A simile, though it will not be perfect, may help you to understand. When we speak of God, we can never give a true and perfect example; for we cannot find anything exactly like him to compare to him. If I discharge a great cannon in a city, every one of the inhabitants will hear the report; not in such a way that each hearer gets his share of the sound, but each hears the whole report, just is if he were the only one to hear it. Now, how is that? There are not as many reports as there are persons listening; and yet each person hears the whole report.

16. **If God is everywhere, why do we not see him?**

We do not see God, because he is a pure Spirit and cannot be seen with bodily eyes.

Pure Spirit, that is, not clothed with any material body—Spirit alone.

17. **Does God see us?**

God sees us and watches over us.

Watches to protect, to reward or punish us. He watches continually; he not only watches, but keeps us alive. God might have created us and then paid no more attention to us; but if he had done so, we should have fallen back again into nothingness. Therefore, he preserves us every moment of our lives. We cannot draw a breath without him. If a steam engine be required to work ceaselessly, you cannot, after setting it in motion, leave it henceforth entirely to itself. You must keep up the supply of water and fire necessary for the generation of steam, you must oil the machinery, guard against overheating or cooling, and, in a word, keep a constant watch that nothing may interfere with its motion. So also God not only watches his creatures, but likewise provides for them. Since we depend so much upon him, is it not great folly to sin against him, to offend, and tempt him as it were? There are some birds that build their nests on the sides of great rocky precipices by the seacoast. Their eggs are very valuable, and men are let down by long ropes to take them from the nest. Now, while one of these men is hanging over the fearful precipice, his life is entirely in the hands of those holding the rope above. While he is in that danger, do you not think he would be very foolish to tempt and insult those on whom his life depends, when they could dash him to pieces by simply dropping the rope?

While we live here upon earth, we are all hanging over a great precipice, namely, eternity; God holds us up by the little thread of our lives, and if he pleased to drop it, we should be hurled into eternity. If we tempt or insult him, he might drop or cut the thread while we are in mortal sin, and then, body and soul, we go down into hell.

18. **Does God know all things?**

God knows all things, even our most secret thoughts, words, and actions.

Certainly, God *knows all things*. First, because he is infinitely wise, and, if he were ignorant of anything, he would not be so. Secondly, because he is everywhere and sees and hears all. Darkness does not hide from his view, nor noise prevent him from hearing. How could we sin if we thought of this! God is just here, looking at me and listening to me. Would I do what I am going to do now if I knew my parents, relatives, and friends were watching me? Would I like them to know that I am thinking about things sinful, and preparing to do shameful acts? No! Why then should I not feel ashamed to let God see and know of this wicked thought or action? They might know it and yet be unable to harm me, but he, all-powerful, could destroy me instantly. Nay, more: not only will God see and know this evil deed or thought; but, by his gift, the Blessed Mother, the angels, and saints will know of it and be ashamed of it before God, and, most of all, my guardian angel will deplore it. Besides, this sin will be revealed to the whole world on the last day, and my friends, relatives, and neighbors will know that I was guilty of it.

19. **Can God do all things?**

God can do all things, and nothing is hard or impossible to him.

20. **Is God just, holy, and merciful?**

God is all-just, all-holy, all-merciful, as he is infinitely perfect.

All just—that is, most just. *Just* means "to give to everyone what belongs to him"—to reward, if it is merited, or to punish, if it is deserved. *Holy*—that is, good. *Merciful* means "compassionate, forgiving, less exacting than severe justice demands." In a court, a just judge is one who listens patiently to all the arguments for and against the prisoner, and then, comparing one with the other, gives the sentence exactly in accordance with the guilt. If he inflicts more or less punishment than the prisoner deserves, or for money or anything else gives an unfair sentence, then he is an unjust judge. The judge might be merciful in this way. The laws say that for the crime of which this prisoner is proved guilty he can be sent to prison for a term not longer than ten years and not shorter than five; that is, for anything between ten and five years. The judge could give him the full ten years that the law allows and be just. But suppose he believed that the prisoner did not know the law and did not intend to be as wicked as he was proved; or that it was his first offense, or that he heard the prisoner's mother, who was old and infirm, pleading for him and saying he was her only support; or other extenuating circumstances that could awaken sympathy: the judge might be merciful and sentence him for the shortest term the law allows. But if the judge dismissed every prisoner, no matter how guilty, without punishment, he would not be a merciful but an unjust judge, who would soon be forced to leave the court. In the same way, God is often merciful to sinners and punishes them less than he could in strict justice. But if he were to allow every sinner to go without any punishment whatsoever—as unbelievers say he should do, by having no hell for the wicked—then he would not be just. For as God is an infinite being, all his perfections must be infinite; that is, he must be as infinitely just as he is infinitely merciful, true, wise, or powerful.

Now he has promised to punish sin; and since he is infinitely true, he must keep his promise.

LESSON THIRD

On the Unity and Trinity of God

Unity means "to be one," and *trinity*, "three in one."

21. **Is there but one God?**

Yes; there is but one God.

22. **Why can there be but one God?**

There can be but one God because God, being supreme and infinite, cannot have an equal.

Supreme, that is, the highest. *Equal*, when two are equal, one has everything the other has. You could say one pen is the equal of another if it is just as nice and will write just as well; one mechanic is the equal of another if he can do the work equally well. Two boys are equal in class if they have exactly the same marks at the end of the month or year. You could not have two persons chief. For example, you could not have two chief generals in an army; two presidents in the nation, or two governors in a state, or two mayors in a city, or two principals in a school, unless they divide equally their power, and then they will be equals and neither of them chief. God cannot divide his power with anyone—so as to give it away entirely—because we say he is infinite, and that means to have all. Others have only the loan of their power from God. Therefore, all power and authority come from God; so that when we disobey our parents or superiors who are placed over us, we disobey God himself.

23. **How many Persons are there in God?**

In God, there are three divine Persons, really distinct and equal in all things—the Father, the Son, and the Holy Ghost.

Distinct, not mingled together. We call the first and second Persons "Father" and "Son," because the second is begotten by the first Person, and not to indicate that there is any difference in their age. We always see in the world that a father is older than his son, so we get the idea perhaps that it is the same in the Holy Trinity. But it is not so. God the Father, and God the Son, and God the Holy Ghost existed from all eternity, and one did not exist before the other. God the Son is just as old as God the Father, and this is another great mystery. Even in nature we see that two things may begin to exist at the same time, and yet one be the cause of the other. You know that fire is the cause of heat; and yet the heat and the fire begin at the same time. Though we cannot understand this mystery of the Father and Son, we must believe it on the authority of God, who teaches it. "First," "second," and "third" Person in the Blessed Trinity does not mean, therefore, that one Person was before the other, or brought into existence by the other.

24. **Is the Father God?**

The Father is God and the first Person of the Blessed Trinity.

25. **Is the Son God?**

The Son is God and the second Person of the Blessed Trinity.

26. **Is the Holy Ghost God?**
The Holy Ghost is God and the third Person of the Blessed Trinity.

27. **What do you mean by "the Blessed Trinity"?**
By "the Blessed Trinity," I mean one God in three divine Persons.

28. **Are the three divine Persons equal in all things?**
The three divine Persons are equal in all things.

29. **Are the three divine Persons one and the same God?**
The three divine Persons are one and the same God, having one and the same divine nature and substance.

Though they are one and the same, we sometimes attribute different works to them. For example, works of creation we attribute to God the Father; works of mercy to God the Son; and works of love and sanctification to the Holy Ghost; and you will often find them thus spoken of in pious books; but all such works are done by all the Persons of the Trinity; because such works are the works of God, and there is but one God.

30. **Can we fully understand how the three divine Persons are one and the same God?**
We cannot fully understand how the three divine Persons are one and the same God, because this is a mystery.

Fully—entirely. We can partly understand it. We know what one God is and we know what three Persons are: but how these two things go together is the part we do not understand—the mystery.

31. **What is a mystery?**
A mystery is a truth which we cannot fully understand.

A truth, that is, a revealed truth—one made known to us by God or his Church. It is a truth which we must believe though we cannot understand it. Let us take an example. When a boy goes to school, he is taught that the earth is round like an orange and revolving in two ways, one causing day and night and the other producing the seasons: spring, summer, autumn, winter. The boy goes out into the country where he sees miles of level land and mountains thousands of feet in height. Again, he goes out on the ocean where sailors tell him it is several miles in depth.

Now he may say: "How can the earth be round if deep valleys, high mountains, and level plains prove to my senses the very opposite, and the countless things at rest upon its surface tell me it is motionless?" Yet he believes even against the testimony of his senses that the earth is round and moving, because his teacher could have no motive in deceiving him; knows better than he, having learned more, and besides has been taught by others who, after long years of careful study and research, have discovered these things and know them to be true. If, therefore, we have to believe things that we do not understand on the authority of men, why should we not believe other truths on the authority of God? Yes, we must believe him.

If a boy knew all his teacher knew, there would be no need of his going to school; he would be the equal in knowledge of his teacher: and if we knew all that God knows, we would be as great as he. As well might we try to empty the whole ocean into the tiny holes that children dig in the sand by its shore, as fully to comprehend the wisdom of God. This is the mistake unbelievers make when they wish to understand with their limited intelligence the boundless knowledge and mysterious ways of God, and, when they cannot understand, refuse to believe. Are they not extremely foolish? Would you not ridicule the boy who refuses to believe that the earth is round and moving because he cannot understand it? As he grows older and learns more, he will comprehend it better; so we, when we leave this world and come into the presence of God, shall see clearly many things that are unintelligible now. For the present, we have only to believe them on the authority of God teaching us.

Another example. We take two little black seeds that look just alike and place them in the same kind of soil; we put the same kind of water upon them; they have the same sunlight and air; and yet when they grow up, one has a red flower and one a blue. Where did the red and where did the blue come from? From the black seed, or the brown soil, or the pure water, air and sunlight? We do not know. It is there, and that is all. We see it and believe it, though we do not understand it.

So, if we refuse to believe everything we do not understand, we shall soon believe very little and make ourselves ridiculous.

LESSON FOURTH

On Creation

This lesson treats of God bringing everything into existence. The chief things created may be classed as follows: 1) The things that simply exist, as rocks and minerals, gold, silver, iron, etc. 2) Things that exist, grow, and live, like plants and trees. 3) Things that grow, live, and feel, like animals. 4) Things that grow, live, feel, and understand, like men. Besides these we have the sun, moon, stars, etc.; all things too that we can see, and also heaven, purgatory, hell, and good and bad angels. All these are the works of God's creation. All these he has called into existence by merely wishing for them.

32. **Who created heaven and earth, and all things?**
God created heaven and earth, and all things.

Heaven, where God is and will always be. It means, too, everything we see in the sky above us. *Earth*, the globe on which we live.

33. **How did God create heaven and earth?**
God created heaven and earth from nothing, by his Word only; that is, by a single act of his all-powerful will.

34. **Which are the chief creatures of God?**
The chief creatures of God are angels and men.

35. **What are angels?**
Angels are pure spirits without a body, created to adore and enjoy God in heaven.

Angels are not the same as saints. Saints are those who at one time lived upon the earth as we do, and who, on acccount of their very good lives, are now in heaven. They had bodies as we have. The angels, on the contrary, never lived visibly upon the earth. In the beginning, God was alone. We take great pleasure in looking at beautiful things. God, seeing his own beauty, and knowing that others would have very great pleasure and happiness in seeing him, determined to create some beings who could enjoy this happiness; and thus he wished to share with them the happiness which he himself derived from seeing his own beauty. Therefore, he created angels who were to be in heaven with him, singing his praises and worshipping before his throne.

The angels are not all equal in dignity, but are divided into nine classes, or choirs, according to their rank or office, and, as theologians tell us, arranged from the lowest to the highest and named as follows: angels, archangels, virtues, powers, principalities, dominations, thrones, cherubim, and seraphim. Archangels are higher than angels and are so called because sent to do the most important works. It was the archangel Michael who drove Lucifer from heaven and the archangel Gabriel who announced to the Blessed Virgin that she was to be the Mother of God. The angels receive their names from the duties they perform. The word *angel* signifies "messenger."

36. **Were the angels created for any other purpose?**

The angels were also created to assist before the throne of God and to minister unto him; they have often been sent as messengers from God to man; and are also appointed our guardians.

The duties of the angels are many. Some remain always in heaven with God; some are sent to earth to be our guardians and to remain with us. Each of us has an angel to take care of us. He is with us night and day, and offers our prayers and good works to God. He prays for us, exhorts us to do good and avoid evil; and he protects us from dangers spiritual and temporal. How unfortunate then must one be to cause him to return to heaven with sad complaints to God; such as: "The one whom I have in charge will not obey laws or use the graces thou sendest him: with all my efforts to save him, he continues to do wrong." He will be doubly sad when he sees other angels returning with good reports and receiving new graces for those whom God has committed to their care. If you love your guardian angel, never impose on him the painful duty of bringing to God the report of your evil doings.

Now, how do we know that the angels offer our prayers and good works to God? We know it from the beautiful story of Tobias, told in the holy scripture.[11] This holy man loved and feared God. He lived at a time when his people were persecuted by a most cruel king, who wished to force them to give up the true God and worship idols, but many of these good people suffered death rather than deny God and obey the wicked king. When they were put to death, their bodies were left lying on the ground, to be devoured by birds of prey or wild animals. Anyone caught burying them was to be put to death by the king's servants. Tobias used to carry the dead bodies of these holy martyrs into his house and bury them at night.

One day, when he returned very tired, he lay down by the wall of his house to rest, and, while lying there, some dirt fell into his eyes and he became blind. This Tobias had a young son whose name was also Tobias; and as he himself was now blind and poor, he wished to send his son into a certain city, at a good distance off, to collect some money that he had formerly loaned to a friend. As the young man did not know the way, his father sent him out to look for a guide. Young Tobias went out and found a beautiful young man standing on the road near his house. Tobias asked the young man to be his guide and he consented, and he brought Tobias to the distant city. As they were on their way, they sat down by the bank of a river. Tobias went into the water near the edge, and soon a great fish rushed at him. Tobias called to his guide. The guide told him to take hold of the fish and drag it out upon the shore. There they killed it, and kept part of its flesh for food and part for medicine. Then they went on to the city, got the money, and returned.

The guide told young Tobias to rub the part of the fish he had taken for medicine upon his father's eyes. He did so, and immediately his father's eyes were cured and he saw. Then both the father and son were so delighted with this young guide that they offered to give him half of all they had. He

[11] Cf. Tobias

refused to take it and then told them he was the angel Raphael, sent from God to be the guide of this good man's son. He told the old Tobias how he (the angel) had carried up to God his prayers and good works while he was burying the dead. When they heard he was an angel, they fell down and reverenced him, being very much afraid. From this beautiful history, we know that the angels carry our prayers and good works to God.

Again, we learn from the holy scripture,[12] in the history of another good man, almost the same thing. The patriarch Jacob was on a journey, and being tired, he lay down to rest with his head upon a stone. As he lay there, he had a vision in which he saw a great ladder reaching up from earth to heaven. At the top, he saw Almighty God standing, and, on the ladder itself, angels ascending and descending. Now the holy fathers of the Church tell us this is what is really taking place: the angels are always going down and up from God to man, though not on a ladder and not visibly as they appeared to Jacob. Besides the guardian angel for each person, there are also guardian angels for each city and for each nation.

Again angels appeared to Lot to warn him about the destruction of the wicked cities of Sodom and Gomorrha.[13] Angels appeared also to the shepherds on the night our Lord was born.[14] The catechism says angels have no bodies; how then could they appear? They took bodies made of some very light substance which would make them visible, and appeared just like beautiful young men, clad in flowing garments, as you frequently see them represented in pictures. Angels were sometimes sent to punish men for their sins, as the angel who killed in one night 185,000 men in the army of the wicked king, Sennacherib, who blasphemed God, and was endeavoring to destroy Jerusalem, God's city.[15]

But here is a difficulty. If God himself watches over us and sees all things, why should the angels guard us? It is on account of God's goodness to us; though it is not necessary. He does not wish us to have any excuse for being bad, so he gives us each a special heavenly servant to watch and

[12] Cf. Gn 28

[13] Cf. Gn 19

[14] Cf. Lk 2

[15] Cf. 4 Kgs 19

assist us by his prayers. If a friend received us into his house and did all he could for us himself, we should certainly be satisfied; but if he gave us a special servant, though it would not be necessary, he would show us great respect and kindness. Moreover, whatever the angels do for us, we might say God himself does, for the angels are only obeying his commands.

37. **Were the angels, as God created them, good and happy?**
The angels, as God created them, were good and happy.

38. **Did all the angels remain good and happy?**
All the angels did not remain good and happy; many of them sinned and were cast into hell; and these are called "devils" or "bad angels."

God did not admit the angels into his presence at once. He placed them for a while on probation, as he did our first parents.

One of these angels was most beautiful, and was named Lucifer, which means "Light-bearer." He was so perfect that he seems to have forgotten that he received all his beauty and intelligence from God, and, not content with what he had, became sinfully proud and wished to be equal to God himself. For his sin, he and all his followers were driven out of heaven, and God then created hell, in which they were to suffer for all eternity. This same Lucifer is now called "Satan," and more commonly, "the devil," and those who accompanied him in his fall, "devils" or "fallen angels."

LESSON FIFTH

On Our First Parents and Their Fall

39. **Who were the first man and woman?**
The first man and woman were Adam and Eve.

In the beginning, God created all things; something particular on each of the six days of creation.[16] On the first day, he made light; on the second, the firmament, or the heavens; and on the sixth day, he created man, and

[16] Cf. Gn 1

called him "Adam." God wished Adam to have a companion; so, one day, he caused Adam to fall into a deep sleep, and then took from his side a rib, out of which he formed Eve. Now God could have made Eve as he made Adam, by forming her body out of the clay of the earth and breathing into it a soul, but he made Eve out of Adam's rib to show that they were to be husband and wife, and to impress upon their minds the nature and sacredness of the love and union that should exist between them.

40. **Were Adam and Eve innocent and holy when they came from the hand of God?**
Adam and Eve were innocent and holy when they came from the hand of God.

God placed Adam and Eve in paradise, a large, beautiful garden, and gave them power over all the other creatures. Adam gave all the animals their appropriate names and they were obedient to him. Even lions, tigers, and other animals that we now fear so much came and played about him. Our first parents, in their state of original innocence, were the happy friends of God, without sorrow or suffering of any kind.

41. **Did God give any command to Adam and Eve?**
To try their obedience, God commanded Adam and Eve not to eat of a certain fruit which grew in the garden of paradise.

He told them[17] they could take of all the fruits in the garden except the fruit of one tree, and if they disobeyed him by eating the fruit of that tree, they should surely die. God might have pointed out any tree, because it was simply a test of their obedience. He gave them a very simple command, for if we are faithful in little things we shall surely be faithful in greater. Moreover, it is not precisely the consideration of what is forbidden, but of the authority by which it is forbidden that should deter us from violating the command and prove our fidelity. Thus, disobedience to our parents and superiors, even in little things, becomes sinful. Someone might say: "Why did God not try their obedience by one of the ten commandments?" Let us examine them. "Remember the

[17] Cf. Gn 2

sabbath." That one would be unnecessary: for every day was sabbath with them; the only work was to praise and serve God. "Thou shalt not steal." They could not; everything was theirs; and so for the other commandments. Therefore, God gave them a simple command telling them: "If you obey, you and all your posterity will be happy; every wish will be gratified, neither sorrow nor affliction shall come upon you, and you shall never die; but if, on the contrary, you disobey, countless evils, misery, and death will be your punishment. The earth, now so fruitful, shall bring forth no crops without cultivation, and, after years of toil, the dead bodies of yourselves and children must lie buried in its soil." So, having the gift of free will, they could take their choice, and either keep his command and be happy, or disobey him and be miserable.

42. **Which were the chief blessings intended for Adam and Eve, had they remained faithful to God?**

The chief blessings intended for Adam and Eve, had they remained faithful to God, were a constant state of happiness in this life and everlasting glory in the next.

Our first parents and their children were not to remain in the garden of paradise forever, but were, after spending their allotted time of trial or probation upon earth, to be taken body and soul into heaven without being obliged to die.

43. **Did Adam and Eve remain faithful to God?**

Adam and Eve did not remain faithful to God, but broke his commandment by eating the forbidden fruit.

As it is told in the Bible,[18] Eve went to the forbidden tree and was standing looking at it, when the devil came in the form of a serpent and, tempting, told her to take some of the fruit and eat. It does not appear that she went and tasted the fruit of all the other trees and finally came to this one, but rather that she went directly to the forbidden tree first. Do we not sometimes imitate Eve's conduct? As soon as we know a certain thing is forbidden, we are more strongly tempted to try it.

[18] Cf. Gn 3

See, then, what caused Eve's sin. She went into the dangerous occasion, and was admiring the forbidden fruit when the tempter came. She listened to him, yielded to his wicked suggestions, and sinned. So will it be with us if, through curiosity, we desire to see or hear things forbidden; for, once in the danger, the devil will soon be on hand to tempt us—not visibly indeed, for that would alarm us and defeat his purpose, but invisibly, like our guardian angels; for the devil is a fallen angel who still possesses all the characteristics of an angel except goodness. But this is not all. Eve not only took and ate the fruit herself, but induced Adam to do likewise. Most sinners imitate Eve in that respect. Not satisfied with offending God themselves, they lead others into sin.

Why should the devil tempt us? God created man to be in heaven, but the fallen angels were jealous of man, and tempted him to sin so that he too should be kept out of heaven and might never enjoy what they lost; just as envious people do not wish others to have what they cannot have themselves.

44. **What befell Adam and Eve on account of their sin?**
Adam and Eve on account of their sin lost innocence and holiness, and were doomed to sickness and death.

They were innocent and holy because they were the friends of God and in a state of grace, but by their sin they lost his grace and friendship. *Doomed* means "sentenced" or "condemned." The first evil result, then, of Adam's sin was that he lost innocence and made his body a rebel against his soul. Then he was to suffer poverty, hunger, cold, sickness, death, and every kind of ill; but the worst consequence of all was that God closed heaven against him. After a few years' trial, as we said, God was to take him into heaven; but now he has closed it against Adam and his posterity. All the people in the world could never induce God to open it again; for he closed it in accordance with his promise, and man was an exile and outcast from his heavenly home.

45. **What evil befell us on account of the disobedience of our first parents?**
On account of the disobedience of our first parents, we all share in their sin and punishment, as we should have shared in their happiness if they had remained faithful.

Does it not seem strange that we should suffer for the sin of our first parents, when we had nothing to do with it? No. It happens every day that children suffer for the faults of their parents and we do not wonder at it. Let us suppose a man's father leaves him a large fortune—houses, land, and money—and that he and his children are happy in the enjoyment of their inheritance. The children are sent to the best schools, have everything they desire now, and bright hopes of happiness and prosperity in the future. But alas! their hopes are vain. The father begins to drink or gamble, and soon the great fortune is squandered. House after house is sold and dollar after dollar spent, till absolute poverty comes upon the children, and the sad condition of their home tells of their distress. Do they not suffer for the sins of their father, though they had nothing to do with them? Indeed, many families in the world suffer thus through the faults of others, and most frequently of some of their members. Could you blame the grandfather for leaving the estate? Certainly not; for it was goodness on his part that made him give. Let us apply this example. What God gave Adam was to be ours also, and he squandered and misused it because he had free will, which God could not take from him without changing his nature; for it is our free will and intelligence that make us men, distinct from and superior to all other animals. They can live, grow, feel, hear, see, etc., as we can, but the want of intelligence and free will leaves them mere brutes. Therefore, if God took away Adam's intelligence and free will, he would have made him a mere animal, though the most perfect.

When a man becomes insane or loses the use of his intelligence and free will, we place him in an asylum and take care of him as we would a tame animal, seldom allowing him to go about without being watched and guarded.

Let us take another example. Suppose I have a friend who is addicted to the excessive drinking of strong liquor, and I say to him: "If you give up that detestable habit for one year, I will make you a present of this beautiful house worth several thousand dollars. It will be yours as long as you live, and at your death you may leave it to your children. I do not owe you anything, but offer this as a free gift if you comply with my request." My friend accepts the offer on these conditions, but the very next day deliberately breaks his promise. I do not give him the house, because he did not keep his agreement: And can anyone say on that account that I am unjust or unkind to him or his children? Certainly not. Well, God acted in the same manner with Adam. He promised him heaven, a home more beautiful than any earthly palace—the place our Lord calls his Father's house[19] and says there are many mansions, that is, dwelling places, in it. God promised this home to Adam on condition that he would observe one simple command. He had no right to heaven, but was to receive it, according to the promise, as a free gift from God, and therefore God, who offered it conditionally, was not obliged to give it when Adam violated his part of the agreement.

The example is not a perfect one, for there is this difference in the cases between Adam and my friend: when my friend does not get the house, he sustains a loss, it is true; but he might still be my friend as he was before, and live in my house; but when Adam lost heaven, he lost God's friendship and grace, and the loss of all grace is to be in sin. So that Adam by breaking the command, was left in sin; and as all his children sustain the same loss, they too are all left in sin till they are baptized.

46. **What other effects followed from the sin of our first parents?**
Our nature was corrupted by the sin of our first parents, which darkened our understanding, weakened our will, and left us a strong inclination to evil.

Our *nature was corrupted* is what I have said of the body rebelling against the soul. Our *understanding darkened*. Adam knew much more without study than the most intelligent men could learn now with constant application. Before his fall, he saw things clearly and understood them well, but after his sin, everything had to be learned by the slow process of study. Then the *will was weakened*. Before he fell, he could easily resist temptation, for his will was strong. You know we sin by the will, because, unless we wish to do the evil, we commit no sin; and if absolutely forced by others to do wrong, we are free from the guilt as long as our will despises and protests against the action. If forced, for example, to break my neighbor's window, I have not to answer in my conscience for the unjust act, because my will did not consent. So, on every occasion on which we sin, it is the will that yields to the temptation. After Adam's sin, his will became weak and less able

[19] Cf. Jn 14:2

to resist temptation; and as we are sharers in his misfortune, we find great difficulty at times in overcoming sinful inclinations. But no matter how violent the temptation or how prolonged and fierce the struggle against it, we can always be victorious if determined not to yield; for God gives us sufficient grace to resist every temptation; and if anyone should excuse his fall by saying he could not help sinning, he would be guilty of falsehood.

A strong inclination to do wrong—that is, unless always on our guard against it. Our Lord once cautioned his apostles to watch and pray lest they fall into temptation;[20] teaching us also by the same warning that, besides praying against our spiritual enemies, we must watch their maneuvers and be ever ready to repel their attacks.

47. **What is the sin called which we inherit from our first parents?**
The sin which we inherit from our first parents is called "original sin."

48. **Why is this sin called "original"?**
This sin is called "original," because it comes down to us from our first parents, and we are brought into the world with its guilt on our souls.

49. **Does this corruption of our nature remain in us after original sin is forgiven?**
This corruption of our nature and other punishments remain in us after original sin is forgiven.

It remains that we may merit by overcoming its temptations; and also that we may be kept humble by remembering our former sinful and unhappy state.

50. **Was anyone ever preserved from original sin?**
The Blessed Virgin Mary, through the merits of her divine Son, was preserved free from the guilt of original sin, and this privilege is called her "immaculate conception."

The Blessed Virgin was to be the Mother of the Son of God. Now it would not be proper for the Mother of God to be even for one moment

[20] Cf. Mt 26:41

the servant of the devil, or under his power. If the Blessed Virgin had been in original sin, she would have been in the service of the devil. Whatever disgraces a mother disgraces also her son; so our Lord would never permit his dear Mother to be subject to the devil, and consequently he, through his merits, saved her from original sin. She is the only one of the whole human race who enjoys this great privilege, and it is called her *immaculate conception*, that is, she was conceived—brought into existence by her mother—without having any spot or stain of sin upon her soul, and hence without original sin.

Our Lord came into the world to crush the power which the devil had exercised over men from the fall of Adam. This he did by meriting grace for them and giving them this spiritual help to withstand the devil in all his attacks upon them. As the Blessed Mother was never under the devil's power, next to God, she has the greatest strength against him, and she will help us to resist him if we seek her aid. The devil himself knows her power and fears her, and, if he sees her coming to our assistance, will quickly fly. Never fail, then, in time of temptation to call upon our Blessed Mother; she will hear and help you and pray to God for you.

LESSON SIXTH

On Sin and Its Kinds

51. **Is original sin the only kind of sin?**

Original sin is not the only kind of sin; there is another kind of sin which we commit ourselves, called "actual sin."

Sin is first or chiefly divided into original and actual; that is, into the sin we inherit from our first parents and the sin we commit ourselves. We may commit *actual* sin in two ways: either by doing what we should not do—stealing, for example—and thus we have a sin of commission, that is, a bad act committed; or by not doing what we should do—not hearing Mass on Sunday, for example—and thus we have a sin of omission, that is, a good act omitted. So, it is not enough to simply do no harm; we must also do some good. Heaven is a reward, and we must do something to merit it. Suppose a man employed a boy to do the work of his office, and, when he came in the morning, found that the boy had neglected the work assigned to him, and, when spoken to about it, simply answered: "Sir, I did no harm." Do you think he would be entitled to his wages? Of course, he did not and should do no harm; but is his employer to pay him wages for that? Certainly not. In like manner, God is not going to reward us for doing no harm; but on the contrary, he will punish us if we do wrong, and give no reward unless we perform the work he has marked out for us. Neither would the office boy deserve any wages if he did only what pleases himself, and not the work assigned by his master.

In the same way, God will not accept any worship or religion but the one he has revealed. He tells us himself how he wishes to be worshipped, and our own invented methods will not please him. Hence, we see the folly of those who say that all religions are equally good, and that we can be saved by practicing any of them. We can be saved only in the one religion which God himself has instituted, and by which he wishes to be honored. Many also foolishly believe, or say they believe, that if they are honest, sober, and the like, doing no injury to anyone, they shall be saved without the practice of any form of religious worship. But how about God's laws and commands? Are they to be despised, disregarded, and neglected entirely, without any fear of punishment? Surely not! And persons who thus think they are doing no harm are neglecting to serve God—the greatest harm they can do, and for which they will lose heaven.

God, we are told, assigned to everyone in this world a certain work to perform in a particular state of life, and this work is called "vocation." One, for instance, is to be a priest; another, a layman; one married; another single, etc. It is important for us to discover our true vocation; for if we are in the state of life to which God has called us, we shall be happy; but if we select our own work, our own state of life without consulting him, we shall seldom be happy in it. How are we to know our vocation? Chiefly by praying to God and asking him to make it known to us. Then if he gives us a strong inclination—constant, or nearly constant—for a certain state of life, and the ability to fulfill its duties, we may well believe that God wishes us to be in that state.

After we have begged God's assistance, we must ask our confessor's advice in the matter, and listen attentively to what the Holy Ghost inspires him to say. The signs of our vocation are, therefore, as stated: first, a strong desire;

and second, an aptitude for the state to which we believe we are called. For example, a young man might be very holy, but if unable to learn, he could never be a priest. Another might be very learned and holy, but if too sickly to perform a priest's duties, he could not, or at least would not, be ordained. Another might be learned and healthy, but not virtuous, and so he could never be a priest. Aptitude, therefore, means all the qualities necessary, whether of mind, or soul, or body. The same is true for a young girl who wishes to become a religious; and the same, indeed, for any person's vocation.

We should never enter a state of life to which we are not called, simply to please parents or others. Neither should we be persuaded by them to give up a state to which we are called; for we should embrace our true vocation at any sacrifice, that in it we may serve God better, and be more certain of saving our souls. Thus, parents and guardians who prevent their children from entering the state to which they are called may sin grievously by exposing them to eternal loss of salvation. Their sin is all the greater when they try to influence their children in this matter for selfish or worldly motives. As they may be selfish and prejudiced without knowing it, they too should ask the advice of their confessor, and good persons of experience. Oh! how many children, sons and daughters, are made unhappy all the days of their life by parents or superiors forcing them into some state to which they were not called, or by keeping them from one to which they were called. This matter of your vocation rests with yourselves and Almighty God, and you are free to do what he directs without consideration for anyone.

52. **What is actual sin?**

Actual sin is any willful thought, word, deed, or omission contrary to the law of God.

Three ways we may sin: by *thought*—allowing our minds to dwell on sinful things; *word*—by cursing, telling lies, etc.; *deed*—by any kind of bad action. But to be sins, these thoughts, words, and deeds must be willful; that is, we must fully know what we are doing, and be free in doing it. Then they must be *contrary to the law of God*; that is, violate some law he commands us to obey, whether it be a law he gave directly himself, or through his Church. We can also violate God's law by neglecting to observe it, and thus sin, provided the neglect be willful, and the thing neglected commanded by God or by his Church.

53. **How many kinds of actual sin are there?**

There are two kinds of actual sin—mortal and venial.

Mortal, that is, the sin which kills the soul. When a man receives a very severe wound, we say he is mortally wounded; that is, he will die from the wound. As breath shows there is life in the body, so grace is the life of the soul; when all the breath is out of the body, we say the man is dead. He can perform no action to help himself or others. So, when all grace is out of the soul, we say it is dead, because it is reduced to the condition of a dead body. It can do no action worthy of merit, such as a soul should do; that is, it can do no action that God is bound to reward—it is dead. "But," you will say, "the soul never dies." You mean it will never cease to exist; but we call it "dead" when it has lost all its power to do supernatural good.

Venial sin does not drive out all the grace: it wounds the soul; it weakens it just as slight wounds weaken the body. If it falls very frequently into venial sin, it will fall very soon into mortal sin also; for the holy scripture says that "he that contemneth small things shall fall by little and little."[21] A venial sin seems a little thing, but if we do not avoid it, we shall by degrees fall into greater, or mortal, sin. Venial sin makes God less friendly to us and displeases him. Now if we really love God, we will not displease him even in the most trifling things.

54. **What is mortal sin?**

Mortal sin is a grievous offense against the law of God.

Grievous—that is, very great or serious. *Against the law.* If we are in doubt whether anything is sinful or not, we must ask ourselves: Is it forbidden by God or his Church? And if we do not know of any law forbidding it, it cannot be a sin, at least, for us.

Suppose, for example, a boy should doubt whether it is sinful or not to fly a kite. Well, is there any law of God or of his Church saying it is sinful

[21] Ecclus 19:1

to fly a kite? If not, then it cannot be a sin. But it might be sinful for another reason, namely, his parents or superiors might forbid it, and there is a law of God saying you must not disobey your parents or superiors. Therefore, a thing not sinful in itself, that is, not directly forbidden by God or his Church, may become sinful for some other reason well known to us.

We must not, however, doubt concerning the sinfulness or lawfulness of everything we do; for that would be foolish and lead us to be scrupulous. If we doubt at all, we should have some good reason for doubting, that is, for believing that the thing we are about to do is or is not forbidden. When, therefore, we have such a doubt, we must seek information from those who can enlighten us on the subject, so that we may act without the danger of sinning. It is our intention that makes the act we perform sinful or not. Let me explain. Suppose a person should mistake Friday for Thursday and should eat meat, that person would not commit a real sin, because it is not a sin to eat meat on an ordinary Thursday. He would commit what we call a "material sin"; that is, his action would be a sin if he really knew what he was doing. On the other hand, if the person, thinking it was Friday when it was really Thursday, ate meat, knowing it to be forbidden, that person would commit a mortal sin, because he intended to do so. Therefore, if what we do is not known to be a sin while we do it, it is no sin for us and cannot become a sin afterward. But as soon as we know or learn that what we did was wrong, it would be a sin if we did the same thing again. In the same way, everything we do thinking it to be wrong or sinful is wrong and sinful for us, though it may not be wrong for those who know better. Again, it is sinful to judge others for doing wrong, because they may not know that what they do is sinful. It would be better for us to instruct than to blame them. The best we can do, therefore, is to learn well all God's laws and the laws of his Church as they are taught in the catechism, so that we may know when we are violating them or when we are not, i.e., when we are sinning and when we are not.

55. **Why is this sin called "mortal"?**

This sin is called "mortal," because it deprives us of spiritual life, which is sanctifying grace, and brings everlasting death and damnation on the soul.

When the soul is sent to hell, it is dead forever, because never again will it be able to do a single meritorious act.

56. **How many things are necessary to make a sin mortal?**

To make a sin mortal, three things are necessary: a grievous matter, sufficient reflection, and full consent of the will.

Grievous matter. To steal is a sin. Now, if you steal only a pin, the act of stealing in that case could not be a mortal sin, because the "matter," namely, the stealing of an ordinary pin, is not grievous. But suppose it was a diamond pin of great value, then it would surely be "grievous matter." *Sufficient reflection*, that is, you must know what you are doing at the time you do it. For example, suppose while you stole the diamond pin you thought you were stealing a pin with a small piece of glass, of little value: you would not have sufficient reflection and would not commit a mortal sin till you found out that what you had stolen was a valuable diamond; if you continued to keep it after learning your mistake, you would surely commit a mortal sin. *Full consent.* Suppose you were shooting at a target and accidentally killed a man: you would not have the sin of murder, because you did not will or wish to kill a man.

Therefore, three things are necessary that your act may be a mortal sin: 1) The act you do must be bad, and sufficiently important. 2) You must reflect that you are doing it, and know that it is wrong. 3) You must do it freely, deliberately, and willfully.

57. **What is venial sin?**

Venial sin is a slight offense against the law of God in matters of less importance; or, in matters of great importance, it is an offense committed without sufficient reflection or full consent of the will.

Slight, that is, a small offense or fault; called *venial*, not because it is not a sin, but because God pardons it more willingly or easily than he does a mortal sin. *Less importance*, like stealing an ordinary, common pin. *Great importance*, like stealing a diamond pin. Without *reflection* or *consent*, when you did not know it was a diamond and did not intend to steal a diamond.

58. **Which are the effects of venial sin?**

The effects of venial sin are the lessening of the love of God in our heart, the making us less worthy of his help, and the weakening of the power to resist mortal sin.

Lessening of the love, because it lessens grace, and grace increases the love of God in us. It displeases God, and though we do not offend him very greatly, we still offend him. *Weakening of the power to resist*. If a man is wounded, it will be easier to kill him than if he is in perfect health. So mortal sin will more easily kill a soul already weakened by the wounds of venial sin.

59. **Which are the chief sources of sin?**

The chief sources of sin are seven: pride, covetousness, lust, anger, gluttony, envy, and sloth; and they are commonly called "capital sins."

A *source* is that from which anything else comes. The source of a river is the little spring on the mountain side where the river first begins. This little stream runs down the mountain, and, as it goes along, gathers strength and size from other little streams running into it. It cuts its way through the meadows, and marks the course and is the beginning of a great river, sweeping all things before it and carrying them off to the ocean. Now, if someone in the beginning had stopped up the little spring on the mountain—the first source of the river—there would have been no river in that particular place. It is just the same with sin. There is one sin that is the source, and as it goes along like the stream, it gathers strength; other sins follow it and are united with it. Again: each of these *capital sins*, as they are called, is like a leader or a captain in an army, with so many others under him and following him. Now, if you take away the head, the other members of the body will perish; so if you destroy the capital sin, the other sins that follow it will disappear also. Very few persons have all the capital sins: some are guilty of one of them, some of two, some of three, but few if any are guilty of them all. The one we are guilty of, and which is the cause of all our other sins, is called our "predominant sin" or our "ruling passion." We should try to find it out, and labor to overcome it.

Every one of these capital sins has a great many other sins following it.

Pride is an inordinate self-esteem. Pride comes under the first commandment; because, by thinking too much of ourselves, we neglect God, and give to ourselves the honor due to him. Of what have we to be proud? Of our personal appearance? Disease may efface in one night every trace of beauty. Of our clothing? It is not ours; we have not produced it; most of it is taken from the lower animals—wool from the sheep, leather from the ox, feathers from the bird, etc. Are we proud of our wealth, money, or property? These may be stolen or destroyed by fire. The learned may become insane, and so we have nothing to be proud of but our good works. All that we have is from God, and we can have it only as long as he wishes. We had nothing coming into the world, and we leave it with nothing but the shroud in which we are buried; and even this does not go with the soul, but remains with the body to rot in the earth. Soon after death, our bodies become so offensive that even our clearest friends hasten to place them underground, where they become the food of worms, a mass of corruption, loathsome to sight and smell. Why, then, should we be so proud of this body, and commit so much sin for it, pamper it with every delicacy, only to be the food of worms? This does not mean, however, that we are not to keep our bodies clean, and take good care of them. We are bound to do so, and could not neglect it without committing sin. The one thing to be avoided is taking too much care of them, and neglecting our soul and God on their account. The followers of pride are: conceit, hypocrisy, foolish display in dress or conduct, harshness to others, waste of time on ourselves, etc.

Covetousness, the same as avarice, greed, etc., is an inordinate desire for worldly goods. Inordinate, because it is not avarice to prudently provide for the future either for ourselves or others. Covetousness comes under the tenth commandment, and is forbidden by it. We must be content with what we have or can get honestly. The followers of covetousness are: want of charity, dishonest dealing, theft, etc.

Lust is the desire for sins of the flesh; for impure thoughts, words, or actions. It comes under the sixth and ninth commandments, and includes all that is forbidden by those commandments. It is the habit of always violating, or of desiring to violate, the sixth and ninth commandments.

Lust and *impurity* mean the same thing. The followers of lust are, generally: neglect of prayer, neglect of the sacraments, and final loss of faith.

Anger comes under the fifth commandment. It is followed by hatred, the desire of revenge, etc.

Gluttony is the sin of eating or drinking too much. With regard to eating, it is committed by eating too often; by being too particular about what we eat; by being too extravagant in always looking for the most costly things that we think others cannot have. With regard to drinking, it is generally committed by taking too much of intoxicating liquors. The drunkard is a glutton and commits the sin of gluttony every time he becomes intoxicated.

Gluttony, especially in drink, comes in a manner under the first commandment, because, by depriving ourselves of our reason, we cannot give God the honor and respect which is his due. Think of how many sins the drunkard commits. He becomes intoxicated, which in itself is a sin. He deprives himself of the use of reason, abuses God's great gift, and becomes like a brute beast. Indeed, in a way he becomes worse than a beast; for beasts always follow the laws that God has given to their nature, and never drink to excess. They obey God, and man is the only one of God's creatures that does not always keep his laws. Think too of the number of insane persons confined in asylums, who would give all in this world for the use of their reason, if they could only understand their miserable condition. Yet the drunkard abuses the gift that would make these poor unfortunate lunatics happy. Again, the drunkard injures his health and thus violates the fifth commandment by committing a kind of slow suicide. He loses self-respect; makes use of sinful language; frequently neglects Mass and all his religious duties; exposes himself to the danger of death while in a state of sin; gives scandal to his family and neighbors; and, by his bad example, causes some to leave or remain out of the true Church. By continued intemperance, he may become insane and remain in that condition till death puts an end to his career and he goes unprepared before the judgment seat of God. Besides all this, he squanders the money he should put to a better use and turns God's gifts into a means of offending him. If a father, he neglects the children and wife for whom he has promised to provide; leaves them cold and hungry while he commits sin with the means that would make them comfortable. Drunkenness therefore is a sin accompanied by many deplorable evils.

There are three great sins you should always be on your guard against during your whole lives, namely: drunkenness, dishonesty, and impurity. If you avoid these, you will almost surely avoid all other sins; for nearly all sins can be traced back to these three. They are the most dangerous, first, because they have most followers; and, secondly, because they grow upon us almost without our knowing it. The drunkard begins perhaps as a boy by taking a little, even very little; the second time he takes a little more; the next time still more, then he begins to be fond of strong drink and can scarcely do without it; finally, he becomes the slave of intemperance and sells his soul and body for it. The passions of dishonesty and impurity grow by degrees in the same manner. Therefore, avoid them in the beginning and resist them while they are under your power. If you find yourself inclined to any of these sins in your youth, stop them at once.

Envy is the desire to see another meet with misfortune that we may be benefited by it. We are glad when he does not succeed in his business, we are sorry when anyone speaks well of him, etc. Envy comes under the eighth commandment.

Sloth is committed when we idle our time, and are lazy; when we are indifferent about serving God; when we do anything slowly and poorly and in a way that shows we would rather not do it. They are slothful who lie in bed late in the morning and neglect their duty. Slothful people are often untidy in their personal appearance; and they are nearly always in misery and want, unless somebody else takes care of them. Sloth comes under the first commandment, because it has reference in a special manner to the way in which we serve God.

How, then, shall we best destroy sin in our souls? By finding out our chief capital sin and rooting it out. If a strong oak tree is deeply rooted in the ground, how will you best destroy its life? By cutting off the branches? No. For, with each returning spring, new branches will grow. How then? By cutting the root, and then the great oak with all its branches will die. In the same way our capital sin is the root, and as long as we leave it in our souls, other sins will grow out of it. While we are trying to destroy our sins without touching our capital sin—our chief sin—we are only cutting off branches that will grow again. Indeed, a great many people are only cutting off branches all the time, and that is why they are not benefited as much as they could be by the prayers they say, Masses they hear, sacraments they receive, and sermons they listen to.

But do not imagine that because you are not becoming better, when you pray, hear Mass, and receive the sacraments, you are doing no good at all. That would be a great mistake, and just such a thing as the devil would suggest to make persons give up their devotions. "What is the use," he might say, "of your trying to be good? You are just as bad as you were a year ago." Do not listen to that temptation. Were it not for your prayers and your reception of the sacraments, you would become a great deal worse than you are. Suppose a man is rowing on the river against a very strong tide. He is rowing as hard as he can and yet he is not advancing one foot up the stream. Is he doing nothing therefore? Ah! he is doing a great deal: he is preventing himself from being carried with the current out into the ocean. He is keeping himself where he is till the force of the tide diminishes, and then he can advance. So, they who are trying to be good are struggling against the strong tide of temptation. If they cease to struggle against it, they will be carried out into the great ocean of sin and lost forever. Someday the temptation will grow weaker and then they will be able to advance toward heaven. We feel temptations most when we are trying to resist them and lead good lives, because we are working against our evil inclinations—the strong tide of our passions. We have no trouble going with them.

LESSON SEVENTH

On the Incarnation and Redemption

Incarnation means "to take flesh," as a body. Here it means our Lord's taking flesh, that is, taking a body like ours, when he became man. *Redemption* means "to buy back." Let us take an example. Slaves are men or women that belong entirely to their masters, just as horses, cows, or other animals do. Slaves are bought and sold, never receive any wages for their work, get their food and clothing and no more. As they never earn money for themselves, they can never purchase their own liberty. If ever they are to be free, someone else must procure their liberty. Now, suppose I am in some country where slavery exists. I am free, but I want one hundred dollars; so I go to a slave owner and say: "I want to sell myself for one hundred dollars." He buys me and I soon squander the one hundred dollars. Now I am his property, his slave; I shall never earn any wages and shall never be able to buy my freedom. No other slave can help me, for he is just in the same condition as I myself am. If I am to be free, a free man who has the money must pay for my liberty. This is exactly the condition in which all men were before our Lord redeemed them. Adam sold himself and all his children to the devil by committing sin. He and they therefore became slaves. They could not earn any spiritual wages, that is, grace of God to purchase their liberty; and as all men were slaves, one could not help another in this matter.

Then our Lord himself came and purchased our freedom. He bought us back again, and the price he paid was his own life and blood given up upon the cross. In his goodness, he did more than redeem us; he gave us also the means of redeeming ourselves in case we should ever have the misfortune of falling again into the slavery of the devil—into sin. He left us the sacrament of penance to which we can go as to a bank, and draw out enough of our Lord's grace—merited for us and deposited in the power of his Church—to purchase our redemption from sin.

60. **Did God abandon man after he fell into sin?**

God did not abandon man after he fell into sin, but promised him a Redeemer, who was to satisfy for man's sin and reopen to him the gates of heaven.

Abandon means "to leave to one's self." Adam and his posterity were slaves, but God took pity on them. He did not leave them to themselves, but promised to help them.

Gates of heaven. Heaven has no gates, because it is not built of material—of stone, or iron, or wood. It is only our way of speaking; just as we say, "hand of God," although he has no hands. Heaven is the magnificent home God has prepared for us, and its gates are his power by which he keeps us out or lets us in as he pleases. Our Lord, therefore, obtained admittance for us.

61. **Who is the Redeemer?**

Our Blessed Lord and Savior Jesus Christ is the Redeemer of mankind.

62. **What do you believe of Jesus Christ?**

I believe that Jesus Christ is the Son of God, the second Person of the Blessed Trinity, true God and true man.

True God. He was true God, equal to his Father from all eternity. He became man when he came upon the earth about two thousand years ago, and was born on Christmas day. Now he is in heaven as God and man. Therefore, he was God always, but man only from the time of his incarnation.

63. **Why is Jesus Christ true God?**

Jesus Christ is true God because he is the true and only Son of God the Father.

God the Father, first Person of the Blessed Trinity, is his real Father, and St. Joseph was his foster father, selected by the heavenly Father to take care of our Lord and watch over him while on earth. A foster father is not the same as a stepfather. A stepfather is a second father that one gets when his real father dies. A foster father is one who takes a person, whether a relative or a stranger, and adopts him as his son. It was a very great honor for St. Joseph to be selected from among all men to take care of the Son of God; to carry in his arms the great one of whom the prophets spoke; the one for whom the whole world longed during so many thousand years; so that, next to our Blessed Mother, St. Joseph deserves our greatest honor.

64. **Why is Jesus Christ true man?**

Jesus Christ is true man because he is the Son of the Blessed Virgin Mary, and has a body and soul like ours.

He has all that we have by nature, but not the things we have acquired; such as deformities, imperfections, and the like. Everything in our Lord was perfect. Above all, he had no sin of any kind, nor even inclination to sin. He could be hungry, as he was when he fasted forty days in the desert.[22] He was

[22] Cf. Mt 4:2

thirsty, as he said on the cross.[23] He could be wearied, as we read in the holy scripture[24] that he sat down by a well to rest, while his disciples went into the city to buy food. All these sufferings come from our very nature. We say a thing comes from our very nature when everybody has it. Now, everyone in the world may at times be hungry, thirsty, or tired; but everybody in the world need not have a toothache or headache, because such things are not common to human nature, but due to some defect in our body; and such defects our Lord did not have, because he was a perfect man. Therefore, our Lord had a body like ours, not as it usually is with defects, but as it should be, perfect in all things that belong to its nature, as Adam's was before he sinned.

65. **How many natures are there in Jesus Christ?**

In Jesus Christ, there are two natures: the nature of God and the nature of man.

He was perfect God and perfect man. His human nature was under the full power of his divine nature, and could not do anything contrary to his divine will. You cannot understand how there can be two natures and two wills in one Person, because it is another of the great mysteries; but you must believe it, just as you believe there are three Persons in one God, though you do not understand it. Those who learn theology and study a great deal may understand it better than you, but never fully. It will be enough, therefore, for you to remember and believe that there are two natures, the divine nature and the human nature, in the one Person of our Lord.

66. **Is Jesus Christ more than one Person?**

No, Jesus Christ is but one divine Person.

But one, so that "the second Person of the Blessed Trinity," "the Son of God," "the Messias," "Christ," "Jesus," "our Lord," "our Savior," "our Redeemer," etc., are all names for the one Person; and, besides these, there are many other names given to our Lord in the holy scripture, both in the old and the new testament.

[23] Cf. Jn 19:28

[24] Cf. Jn 4:6

67. **Was Jesus Christ always God?**

Jesus Christ was always God, as he is the second Person of the Blessed Trinity, equal to his Father from all eternity.

68. **Was Jesus Christ always man?**

Jesus Christ was not always man, but became man at the time of his incarnation.

69. **What do you mean by "the incarnation"?**

By "the incarnation," I mean that the Son of God was made man.

70. **How was the Son of God made man?**

The Son of God was conceived and made man by the power of the Holy Ghost, in the womb of the Blessed Virgin Mary.

71. **Is the Blessed Virgin Mary truly the Mother of God?**

The Blessed Virgin Mary is truly the Mother of God, because the same divine Person who is the Son of God is also the Son of the Blessed Virgin Mary.

72. **Did the Son of God become man immediately after the sin of our first parents?**

The Son of God did not become man immediately after the sin of our first parents, but he was promised to them as a Redeemer.

God did not say to Adam when he would send the Redeemer, and so the Redeemer did not come for about four thousand years after he was first promised. God permitted this long time to elapse in order that mankind might feel and know how great an evil sin is, and what misery it brought upon the world. During these four thousand years, men were becoming gradually worse. At one time—about sixteen hundred years after Adam's sin—they became so bad that God destroyed by a deluge, or great flood of water, all persons and living things upon the earth, except Noe, his wife, his three sons and their wives, and the animals they had in the ark with them.[25] Let me now give you more particulars about this terrible punishment.

[25] Cf. Gn 6

After God determined to destroy all living things on account of the wickedness of men, he told Noe, who was a good man, to build a great ark, or ship, for himself and his family, and for some of all the living creatures upon the earth.[26] When the ark was ready, Noe and his family went into it, and the animals that were to be saved came by God's power, and two by two were taken into the ark. Besides the two of each kind of animals, Noe was required to take with him five more of each kind of clean animals. Clean animals were certain animals which, according to God's law, could be offered in sacrifice or eaten; they were such animals as the ox, the sheep, the goat, etc. Therefore, seven of each of the clean animals, and two of each of the other kinds. Why did he have seven clean animals? Two were to be set free upon the dry earth with the other animals, and the other five were for food or sacrifice.

Noe spent a hundred years in making the ark. At that time men lived much longer than they do now. Adam lived over 900 years and Mathusala, the oldest man, lived to be 969 years old. There are many reasons why men live a shorter time now than then.

When the door of the ark was closed, God sent a great rain that lasted for forty days and forty nights. All the springs of water broke forth, and all the rivers and lakes overflowed their banks. Men ran here and there to high places, while the water rose higher and higher till it covered the tops of the mountains, and all not in the ark were drowned. The big ark floated about for about a year; for although it stopped raining after forty days, just think of the quantity of water that must have fallen! Think of the rain that would fall during the whole of Lent from Ash Wednesday to Easter Sunday—forty days. It took a long time, therefore, for the waters to go down and finally disappear. When the waters began to go down, Noe, wishing to know if any land was as yet above the water, opened the little window, and sent out a raven or crow over the waters. The raven did not come back, because it is a bird that eats flesh, and it found plenty of dead bodies to feed upon. Then Noe sent out a dove, and the dove came back with the bough of an olive tree in its mouth. From this Noe knew that the earth was becoming dry again. After some days, the ark rested on the top of a mountain named Ararat. When all the waters had dried up, Noe and

[26] Cf. Gn 7

his family and all the animals passed out of the ark. He offered a sacrifice of thanksgiving, and he and his family settled once more upon the earth.

For a while, the descendants of Noe were good, but when they became numerous, they soon forgot the deluge and its punishments, and became very wicked. Many forgot the true God altogether, and began to worship the sun, moon, and stars. Some worshipped animals, and others idols of wood or stone. They offered up human victims and committed all kinds of sins most displeasing to God. Many were in slavery; masters were cruel; and things were becoming daily worse; till just before the coming of our Lord, the world was in a terrible condition of misery and sin. The lawmakers tried to remedy these evils by their laws, and the teachers and professors by their teaching; but all was of no avail. God himself must save the world.

God gave many promises of the Redeemer. The first one was given in the garden to our first parents. God said to the serpent: "I will put enmities," that is hatred, "between thee and the woman"; that is, between the devil and the Blessed Virgin—whom the holy writers call the "second Eve," because as the first Eve caused our fall, the second Eve helped us to rise again. "I will put also a great hatred between the devil and your Redeemer."[27] The next promise of the Redeemer was made to Abraham.[28] Another was made to Isaac, and another to Jacob; and later these promises were frequently renewed through the prophets; so that, during the four thousand years, God encouraged the good people, by promising from time to time the Redeemer.

Some of the prophets foretold to what family he would belong, and when he would be born, and when and what he would suffer, and how he would die. They also foretold signs or things that would come to pass just before the advent or coming of the Messias;[29] so that, when the people saw these things coming to pass, they could know that the time of the Messias was at hand. Thus, when our Lord came, the whole world was waiting and looking for the promised Redeemer, because the signs foretold had appeared or were taking place. But the majority did not recognize our Lord when he came, on account of the quiet, humble, and poor way in which

[27] Cf. Gn 3:15

[28] Cf. Gn 15

[29] Cf. Gn 49:10

he came. They were expecting to see the Redeemer come as a great and powerful king, with mighty armies conquering the world; and in this they were mistaken. If they had studied the holy scriptures, they would have learned how he was to come—poor and humble.

73. **How could they be saved who lived before the Son of God became man?**
They who lived before the Son of God became man could be saved by believing in the Redeemer to come, and by keeping the commandments.

We have seen that God promised the Redeemer during four thousand years. Now, those who believed these promises and kept all God's commandments, and observed all his laws as they knew them, could be saved. They could not, it is true, enter into heaven after their death, but they could wait in limbo without suffering till our Lord opened heaven for them. They were saved only through the merits of our Lord. And how could this be when our Lord was not yet born? Do you know what a promissory note is? It is this: when a man is not able to pay his debts just now, but will be able afterward, he gives those to whom he owes the money a promissory note, that is, a written promise that he will pay at a certain time. Now, those who died before our Lord was born had the holy scriptures promising that Christ would pay for them and for their sins when he would come. So, God saved them on account of this promise and kept them free from suffering till our Lord came. If any died when they were little infants, their parents answered for them as godfathers and godmothers do now for infants at baptism.

74. **On what day was the Son of God conceived and made man?**
The Son of God was conceived and made man on Annunciation day, the day on which the angel Gabriel announced to the Blessed Virgin Mary that she was to be the Mother of God.

Annunciation day is the 25th of March. You can easily remember that feast. Everybody knows that St. Patrick's day is on the 17th of March, and therefore, eight days after it comes Annunciation day. There is another feast coming in between them, the feast of St. Joseph, on the 19th of March. Therefore, it is easy to remember these three feasts coming all in March and almost together. *Annunciation* is the name given to that day after the angel came, but it was not called so before. *Annunciation* means "to tell or make known," and this is the day the angel made known to the Blessed Virgin that she was selected for the high office of Mother of God. The Blessed Virgin was expecting the Messias, and was probably praying for his speedy arrival, as were the rest of her people, when suddenly the angel came and said: "Hail, full of grace."[30]

75. **On what day was Christ born?**

Christ was born on Christmas day, in a stable at Bethlehem, nearly nineteen hundred years ago.

Christmas day is the 25th of December, one week before the New Year. It is called "Christmas day" since the time our Lord was born, nearly nineteen hundred years ago. *In a stable at Bethlehem.* The story of our Lord's birth is in every way a very sad one.

The Blessed Virgin and St. Joseph lived in Palestine—called also "the Holy Land" since our Lord lived there. Palestine was the country where God's people, the Jews, lived, and at the time we are speaking of, it was under the power of the Roman Emperor, who had his soldiers and governor there. He wished to find out how many people were there, and so he ordered a census or count of the people to be made.[31] We take the census very differently now from what they did then. We in the United States, by order of the government, send men around from house to house to write down the names; but in Palestine, when they wanted the number of the people, every one, no matter where he lived, had to go to the city or town where his forefathers had lived and there register his name with all the others who belonged to the same tribe or family. Now, the forefathers of St. Joseph and the Blessed Virgin belonged to the little town of Bethlehem;[32] so they had to leave Nazareth where they were then living and go to Bethlehem. This was shortly before Christmas.

When they got to Bethlehem, they found the place crowded with people who also came to enroll their names. They went to the inn or hotel to seek for lodging for the night. The hotels there were not like ours. They were simply large buildings with small rooms and no furniture; they were

[30] Lk 1:28. See the Hail Mary explanation, above.
[31] Cf. Lk 2
[32] Cf. Ibid.

called "caravansaries." A man was in charge of the building, and by paying him something, persons were allowed the use of a room. No food was sold there, so travelers had to do their cooking at home and bring whatever they needed with them. When the Blessed Virgin and St. Joseph went to the inn, they found all the rooms occupied. Then they went up and down the streets looking for some house where they might stay. Nobody would take them in, because St. Joseph was old and poor and had no money, or little, to give. They were refused at every door, a very sad thing indeed. What were they to do?

It was growing dark, and the lights most likely were being lighted here and there in the houses. The old towns were not built as ours are, with houses on the outskirts growing fewer as we advance into the country. They were surrounded by great walls to keep out their enemies. There were several large gates in these walls, through which the people entered or left the city. At night, these gates were closed and guarded. Nearly all the people lived within the walls, and the country was lonely and almost deserted. Only shepherds were to be found in the country, and they lived in tents, which they carried about from place to place, as soldiers do in time of war. Such was the country about Bethlehem.

As St. Joseph and the Blessed Virgin could not find any place to stay in the town, they were forced to go into the country. They must have suffered also from fear because the country was infested with wolves and wild dogs, so fierce that they sometimes came into the towns and attacked the people in the streets. Besides, many robbers were wandering about waiting for victims. Palestine is a hilly country, and there were on the sides of some of the hills large caves in which these robbers frequently took refuge or divided their spoils. Because the shepherds at times, especially in bad weather, brought their animals into these caves, they are often called "stables." The Blessed Virgin and St. Joseph found, we are told, one of these cold, dark places, went into it for the night, and there our Lord was born.

It was the month of December and must have been quite cold, so the little infant Jesus must have suffered greatly from the cold. If it had been a stable such as we see in our days it would have been bad enough; but think of this cold, dark, miserable cave, and yet it was our Lord, the King of heaven and earth, who was born there. There are few people so poor that they have to live in a cave. What wonderful humility, then, on the part of our Lord. He could have been born, if he wished, in the grandest palace man could construct, and have had thousands of angels to bring him whatever he needed, for they are his servants in heaven. But our Lord became so humble to teach us. What impression should this make on those who are too fond of dress and too vain about their homes.

It was foretold by the prophets that our Lord would be born in Bethlehem, and, when the time was near at hand, his parents were living in Nazareth; then the Roman emperor gave the decree that the census be taken, which obliged our Lord's parents to go to Bethlehem, and thus our Lord was born there, and the words of the prophets fulfilled. See how God moves the whole world, if necessary, to accomplish what he desires. But how naturally he does everything. Nobody knew, not even the Roman emperor himself, that he was giving an edict to fulfill the prophecies and the promises of God. So, at times, people do many things to carry out the designs of God, though they know it not. We should never complain therefore or do unwillingly whatever work we have to perform, because it may be something that God wishes us to do for some very special end. If you look back upon your lives, you can see that God guided and directed you upon many occasions.

76. **How long did Christ live on earth?**

Christ lived on earth about thirty-three years, and led a most holy life in poverty and suffering.

The life of our Lord was spent in the following manner. At the time our Lord was born in Bethlehem, wise men or kings, called "Magi," came from the East—perhaps from Persia or Arabia—to adore him. They saw a strange star, and, leaving their own country, came to Palestine. When they came as far as Jerusalem, they went to King Herod and asked him where the young King was born. Herod was troubled, for he was afraid the new King would deprive him of his throne. He called together all the priests and asked them about this royal child. They told him and the Magi that, according to the prophecies, the Savior should be born in Bethlehem. The wise men saw the star once more, and followed it to Bethlehem, where it stood over the stable in which our Lord lay. They entered, and adored the infant Jesus, and offered him presents.

Now, Herod told them to come back after they had found the newborn King, and tell him where he was, that he too might go and adore him. But such was not Herod's real intention. He wished not to adore but to kill him. See, then, how the wicked pretend at times to do good, that they may deceive us and lead us astray. Be always on your guard against a person if you suspect his goodness. But Herod could not deceive God, who, knowing his heart, warned the wise men not to return to Herod, but to go back to their own country by another way, which they did.

We celebrate the day on which the wise men adored the infant Jesus on the feast of the Epiphany (six days after New Year's day). When the Magi did not return, Herod knew that they had avoided him. He was very angry indeed, and in order to be sure of killing the poor little infant Jesus, he had all the infants or children in or near Bethlehem who were not over two years old put to death. We honor these first little martyrs who suffered for Christ on the feast of Holy Innocents—three days after Christmas.

After the departure of the wise men, God sent an angel to St. Joseph, warning him of Herod's evil designs, and telling him to fly with Jesus and Mary into Egypt. Then St. Joseph, with the Blessed Virgin and the infant, set out for Egypt. St. Joseph did not ask the angel how long he would have to stay there; nor did he ask to be allowed to wait till morning. He obeyed promptly; he arose in the night, and started at once. What an example of obedience for us! They must have had many hardships on the way. They must have suffered much from hunger, cold, and fear. They dare not go on the best roads, for we may well suppose that Herod had his spies out watching for any that might escape. So, they went by the roughest roads and longest way. In Egypt, they were among strangers, and how could a poor old carpenter like St. Joseph find enough work there! The Holy Family must at times have suffered greatly from want. They remained in Egypt for some time. Afterward, when Herod died, they returned to Nazareth.[33]

At twelve years of age, our Lord went to the Temple of Jerusalem to offer sacrifice with his parents.[34] He afterward returned to Nazareth, and then for

[33] Cf. Mt 2

[34] Cf. Lk 2:42ff

eighteen years—called his "hidden life"—we do not hear anything of him. Most likely he worked in the carpenter shop with his foster father, St. Joseph.

At the age of thirty,[35] our Lord began his public life; that is, his preaching, miracles, etc. His public life lasted a little over three years, and then he was put to death on the cross.

77. **Why did Christ live so long on earth?**
Christ lived so long on earth to show us the way to heaven by his teaching and example.

Christ went through all the stages of life, that each might have an example. He was an infant; then a child; then a young man; and finally, a man. He did not become an old man to set an example to the old, because, if men follow his example in their youth and manhood, they will be good in old age. Youth is the all-important time to learn. If you want a tree to grow straight, you must keep it straight while it is only a little twig. You cannot straighten an old oak tree that has grown up crooked. So you must be taught to do right in your youth, that you may do the same when old. Of the hidden or private life of our Lord, we, as I have said, know nothing, except that he was obedient to his parents; for he wished to give an example also to those holy persons who lead a life hidden from the world. Some books have given stories about what our Lord did in school, etc., but these stories are not true. The only true things we know of our Lord are those told in the holy scripture, or handed down to us by the Church in her teachings, or those certainly revealed to God's saints. Remember, then, that others are taught best by example, and be careful of the example you give.

LESSON EIGHTH

On Our Lord's Passion, Death, Resurrection, and Ascension

The passion, that is, the terrible sufferings of our Lord, began after the last supper, and ended at his death. On Thursday evening, our Lord sat down

[35] Cf. Lk 3:23

for the last time with his dear apostles. He had been talking, eating, and living with them for over three years; and now he is going to take his last meal with them before his death. He told them then how he was to suffer, and that one of them was going to betray him. They were very much troubled, for only Judas himself knew what he was about to do.

78. **What did Jesus Christ suffer?**

Jesus Christ suffered a bloody sweat, a cruel scourging, was crowned with thorns, and was crucified.

After the supper, our Lord went with his apostles to a little country place just outside Jerusalem, and separated from it by a small stream. He told the three apostles, Peter, James, and John, to stay near the entrance, and to watch and pray, while he himself went further into the Garden of Olives, or Gethsemani, as this place was called, and, throwing himself upon his face, prayed long and earnestly, but the apostles fell asleep.

We often find persons who are in great anguish or dread covered with a cold perspiration. Now, our Lord's agony in the garden was so intense that great drops, not of sweat, but of blood, oozed from every pore, and trickled to the ground. There are three reasons given for this dreadful agony.

1. The clear, certain knowledge of the sufferings so soon to be endured. If we were to be put to death tomorrow and knew exactly the manner of our death and the pain it would inflict, how great would be our fear! Our Lord, knowing all things, knew in every particular what he would have to undergo. Moreover, his sufferings were greater than ours could be, even if we suffered the same kind of death; because his body was most perfect, and therefore more susceptible of pain than ours. A wound in the eye, because the most sensitive and delicate part of the body, would cause us greater pain than a wound on the foot or hand. Thus, all the parts of our Lord's body, being so perfect and sensitive, we can scarcely imagine his dreadful torments, the very thought of which caused him such agony.

2. The sins, past, present, and future of all men. He knew all things, as we have said, and looking back upon the world, he saw all the sins committed, of thought, word, and deed, from the time of Adam down to his own; and seeing all these offenses against his Father, he was very much grieved.

3. The third reason why he grieved: he looked forward and saw how little many persons would profit by all the sufferings he was about to endure. He saw all the sins that would be committed from the time of his death down to the end of the world. He saw us also sinning with the rest. No wonder then that he suffered so much in the garden. This suffering on that night is called our Lord's "agony in the garden."

That night, Judas, who had betrayed him to his enemies, came with a great band of soldiers and people, with swords and clubs, to make our Lord a prisoner. He did not try to escape, but stood waiting for them, though all his apostles, who had promised to stay with him, ran away. Then the soldiers led our Lord to the house of the chief priest. Then they gathered the priests, and gave him a kind of trial, and said he was guilty of death. But at that time, the Jews had no power to put persons to death according to the law; so they had to send our Lord to Pontius Pilate, the Roman governor, to be condemned, because they were under the power of the Romans. The Jews acted against their laws in the trial of our Lord.

1) They tried him at night; and 2) they allowed him no witnesses in his defense, but even employed false witnesses to testify against him, and thus acted against all law and justice. Early in the morning, they led him to Pilate, who commanded that he should be scourged. Then they stripped our Lord of his garments, fastened his hands to a low stone pillar, and there he was scourged by the Roman soldiers. The lashes used by the Romans were made of leather, with pieces of bone, iron, or steel fastened into it, so that every stroke would lay open the flesh. It is most likely these were the lashes used upon our Lord till every portion of his body was bruised and bleeding, and they replaced his garments upon him. Now, you know if you put a cloth upon a fresh wound, the blood will soak into it and cause it to adhere to the mangled flesh. Our Blessed Lord's garment, thus saturated with his blood, adhered to his wounded body, and, when again removed, caused him unspeakable pain.

Next, the soldiers, because our Lord had said he was a king—meaning a spiritual king—led him into a large hall and mocked him. They made a crown of long, sharp thorns, and forced it down upon his brow with a heavy rod or reed; every stroke driving the thorns into his head, and causing the blood to roll down his sacred face. They again took off his garments, and opened anew the painful wounds. Because kings wore purple, they put an old purple garment upon him, and made him a mock king, genuflecting in ridicule as they passed before him. They struck him in the face and spat upon him; and yet it seems our patient Lord said not a word in complaint.

Then they put his garments upon him, and Pilate asked the people what he should do with him, and they cried, "Crucify him." It was then Friday morning, and probably about ten or eleven o'clock. They made a cross of heavy beams, and, laying it upon his shoulders, forced him to carry it to Calvary—the place of execution, just outside the city; for it was not allowed to execute anyone in the city. Our Lord had not eaten anything from Thursday evening, and then, with all he suffered and the loss of blood, he must have been very weak at eleven o'clock on Friday morning. He was weak, and fell many times under the cross. His suffering was increased by seeing his Blessed Mother looking at him. When he arrived at Calvary, they tore off his garments and nailed him to the cross, driving the rough nails through his hands and feet. It was then about twelve o'clock.

From twelve to three in the afternoon, our Blessed Savior was hanging on the cross, with a great multitude of his enemies about him mocking him and saying cruel things. Even the two thieves that were crucified with him reviled him, though one of them repented and was pardoned before death. Our Lord's poor Mother and his few friends stood at a little distance, witnessing all that was going on. When our Lord was thirsty, his executioners gave him gall to drink. At three o'clock, he died, and there was an earthquake and darkness, and the people were sorely afraid.

But you will ask: "How could these soldiers be so cruel?" They were Romans; and in those days, men, called "gladiators," used to fight with swords before the Roman emperor and all the people—just as actors play now for the amusement of their audience. People who could enjoy such scenes as men slaying one another in deadly conflict would scarcely be moved to pity by seeing a man scourged. Again, in the early ages of the Church, during the persecutions, the emperors used to order the Christians to be thrown to wild beasts to be torn to pieces in the presence of the people—who applauded these horrible sights. They who could see so many put to death would not mind putting one to death, even in the most terrible manner.

79. **On what day did Christ die?**

Christ died on Good Friday.

Good Friday, so called since that time.

80. **Why do you call that day "good" on which Christ suffered so sorrowful a death?**

We call that day "good" on which Christ died, because by his death he showed his great love for man, and purchased for him every blessing.

81. **Where did Christ die?**

Christ died on Mount Calvary.

Mount Calvary, a little hill just outside the city of Jerusalem. For every city they have a special prison or place where all their criminals are executed. Now, as the great Temple of God was in Jerusalem, the city itself was called "the city of God," because, in the Temple, God spoke to the priests in the holy of holies. The Temple was divided into two parts: one part, something like the body of our churches, called "the holy," and the other part, where the ark of the covenant was kept, called "the holy of holies." It had about the same relation to the Temple as our altar and sanctuary have to our churches. The ark of the covenant was a box about four feet long, two and a half feet high, and two and a half feet wide, made of the finest wood, and ornamented with gold in the most beautiful manner. In it were the tables of stone, on which were written the commandments of God; also, the rod that Aaron—Moses' brother—changed into a serpent before King Pharao; also, some of the manna with which the people were miraculously fed during their forty years' journey in the desert when they fled out of Egypt.

All these things were figures of the true religion. The ark itself was a figure of the tabernacle, and the manna of the Holy Eucharist. The holy of holies was hidden from the people by a veil. Only the chief priest was allowed into that sacred place, and but once a year. The veil—called "the veil of the Temple"—hiding that holy of holies, though the things mentioned above were no longer in it, was torn asunder when our Lord died on the cross;[36] because, after his death, there was no need any longer of figures; for, after his death, we have the tabernacle itself and the real manna, the real bread from heaven, namely, the body of our Lord. The veil was rent to show also that God would not remain any longer in the Temple, but would be for the future only in the Christian Church. On account of all these things, therefore, Jerusalem was called "the holy city," and no criminals were put to death in it, but were conducted to Calvary—which means "the place of skulls"—and were there put to death.

I now call your attention to one thing. If the Jews showed such great respect and reverence for the ark containing only figures of the Blessed Sacrament, how should we behave in the presence of the tabernacle on the altar containing the Blessed Sacrament itself!

82. **How did Christ die?**

Christ was nailed to a cross and died on it, between two thieves.

Two thieves, because they thought this would make his death more disgraceful—making him equal to common criminals. One of these thieves, called "the penitent thief," repented of his sins and received our Lord's pardon before his death. The other thief died in his sins. Holy writers tell us that one of these thieves was saved to give poor sinners hope, and to teach them that they may save their souls at the very last moment of their lives if only they are heartily sorry for their sins and implore God's pardon for them. The other thief remained and died impenitent, that sinners may fear to put off their conversion to the hour of death, thus rashly presuming on God's mercy. Persons who willfully delay their conversion and put off their repentance to the last moment, living bad lives with the hope of dying well, may not accept the grace to repent at the last moment, but may, like the unfortunate, impenitent thief, die as they lived, in a state of sin.

83. **Why did Christ suffer and die?**

Christ suffered and died for our sins.

[36] Cf. Mt 27:51

It was not necessary for our Lord to suffer so much, but he did it to show how much he loved us and valued our souls, and how much he was willing to give for them. We, alas! do not value our souls as Christ did; we sometimes sell them for the merest trifle—a moment's gratification. How sinful!

84. **What lessons do we learn from the sufferings and death of Christ?**
From the sufferings and death of Christ, we learn the great evil of sin, the hatred God bears to it, and the necessity of satisfying for it.

We learn *the great evil of sin* also from the misery it brought into the world; *the hatred God bears to it*, from the punishment he inflicted on the wicked angels and on our first parents for it; and lastly, *the necessity of satisfying for it*, from the fact that God allowed his dear and only Son to suffer death itself for the sins even of others.

85. **Whither did Christ's soul go after his death?**
After Christ's death, his soul descended into hell.

86. **Did Christ's soul descend into the hell of the damned?**
The hell into which Christ's soul descended was not the hell of the damned, but a place or state of rest called "limbo," where the souls of the just were waiting for him.

Hell had many meanings in olden times. The grave was sometimes called "hell." Jacob, when he heard that wild beasts had devoured his son Joseph, said: "I will go down with sorrow into hell."[37] He meant the grave. *Limbo* is not the same as purgatory. It does not exist now, or, if it does, is only for little children who have never committed actual sin and who have died without baptism. They will never get into heaven or see God, but they will not have to suffer pains as they who are in purgatory or hell endure.

87. **Why did Christ descend into limbo?**
Christ descended into limbo to preach to the souls who were in prison—that is, to announce to them the joyful tidings of their redemption.

[37] Gn 37:35

88. **Where was Christ's body while his soul was in limbo?**

While Christ's soul was in limbo, his body was in the holy sepulchre.

Sepulchre is the same as "tomb." It is like a little room. In it, the coffin is not covered up with earth as it is in the grave, but is placed upon a stand. We call such places "vaults," and you can see many of them in any cemetery or burying ground. Sometimes they are cut in the side of elevated ground with their entrance level with the road; and sometimes they are built altogether under the ground. The one in which our Lord was placed was cut out of the side of a rock, and had for a door a great stone against the entrance. Our Lord was not placed in a coffin, but was wrapped in a linen cloth. It was the custom of the Jewish people and of many other ancient nations to embalm the bodies of the dead, wrap them in cloths, and cover them with sweet spices.[38] Thus it was that Mary Magdalene and other good women came early in the morning to anoint the body of our Lord.

"But," you will say, "why did they not do it on Friday evening or night?" The reason was this: the day with the Jews began at sunset—generally about six o'clock—and ended at sunset on the next evening. We count our twenty-four hours, or day, from twelve at midnight till twelve the next night. Therefore, with the Jews, six o'clock on Friday evening was the beginning of Saturday. They kept Saturday, or the sabbath, instead of Sunday as a day of worship. On that day, which they kept very strictly, it was not allowable to do work of any kind; so they could not anoint our Lord's body till the sabbath ended, which was about six o'clock, or sunset on Saturday evening. So, as the holy scripture tells us, they came very early in the morning; for Mary Magdalene and these good women were Jews, and strictly observed the Jewish law.

You must know that our Lord himself, the Blessed Virgin, St. Joseph, and the apostles were Jews; and that the Jewish religion was the true religion up to the coming of our Lord; but as it was only a figure and a promise of the Christian religion, it ceased to have any meaning or to be the true religion when the Christian religion itself was established by our Lord.

[38] Cf. Mt 27:59

89. **On what day did Christ rise from the dead?**

Christ rose from the dead, glorious and immortal, on Easter Sunday, the third day after his death.

Rose by his own power. This is the greatest of all our Lord's miracles, because all he taught is confirmed by it and depends upon it. A miracle is a work that can be performed only by God, or by someone to whom he has given the power. If anyone performs a real miracle to prove what he says, his words must be true; for God, who is infinite truth, could not sanction a lie—could not help an impostor to deceive us. Now our Lord said he was the Son of God; that he could forgive sins, etc.; and he performed miracles to prove what he said. Therefore, he must have told the truth. So all those whom God sent to do any great work were given the power to perform miracles that the people might know they were really messengers from God. They, on the other hand, who claim, as many have done from time to time in the world, that they have been sent by God to do some great work, and can give no convincing proof of their mission, are not to be believed. Thus, when Martin Luther claimed that he was sent by God to reform the Catholic Church—which had existed nearly fifteen hundred years before he was born—he performed no miracles, nor did he give any other proof that he had any such commission from God; and he cannot therefore be believed.

God has established all the laws of nature permanently. They will not vary or change, so that we can depend upon them. We can always be sure that the sun will rise and set; that the seasons will come; that fire will burn, etc. Now, if we see three young men in a great fiery furnace without being burned,[39] we say it is a great miracle; because naturally the fire would burn them up if God did not prevent it. Again, water will not stand up like a high wall without something keeping it back; it will always run about and fill every empty spot near it. If, therefore, we see water standing up like a high wall, as it did in the Red Sea at the command of Moses, and in the river Jordan, we say it is a miracle. So in all cases where the laws of nature do not work in the ordinary manner, we say a miracle is being performed. Now our Lord performed many such miracles—many times he suspended

[39] Cf. Dn 3

the laws of nature—which God alone can do, since he alone established them. Our Lord called back the soul to the body after death, thus raising the dead. He healed the sick, gave sight to the blind, cured the lame, etc., when all medicine and natural means were useless. He did all these things instantly as a rule, and without remedies. Therefore, his miracles prove his divine power. Since the resurrection was a great miracle, and our Lord performed it to prove that he was the true and only Son of God, he must have been just what he said he was.

Glorious. Our Lord rose in the same body he had before his death; but when he rose, it had new qualities—it was glorified. The qualities of a glorified body are four, namely: brilliancy, agility, subtility, and impassibility.

1. It has brilliancy; that is, it shines like a light; it gives forth light; the soul shines through the body. You have heard of the transfiguration of our Lord. One day, he took three of his apostles—Peter, James, and John—unto a high mountain;[40] and as he was speaking to them, suddenly his whole body began to shine like the sun. Then Moses and Elias—two great and holy men of the old law—came and conversed with him. The apostles were astonished and delighted at the sight, and wished to remain there always. Our Lord's body at that time showed one of the qualities of a glorified body. The same three apostles that saw him thus transfigured and heard the voice of the heavenly Father saying, "This is my beloved Son," were present in the garden during our Lord's agony. He allowed them to see the transfiguration, so that, when they should see him suffering as man, they would remember that they saw him on the mountain glorified as God.

2. Agility; that is, a glorified body can move rapidly from one place to another, like the lightning itself. After his resurrection, our Lord was in Jerusalem, and almost immediately he appeared near the village of Emmaus to two disciples going there.[41] They had left Jerusalem after the crucifixion, probably through fear, and were going along together talking about what had happened during the days of our Lord's passion. Suddenly our Lord came and walked and talked with them, but they did not know him. They asked him to stay that

[40] Cf. Mt 17

[41] Cf. Lk 24

night at their house, for it was growing dark. He did stop with them, and, at supper, they knew him, and then he vanished from their sight. An ordinary person would have to get up and walk away; but he vanished, showing on this occasion the second quality of his glorified body—agility.

3. Subtility; that is, such a body can go where it pleases and cannot be resisted by material things. It can pass through closed doors or gates, and even walls cannot keep it out. It passes through everything, as light does through glass without breaking it. At one time, after our Lord's resurrection, the apostles were gathered together in a room, for they were still afraid of being put to death, and the doors were tightly closed. Suddenly, our Lord stood in the midst of them and said: "Peace be to you."[42] They did not open the door for him; neither wood nor stone could keep him out; and thus, he showed that his body had the third quality.

4. His body had the fourth quality also—impassibility, which means that it can no longer suffer. Before his death, and at it, our Lord suffered dreadful torments, as you know; but after his resurrection, nothing could injure or hurt him. The spear could not hurt his side, nor the nails his hands, nor the thorns his head. Shortly after his resurrection, our Lord appeared to his apostles while Thomas, one of them, was absent.[43] When Thomas returned, the other apostles told him that they had seen the Lord risen from the dead; but he would not believe them, saying, "Unless I see the holes where the nails were in his hands and feet, and put my finger into his side, I will not believe." Now our Lord, knowing all things, knew this also; so he came again when Thomas was present, and said to him: "Now, Thomas, put your hand into my side." Thomas cried out: "My Lord and my God!" He believed then, because he saw. Now if this body of our Lord's had been an ordinary body, it would have caused him pain to allow anyone to put his hand into the wound; but it was impassible. It seems very strange, does it not, that Thomas would not believe what the other apostles told him? God permitted this. Why? Because, if they all believed easily, some enemies of our Lord might say the apostles were simple men that believed everything without any proof. Now they cannot

[42] Jn 20:19
[43] Cf. Jn 20:24

truly say so, because here was one of the apostles, Thomas, who would not believe without the very strongest kind of proof. Another person, one would think, would have been satisfied with seeing our Lord's wounds; but Thomas would not trust even his eyes—he must also touch before he would believe: showing, therefore, that the apostles were not deceived in anything our Lord did in their presence, for they had always the most convincing proofs.

After the resurrection, at the last day, the bodies of all those who are to be in heaven will have the qualities I have mentioned; that is, they will be glorified bodies.

Speaking of our Lord's wounds, I might tell you what the *stigmata* means, if you should ever hear or read of it. There have been some persons in the world—saints, of course—who have had upon their hands, feet, and side wounds just like those our Lord had, and these wounds caused them great pain. For example, St. Francis of Assisi.[44] Up to 1883—that is, only a few years ago—there lived in Belgium a young girl named Louise Lateau who had the stigmata. We have the most positive proof of it, as you may see in the accounts of her life now published. Her wounds caused her great pain and bled every Friday for many years. She was a delicate seamstress, and lived with her mother and sisters in almost continual poverty. She had always been remarkable for her true piety, patience in suffering, and charity to the sick. I mention this young girl because she lived in our own time, and is the latest person we know of who had the stigmata, or wounds of our Lord. So, if you ever hear of the stigmata of St. Francis or others, you will know that it means "wounds, like those of our Lord, impressed on their bodies in a miraculous manner."

Immortal—that is, never to die again, as it will be with us also after the resurrection.

The third day. It was not three full days, but the parts of three days. Suppose someone should ask you on Friday evening how long from now to Sunday; you would answer: "Sunday will be the third day from today." You would count thus: Friday one, Saturday two, and Sunday itself three. So it was with our Lord. He died on Friday at about three in the afternoon, and remained in the sepulchre till Sunday morning.

[44] See *Butler's Lives of the Saints*, Oct. 4th.

90. How long did Christ stay on earth after his resurrection?

Christ stayed on earth forty days after his resurrection, to show that he was truly risen from the dead, and to instruct his apostles.

After our Lord's resurrection, he remained on earth forty days: but you must not think he was visible all that time. No. He did not appear to everybody, but only to certain persons, and not all the time to them either. He appeared to his apostles and others in all about nine times; at least, we know for certain that he appeared nine times, though he may have appeared oftener. He showed that *he was truly risen*, for he ate with his apostles and conversed with them.[45] It was after the resurrection that he breathed on them and gave them the power to forgive sins.[46]

91. After Christ had remained forty days on earth, whither did he go?

After forty days, Christ ascended into heaven, and the day on which he ascended into heaven is called "Ascension day."

One day, he was on a mountain with his apostles and disciples; and as he was talking to them, he began to rise up slowly and quietly, just as you have sometimes seen a balloon soar up into the air without noise. Higher and higher he ascended; and as they gazed up at him, the clouds opened to receive him, then closed under him: and that was the last of our Lord's mission as man upon earth. The ascension took place forty days after the resurrection.[47]

92. Where is Christ in heaven?

In heaven, Christ sits at the right hand of God the Father Almighty.

93. What do you mean by saying that Christ sits at the right hand of God?

When I say that Christ sits at the right hand of God, I mean that Christ as God is equal to his Father in all things, and that as man he is in the highest place in heaven next to God.

[45] Cf. Lk 24:42
[46] Cf. Jn 20
[47] Cf. Acts 1

LESSON NINTH

On the Holy Ghost and His Descent upon the Apostles

94. **Who is the Holy Ghost?**
The Holy Ghost is the third Person of the Blessed Trinity.

95. **From whom does the Holy Ghost proceed?**
The Holy Ghost proceeds from the Father and the Son.

96. **Is the Holy Ghost equal to the Father and the Son?**
The Holy Ghost is equal to the Father and the Son, being the same Lord and God as they are.

97. **On what day did the Holy Ghost come down upon the apostles?**
The Holy Ghost came down upon the apostles ten days after the ascension of our Lord; and the day on which he came down upon the apostles is called "Whitsunday" or "Pentecost."

We have seen already that the apostles fled and were very much afraid when our Lord was taken prisoner. Even Peter, the chief of the apostles, who said he would die rather than leave our Lord, shamefully denied him; and St. John, the beloved disciple, stood near the cross, but offered no resistance to our Lord's enemies. After the crucifixion of our Lord, the apostles, afraid of being put to death, shut themselves up in a room. Ten days after our Lord's ascension, they were praying as usual in their room, when suddenly they heard the sound as it were of a great wind, and then they saw tongues the shape of our own, but all on fire, coming, and one tongue resting on the head of each apostle present.[48]

This was the Holy Ghost coming to them. The Holy Ghost, being a pure Spirit without a body, can take any form he pleases. He sometimes came in the form of a dove; so, when you see a dove painted in a church near the altar, it is there to represent the Holy Ghost. You could not paint

[48] Cf. Acts 2

a spirit, so angels and God himself are generally represented in pictures as they at some time appeared to men.

Whitsunday, or White-Sunday; probably so called because in the early ages of the Church converts were baptized on the day before, and, after their baptism, wore white robes or garments as a mark of the soul's purity after baptism.

Pentecost means the fiftieth day, because the feast comes fifty days after the resurrection of our Lord. After his resurrection, he remained forty days upon earth, and ten days after he ascended into heaven, the Holy Ghost came, thus making the fifty days. After the Holy Ghost came down upon the apostles, they were no longer timid men. They went forth boldly into the streets and preached Christ crucified; telling the people how the Son of God—the true Messias promised—had been put to death. Many who heard them believed and were baptized. The first time St. Peter preached to the people, three thousand were converted;[49] so that, when all the apostles preached, the number of Christians increased rapidly, and the Christian religion was soon carried to distant parts of the world.

At the time our Lord was put to death, the Jews were celebrating a great feast in Jerusalem. The Jews were not like us in this respect. We have many churches, and in all of them sacrifice, that is, the Holy Mass, is offered. The Jews had only one Temple where sacrifice could be offered, and that was in Jerusalem. They had synagogues or meeting houses throughout the land in which they assembled to pray and hear the holy scriptures read; but they could not offer sacrifice in them. Three times a year, they went to Jerusalem to celebrate their great feasts. One of these feasts was called the "Pasch" or "Passover," and it was during the celebration of that feast that our Lord was put to death; so that there were many persons from all parts of the nation present at the sad execution. I must now tell you why they celebrated the Pasch.

We generally celebrate a feast to commemorate—to remind us of—some great event; and the Jews celebrated this feast to remind them of their deliverance from the slavery of the Egyptians, in which their ancestors had been suffering for about two hundred years. At the end of

[49] Cf. Acts 2:41

that time, God sent Moses to deliver them. You should know, then, who Moses was and what he did to deliver his people, and you should know also something of the history of his people—the Israelites—and how they came to be in Egypt.

At the time I am now going to speak of, the old patriarch Jacob, Abraham's grandson, had eleven sons—for Benjamin, the twelfth son, was born afterward—and the youngest was called "Joseph." Joseph was the favorite of his father, and his brothers were jealous of him. The brothers were shepherds, and used to take their flocks to feed at a great distance from home, and did not return for a long time. One day, the father sent Joseph to his brothers to see if all were well. They hated Joseph because his father loved him best; and when they saw him coming, they agreed never to let him return to his father.[50] They intended to kill him. While they were debating about how they should put him to death—he was then only sixteen years old—some merchants passed on their way to Egypt; so, instead of killing him, they sold him as a slave to the merchants. Then they took Joseph's coat and dipped it in the blood of a kid, and sent it to their poor old father, saying they had found it, and making him believe that some wild beast on the way had eaten Joseph.

When the merchants arrived in Egypt, Potiphar, one of the king's officers, bought Joseph, and brought him as a slave to his own house. While there, Joseph was falsely accused of a great crime, and cast into prison. While Joseph was in prison, the king had a dream.[51] He saw in the dream seven fat cows coming up out of a river, followed by seven lean cows; and the lean cows ate up the fat cows. He saw also seven fat ears of corn and seven lean ears of corn; and the seven lean ears ate up the seven fat ears. The king was very much troubled, and called together all his wise men to tell him what the dream meant, but they could not. Then the king heard of Joseph, and sent for him. Now, Joseph was a very good young man, and God showed him the meaning; so he told the king that the seven fat ears of corn and the seven fat cows meant seven years of great abundance in

[50] Cf. Gn 37
[51] Cf. Gn 41

Egypt, and that the seven lean ears and the seven lean cows meant seven years of famine that would follow, and all the abundance of the previous seven years would be consumed. So he advised the king to build great barns during the years of plenty, and gather up all the corn everywhere to save it for the years of famine. The king was delighted at Joseph's wisdom, and made him after himself the most powerful in the kingdom, giving him charge of everything, so that Joseph himself might do what he had advised.

Now, it happened years after this that there was a famine in the country where Joseph's father lived, and he sent all his sons down into Egypt to buy corn.[52] They did not know their brother Joseph, but he knew them; and after forgiving them for what they had done to him, he sent them home with an abundance of corn. Afterward, Joseph's father and brothers left their own country and came to live near Joseph in Egypt. The king gave them good land,[53] and they lived there in peace and happiness. Learn from this beautiful history of Joseph how God protects those that love and serve him no matter where they are or in what danger they may be placed; and how he even turns the evil deeds of their enemies into blessings for them.

After the death of Joseph and his brothers, their descendants became very numerous, and the new king of the Egyptians began to persecute them.[54] He imposed upon them the hardest works, and treated them most cruelly. He ordered that all their male infants should, as soon as born, be thrown into the river Nile. Now, about that time, Moses was born.[55] His mother did not obey the king's order, but hid him for about three months. When she could conceal him no longer, she made a little cradle of rushes, and covering it over with pitch or tar to keep out the water, placed him in it, and then laid it in the tall grass by the edge of the river, sending his little sister to watch what would become of him. Just then the king's daughter came down to bathe, and seeing the little child, ordered one of her servants to bring him to her. At that moment, Moses' little sister, pretending not to know him, ran up and asked the king's daughter if she wished to procure a

[52] Cf. Gn 42
[53] Cf. Gn 47
[54] Cf. Ex 1
[55] Cf. Ex 2

nurse for him. The king's daughter replied in the affirmative and permitted her to bring one; so Moses' own mother was brought and engaged to be his nurse: but he was not known as her son, but as the adopted son of the king's daughter. When Moses grew up, he was an officer in the king's army; but, because he took the part of his persecuted countrymen, he offended the king, and had to fly from the palace. He then went into another country and became a shepherd.

During all this time, the persecuted Israelites were praying to the true God to be delivered from the slavery of the Egyptians, who were idolaters. One day, Moses saw a bush burning; and as he came near to look at it, he heard a voice telling him not to come too near, and bidding him take off his shoes, for he was on holy ground.[56] It was God who thus appeared and spoke to him, and he ordered him to take off his shoes as a mark of respect and reverence. When we want to show our respect for any person or place, we take off our hats; but the people of that country, instead of their hats, took off their shoes. It was the custom of the country and did not seem strange to them.

Then God told Moses that he was going to send him to deliver his people from the Egyptians and lead them back to their own country; and he sent Aaron, the brother of Moses, with him. Then Moses said to God, "The king of Egypt will not let the people go, and what can I do?" God gave Moses two signs or miracles to show the king, so that he could know that Moses was really sent by him. He gave him power to change a rod into a serpent, and back again into a rod; power also to bring a disease instantly upon his hand, and to heal it instantly.[57] "Do these," said Almighty God, "in the presence of the king." Then Moses and Aaron went to the king and did as God commanded them; and when the rod of Aaron became a serpent, the king's magicians—that is, men who do apparently wonderful things by sleight of hand or the power of the devil—cast their rods upon the ground, and they also became serpents—not that their rods were changed into serpents, but the devil, who was helping them, took away instantly their rods and

[56] Cf. Ex 3
[57] Cf. Ex 4

put real serpents in their place—but Aaron's serpent swallowed them up.[58] After these signs, the king would not let the people go with Moses; for God permitted the king's heart to be hardened, so that all the Egyptians might see the great work God was going to do for his people.

Then God sent the ten plagues upon the Egyptians, while the Israelites—God's people—suffered nothing from these plagues.

The first plague was blood. All the water in the land was converted into blood.[59] The king then sent for Moses, and promised that if he would take away the plague, he would allow all the people to depart. Moses prayed to God, and the plague was removed. But after it was taken away, the king's heart was hardened again and he would not keep his promise. Just as people in sickness, distress, or danger sometimes promise God they will lead better lives if only he will help them, and, when they are saved, they do not keep their promises, so did Pharao; and therefore, God sent another plague. The second plague was frogs. Great numbers of them came out of the rivers and lakes, and filled all the houses of the Egyptians, and crawled into their food, beds, etc. Again the king sent for Moses and did as before; and again Moses prayed, and all the frogs went back into the waters or died.[60] But the king again hardened his heart and did not keep his promise.

The third plague was sciniphs[61]—very small flies, that filled the land. Imagine our country filled with mosquitoes so numerous that you could scarcely walk through them; it would be a dreadful plague. As it is, two or three might cause you considerable annoyance and pain: What then if there were millions doubly venomous, because sent to punish you? So these little flies must have greatly punished the Egyptians. The fourth plague was flies that filled the land and covered everything, to the great disgust of the people. The fifth plague was murrain—a disease that broke out among the cattle. The sixth plague was a disease—boils—that broke out on men and beasts, so that scarcely any one could move on account of the pains and suffering. The seventh plague was hail that fell in large pieces and destroyed

[58] Cf. Ex 7
[59] Cf. Ibid.
[60] Cf. Ex 8
[61] Cf. Ibid.

all their crops. The eighth plague was locusts. These are very destructive little animals. They look something like our grasshoppers, but are about two or three times their size. They fly and come in millions. They come to this country in large numbers—almost a plague—every fifteen or twenty-five years, and the farmers fear them very much. They eat up every green blade or leaf, and thus destroy all the crops and trees. When the locusts came upon Egypt, Moses, at the king's request, prayed, and God sent a strong wind that swept them into the sea, where they perished in the water. The ninth plague was a horrible darkness for three days in all the land of Egypt.

The tenth plague, the last, was the most terrible of all—the killing of the firstborn in all the land of Egypt.[62] God instructed Moses to tell the Israelites in the land that on a certain night they were to take a lamb in each family, kill it, and sprinkle its blood on the doorposts of their houses. They were then to cook the lamb and eat it standing, with their garments ready as for a journey.[63] The lamb was called "the paschal lamb," and was, after that, to be eaten every year, at about what is with us Easter time, in commemoration of this event. That night, God sent an angel through all the land, and he killed the firstborn of man and beast in all the houses of the Egyptians. That is, he killed the eldest son in the house; and if the father was the firstborn in his father's family, he was killed also; and the same for the beasts. This was a terrible punishment. In the house of every Egyptian there were some dead, but not one in the houses of the Israelites; for when the angel saw the blood of the lamb on the doorposts, he passed over and did not enter into their houses, so that this event, called "Passover" or "Pasch," was kept always as a great feast by God's people. This paschal lamb was a figure of our Blessed Lord, for as its blood saved the Israelites from death, so our Lord's blood saved and still saves us from eternal death in hell.

After that dreadful night, Pharao allowed the people to depart with Moses; but when they had gone as far as the Red Sea, he was sorry he let them go, and set out with a great army to bring them back. There the people stood, with the sea before them and Pharao and his army coming

[62] Cf. Ex 12

[63] Cf. Ibid.

behind them; but God provided for them a means of escape. At God's command, Moses stretched his rod over the sea, and the waters divided and stood like great walls on either side; and all the people passed through the opening in the waters, on the dry bed of the sea.[64]

Pharao attempted to follow them, but when he and his army were on the dry bed of the sea, between the two walls of water, God allowed the waters to close over them, and they were all drowned. Then the Israelites began the great journey through the desert, in which they traveled for forty years. During all that time, God fed them with manna. He himself, as a guide, went with them in a cloud, that shaded them from the heat of the sun during the day and was a light for them at night. But you will ask: "Was the desert so large that it took forty years to cross it?" No, but these people, notwithstanding all God had done for them, sinned against him in the desert; so, he permitted them to wander about through it till a new generation of people grew up, who were to be led into the promised land by Josue, the successor of Moses. From this we may learn a lesson for ourselves: God will always punish those who deserve it, even though he loves them and may often have done great things to save them; but he will wait for his own time to punish.

The Israelites then, as I have said, went from every part of the land up to the Temple in Jerusalem to celebrate the Pasch each year. It was during one of these celebrations that our Lord was put to death, and during another feast that St. Peter preached to the people after our Lord's death. He spoke only in one language, and yet all his hearers understood, for each heard his own language spoken.[65] This was called the "gift of tongues," and was given to the apostles when the Holy Ghost came upon them. For example, if each of you came from a different country and understood the language only of the country from which you came, and I gave the instructions only in English, then if everyone thought I was speaking his language—German, French, Spanish, Italian, etc.—and understood me,

[64] Cf. Ex 14

[65] Cf. Acts 2:6

I would have what is called the "gift of tongues," and it would be a great miracle, as it was when bestowed upon the apostles.

In the first ages of the Church, God performed more miracles than he does now, because they are not now so necessary. These miracles were performed only to make the Church better known, and to prove that she was the true Church, with her power and authority from God. That can now be known and seen in Christian countries without miracles. These special gifts, like the gift of tongues, were given also to some of the early Christians by the Holy Ghost, when they received confirmation; but they were not a part of or necessary for confirmation, but only to show the power of the true religion. Those who heard St. Peter preach, when they went back to their own countries, told what they had seen and heard, and thus their countrymen were prepared to receive the gospel when the apostles came to preach it.

98. **How did the Holy Ghost come down upon the apostles?**
The Holy Ghost came down upon the apostles in the form of tongues of fire.

99. **Who sent the Holy Ghost upon the apostles?**
Our Lord Jesus Christ sent the Holy Ghost upon the apostles.

100. **Why did Christ send the Holy Ghost?**
Christ sent the Holy Ghost to sanctify his Church, to enlighten and strengthen the apostles, and to enable them to preach the gospel.

Sanctify, to make more holy by the grace which he would give to the members of the Church. *To enlighten.* The apostles did not understand very well everything our Lord taught while he was with them; but after the Holy Ghost came upon them, they understood perfectly, and remembered many things which our Lord said to them, and understood the true meaning of all. The prophets foretold that when the Messias, Christ, would come, he would bring all the world under his power. The prophets meant in a spiritual sense; but most of the people understood that he was to be a great general, with powerful armies, who would subdue all the nations of the earth, and bring them under the authority of the Jews. We know they thought that the great kingdom he was to establish upon earth would be a temporal kingdom from many of their sayings and actions. One day, the mother of two of our Lord's apostles came to ask him if, when he had established his kingdom upon the earth, he would give her sons honorable positions in it, and place them high in authority.[66] Our Lord told her she did not understand what she was asking. This shows that even some of the apostles—much less the people—did not understand the full nature of our Lord's mission upon earth, nor of his kingdom, the Church. Often too, when he preached to the people, the apostles asked him on his return what his sermon meant.[67] But after the Holy Ghost came, they were enlightened, and understood all without difficulty.

Strengthen. I told you already that, before the Holy Ghost came, they were timid and afraid of being arrested, but that afterward they went out boldly, and taught all they had learned from our Lord. They were often taken prisoners and scourged, but it mattered not—they were firm in their faith, and could suffer anything for Christ after they had been enlightened and strengthened by the Holy Ghost. Finally, they were all, with the exception of St. John, put to death for their holy faith. St. Peter and St. Paul were crucified at Rome about the year 65, that is, about thirty-two years after the death of our Lord. St. James was beheaded by order of King Herod; St. John lived the longest, and was the only one of the apostles who was not put to death, though he was cast into a large vessel of boiling oil, but was miraculously saved.

Certainly, by dying for their faith, the apostles showed that they were not impostors or hypocrites. They must really have believed what they taught, otherwise they would not have laid down their lives for it. They were certain of what they taught, as we saw when speaking of St. Thomas.

101. **Will the Holy Ghost abide with the Church forever?**

The Holy Ghost will abide with the Church forever, and guide it in the way of holiness and truth.

Abide means "to stay with us."

[66] Cf. Mt 20:20
[67] Cf. Lk 8:9

LESSON TENTH

On the Effects of the Redemption

102. **Which are the chief effects of the redemption?**

The chief effects of the redemption are two: the satisfaction of God's justice by Christ's sufferings and death, and the gaining of grace for men.

An *effect* is that which is caused by something else. If you place a danger signal on a broken railroad track, the effect will be preventing the wreck of the train, and the cause will be your placing the signal. Many effects may flow from one cause. In our example, see all the good effects that may follow your placing the signal—the cars are not broken, the passengers are not killed, the rails are not torn out of their places, etc. Thus, the redemption had two effects, namely: to satisfy God for the offense offered him by the sins of men, and to merit grace to be used for our benefit.

103. **What do you mean by "grace"?**

By "grace," I mean a supernatural gift of God bestowed on us, through the merits of Jesus Christ, for our salvation.

Supernatural, that is, above nature. *A gift*—something, therefore, that God does not owe us. He owes us nothing, strictly speaking. Health, talents, and such things are natural gifts, and belong to our nature as men; but grace is something above our nature, given to our soul. God gives it to us on account of the love he has for his Son, our Lord, who merited it for us by dying for us. *Merits*. A merit is some excellence or goodness which entitles one to honor or reward.

Grace is a help we get to do something that will be pleasing to God. When there is anything in our daily works that we cannot do alone, we naturally look for help; for example, to lift some heavy weight is only a natural act, not a supernatural act, and the help we need for it is only natural help. But if we are going to do something above and beyond our nature, and cannot do it alone, we must not look for natural, but for supernatural, help; that is, the help must always be like the work to be done. Therefore, all spiritual works need spiritual help, and spiritual help is grace.

104. **How many kinds of grace are there?**

There are two kinds of grace—sanctifying grace and actual grace.

105. **What is sanctifying grace?**

Sanctifying grace is that grace which makes the soul holy and pleasing to God.

Sanctifying, that is, making us holy by cleansing, purifying our souls. Sin renders the soul ugly and displeasing to God, and grace purifies it. Suppose I have something bright and beautiful given to me, and take no care of it, but let it lie around in dusty places until it becomes tarnished and soiled, loses all its beauty, and appears black and ugly. To restore its beauty, I must clean and polish it. Thus, the soul blackened by sin must be cleaned by God's grace. If the soul is in mortal sin—altogether blackened—then sanctifying grace brings back its brightness and makes it pleasing to God; but if the soul is already bright, though stained or darkened a little by venial sin, then grace makes it still brighter.

106. **What do you call those graces or gifts of God by which we believe in him, hope in him, and love him?**

Those graces or gifts of God by which we believe in him, and hope in him, and love him, are called the "divine virtues" of faith, hope, and charity.

Virtues. Virtue is the habit of doing good. The opposite to virtue is vice, which is the habit of doing evil. We acquire a habit, bad or good, when we do the same thing very frequently. We then do it easily and almost without thinking; as a man, for instance, who has the habit of cursing, curses almost without knowing it, though that does not excuse him, but makes his case worse, by showing that he must have cursed very often to acquire the habit. If, however, he is striving to overcome the bad habit, and should unintentionally curse now and then, it would not be a sin, since he did not wish to curse, and was trying to overcome the vice. One act does not make a virtue or a vice. A person who gives alms only once cannot be said to have the virtue of charity. A man who curses only once a year cannot be said to have the vice of cursing. Faith, hope, and charity are infused by God into our souls, and are therefore called "infused virtues," to distinguish them from the virtues we acquire.

107. **What is faith?**

Faith is a divine virtue by which we firmly believe the truths which God has revealed.

A divine virtue is one that is heavenly or holy. Faith is the habit of always believing all that God has revealed and the Church teaches. *Firmly*, that is, without the slightest doubt. *Revealed*, that is, made known to us. Revelation is the collection of all the truths that God has made known to us. But why do we believe? Because we clearly see and know the truth of what is revealed? No, but because God reveals it; we believe it though we cannot see it or even understand it.

If we see it plainly, then we believe it rather because we see it than because God makes it known to us. Suppose a friend should come and tell you the church is on fire. If he never told you lies, and had no reason for telling you any now, you would believe him—not because you know of the fire, but because he tells you; but afterward, when you see the church or read of the fire in the papers, you have proof of what he told you, but you believed it just as firmly when he told you as you do afterward.

In the same way, God tells us his great truths and we believe them; because we know that since God is infinitely true, he cannot deceive us or be deceived. But if afterward, by studying and thinking, we find proof that God told us the truth, we do not believe with any greater faith, for we always believed without doubting, and we study chiefly that we may have arguments to prove the truth of God's revelations to others who do not believe. Suppose some person was present when your friend came and said the church is burning, and that that person would not believe your friend. What would you do? Why, convince him that what your friend said was true by showing him the account of the fire in the papers. Thus, learning does not change our faith, which, as I have said, is not acquired by study, but is infused into our souls by God. The little boy who hears what God taught, and believes it firmly because God taught it, has as good a faith as his teacher who has studied all the reasons why he should believe.

108. **What is hope?**

Hope is a divine virtue by which we firmly trust that God will give us eternal life and the means to obtain it.

Eternal—that is, everlasting life—life without end. *Means*—that is, his grace, because without God's grace we cannot do any supernatural thing.

109. **What is charity?**

Charity is a divine virtue by which we love God above all things for his own sake, and our neighbor as ourselves for the love of God.

The virtue of charity makes us *love God*, because he is so good and beautiful, wise and powerful in himself; therefore, for his own sake and without any other consideration. *Above all things*, in such a way that we would rather lose anything than offend him. But someone may say he thinks he loves his parents more than God. Well, let us see. To repeat an example already given, suppose his parents told him to steal, and he knew stealing to be a sin; if he would not steal, that would show, would it not, that he loved God more than his parents, for he would rather offend his parents than God. That is the kind of love we must have for God; not mere feeling, but the firm belief that God is the best of all, and when we have to choose between offending God and losing something, be it goods or friends, we would rather lose anything than offend God.

Neighbor. Not merely the person living near us, but all men of every kind and nation—even our enemies. The people who lived at the time of our Lord in his country used to dispute about just what persons were to be considered their neighbors; so one day, they asked our Lord, and he answered them by telling them the following.[68] Said he: "A man was once going down from Jerusalem, and, on the way, robbers beat him, robbed him, and left him on the wayside, dying. First, one man came by, looked at the wounded man, and passed on; then another came and did the same; finally, a third man came, who was of a different religion and nationality from the wounded man. But he did not consider these things. He dressed the poor man's wounds, placed him upon his horse and brought him to an inn or hotel, and paid the innkeeper to take care of him. Now," said our Lord, "which of these three was neighbor to the wounded man?" And they answered rightly: "The man that helped him." Our Lord, by this

[68] Cf. Lk 10:30

example, wished to teach them and us that everybody is our neighbor who is in distress of any kind and needs our help. *Neighbor*, therefore, means every human being, no matter where he lives or what his color, learning, manners, etc., for every human being in the world is a child of God and has been redeemed by our Lord. Therefore, every child of God is my neighbor, and even more—he is my brother; for God is his father and mine also, and if he is good enough for God to love, he should be good enough for me.

As ourselves. Not with as much love, but with the same kind of love; that is, we are to follow the rule laid down by our Lord: "Do unto others as you would have others do unto you." Never do to anyone what you would not like to have done to yourself; and always do for another just what you would wish another to do for you, if you were in the same position. Our neighbor is our equal and gifted with all the gifts that we ourselves have. When we come into the world, we are all equal. We have a body and a soul, with the power to develop them. Money, learning, wealth, fame, and all else that makes up the difference between men in the world are acquired in the world; and when men die, they go out of the world without any of these things, just as they came into it. The real difference between them in the next world will depend upon the things they have done, good or bad, while here. We should love our neighbor also on another account, namely: that he is one day to be in heaven with us; and if he is to be with us for all eternity, why should we hate him now? On the other hand, if our neighbor is to be in hell on account of his bad life, why should we hate him? We should rather pity him, for he will have enough to suffer without our hatred.

110. **What is actual grace?**

Actual grace is that help of God which enlightens our mind and moves our will to shun evil and do good.

Actual. Sanctifying grace continues with us, but when grace is given just so that we may do a good act or avoid a bad one, it is called "actual grace." Suppose, for example, I see a poor man and am able to aid him. When my conscience tells me to give him assistance, I am just then receiving an actual grace, which moves me and helps me to do that good act; and just as soon as I give the help, the actual grace ceases, because no longer needed. It was given for that one good act, and now that the act is done, the actual grace has produced its effect. Again, a boy is going to Mass on Sunday and meets other boys who try to persuade him to remain away from Mass and go to some other place. When he hears his conscience telling him to go to Mass by all means, he is receiving just then an actual grace to avoid the mortal sin of missing Mass, and the grace lasts just as long as the temptation. Sacramental grace is sanctifying grace—given in the sacraments—which contains for us a right to actual graces when we need them. These actual graces are given to help us to fulfill the end for which each of the sacraments was instituted. They are different for each sacrament, and are given just when we need them; that is, just when we are tempted against the object or end for which the sacrament was instituted.

111. **Is grace necessary for salvation?**

Grace is necessary for salvation, because without grace we can do nothing to merit heaven.

112. **Can we resist the grace of God?**

We can and unfortunately often do resist the grace of God.

Grace is a gift, and no one is obliged to take a gift; but if God offers a gift and we refuse to take it, we offend and insult him. To insult God is to sin. Therefore, to refuse to accept, or to make bad use of the grace God gives us, is to sin.

113. **What is the grace of perseverance?**

The grace of perseverance is a particular gift of God which enables us to continue in the state of grace till death.

Perseverance here does not mean perseverance in our undertakings, but perseverance in grace—never in mortal sin; always a friend of God. Now, if God keeps us from all sin till the day of our death and takes us while we are his friends, then he gives us what we call the "gift of final perseverance." We cannot, strictly speaking, merit this great grace, but only pray for it; so, anyone who commits mortal sin may be taken just in that state and be lost for all eternity.

LESSON ELEVENTH

On the Church

Before speaking of the Church, I wish to give you a short account of the true religion before the coming of our Lord.

When Adam was created in a state of grace, God communicated with him freely; he knew God even better than we do now. But after their sin, our first parents fell from the friendship of God. Cain—one of Adam's sons—murdered his brother Abel, and, for this, he and his posterity were cursed by God, and all his descendants became very wicked.[69] The other children of Adam remained faithful to God as long as they kept away from the children of Cain; but just as soon as they associated and intermarried with them, they also became wicked. This should teach us to avoid evil company, for there is always more likelihood that the good will become bad than that the bad will be converted by the good. You know the old saying, that if you take a basket of good apples and place a bad one among them, in a short time they will all be spoiled.

After the deluge, Noe and his family settled once more upon the land, and, for a time, their descendants remained faithful to God; but later, they became wicked and undertook to build a great tower,[70] which they thought would reach up to heaven. They believed, perhaps, that if ever there should be another deluge upon the earth, they could take refuge in the tower. But God was displeased with their conduct and prevented them from completing the tower by confusing their tongues or language so that they could not understand one another. Then those who spoke the same language went to live in the same part of the country, and thus the human race was scattered over the earth, and the different nations had different languages.

After a time, they were all losing the knowledge of the true God and beginning to worship idols. God did not wish that the whole human race should forget him, so he selected Abraham to be the father and head of one chosen people who should always worship the true God. He sent Abraham

[69] Cf. Gn 4:11
[70] Cf. Gn 11

from his own country into another, and promised him great things, and renewed to him the promises of the Redeemer first made to Adam and Eve. After the death of Abraham, God raised up, from time to time, prophets to tell the people his holy will, to warn them of their sins and the punishment they would receive, and to remind them of the promised Messias. Prophets are men that God inspires to tell the future. They tell what will happen often hundreds of years after their own death. They do not guess at these things, but tell them with certainty. At times, statesmen can foresee that there will be a war in a country at a certain time; but they are not prophets, because they only guess at such things, or know them by natural signs; and very often things thus foretold do not occur. True prophecy is the foretelling of something which could not be known by any means but inspiration from God.

Neither are persons who call themselves fortune tellers prophets, but only sinful people, who for money tell lies or guess at the future. It is a great sin to go to them or listen to them, as we shall see later in another question.

At the time promised, God sent his Son—our Lord—to redeem the world and save all men. He came to save all men, and yet he remained upon earth only thirty-three years. We can easily understand that by his death he could save all those who lived before he did; but how were they to be saved who should live after him, down to the end of the world? How was his grace to be given to them? How were they to know of him, or of what he taught? All this was to be accomplished by his Church.

114. **Which are the means instituted by our Lord to enable men at all times to share in the fruits of the redemption?**

The means instituted by our Lord to enable men at all times to share in the fruits of the redemption are the Church and the sacraments.

Our Lord instituted the Church to carry on the work he himself was doing upon the earth—teaching the ignorant, visiting the sick, helping the poor, forgiving sins, etc. He commanded all men to hear the Church teaching, just as they would hear himself. But suppose some persons should establish a false church and claim that it was the true Church of our Lord, how could people know the true Church from false churches? When a man invents anything to be sold, what does he do that people may know the true article—say a pen? Why, he puts his trademark upon it. Now the trademark is a certain sign which shows that the article bearing it is the genuine article; and if others use the trademark on imitation articles, they are liable to be punished by law. Now our Lord did the same. He gave his Church four marks or characteristics to distinguish it from all false churches. He said, "My Church will be one; it will be holy; it will be catholic; it will be apostolic; and if any church has not these four marks, you may be sure it is not my Church." Some false church may seem to have one or two, but never all the marks; so, when you find even one of the marks wanting, you will know it is not the true Church established by Christ.

Therefore, all the religions that claim to be the true religion cannot be so. If one man says a thing is white and another says it is black, or if one says a thing is true and another says it is false, they cannot both be right. Only one can be right, and if we wish to know the truth, we have to find out which one it is. So, when one religion says a thing is true and another religion says the same thing is false, one of them must be wrong, and it is our duty to find out the one that is right. Therefore, of all the religions claiming to be the true religion of our Lord, only one can be telling the truth, and that one is the religion or Church that can show the four given marks. The Roman Catholic Church is the only one that can show these marks, and is, therefore, the only true Church, as we shall see in the next lesson.

Fruits of his redemption—that is, to receive the grace merited by our Lord when he redeemed us by his death.

115. **What is the Church?**

The Church is the congregation of all those who profess the faith of Christ, partake of the same sacraments, and are governed by their lawful pastors under one visible head.

Congregation. Not the building, therefore; because if Mass was offered up in an open field, with the people kneeling about, it would still be the church of that place. The buildings that we use for churches might have been used for anything else—a public hall, theatre, or school, for example; but when these buildings we call churches are blessed or consecrated, they become holy. They are holy also because the gospel is preached in them, the sacraments are administered in them, and the Holy Sacrifice of the Mass is offered in them. But they are holy especially because our Lord dwells in them in the tabernacle, where he lives and sees and hears just as truly as he did when he was man upon earth.

In the early ages, the Christians had no churches—they met secretly in private houses. Later, when the cruel pagan emperors began to persecute and put to death the Christians, they made large tunnels underground, and in these places, they heard Mass and received the sacraments. These underground churches were called the "catacombs," and some of them may still be seen at Rome. In these catacombs, too, the Christians buried their dead, especially the bodies of the holy martyrs. On their tombs—generally of stone—Mass was celebrated. In every altar, the table, or flat part on which the priest celebrates Mass, should be of stone; but if the altar is made of wood, then at least the part just in front of the tabernacle must be of stone and large enough to hold, say, two chalices—that is, about ten or twelve inches square. In this stone are placed some relics of the holy martyrs. A piece is cut out of the stone and the relic placed in the opening. Then the bishop puts the little piece of stone back into its place over the relic, seals the opening, blesses the stone, and gives it to the church. This is called the "altar stone." You cannot see it, because it is covered with the altar cloth; but unless it is in the altar, the priest cannot say Mass. This stone reminds us of the stone tombs of the saints upon which Mass was celebrated.

The Church—that is, the Christians—was persecuted for about three hundred years after the death of our Lord. These persecutions took place at ten different times and under different Roman emperors. Orders were given to put to death all the Christians wherever they could be found. Some were cast into prison, some exiled, some taken to the Roman Coliseum—an immense building constructed for public amusements—where they were put to death in the most terrible manner in the presence of the emperor and people assembled to witness these fearful scenes. Some were stripped of their clothing and left standing alone, while savage beasts, wild with hunger, were let loose upon them. Sometimes by a miracle of God, the animals would not harm them, and then the Christians were either put to death by the sword, mangled by some terrible machine, or burned. In these dreadful sufferings, the Christians remained faithful and firm, though they could have saved their lives by denying our Lord or offering sacrifice to idols. The few who, through fear, did deny their faith are now forgotten and unknown; while those who remained steadfast are honored as saints in heaven and upon earth; the Church sings their praises and tells every year of their holy lives and triumph over all their enemies.

Even some pagans who came to see the Christians put to death were so touched by their patience, fortitude, courage, and constancy, that they also declared themselves anxious to become Christians, and were put to death, thus becoming martyrs, baptized in their own blood. How many lessons we may learn from all this: 1) How very respectful we should be in the church, which is holy for all the reasons I have given. 2) What a shame it is for us not to hear Mass when we can do so easily. Our churches are never very far from us, and generally well lighted, ventilated, furnished with seats and every convenience, and, in these respects, unlike the dark, damp, underground churches of the early Christians. Moreover, we may attend our churches freely and without the least danger to our lives; while the Christians of the early ages were constantly in dread and danger of being seized and put to death. Even at the present day, in many countries where holy missionaries are trying to teach the true religion, their converts sometimes have to go great distances to hear Mass, and even then, it is not celebrated in comfortable churches, but probably on the slope of a rugged mountain or in some lonely valley or wood where they may not be seen, for they fear if they are captured—as often happens—both they and their priest will be put to death. You can read in the account of foreign missions that almost every year some priests and many people are martyred for their faith. Is it not disgraceful, then, to see some Catholics giving up their holy faith and the practice of their religion so easily—sometimes for a little money, property, or gain; or even for a bad habit, or for irreligious companions and friends? What answer will they make on the day of judgment when they stand side by side with those who died for the faith?

All those who profess the faith, etc. The pope, bishops, priests, and people all taken together are the Church, and each congregation or parish is only a part of the Church.

Partake—that is, receive. *Lawful pastors*—that is, each priest in his own parish, each bishop in his own diocese, and the pope throughout the world. *Visible head*—that is, one who can be seen, for *invisible* means "cannot be seen."

116. **Who is the invisible head of the Church?**

Jesus Christ is the invisible head of the Church.

Invisible head. If, for example, a merchant of one country wishes to establish a branch of his business in another, he remains in the new country long enough to establish the branch business, and then appointing someone to take his place, returns to his own country. He is still the head of the new establishment, but its invisible head for the people of that country, while its visible head is the agent or representative he has placed in charge to carry on the business in his name and interest. When our Lord wished to establish his Church, he came from heaven; and, when about to return to heaven, appointed St. Peter to take his place upon earth and rule the Church as directed. You see, therefore, that our Lord, though not on earth, is still the real head and owner of the Church, and whatever his agent or vicar—that is, our holy father, the pope—does in the Church, he does it with the authority of our Lord himself.

117. **Who is the visible head of the Church?**

Our holy father the pope, the bishop of Rome, is the vicar of Christ on earth and the visible head of the Church.

The *bishop of Rome* is always pope. If the bishop of New York, or of Baltimore, or of Boston, became pope, he would become the bishop of Rome and cease to be the bishop of New York, Baltimore, or Boston, because St. Peter, the first pope, was bishop of Rome; and therefore, only the bishops of Rome are his lawful successors—the true popes—the true visible heads of the Church. The bishops of the other dioceses of the world are the lawful successors of the other apostles who taught and established churches throughout the world. The bishops of the world are subject to the pope, just as the other apostles were subject to St. Peter, who was appointed their chief by our Lord himself.

Vicar—that is, one who holds another's place and acts in his name.

118. **Why is the pope, the bishop of Rome, the visible head of the Church?**
The pope, the bishop of Rome, is the visible head of the Church, because he is the successor of St. Peter, whom Christ made the chief of the apostles and the visible head of the Church.

Of Rome. That is why we are called "Roman" Catholics; to show that we are united to the real successor of St. Peter, and are therefore members of the true apostolic Church.

119. **Who are the successors of the other apostles?**
The successors of the other apostles are the bishops of the holy Catholic Church.

We know the apostles were bishops, because they could make laws for the Church, consecrate other bishops, ordain priests, and give confirmation—powers that belong only to bishops, and are still exercised by them.

120. **Why did Christ found the Church?**
Christ founded the Church to teach, govern, sanctify, and save all men.

Teach religion. *Govern* in things that regard salvation. *Sanctify*, make good. *Save* all who wish to be saved.

121. **Are all bound to belong to the Church?**
All are bound to belong to the Church, and he who knows the Church to be the true Church and remains out of it cannot be saved.

Anyone who knows the Catholic religion to be the true religion and will not embrace it cannot enter into heaven. If one not a Catholic doubts whether the church to which he belongs is the true Church, he must settle his doubt, seek the true Church, and enter it; for if he continues to live in doubt, be becomes like the one who knows the true Church and is deterred by worldly considerations from entering it.

In like manner, one who, doubting, fears to examine the religion he professes lest he should discover its falsity and be convinced of the truth of the Catholic faith cannot be saved.

Suppose, however, that there is a non-Catholic who firmly believes that the church to which he belongs is the true Church, and who has never—even in the past—had the slightest doubt of that fact—what will become of him?

If he was validly baptized and never committed a mortal sin, he will be saved; because, believing himself a member of the true Church, he was doing all he could to serve God according to his knowledge and the dictates of his conscience. But if ever he committed a mortal sin, his salvation would be very much more difficult. A mortal sin once committed remains on the soul till it is forgiven. Now, how could his mortal sin be forgiven? Not in the sacrament of penance, for the protestant does not go to confession; and if he does, his minister—not being a true priest—has no power to forgive sins. Does he know that without confession it requires an act of truly perfect contrition to blot out sin, and can he easily make such an act? What we call "contrition" is generally only imperfect contrition—that is, sorrow for our sins because we fear their punishment in hell or dread the loss of heaven. If a Catholic, with all the graces he has received in the sacraments, finds it difficult to make an act of perfect contrition—that is, sorrow for sin out of pure love for God, who is so good in himself—how much more difficulty will the protestant, who does not receive such graces, experience in making it? It is to be feared either he would not know of this necessary means of regaining God's friendship, or he would be unable to elicit the necessary act of perfect contrition, and thus the mortal sin would remain upon his soul and he would die an enemy of God.

If, then, we found a protestant who never committed a mortal sin after baptism, and who never had the slightest doubt about the truth of his religion, that person would be saved; because, being baptized, he is a member of the Church, and, being free from mortal sin, he is a friend of God and could not in justice be condemned to hell. Such a person belongs to what we call the "soul of the Church." He would belong to the body of the Church—that is, he would attend Mass and receive the sacraments—if he knew the Catholic Church to be the only true Church.

I am giving you an example, however, that is rarely found, except in the case of infants or very small children baptized in protestant sects. All infants rightly baptized by anyone are really children of the Church, no matter what religion their parents may profess. Indeed, all persons who are baptized are children of the Church; but those among them who deny its teaching, reject its sacraments, and refuse to submit to its lawful pastors, are rebellious children known as heretics.

I said I gave you an example that can scarcely be found, namely, of a person not a Catholic, who really never doubted the truth of his religion, and who, moreover, never committed during his whole life a single mortal sin. There are so few such persons that we can practically say for all those who are not members of the body of the Catholic Church, believing its doctrines, receiving its sacraments, and being governed by its visible head, our holy father, the pope, salvation is an extremely difficult matter.

I do not speak here of pagans who have never heard of our Lord or his holy religion, but of those outside the Church who claim to be good Christians without being members of the Catholic Church.

LESSON TWELFTH

On the Attributes and Marks of the Church

An attribute is any characteristic or quality that a person or thing may be said to have. All good qualities are good attributes, and all bad qualities are bad attributes. All perfections or imperfections are attributes. If I can say of you that you are good, then goodness is one of your attributes. If I can say you are beautiful, then beauty is one of your attributes. We have seen already that the Church has four marks; but besides these, it has three attributes, which flow from its marks. It is easier to see the marks of the Church than its attributes. It is easier to see, for instance, that the Church is one than that it is indefectible.

122. **Which are the attributes of the Church?**
The attributes of the Church are three: authority, infallibility, and indefectibility.

123. **What do you mean by "the authority of the Church"?**
By "the authority of the Church," I mean the right and power which the pope and the bishops, as the successors of the apostles, have to teach and govern the faithful.

Authority is the power which one person has over another, so as to be able to exact obedience. A teacher has authority over his scholars, because they must obey him; but the teacher need not obey the scholars, because they have no authority over him. God alone has authority of himself and from himself. All others who have authority receive it from God, either directly or through someone else. The pope has authority from God himself, and the priests get theirs through their bishops. Therefore, to resist or disobey lawful authority is to resist and disobey God himself. If one of you were placed in charge of the class in my absence, he would have lawful authority, and the rest of you should obey him—not on account of himself, but on account of the authority he has. Thus, the president of the United States, the governor, the mayor, etc., are only ordinary citizens before their election; but after they have been elected and placed in office, they exercise lawful authority over us, and we are bound as good citizens and as good Catholics to respect and obey them.

124. **What do you mean by "the infallibility of the Church"?**
By "the infallibility of the Church," I mean that the Church cannot err when it teaches a doctrine of faith or morals.

Infallibility. When we say the Church is infallible, we mean that it cannot make a mistake or err in what it teaches; that the pope, the head of the Church, is infallible when he teaches *ex cathedra*—that is, as the successor of St. Peter, the vicar of Christ. *Cathedra* signifies "a seat," *ex* stands for "out of"; therefore, *ex cathedra* means "out of the chair or office of St. Peter," because *chair* is sometimes used for *office*. Thus, we say, "The presidential chair is opposed to this or that," when we intend to say, "The president, or the one in that office, is opposed to it." The cathedral is the church in which the bishop usually officiates, so called on account of the bishop's *cathedra*, or throne, being in it.

125. **When does the Church teach infallibly?**
The Church teaches infallibly when it speaks through the pope and bishops united in general council, or through the pope alone when he proclaims to all the faithful a doctrine of faith or morals.

But how will we know when the pope speaks *ex cathedra*, when he is speaking daily to people from all parts of the world? To speak *ex cathedra* or infallibly, three things are required:

1. He must speak as the head of the whole Church, not as a private person; and in certain forms of words by which we know he is speaking *ex cathedra*.

2. What he says must hold good for the whole Church—that is, for all the faithful, and not merely for this or that particular person or country.

3. He must speak on matters of faith or morals—that is, when the holy father tells all the faithful that they are to believe a certain thing as a part of their faith; or when he tells them that certain things are sins, they must believe him and avoid what he declares to be sin. He could not make a mistake in such things. He could not say that our Lord taught us to believe and do such and such, if our Lord did not so teach, because our Lord promised to be with his Church for all time, and to send the Holy Ghost, who would teach it all truth and abide with it forever. If then the Church could make mistakes in teaching faith and morals, the Holy Ghost could not be with it, and our Lord did not tell the truth—to say which would be blasphemy.

But remember, the pope is not infallible unless he is teaching faith or morals; that is, what we have to believe or do in order to save our souls. If the holy father wrote a book on astronomy, mathematics, grammar, or even theology, he could make mistakes as other men do, because the Holy Ghost has not promised to guide him in such things. Nevertheless, whatever the pope teaches on anything you may be pretty sure is right. The pope is nearly always a very learned man of many years' experience. He has with him at Rome learned men from every part of the world, so that we may say he has the experience of the whole world. Other rulers cannot and need not know as much as the holy father, because they have not to govern the world, but only their own country. Moreover, there is no government in the whole world as old as the Church, no nation that can show as many rulers without change; so we may say the pope has also the experience of all the popes who preceded him, from St. Peter down to our present holy father, Leo XIII—263 popes.

Therefore, considering all this, we should have the very greatest respect for the opinions and advice of the holy father on any subject. We should not set up our limited knowledge and experience against his, even if we think that we know better than he does about certain political events taking place in our country, for we are not sure that we do. The holy father knows the past history of nations; he knows the nature of mankind; he knows that what takes place in one nation may, and sometimes does, take place in another under the same circumstances. Thus, the holy father has greater foresight than we have, and we should be thankful when he warns us against certain dangers in politics or other things. He does not teach politics; but as everything we do is either good or bad, every statesman or politician must consider whether what he is about to do be right or wrong, just or unjust. It is the business and duty of the holy father to declare against the evil or unjust actions of either individuals or nations, and for that reason he seems at times to interfere in politics when he is really teaching morals. At times, too, governments try to deprive the Church or the holy father of their rights; and when he defends himself against such injustice and protests against it, his enemies cry out that he is interfering with the government.

You understand now what the infallibility of the pope implies, and that it does not mean, as the enemies of the Church say, that the pope cannot sin, cannot be mistaken in anything. The pope can sin just the same as anyone else; he could be a very bad man if he wanted to be so, and take the punishment God would inflict for his sins. Could he not be very angry, entirely neglect prayer, or pray with willful distraction; could he not be proud, covetous, etc.?—and these are sins. Therefore, he could sin; and hence he has to go to confession and seek forgiveness just as we do. Therefore, remember this: whether the pope be a bad man or a good man in his private life, he must always tell the truth when he speaks *ex cathedra*, because the Holy Ghost is guiding him and will not permit him to err or teach falsehood in faith or morals.

We have examples in the Bible[71] where God sometimes makes even bad men foretell the truth. Once he gave an ass the power to speak, that it might protest against the wrongdoing of its wicked and cruel rider.

[71] Cf. Nm 22-23

We have seen how governments interfere with the rights of the holy father, and thus he has need of his temporal power that he may be altogether independent of any government. Now let me explain to you what is meant by "the temporal power of the pope." Well, then, the holy father should have some city or states, not belonging to any government, in which he would be the chief and only ruler. Up to the year 1870, the holy father did have such states: they were called the "Papal States," and the power he had over them—just like that of any other ruler—was called the "temporal power." Now how did he get those states and how did he lose them? He got them in the most just manner, and held possession of them for about a thousand years.

Hundreds of years ago, the people of Rome and the surrounding countries elected the pope their sole ruler. He was already their spiritual ruler, and they made him also their temporal ruler. Then the pope protected and governed them as other rulers do. Later, kings and princes added other lands, and thus by degrees the possessions of the pope became quite extended.

How did he lose these possessions? The Italian government took them from him in the most unjust manner. Besides the lands, they deprived the Church of other property donated to it by its faithful children. No ruler in the world had a more just claim or better right to his possessions than the holy father, and a government robbed him of them as a thief might take forcibly from you whatever had been justly given to you, when he found you were unable to defend yourself against him.

But has the holy father need of his temporal power? Yes, the holy father has need of some temporal power. He must be free and independent in governing the Church. He must be free to say what he wishes to all Catholics throughout the world, and free to hear whatever they have to say to him. But if the pope is under another ruler he cannot be free. That ruler may cast him into prison, and not allow him to communicate with the bishops of the world. At least, he can say nothing about the injustice of the ruler who is over him. Therefore, the pope must have some possessions of his own, that he may not be afraid of the injustice of any ruler, and may speak out the truth boldly to the whole world, denouncing bad rulers and praising good ones as they deserve.

Mind, I do not say what possessions the holy father should have, but simply that he should have some, in which he would be altogether independent.

In justice, he should have all that was taken from him. We have a good example here in the United States to illustrate the need of the independence of the pope. You know every state in the United States is a little government in itself, with its own governor, legislature, laws, etc. Now over all these little governments or states we have the government of the United States, with the president at its head. In the beginning, the members of the United States Government assembled to transact the business of the nation sometimes in one state and sometimes in another—sometimes in New York and sometimes in Pennsylvania, etc. But they soon found that in order to be independent of every state and just to all, they must have some territory or possessions of their own not under the power of any state. So, some of the states granted them Washington and the country about it for ten miles square, now called the "District of Columbia"—in which the United States Government could freely perform its duties. In a similar manner, the holy father is over all the governments of the world in matters of religion—in matters of justice and right; and just as the United States Government has to decide between the rights of one state and the rights of another, so the holy father has sometimes to decide between the rights of one government and the rights of another, and must, in order to be just with all, be free and independent of all.

Again, the temporal power of the pope is very useful to the Church; for with the money and goods received from his possessions, the holy father can educate priests and teachers, print books, etc., for the foreign missions. He can also support churches, schools, and institutions in poor countries, and especially where the missionaries are laboring for the conversion of the native heathens. When the holy father had his own possessions, he could do much that he cannot now do for the conversion of pagan nations. At present, he must depend entirely upon the charitable offerings of the faithful for all good works, even for his own support. The offering we make once a year for the support of the holy father is called "Peter's pence," because it began by everyone sending yearly a penny to the pope, the successor of St. Peter.

126. **What do you mean by "the indefectibility of the Church"?**

By "the indefectibility of the Church," I mean that the Church, as Christ founded it, will last till the end of time.

Therefore, *indefectibility* means that the Church can never change any of the doctrines that our Lord taught, nor ever cease to exist. When we say it is infallible, we mean that it cannot teach error while it lasts; but when we say it is indefectible, we mean that it will last forever and be infallible forever, and also that it will always remain the same as our Lord founded it. There are two things that you must clearly understand and not confound, namely, the two kinds of laws in the Church—those which our Lord gave it and those which it made itself. The laws that our Lord gave it it can never change. For example, the Church could not abolish one of the sacraments, leaving only six; neither could it add a new one, making eight. But when, for example, the Church declares that on a certain day we cannot eat flesh meat, it makes the law itself, and can change it when it wishes. Our Lord left his Church free to make certain laws, just as they would be needed. It has always exercised this power, and made laws to suit the circumstances of the place or times. Even now it does away with some of its old laws that are no longer useful, and makes new ones that are more necessary. But the doctrines, the truths of faith or morals, the things we must believe and do to save our souls, it never changes and never can change: it may regulate some things in the application of the divine laws, but the laws themselves can never change in substance.

127. **In whom are these attributes found in their fullness?**

These attributes are found in their fullness in the pope, the visible head of the Church, whose infallible authority to teach bishops, priests, and people in matters of faith or morals will last to the end of the world.

128. **Has the Church any marks by which it may be known?**

The Church has four marks by which it may be known: it is one; it is holy; it is catholic; it is apostolic.

129. **How is the Church one?**

The Church is one because all its members agree in one faith, are all in one communion, and are all under one head.

The Catholic Church is *one*, first in government and second in doctrine. In government, every pastor has a certain parish or territory in which all the people belong to his congregation—they form his flock. He has to take care only of these, to teach them, give them the sacraments, etc. He has not to be responsible for those outside his parish. Then, over the pastor, we have the bishop, who looks after a certain number of pastors; then comes the archbishop, over a certain number of bishops; next comes the primate, who is head of all the archbishops in the country; and over all the primates of the world, we have the holy father. Thus, when the holy father speaks to the bishops, the bishops speak to the priests, and the priests to the people. The Church is therefore one in government, like a great army spread over the world. We can go up step-by-step from the lowest member of the Church to the highest—the holy Father; and from him to our Lord himself, who is the invisible head of all. This regular body of priests, bishops, archbishops, etc., so arranged, one superior to the other, is called the "hierarchy of the Church."

The Church is one also in doctrine—that is, every one of the three hundred million Catholics in the world believes exactly the same truths. If any Catholic denies only one article of faith, though he believes all the rest, he ceases to be a Catholic, and is cut off from the Church. If, for example, you would not believe matrimony or holy orders a sacrament, or that our Lord is present in the Holy Eucharist, you would not be a Catholic, though you believed all the other teachings of the Church.

Therefore, the Church is one both in government and teaching or doctrine. Now, has any other Church claiming to be Christ's Church that mark? No. The protestant religions are not one either in government or belief. The protestants of England have no authority over the protestants of America, and those of America have nothing to say over those of Germany or France. So, every country is independent, and they have no chief head. Neither are they one in belief. In the same country, there are many kinds of protestants—Episcopalians, Presbyterians, Methodists, etc.—who do not believe the same thing. Even those who attend the same church and profess the same religion do not all believe the same. Everyone, they say, has a right to interpret the holy scriptures according to his own views, so they take many different meanings out of the very same words. There must be some chief person to tell the true meaning of the holy scriptures when there is a dispute about it; but they have no such chief, and the result is they are never done disputing.

The United States has a constitution and laws. Now, suppose every citizen was allowed to construe the laws to suit himself, without any regard for the rights of others, what a fine state of affairs we should soon have. But the wise makers of the Constitution and laws of the United States did not leave us in such danger. They appointed judges to interpret or explain the laws and give the correct meaning when disputes arise. Then, in Washington, there is a chief judge for the whole United States; and when he says the words of the law mean this or that, every citizen must abide by his decision, and there is no appeal from it. Just in the same way our Lord made laws for all men, and while he was upon earth, he explained them himself. He never left all men free to take their own meaning out of them. He appointed judges—the bishops; and a chief judge for the whole world—the pope. The Holy Ghost guides him, as we have seen above, so that he cannot make mistakes in the meaning of Christ's laws; and when he says, "This is what the words of our Lord in his law signify," no one who is a true Christian can refuse to believe, or can appeal from his decision.

130. **How is the Church holy?**

The Church is holy because its founder, Jesus Christ, is holy; because it teaches a holy doctrine, invites all to a holy life, and because of the eminent holiness of so many thousands of its children.

Protestant religions have not holy doctrines if we examine them closely. They teach, for example, that faith without good works will save us, and thus take away the motives for doing good; that marriage is not binding for life—the husband and wife may for some causes separate, or get a divorce and marry again. This would leave the children without the care of their proper parents, sometimes without a home, and nearly always without religious instruction. The same persons might separate again and marry another time, and thus there would be nothing but confusion and immorality in society. Again, some of their doctrines teach that we cannot help sinning; so, everyone could excuse himself for his sins by saying he could not help them, which you can easily see would lead to the worst of consequences. Lastly, their doctrines have never made one saint—acknowledged as such from miracles performed. Protestants are so called because, when their ancestors rebelled against the Church about three hundred years ago, the Church made certain laws and they protested against them, separated from the Church, and formed a new religion of their own.

131. **How is the Church catholic or universal?**

The Church is catholic or universal because it subsists in all ages, teaches all nations, and maintains all truth.

Subsists means "to have existence." *Catholic.* The word *catholic* signifies "universal." The Church is universal in three ways, namely: in time, in place, and in doctrine. It is universal in time; for from the day our Lord commissioned his apostles to preach to the whole world down to the present, it has existed, taught, and labored in every age. It is universal in place; that is, it is not confined to one part of the world, but teaches throughout the entire world. It is universal in doctrine, for it teaches the same doctrines and administers the same sacraments everywhere; and its doctrines are suited to all classes of men—to the ignorant as well as the learned, to the poor as well as the rich. It teaches by the voice of its priests and bishops, and all, civilized or uncivilized, to whom its voice reaches, can learn its doctrines, receive its sacraments, and practice its devotions.

It has converted all the pagan nations that have ever been converted, and the title *Catholic* belongs to the Roman Catholic Church alone. All protestant churches that claim this title do so unjustly. They are not universal in time, and cannot be called "the Church of all ages," because they were established only three hundred or four hundred or less years ago. They are not catholic in place, because they are mostly confined to particular countries. They are not universal in doctrine, because what they teach in one country, they reject in another; and even in the same country, what they teach at one time, they reject at another. Wherever it is possible for civilized people to go, there you will find a priest saying Mass in just the same way you see him saying it here. It is a great consolation for one in a strange country to enter a church and hear Mass, perceiving no difference in the vestments, ceremonies, or language of the priest. A little altar boy from the United States could serve Mass in any part of the world. See, therefore, the great advantage the Church has in using the Latin language instead of the vernacular or ordinary language of the people. If the Church used the usual language of the people, the Mass would seem different in every country; while natives would understand the words of the priest, strangers would not.

The Latin language is now what we call a "dead language"; that is, it is not the common language of any country; and because it is a dead language does not change: another reason why the Church uses it, that nothing may change in its divine service. The prayers used in the Church are exactly the same today as they were when they were written, many centuries ago. The living languages—that is, those in use, such as English, French, German, etc., are always changing a little—new words are being added, and the meaning of old ones changed. The Church uses the same language all over the world to show that it is not the Church of any particular country, but the true Church of all men everywhere.

Again, using only one language, the Church can hold its great councils, call together all the bishops of the world, that they may condemn errors or make wise laws. When the holy father addresses them in Latin, they can all understand and answer him. If, therefore, the Church did not use the same language everywhere, how could this be done, unless every one present understood all the languages of the world—which is a thing nearly impossible. But someone might say, "If the Mass was said in English, we could follow it better." You can follow just as well in Latin, for in nearly all prayer books you have besides the Latin said by the priest the meaning of it in English on the same page, or you have the English alone.

132. **How is the Church apostolic?**

The Church is apostolic because it was founded by Christ on his apostles and is governed by their lawful successors, and because it has never ceased, and never will cease, to teach their doctrine.

Apostolic, which means that the Church was founded at the time of the apostles, and has been the same ever since. Since the time of St. Peter, the first pope, there have been 263 popes. You can go back from our present holy father, Leo XIII, to Pius IX, who was before him, to Gregory XVI, who was before him, to Pius VIII, before him, and so on, one by one, till you come to St. Peter himself, who lived at the time of our Lord. Thus, the Church is apostolic in its origin or beginning.

It is also apostolic in its teaching; for all the doctrines it teaches now were taught by the apostles. The Church does not make new doctrines, but it teaches its truths more clearly and distinctly when someone denies them. For example, it would not be necessary for you to prove yourself good and honest till somebody said you were bad and dishonest. You prove your honesty when it is denied, but both you and your friends believed it always, though you did not declare it till it was denied. In just the same way, the Church always believed that our Lord is the Son of God; that there are seven sacraments; that the pope is infallible, etc. These truths and all the others were believed by the apostles, and the Church proclaimed them in a special manner when they were denied. Then it called together in council all its bishops, and they, with the holy father, proclaimed these truths—not as new doctrines, but as truths always believed by the Church, and now defined because denied.

Protestants have not for their churches the mark *apostolic*. How could their churches be founded by the apostles, when the apostles were dead more than fourteen hundred years before there were any protestant churches? What is more, they have changed the teachings of the apostles; and so they have not the mark *apostolic* either in their origin or teaching.

But they say the Catholic Church fell into error and made mistakes, and that God wished reformers to correct these errors. How could the Church fall into error when our Lord promised to remain always with it, and to send the Holy Ghost to guide and teach it forever? And, secondly, if God sent the protestants to correct the mistakes of the Catholic Church, what proof do they give us that they have such power from God? When, as we have seen, God sends anyone to do a special work, he always gives him power to prove his mission. When he sent Moses, he gave him signs—the plagues of Egypt. When he sent his prophets, they called down fire and rain from heaven.[72] But protestants have shown us no signs and performed no miracles; therefore, we cannot believe their assertion that God sent them to correct the Catholic Church. Neither can we believe that our Lord broke his promise to stay with the Church. We shall see the whole truth of the matter if we go back to the establishment of the protestant religion and consider the life of Luther and the others who founded it.

Luther, then a young man, while out one day, saw his friend killed at his side by a stroke of lightning. Much affected by that sad event, Luther became a priest in the Order of the Augustinians. He was a learned man and a great preacher, but very proud. The holy father was completing St. Peter's Church in Rome, and about that time granted an indulgence to those giving alms for the purpose: just as pastors now offer Masses for those who contribute means to build a new church, or hospital, asylum, etc.

The holy father sent Dominican priests to preach about this indulgence and collect this money. Then Luther, when he found that he, a great preacher, was not appointed, was probably jealous. He first began to preach against the abuses of indulgences; but pride made him go further, and soon he began to preach against the doctrine of indulgences, and thus became a heretic. Then he was condemned by the pope, and cut off from the Church. Being proud, he would not submit, but began to form a new religion, now called "protestant." But how did he get the people to follow him? Oh, very easily. Then, as now, there were plenty of bad and indifferent Catholics. At that time, the Church was rich and had much property and lands; because when rich Catholics died, they often left to the Church property for its own support and the support of its institutions. Even during their lifetime, kings and princes sometimes gave the Church large donations of lands and money. The Church, then, was supported by these gifts and the income or rents of the lands, and did not need to look for collections from the people, as it has to do now. Here, then, is how Luther got many to follow him. He told greedy princes that if they came with him, they could become rich by seizing the property of all the churches, and the greedy

[72] Cf. 3 Kgs 18

princes, glad of an excuse, went with him. Then he told the people—the bad Catholics—that fasting was too severe; going to confession too hard; hearing Mass every Sunday too difficult; and if they renounced their faith and embraced his new religion, he would do away with all these things: so, they also followed him. He himself broke his solemn vows made to God, and the people easily followed his example.

Those attending the protestant churches in our times are generally rich and refined people, but you must not think that the first protestants of three hundred years ago were just like them. No. Many of them were from the lowest and worst—I do not say poorest—classes in society; and when they got an excuse, they went about destroying churches and institutions, burning beautiful statues, paintings, music, books, and works of art that the Church had collected and preserved for centuries. This you may read in any of the histories of the Church and times. The protestants of the present day praise all these works of art now; but if their ancestors had had their way, every beautiful work of art would have been destroyed.

Some persons say they would not be members of the Catholic Church, because so many poor people attend it. Then they do not want to belong to the Church of our Lord, because his Church is the Church of both poor and rich. When St. John the Baptist sent his disciples to ask our Lord if he were really the Messias, our Lord did not say, "Yes" or "No," but told them to relate to John what they had heard and seen,[73] namely, that he (Christ) cured the blind, the lame, and the deaf, and preached to the poor. Therefore, our Lord gave preaching to the poor as a proof that he is the true Redeemer; and since our Lord himself had the poor in his congregation, the Church everywhere must have the poor among its members, for it must do what our Lord did. So, if you see a church to which the poor people never go, and in which they are not welcome, you have good reason to suspect it is not the Church of our Lord—not the true Church. Again, poverty and riches belong only to this world and make a distinction only here. The one who is poorest in this world's goods may be richest in God's grace. Indeed, if most protestants studied the early history of their religion, they would not

[73] Cf. Mt 11:5

be proud, but ashamed of it. How little they would think of their ancestors who gave up God for some worldly gain, while the Catholic martyrs gave up everything, even their lives, rather than forsake God and the true religion.

133. **In which church are these attributes and marks found?**
These attributes and marks are found in the holy Roman Catholic Church alone.

We have seen that some religions may seem to have one or two of the marks; but the Catholic Church alone has them all, and is consequently the only true Church of Christ. The other religions are not one—that is, united over the world; they give no proof of holiness, never having had any great saints whom God acknowledged as such by performing miracles for them. They are not catholic, because they have not taught in all ages and nations. They are not apostolic, because established hundreds of years after the apostles. They are not infallible, for they have now declared things to be false which they formerly declared to be true; they are not indefectible—they are not as our Lord founded them, for he never founded them; and they are constantly making changes in their beliefs and practices.

The marks of the Church are necessary also because the Church must be a visible Church, that all men may be able to see and know it; for our Lord said, "He that will not hear the Church, let him be to thee as the heathen and the publican."[74] Heathens were those who worshipped false gods. Publicans were men who gathered the taxes from the Jews for the Romans; they were generally very cruel to the people, and were much hated and despised by them. Therefore, our Lord meant: if anyone will not obey the Church, you should avoid him as you avoid the heathens and the publicans, whom you despise. Now no one can be blamed for not obeying a church that is invisible and unknown. Therefore, the true Church must be a visible body and easily known to all who earnestly seek it as the Church of Christ. But if some shut their eyes and refuse to look at the light of truth, ignorance will not excuse them; they must be blamed and fall under the sentence of our Lord.

[74] Cf. Mt 18:17

134. **From whom does the Church derive its undying life and infallible authority?**
The Church derives its undying life and infallible authority from the Holy Ghost, the Spirit of truth, who abides with it forever.

135. **By whom is the Church made and kept one, holy, and catholic?**
The Church is made and kept one, holy, and catholic by the Holy Ghost, the Spirit of love and holiness, who unites and sanctifies its members throughout the world.

LESSON THIRTEENTH

On the Sacraments in General

This lesson does not speak of any sacrament in particular, but upon all the sacraments taken together. It explains what we find in all the sacraments.

136. **What is a sacrament?**
A sacrament is an outward sign instituted by Christ to give grace.

Three things are necessary to make a sacrament. There must be: 1) *an outward*, that is, a visible, *sign*; 2) this sign must have been *instituted* or given by our Lord; 3) it must *give grace*. Now, a sign is that which tells us that something else exists. Smoke indicates the presence of fire. A red light on a railroad tells us there is danger at the spot. Therefore, the outward signs in the sacraments tell us that there is in the sacraments something we do not see and which they signify and impart. For example, the outward sign in baptism is the pouring of the water on the head of the person to be baptized, and the saying of the words. Water is generally used for cleaning purposes. Water, therefore, is used in baptism as an outward sign to show that as the water cleans the body, so the grace given in baptism cleans the soul. It is not a mere sign, for at the very moment that the priest pours the water and says the words of baptism, by the pouring of the water and saying of the words, with the proper intention, the soul is cleansed from original sin; that is, the inward grace is given by the application of the outward sign. Again, in confirmation, the outward sign is the anointing with oil, the bishop's prayer, and the placing of his hands upon us. Now, what inward grace is given in confirmation? A grace which strengthens us in our faith. Oil, therefore, is used for the outward sign in this sacrament, because oil gives strength and light.

In olden times, the gladiators—men who fought with swords as prize-fighters do now with their hands—used oil upon their bodies to make them strong. Oil was used also to heal wounds. Thus, in confirmation, the application of this outward sign of strength gives the inward grace of light and strength. Moreover, oil easily spreads itself over anything and remains on it. A drop of water falling on paper dries up quickly; but a drop of oil soaks in and spreads over it. So, oil is used to show also that the grace of confirmation spreads out over our whole lives, and strengthens us in our faith at all times.

Again, in penance, we have the outward sign when the priest raises his hand and pronounces over us the words of absolution.

If we did not have these outward signs, how could anyone know just at what time the graces are given? We can know now, for, at the very moment the outward sign is applied, the grace is given; because it is the application of the sign that by divine institution gives the grace, and thus the two must take place together.

Institution by Christ is absolutely necessary, because he gives all grace, and he alone can determine the manner in which he wishes it distributed. The Church can distribute his grace, but only in the way he wishes. Hence, it cannot make new sacraments or abolish old ones.

137. **How many sacraments are there?**

There are seven sacraments: baptism, confirmation, Holy Eucharist, penance, extreme unction, holy orders, and matrimony.

The life of our soul is in many ways similar to the life of our body. Our bodies must first be born, then strengthened, then fed. When sick, we must be cured; and when about to die, we must be taken care of. Then there must be someone to rule others, and there must be persons to be governed. In like manner, we are spiritually born into a new life by baptism, we are strengthened by confirmation, fed with the Holy Eucharist, and cured of the maladies of our souls by penance. By extreme unction, we are helped at the hour of death; by holy orders, our spiritual rulers are appointed by God; and by matrimony, families, with a father at the head and children to be ruled, are established. Thus, we have our spiritual life similar in many things to our physical or bodily life.

138. **Whence have the sacraments the power of giving grace?**

The sacraments have the power of giving grace from the merits of Jesus Christ.

Our Lord died to merit grace for us, and appointed the sacraments as the chief means by which it was to be given.

139. **What grace do the sacraments give?**

Some of the sacraments give sanctifying grace, and others increase it in our souls.

Baptism and penance give this sanctifying grace when there is not any of it in the soul. But the other sacraments are received while we are in a state of grace, and they therefore increase the quantity of it in our souls.

140. **Which are the sacraments that give sanctifying grace?**

The sacraments that give sanctifying grace are baptism and penance; and they are called "sacraments of the dead."

Of the dead. Not of a dead person; for, when a person is dead, he cannot receive any of the sacraments. It is only while we live upon earth that we are on trial, and can do good or evil, and merit grace. At death, we receive simply our reward or punishment for what we have done while living. Therefore, "sacraments of the dead" mean "sacraments given to a dead soul," that is, to a soul in mortal sin. When grace—its life—is all out of the soul, it can do nothing to merit heaven; and we say it is dead, because the dead can do nothing for themselves. If a person receives—as many do—the sacrament of penance while his soul is not in a state of mortal sin, what then? Then the soul—already living—receives an increase of sanctifying grace, that is, greater spiritual life and strength.

141. **Why are baptism and penance called "sacraments of the dead"?**
Baptism and penance are called "sacraments of the dead," because they take away sin, which is the death of the soul, and give grace, which is its life.

142. **Which are the sacraments that increase sanctifying grace in the soul?**
The sacraments that increase sanctifying grace in the soul are: confirmation, Holy Eucharist, extreme unction, holy orders, and matrimony; and they are called "sacraments of the living."

143. **Why are confirmation, Holy Eucharist, extreme unction, holy orders, and matrimony called "sacraments of the living"?**
Confirmation, Holy Eucharist, extreme unction, holy orders, and matrimony are called the "sacraments of the living," because those who receive them worthily are already living the life of grace.

144. **What sin does he commit who receives the sacraments of the living in mortal sin?**
He who receives the sacraments of the living in mortal sin commits a sacrilege, which is a great sin, because it is an abuse of a sacred thing.

Sacrilege. There are other ways besides the unworthy reception of the sacraments in which a person may commit sacrilege. You could commit it by treating any sacred thing with great disrespect. For example, by making common use of the sacred vessels used at the altar; by stealing from the church; by turning the church into a market, etc. You could commit it also by willfully killing or wounding persons consecrated to God, such as nuns, priests, bishops, etc. Therefore, sacrilege can be committed by willfully abusing or treating with great irreverence any sacred person, sacred place, or sacred thing.

145. **Besides sanctifying grace, do the sacraments give any other grace?**
Besides sanctifying grace, the sacraments give another grace, called "sacramental."

146. **What is sacramental grace?**

Sacramental grace is a special help which God gives to attain the end for which he instituted each sacrament.

For example, what was the end for which penance was instituted? To forgive sins and keep us out of sin. Therefore, the sacramental grace given in penance is a grace that will enable us to overcome temptation and avoid the sins we have been in the habit of committing. When a person is ill, the doctor's medicine generally produces two effects: one is to cure the disease and the other to strengthen the person so that he may not fall back into the old condition. Well, it is just the same in the sacraments; the grace given produces two effects: one is to sanctify us and the other to prevent us from falling into the same sins. Again, confirmation was instituted that we might become more perfect Christians, stronger in our faith. Therefore, the sacramental grace of confirmation will strengthen us to profess our faith when circumstances require it; or when we are tempted to doubt any revealed truth, it will help us to overcome the temptation. So, in all the sacraments we receive the sacramental grace or special help given to attain the end for which the sacraments were separately instituted.

147. **Do the sacraments always give grace?**

The sacraments always give grace, if we receive them with the right dispositions.

Right dispositions; that is, if we do all that God and the Church require us to do when we receive them. For instance, in penance, the right disposition is to confess all our mortal sins as we know them, to be sorry for them, and have the determination never to commit them again. The right disposition for the Holy Eucharist is to be in a state of grace, and—except in special cases of sickness—fasting from midnight.

148. **Can we receive the sacraments more than once?**

We can receive the sacraments more than once, except baptism, confirmation, and holy orders.

Baptism is so important that if we do not receive it, we cannot receive any other of the sacraments. Now, to administer baptism validly, that is, properly, everything must be done exactly as our Lord intended and the Church teaches. The proper kind of water and all the exact words must be used. Also, the water must touch the body, that is, the head, if possible. Now, persons not knowing well how to baptize might neglect some of these things, and thus the person would not be baptized. The Church wishes to be certain that all its children are baptized; so, when there is any doubt about the first baptism, it baptizes again conditionally, that is, the priest says in giving the baptism over again: "If you are not baptized already, I baptize you now." Therefore, if the person was rightly baptized the first time, the second ceremony has no effect; because the priest does not intend to give baptism a second time. But if the first baptism was not rightly given, then the second takes effect. In either case, baptism is given only once; for if the first was valid, the second is not given; and if the first was invalid, the second is given.

Converts to the Church are generally baptized conditionally, because there is doubt about the validity of the baptism they received.

The sacraments may be given conditionally when we doubt if they were or can be validly given.

149. **Why can we not receive baptism, confirmation, and holy orders more than once?**

We cannot receive baptism, confirmation, and holy orders more than once, because they imprint a character in the soul.

A character. It is a spiritual character, and remains forever, so that, whether the person is in heaven or hell, this mark will be seen. It will show that those having it were Christians, who received baptism, confirmation, or holy orders. If they are in heaven, these characters will shine out to their honor, and will show how well they used the grace God gave them. If they are in hell, these characters will be to their disgrace, and show how many gifts and graces God bestowed upon them, and how shamefully they abused all.

150. **What is the character which these sacraments imprint in the soul?**

The character which these sacraments imprint in the soul is a spiritual mark which remains forever.

151. **Does this character remain in the soul even after death?**
This character remains in the soul even after death: for the honor and glory of those who are saved; for the shame and punishment of those who are lost.

LESSON FOURTEENTH

On Baptism

152. **What is baptism?**
Baptism is a sacrament which cleanses us from original sin, makes us Christians, children of God, and heirs of heaven.

Christians, that is, members of the Church of Christ. *Children of God*, that is, adopted children. All men are children of God by their creation, but Christians are children of God, not merely by creation, but also by grace and union with our Lord. *Heirs of heaven*. An heir is one who inherits property, money, or goods at the death of another. These things are left by a will or given by the laws of the state, when the person dies without making a will. A will is a written statement in which a person declares what he wishes to have done, at his death, with whatever he possesses—the charitable objects or the persons to whom he wishes to leave his goods. This will is called also the "last testament." It is signed by witnesses, and after the death of the testator is committed to the care of a person—called the "executor"—whose business it is to see that all stated in the will or testament is carried out. There is an officer in the state to take these things in hand and settle them according to law, when the amount left is large, and there is a dispute about it.

You can understand better now why we call the Bible the old and the new "testament." When our Lord died, we were left an inheritance and spiritual property. The inheritance was heaven, which we had lost through the sin of Adam and regained by the death of our Lord. The spiritual property was God's grace, which he merited for us. The old testament contains the promise of what our Lord would leave us at his death, and the new testament shows that he kept his promise and did leave what he said. The old testament was written before he died, and the new testament after his death. The witnesses of these testaments were the patriarchs, prophets, apostles, and evangelists, who heard God making the promises through the inspiration of the Holy Ghost. The Church is the executor of Christ's will, and it is its business to see that all men receive what Christ left them, namely, God's grace and heaven. It must also see that they are not cheated out of it by their enemies—the devil, the world, and the flesh.

153. **Are actual sins ever remitted by baptism?**
Actual sins and all the punishment due to them are remitted by baptism, if the person baptized be guilty of any.

We know that baptism remits original sin. But suppose a person is not baptized till he is twenty-five or thirty years old; he has surely committed some sins since he was seven years of age—the time at which he received the use of reason. Now the question asks: Are all his sins, those he committed himself as well as the original sin, forgiven by baptism? The answer is: Yes. All his sins are forgiven, so that he has not to confess them. But he must be heartily sorry for them and have the firm determination of never committing them again, just as in confession. Moreover, that he may not have to confess these sins, we must be absolutely certain that he was never baptized before. Besides remitting the sins themselves, baptism remits all the temporal punishment due to them.

In the sacrament of penance, the sinner is saved from the eternal punishment—that is, hell—and from part of the temporal punishment. But although the sins have been forgiven, the sinner must make satisfaction to God for the insult offered by his sins.

Therefore, he must suffer punishment in this world or in purgatory. We call this punishment "temporal," because it will not last forever. You can make this satisfaction to God while on earth, and thus avoid much of the temporal punishment by prayers, fasting, gaining indulgences, alms, and good works; and even by bearing your sufferings, trials, and afflictions patiently, and offering them up to God in satisfaction for your sins.

In baptism, both the eternal and temporal guilt are washed away; so that if a person just baptized died immediately, he would go directly to heaven, not to purgatory: because persons go to purgatory to pay off the temporal guilt. Neither could that person gain an indulgence, because indulgences are only to help us to pay the temporal debt. Neither could that person receive the sacrament of penance, because penance remits only sins committed after baptism, and that person had no sins to remit, because he died just after receiving baptism. See, then, the goodness of our Lord in instituting baptism, to forgive everything and leave us as free from guilt as our first parents were when God created them.

154. **Is baptism necessary to salvation?**

Baptism is necessary to salvation, because without it we cannot enter into the kingdom of heaven.

Those who through no fault of theirs die without baptism, though they have never committed sin, cannot enter heaven—neither will they go to hell. After the last judgment, there will be no purgatory. Where, then, will they go? God in his goodness will provide a place of rest for them, where they will not suffer and will be in a state of natural peace; but they will never see God or heaven. God might have created us for a purely natural and material end, so that we would live forever upon the earth and be naturally happy with the good things God would give us. But then we would never have known of heaven or God as we do now. Such happiness on earth would be nothing compared to the delights of heaven and the presence of God; so that now, since God has given us, through his holy revelations, a knowledge of himself and heaven, we would be miserable if left always upon the earth. Those, then, who die without baptism do not know what they have lost, and are naturally happy; but we who know all they have lost for want of baptism know how very unfortunate they are. Think, then, what a terrible crime it is to willfully allow anyone to die without baptism, or to deprive a little child of life before it can be baptized! Suppose all the members of a family but one little infant have been baptized; when the day of judgment comes, while all the other members of a family—father, mother, and children—may go into heaven, that little one will have to remain out; that little brother or sister will be separated from its family forever, and never, never see God or heaven. How heartless and cruel, then, must a person be who would deprive that little infant of happiness for all eternity—just that its mother or someone else might have a little less trouble or suffering here upon earth.

155. **Who can administer baptism?**

The priest is the ordinary minister of baptism; but in case of necessity, anyone who has the use of reason may baptize.

Ordinary—that is, the one who has a right to baptize and generally does; others can baptize only in case of necessity.

Priest and all above him—bishops and the pope; for they have all the power the priest has, and more besides. *Minister* is the name given here to one who performs any of the sacred rites or ceremonies of the Church. *Necessity.* When the ordinary minister cannot be had and when baptism must be given; for if it is not absolutely necessary to give the baptism, then you must wait for the ordinary minister.

Anyone. Even persons not Catholics or not Christians may, in case of necessity, baptize a person wishing to receive baptism, if they know how to baptize and seriously wish to do what the Church of Christ does when it baptizes. You cannot baptize a person against his will. Neither can you baptize an infant whose parents are unwilling to have the child baptized, or when the child will not be brought up in the Catholic religion. But if the child is dying, it can and should be baptized, even without the consent of the parents.

Use of reason. Because the person must intend to do what our Lord ordered to be done in giving baptism; and a little child could not understand, and could not therefore baptize.

156. **How is baptism given?**

Whoever baptizes should pour water on the head of the person to be baptized, and say, while pouring the water: "I baptize thee in the name of the Father, and of the Son, and of the Holy Ghost."

When the priest baptizes in the church, he uses consecrated water—that is, water blessed for that purpose on Holy Saturday, and mixed with holy oil. When he or any other, in case of necessity, baptizes in a private house, he may use plain, clean water, and he baptizes without the other ceremonies used in the church. Remember, in baptism you can use ordinary clean water, warm or cold. When the priest or anyone baptizes by simply pouring the water and pronouncing the words of baptism, we call it private baptism. The baptism given in church with all the ceremonies is called "solemn baptism." Any person baptized privately should be brought to the church afterward to have the rest of the ceremonies performed.

It will increase your respect for the sacrament to know what ceremonies are used in solemn baptism, and what they signify. The following things must be prepared: the holy oils, a little salt, a little pitcher or something similar to pour the water from, a vessel to receive the water when poured, some cotton, two stoles, one white and one purple, towels, a white cloth, candle, and candlestick. All being ready, the person holding the infant takes it on the right arm, face up, and the priest, having learned the name it is to be given, begins by asking the one to be baptized: "What do you ask of the Church of God?" And the godparents answer for the child: "Faith." If the person receiving baptism is capable of answering for himself, he must do so. Then the priest exhorts the child to keep the commandments and love God; then he breathes three times upon it and bids the evil spirit depart.

He next prays for the child and puts a little salt into its mouth, as a sign of the wisdom that faith gives, and again prays for the child. Then he places the end of his stole over it as a sign that it is led into the Church; for baptism is given in a place called the "baptistery," railed off from the church and near the door, because formerly the ceremony up to this point was performed outside the church, and, at this part of the ceremony, the person was led in to be baptized. Then, before baptism, the person says the Creed and the Our Father; for when a grown person is to be baptized, he must first be instructed in all the truths of religion, and he must say the Creed to show that he believes them. Again, the priest prays and places a little spittle on the ears and nose of the child, using at the same time the words used by our Lord when he spit upon the ground, and rubbing the spittle and clay upon the eyes of the blind man, healed him.[75]

[75] Cf. Jn 9:6

The priest next asks the child if it renounces the devil and all his works and pomps—that is, vanities and empty shows; and having received the answer, anoints it with holy oil on the breast and back. Then he again asks for a profession of faith, and finally baptizes it.

After baptism, he anoints its head with holy chrism, places a white cloth upon it to signify the purity it received in baptism, and as a sign that it must keep its soul free from sin. Then he places in its hand a lighted candle, to signify the light of faith it has received in baptism. We are baptized at the door of the church to show that without baptism we are out of the Church. We are often signed with the sign of the cross to remind us that our salvation is due to the cross and passion of our Lord. The priest's stole is placed over us to show that the Church takes us under its protection and shields us from the power of the devil. We are anointed as a sign that we are freed from our sins and strengthened to fight for Christ. The white cloth or garment is placed upon us to remind us of the glory of the resurrection; the light is placed in our hand to show that we should burn with Christian charity.

157. **How many kinds of baptism are there?**
There are three kinds of baptism: baptism of water, of desire, and of blood.

158. **What is baptism of water?**
Baptism of water is that which is given by pouring water on the head of the person to be baptized, and saying at the same time: "I baptize thee in the name of the Father, and of the Son, and of the Holy Ghost."

159. **What is baptism of desire?**
Baptism of desire is an ardent wish to receive baptism, and to do all that God has ordained for our salvation.

Ardent wish by one who has no opportunity of being baptized—for no one can baptize himself. He must be sorry for his sins and have the desire of receiving the baptism of water as soon as he can; just as a person in mortal sin and without a priest to absolve him may, when in danger of death, save his soul from hell by an act of perfect contrition and the firm resolution of going to confession as soon as possible. Baptism of desire would be useful and necessary if there was no water at hand or no person to baptize; or if the one wishing to be baptized and those about him did not know exactly how baptism was to be given—which might easily happen in pagan lands.

One thing you must especially remember in giving baptism in case of necessity: namely, that it would not do for one person to pour the water and another to say the words. The same person must do both, or the baptism will not be valid. If you are called to baptize in case of necessity, be very careful to observe the following points, otherwise the baptism will not be valid: use clean water and nothing but water—no other liquid would do. Say every one of the exact words: "I baptize thee in the name of the Father, and of the Son, and of the Holy Ghost." It would not do to say, "I baptize thee in the name of God"; or, "I baptize thee in the name of the Blessed Trinity"; nor would it do to say simply, "In the name of the Father, and of the Son, and of the Holy Ghost," without saying, "I baptize thee." Say the words at the same time you pour the water, and be sure the water touches the skin. It would not do to pour the water simply on the hair. You must not sprinkle the water, but pour it upon the head.

When you have followed the above instructions carefully and are sure you have baptized properly, never under any circumstances repeat the baptism on the same person. It is a sin to try to baptize more than once when you know baptism can be given only once. The sight of the person dying and the fact that you are called for the first time may cause you to be somewhat excited; but be calm, remember the importance of the sacrament, and you will administer it as directed. Parents should not baptize their own children in case of necessity, if there is any other person present who can validly do it. Remember those who administer baptism contract a spiritual relationship with the person they baptize and with his parents. If they wished, years afterward, to marry either the person they baptized or the parents of the person, they must make this relationship known to the priest.

Sponsors are not necessary in private baptism. A person may be sponsor for a child in baptism without being present at the baptism, provided someone else holds the child in his name and answers the questions he himself would answer if he were present. Such a sponsor is said to stand for the child by proxy, and he, and not the one who holds the child, is then the real godparent when, at the request of the parents or priest, he has consented to be sponsor.

160. **What is baptism of blood?**

Baptism of blood is the shedding of one's blood for the faith of Christ.

Baptism of blood, called "martyrdom," is received by those who were not baptized with water, but were put to death for their Catholic faith. This takes place even nowadays in pagan countries where the missionaries are trying to convert the poor natives. These pagans have to be instructed before they are baptized. They do everything required of them, let us suppose, and are waiting for the day of baptism. Those who are being thus instructed are called "catechumens." Someday, while they are attending their instructions, the enemies of religion rush down upon them and put them to death. They do not resist, but willingly suffer death for the sake of the true religion. They are martyrs then and are baptized in their own blood; although, as we said above, blood would not do for an ordinary baptism even when we could not get water; so that if a person drew blood from his own body and asked to be baptized with it, the baptism would not be valid. Neither would they be martyrs if put to death not for religion or virtue, but for some other reason—say political.

161. **Is baptism of desire or blood sufficient to produce the effects of baptism of water?**

Baptism of desire or of blood is sufficient to produce the effects of the baptism of water, if it is impossible to receive the baptism of water.

162. **What do we promise in baptism?**

In baptism, we promise to renounce the devil with all his works and pomps.

163. **Why is the name of a saint given in baptism?**

The name of a saint is given in baptism in order that the person baptized may imitate his virtues and have him for a protector.

The saint whose name we bear is called our "patron saint." This saint has a special love for us and a special care over us. People take the names of great men because they admire their good qualities or their great deeds. So, we take saints' names because we admire their Christian virtues and great Christian deeds. We should, therefore, read the life of our patron saint and try to imitate his virtues, and the day on which the Church celebrates the feast of our patron saint should be a great day for us also. The Church generally celebrates the saint's feast on the day on which he died, that is, as we believe, the day on which he entered into heaven.

164. **Why are godfathers and godmothers given in baptism?**
Godfathers and godmothers are given in baptism in order that they may promise in the name of the child what the child itself would promise if it had the use of reason.

165. **What is the obligation of a godfather and a godmother?**
The obligation of a godfather and a godmother is to instruct the child in its religious duties if the parents neglect to do so or die.

This is a very important obligation, and we should be faithful in the fulfillment of it before God. Godfathers and godmothers are also called "sponsors." The following persons cannot be sponsors: 1) All persons not Catholics, because they cannot teach the child the Catholic religion if they do not know it themselves. 2) All persons who are publicly leading bad lives; for how can they give good example and teach their godchild to be good when they themselves are public sinners? 3) All persons who are ignorant of their religion should not take upon themselves the duties of godparents. Therefore, parents should select as sponsors for their children only good, practical Catholics—not Catholics merely in name, but those who live up to their faith, and who will be an example for their children.

To repeat what has already been said, godparents contract a spiritual relationship, and in the event of their marriage, they must make known this relationship to the priest. The godfather and the godmother do not contract a relationship between themselves, but only with the child and its parents; so that neither the godfather nor the godmother could marry the child or its parents without first obtaining a dispensation; that is, permission from the Church granted by the bishop or pope.

With regard to names, parents should never be induced by any motive to give their child some foolish or fancy name taken from books, places, or things. Above all, they should never select the name of any enemy of the Church or unbeliever, but the name of one of God's saints who will be a model for the child. Whatever name is taken, if it be not a saint's name, the name of some saint should be given as a middle name. If this has been omitted in baptism, it should be supplied in confirmation, at which time a new name can be added. Again, if a saint's name has been taken in baptism, it should not be shortened or changed so as to mean nothing; as, for example, Mazie, Miz, etc., for Mary. When your correct name is mentioned, your saint is honored, and I might say, "invoked," because it should remind you of him. For that reason, you should not have meaningless or foolish pet names, known only to your family or your friends.

LESSON FIFTEENTH

On Confirmation

166. **What is confirmation?**

Confirmation is a sacrament through which we receive the Holy Ghost to make us strong and perfect Christians and soldiers of Jesus Christ.

In baptism, we are made Christians, but we are not very strong in our faith till the Holy Ghost comes in confirmation. You remember how timid the apostles were before the coming of the Holy Ghost, and how firm and determined in their faith they were afterward; and how fearlessly they preached even to those who crucified our Lord. *Soldiers*, because we must fight for our salvation against our three enemies: the devil, the world, and the flesh. Our Lord is our great leader in this warfare, and we must follow him and fight as he directs. A soldier that fights as he pleases and not as his general commands will surely be beaten.

167. Who can administer confirmation?

The bishop is the ordinary minister of confirmation.

Ordinary, because in some very distant countries where, on account of the small number of Christians, they have as yet no bishops, the pope allows some priest to give confirmation; but then he must use the holy oil consecrated by a bishop, and cannot consecrate oil himself.

168. How does the bishop give confirmation?

The bishop extends his hands over those who are to be confirmed, prays that they may receive the Holy Ghost, and anoints the forehead of each with holy chrism in the form of a cross.

169. What is holy chrism?

Holy chrism is a mixture of olive oil and balm, consecrated by the bishop. The oil signifies the strength we receive, and the balm that we should be free from the corruption of sin and give forth the sweetness of virtue.

170. What does the bishop say in anointing the person he confirms?

In anointing the person he confirms, the bishop says: "I sign thee with the sign of the cross, and I confirm thee with the chrism of salvation, in the name of the Father, and of the Son, and of the Holy Ghost."

171. What is meant by anointing the forehead with chrism in the form of a cross?

By anointing the forehead with chrism in the form of a cross is meant that the Christian who is confirmed must openly profess and practice his faith, never be ashamed of it, and rather die than deny it.

Openly profess—that is, acknowledge that he is a Catholic when it is necessary to do so. He need not proclaim it in the streets. *Practice* it without regard for what other people think, say, or do. *Ashamed* of a religion so glorious as the Catholic religion? Would we not be proud to belong to a society of which kings and princes were members? Well, a few centuries ago, nearly all the kings, princes, and great men of the earth were Catholics. All the saints were Catholics. All the popes were Catholics. At present, over two hundred million people in the world are Catholics. This Church was founded when

Christ our Lord was on earth, and is nearly two thousand years old. All the other churches are only a few hundred years old. We ought, therefore, to be proud of our religion, for which and in which so many noble persons died. We should feel proud that we are Catholics; while protestants should feel ashamed in our presence, for they have deserted the true standard of Christ, and followed some other leader who set up a religion of his own in opposition to the true Church of our Lord. They will not have the cross or crucifix, the standard of Christ, in their churches or houses or about their persons, and yet they claim to be Christians redeemed by the cross. We are called upon to defend or profess our religion when we have to do what the Church and God require us to do: for example, hear Mass on Sundays and holy days; abstain from the use of flesh meat on Fridays, fast days, and the like, when we are among persons not Catholics.

172. **Why does the bishop give the person he confirms a slight blow on the cheek?**
The bishop gives the person he confirms a slight blow on the cheek to put him in mind that he must be ready to suffer everything, even death, for the sake of Christ.

173. **To receive confirmation worthily, is it necessary to be in the state of grace?**
To receive confirmation worthily, it is necessary to be in the state of grace.

174. **What special preparation should be made to receive confirmation?**
Persons of an age to learn should know the chief mysteries of faith and the duties of a Christian, and be instructed in the nature and effects of this sacrament.

How can one be a good soldier who does not know the rules and regulations of the army nor understand the commands of his general? How can one be a good Christian who does not understand the laws of the Church and the teachings of Christ? The *nature*—that is, understand the sacrament itself. *Effects*—that is, what it does in our souls.

175. **Is it a sin to neglect confirmation?**
It is a sin to neglect confirmation, especially in these evil days when faith and morals are exposed to so many and such violent temptations.

Temptations—from the sayings and writings of the enemies of religion. To neglect it when we have an opportunity of receiving it without any very great difficulty would be a sin. When persons have been unfortunate enough to grow up without confirmation, they should come at any time in their lives to receive it, and not be ashamed to do so on account of their age or condition in life.

LESSON SIXTEENTH

On the Gifts and Fruits of the Holy Ghost

176. **What are the effects of confirmation?**

The effects of confirmation are an increase of sanctifying grace, the strengthening of our faith, and the gifts of the Holy Ghost.

Increase, because we must be in a state of grace, that is, having already sanctifying grace in our souls when we receive confirmation. *Strengthening*, so that we have no doubt about the doctrines we believe.

177. **What are the gifts of the Holy Ghost?**

The gifts of the Holy Ghost are wisdom, understanding, counsel, fortitude, knowledge, piety, and fear of the Lord.

178. **Why do we receive the gift of fear of the Lord?**

We receive the gift of fear of the Lord to fill us with a dread of sin.

On account of the goodness of God and the punishment he can inflict.

179. **Why do we receive the gift of piety?**

We receive the gift of piety to make us love God as a Father, and obey him because we love him.

180. **Why do we receive the gift of knowledge?**

We receive the gift of knowledge to enable us to discover the will of God in all things.

181. **Why do we receive the gift of fortitude?**

We receive the gift of fortitude to strengthen us to do the will of God in all things.

Some know the will of God—what they should do—but they have not the courage to follow the dictates of their conscience. For example, a person goes with bad company: the gift of knowledge will teach him that he should give it up; but the gift of fortitude will enable him to do what his conscience shows him to be right.

182. **Why do we receive the gift of counsel?**

We receive the gift of counsel to warn us of the deceits of the devil, and of the dangers to salvation.

The devil is much wiser than we are, and has much more experience, being among the people of the world ever since the time of Adam—about six thousand years. He could therefore easily deceive and overcome us if God himself, by the gift of counsel, did not enable us to discover his tricks and expose his plots. When at times we are tempted, our conscience warns us, and if we follow the warning, we shall escape the sin. Counsel tells us when persons or places are dangerous for our salvation.

183. **Why do we receive the gift of understanding?**

We receive the gift of understanding to enable us to know more clearly the mysteries of faith.

Mysteries, truths we could never know by reason, but only by the teaching of God; and the gift of understanding enables us to know better what his teaching means. The apostles heard and knew what our Lord taught, but they did not fully understand the whole meaning till the Holy Ghost had come.

184. **Why do we receive the gift of wisdom?**

We receive the gift of wisdom to give us a relish for the things of God and to direct our whole life and all our actions to his honor and glory.

Relish, a liking for, a desire for.

185. **Which are the beatitudes?**

The beatitudes are:

1. Blessed are the poor in spirit, for theirs is the kingdom of heaven.
2. Blessed are the meek, for they shall possess the land.
3. Blessed are they that mourn, for they shall be comforted.
4. Blessed are they that hunger and thirst after justice, for they shall be filled.
5. Blessed are the merciful, for they shall obtain mercy.
6. Blessed are the clean of heart, for they shall see God.
7. Blessed are the peacemakers, for they shall be called the children of God.
8. Blessed are they that suffer persecution for justice' sake, for theirs is the kingdom of heaven.

The beatitudes are part of a sermon our Lord once preached to the people on the mount.[76] When our Lord wished to preach, the Jews would not always allow him to enter their synagogues or meeting houses; so he preached to the people in the open air. Sometimes he stood in a boat by the seashore; sometimes on a little hill, with the people standing or sitting near him. Did you ever think how you would have acted if you lived at that time and were present when our Lord preached? How anxious you would have been to get near to him? How you would have pushed your way through the crowd and listened to every word? Why, then, do you sometimes pay so little attention in church or at instructions when the words of our Lord are repeated to you? Our Lord instituted a Church which, as we know, is sometimes called "the kingdom of heaven." In this sermon, he laid down the condition for being good subjects of his kingdom; that is, he gives the virtues we should practice to be good children of the Church. He tells us what rewards we shall have for practicing these virtues and leading a holy life: namely, God's grace and blessing in this world and everlasting glory in heaven.

1. *Poor in spirit.* One is poor in spirit if he does not set his heart upon riches and the goods of this world in such a way that he would be willing to offend God in order to possess them, or rather than part with them. Thus, one who has no money but who would do anything to get it, would be poor,

[76] Cf. Mt 5

but not poor in spirit, and therefore not among those our Lord calls blessed. If we are really poor and wish to be poor in spirit also, we must be contented with our lot—with what God gives us—and never complain against him. No matter how poor, miserable, or afflicted we may be, we could still be worse, since we can find others in a worse condition than we are. We do not endure every species of misery, but only this or that particular kind; and if the rest were added, how much worse our condition would be! The very greatest misery is to be in a state of sin. If we are poor and in sin, our condition is indeed pitiable, for we have no consolation; but if we are virtuous in poverty, bearing our trials in patience and resignation for the love of God, we have the rich treasures of his grace and every assurance of future happiness. On the other hand, if one is very rich and gives freely and plentifully to the poor and works of charity, and is willing to part with riches rather than offend God, such a one is poor in spirit and can be called "blessed."

It is a great mistake to risk our souls for things we must leave to others at our death. Sometimes those who leave the greatest inheritance are soonest forgotten and despised, because the money or property bequeathed gives rise to numerous lawsuits, quarrels and jealousies among the relatives, and thus becomes a very curse to that family, whose members hate one another on its account. Or it may happen that the heirs thoughtlessly enjoy and foolishly squander the wealth the man, now dead, has labored so hard to accumulate, while he, perhaps, is suffering in hell for sins committed in securing it. Again, how many children have been ruined through the wealth left them by their parents! Instead of using it for good purposes, they have made it a means of sin; often lose their faith and souls on account of it; and in their ingratitude, never offer a prayer or give an alms for the soul of the parent, who in his anxiety to leave all to them left nothing in charity to the Church or the poor. Surely it is the greatest folly to set our hearts upon that which can be of no value to us after death. When a person dies, men ask: "What wealth has he left behind?" But God and the angels ask: "What merits has he sent before him?"

2. *Possess the land*—that is, the promised or Holy Land, which was a figure of the Church. Therefore, it means the meek shall be true members of our Lord's Church here on earth and hereafter in heaven, and be beloved by all.

3. *That mourn.* Suffering is good for us if we bear it patiently. It makes us more like our blessed Lord, who was called the "Man of Sorrows."

4. *Justice*—that is, all kinds of virtue. *Filled*—that is, with goodness and grace. In other words, if we ask and really wish to become virtuous, we shall become so. St. Joseph is called in holy scripture a "just man,"[77] to show that he practiced every virtue.

5. If we are *merciful* to others, God will be merciful to us.

6. *Clean of heart*—that is, pure in thoughts, words, deeds, and looks.

7. *Peacemakers.* If persons who try to make peace and settle disputes are called "the children of God," those who, on the contrary, try to stir up dissensions should be called "the children of the devil." Never tell the evil you may hear of another, especially to the one of whom it was spoken; and never carry stories from one to another: it is contemptible, and sinful as well. If you have nothing good to say of the character of another, be silent, unless your duty compels you to speak. Never be a child of the devil by exciting jealousy, hatred, or revenge in anyone; but, on the contrary, make peace wherever you can, and be one of the children of God.

8. *Suffer persecution.* Therefore, when you are badly treated on account of your piety or religion, remember you are like the martyrs of your holy faith, suffering for virtue and truth, and that you will receive your reward.

186. **Which are the twelve fruits of the Holy Ghost?**

The twelve fruits of the Holy Ghost are charity, joy, peace, patience, benignity, goodness, long-suffering, mildness, faith, modesty, continency, and chastity.

Fruits, the things that grow from the gifts of the Holy Ghost. *Charity*, love of God and our neighbor. *Peace* with God and man and ourselves. With God, because we are his friends. With man, because we deal justly with all and are kind to all. With ourselves, because we have a good conscience, that does not accuse us of sin. *Benignity*, disposition to do good and show kindness. *Long-suffering*—same as patience. *Modesty*, *continency*, and *chastity* refer to purity in thoughts, words, looks, and actions.

[77] Mt 1:19

LESSON SEVENTEENTH

On the Sacrament of Penance

When our Blessed Lord redeemed us, he applied the benefits of the redemption in the sacrament of baptism. By this baptism, he freed us from sin and the slavery of the devil; he restored us to God's grace; he reopened for us heaven; made us once more children of God: in a word, he placed us in the condition in which we were before our fall through the sin of our first parents. This was certainly a great kindness bestowed upon us, and one would think we would never forget it, and never more lose God's friendship by any fault of ours; especially when we had seen the great miseries brought upon the world by sin, and had learned something of hell where we would have been, and of heaven which we would have lost, if our Lord had not redeemed us. Our Blessed Lord saw, however, that we would forget his benefits, and again, even after baptism, go freely into the slavery of the devil. How, then, could we be saved? We could not be baptized again, because baptism can be given only once. Our good Lord in his kindness instituted another sacrament, by which we could once more be freed from sin if we had the misfortune to fall into it after baptism—it is the sacrament of penance. It is called "the plank in a shipwreck." When sailors are shipwrecked and thrown helplessly into the ocean, their only hope is some floating plank that may bear them to the shore. So, when we fall after baptism, we are thrown into the great ocean of sin, where we must perish if we do not rest upon the sacrament of penance, which will bring us once more in safety to the friendship of God. How very thankful the poor shipwrecked sailors would be to anyone who would offer them a plank while they were in danger! Do you think they would refuse to use it? In like manner, how thankful we should be for the sacrament of penance, and how anxious we should be to use it when we are in danger of losing our souls!

The sacrament of penance shows the very great kindness of our Lord. He might have said: "I saved them once, and I will not trouble myself more about them; if they want to sin again, let them perish." But no, he forgives us and saves us as often as we sincerely call on him for help, being truly sorry for our sins. He left this power also to his apostles, saying to them: "As often as any poor sinner shall come to you and show that he is truly sorry for his sins, and has the determination not to commit them again, and confesses them to you, I give you the power to pardon his sins in the sacrament of penance." The forgiveness of your sins is the chief though not the only blessing you receive in the reception of this sacrament, through which you derive so many and great advantages from the exhortation, instruction, or advice of your confessor.

Is it not a great benefit to have a friend to whom you can go with the trials of your mind and soul, your troubles, temptations, sins, and secrets? You have that friend—the priest in the confessional. He is willing to help you, for he consecrated his life to God to help men to save their souls. He is able to help you, for he understands your difficulties, sins, and temptations, and the means of overcoming them. He has made these things the study of his life, and derives still greater knowledge of them from hearing the sad complaints of so many relating their secret sorrows or afflictions, and begging his advice.

Then you are sure that whatever you tell him in the confessional will never be made known to others, even if the priest has to die to conceal it. You might tell your secrets to a friend, and, if you afterward offended him, he would probably reveal all you told him. The priest asks no reward for the service he gives you in the confessional, but loves to help you, because he has pledged himself to God to do so, and would sin if he did not. Some enemies of our holy religion have tried to make people believe that Catholics have to pay the priest in confession for forgiving their sins; but every Catholic, even the youngest child who has been to confession, knows this to be untrue, and a base calumny against our holy religion; even those who assert it do not believe it themselves. The good done in the confessional will never be known in this world. How many persons have been saved from sin, suicide, death, and other evils by the advice and encouragement received in confession! How many persons who have fallen into the lowest depths of sin have by the sacrament of penance been raised up and made to lead good, respectable lives—a blessing to themselves, their families, and society!

187. **What is the sacrament of penance?**

Penance is a sacrament in which the sins committed after baptism are forgiven.

One who has never been baptized could not go to confession and receive absolution, nor indeed any of the sacraments.

188. **How does the sacrament of penance remit sin and restore the soul to the friendship of God?**

The sacrament of penance remits sin and restores the friendship of God to the soul by means of the absolution of the priest.

Absolution means the words the priest says at the time he forgives the sins. *Absolve* means "to loose or free." When ministers or ambassadors are sent by our government to represent the United States in England, France, Germany, or other countries, whatever they do there officially is done by the United States. If they make an agreement with the governments to which they are sent, the United States sanctions it, and the very moment they sign the agreement it is signed and sanctioned by the authority of our government whose representatives they are, and their official action becomes the action of the United States itself. But when their term of office expires, though they remain in the foreign countries, they have no longer any power to sign agreements in the name and with the authority of the United States.

You see, therefore, that it is the power that is given them, and not their own, that they exercise. In like manner, our Lord commissioned his priests and gave them the power to forgive sins, and whatever they do in the sacrament of penance he himself does. At the very moment the priest pronounces the words of absolution on earth, his sentence is ratified in heaven and the sins of the penitent are blotted out.

It may increase your veneration for the sacrament to know the precise manner in which absolution is given. After the confession and giving of the penance, the priest first prays for the sinner, saying: "May Almighty God have mercy on you, and, your sins being forgiven, bring you to life everlasting. Amen." Then, raising his right hand over the penitent, he says: "May the Almighty and merciful Lord grant you pardon, absolution, and remission of your sins. Amen." Then he continues: "May our Lord Jesus Christ absolve you, and I, by his authority, absolve you from every bond of excommunication and interdict, as far as I have power and you stand in need. Then I absolve you from your sins. In the name of the Father, and of the Son, and of the Holy Ghost. Amen." At these last words, he makes the sign of the cross over the penitent. In conclusion, he directs to God a prayer in behalf of the penitent in the following words: "May the passion of our Lord Jesus Christ, the merits of the Blessed Virgin Mary and of all the saints, and whatsoever good you may have done or evil you may have suffered, be to you unto the remission of your sins, the increase of grace, and the recompense of everlasting life. Amen." Then the priest says, "God bless you," "Go in peace," or some other expression showing his delight at your reconciliation with God.

189. **How do you know that the priest has the power of absolving from the sins committed after baptism?**

I know that the priest has the power of absolving from sins committed after baptism, because Jesus Christ granted that power to the priests of his Church when he said: "Receive ye the Holy Ghost. Whose sins you shall forgive, they are forgiven them; whose sins you shall retain, they are retained."[78]

Every Christian knows our Lord himself had power to forgive sins: 1) because he was God, and 2) because he often did forgive them while on earth, and proved that he did by performing some miracle; as, for example,[79] when he cured the poor men who had been sick and suffering for many years, he said to them: "Thy sins are forgiven thee; arise, take up thy bed, and walk," and the men did so. Since our Lord had the power himself, he could give it to his apostles if he wished, and he did give it to them and their successors. For if he did not, how could we and all others who, after baptism, have fallen into sin be cleansed from it? This sacrament of penance was for all time, and so he left the power with his Church,

[78] Jn 20:22-23
[79] Cf. Mk 2; Jn 5

which is to last as long as there is a living human being upon the earth. Our Lord promised to his apostles before his death this power to forgive sins,[80] and he gave it to them after his resurrection, when he appeared to them and breathed on them, and said: "Whose sins you shall forgive, they are forgiven them; and whose sins you shall retain, they are retained."[81]

190. **How do the priests of the Church exercise the power of forgiving sins?**

The priests of the Church exercise the power of forgiving sins by hearing the confession of sins, and granting pardon for them as ministers of God and in his name.

The power to forgive sins implies the obligation of going to confession; because, as most sins are secret, how could the apostles know what sins to forgive and what sins to retain—that is, not to forgive—unless they were told by the sinner what sins he had committed? They could not see into his heart as God can, and know his sins; and so, if the sinner wished his sins forgiven, he had to confess them to the apostles or their successors. Therefore, since we have the sacrament of penance, we must also have confession.

191. **What must we do to receive the sacrament of penance worthily?**

To receive the sacrament of penance worthily, we must do five things:

1. We must examine our conscience.
2. We must have sorrow for our sins.
3. We must make a firm resolution never more to offend God.
4. We must confess our sins to the priest.
5. We must accept the penance which the priest gives us.

When we are about to go to confession, the first thing we should do is to pray to the Holy Ghost to give us light to know and remember all our sins, to fully understand how displeasing they are to God, and to have a great sorrow for them, which includes the resolution of never committing them again. The next thing we should do is:

[80] Cf. Mt 18:18
[81] Jn 20:23

1. *Examine our conscience*; and first of all, we find out how long a time it is since our last confession, and whether we made a good confession then and received Holy Communion and performed our penance. The best method of examining is to take the commandments and go over each one in our mind, seeing if we have broken it, and in what way; for example:

First. "I am the Lord thy God; thou shalt not have strange gods before me." Have I honored God? Have I said my prayers morning and night; have I said them with attention and devotion? Have I thanked God for all his blessings? Have I been more anxious to please others than to please God, or offended him for the sake of others?

Second. "Thou shalt not take the name of the Lord thy God in vain." Have I cursed? Have I taken God's name in vain or spoken without reverence of holy things?

Third. "Remember thou keep holy the sabbath day." Have I neglected to hear Mass through my own fault on Sundays and holy days of obligation? Have I kept others from Mass? Have I been late, and at what part of the Mass did I come in? Have I been willfully distracted at Mass, or have I distracted others? Have I done servile work without necessity?

Fourth. "Honor thy father and thy mother." Have I been disobedient to parents or others who have authority over me—to spiritual or temporal superiors, teachers, etc.? Have I slighted or been ashamed of parents because they were poor or uneducated? Have I neglected to give them what help I could when they were in need of it? Have I spoken of them with disrespect or called them names that were not proper?

Fifth. "Thou shalt not kill." Have I done anything that might lead to killing? Have I been angry or have I tried to take revenge? Have I borne hatred or tried to injure others? Have I given scandal?

Sixth. "Thou shalt not commit adultery." Have I indulged in any bad thoughts, looked at any bad pictures or objects, listened to any bad conversation, told or listened to bad or immodest jokes or stories, or, in general, spoken of bad things? Have I done any bad actions or desired to do any while alone or with others?

Seventh. "Thou shalt not steal." Have I stolen anything myself or helped or advised others to steal? Have I received anything or part of anything that I knew to be stolen? Do I owe money and not pay it when I can? Have I bought anything with the intention of never paying for it or at least knowing I never could pay for it? Have I made restitution when told to do so by my confessor; or have I put it off from time to time? Have I failed to give back what belonged to another? Have I found anything and not tried to discover its owner, or have I kept it in my possession after I knew to whom it belonged? Have I cheated in business or at games?

Eighth. "Thou shalt not bear false witness against thy neighbor." Have I told lies or injured anyone by my talk? Have I told the faults of others without any necessity? It is not allowed to tell the faults of others, even when you tell the truth about them, unless some good comes of the telling.

Ninth. "Thou shalt not covet thy neighbor's wife." This can come into our examination on the sixth commandment.

Tenth. "Thou shalt not covet thy neighbor's goods." This can come into our examination on the seventh commandment.

After examining yourself on the commandments of God, examine yourself on the commandments of the Church.

First. "To hear Mass on Sundays and holy days of obligation." This has been considered in the examination on the third commandment.

Second. "To fast and abstain on the days appointed." Have I eaten meat on Fridays or fast days, remembering that it was Friday or a fast day, and when I had no permission from my confessor to do so on account of poor health or other reason?

Third. "To confess at least once a year." Is it over a year, and how much over it, since I have been to confession?

Fourth. "To receive Holy Eucharist during the Easter time." Did I go to Holy Communion between the First Sunday of Lent and Trinity Sunday? If not, I have committed a mortal sin.

Fifth. "To contribute to the support of our pastors." Have I helped the church and reasonably paid my share of its expenses—given to charity and the like, or have I made others pay for the light, heat, and other things that cost money in the church, and shared in their benefits without giving according to my means? Have I kept what was given me for the church or other charity, or stolen from the church and not stated that circumstance when I confessed that I stole?

Sixth. "Not to marry persons who are not Catholics, or who are related to us within the fourth degree of kindred, or privately without witnesses, nor to solemnize marriage at forbidden times." Have I anything to tell on this commandment?

After examining yourself on the commandments of God and of his Church, examine yourself on the capital sins, especially on *pride*. Have I been impudent and stubborn, vain about my dress, and the like? Have I despised others simply on account of poverty or something they could not help? *Gluttony*. Have I ever taken intoxicating drink to excess or broken a promise not to take it? Have I knowingly caused others to be intoxicated? *Sloth*. Have I wasted my time willfully and neglected to do my duty at school or elsewhere?

After examining yourself on the commandments and capital sins, examine yourself on the duties of your state of life. If you are at school, how have you studied? You should study not alone to please your parents or teachers, but for the sake of learning. If you are at work, have you been faithful to your employer, and done your work well and honestly?

The above method is generally recommended as the best in the examination of conscience. But you need not follow these exact questions; you can ask yourself any questions you please: the above questions are given only as examples of what you might ask, and to show you how to question yourself. It is useless to take any list of sins in a prayer book and examine yourself by it, confessing the sins just as they are given. If you do take such a list and find in it some questions or sins that you do not understand, do not trouble yourself about them. In asking yourself the questions, if you find you have sinned against a commandment, stop and consider how many times. There are few persons who sin against all the commandments. Some sin against one and some against another. Find out the worst sin you have and the one you have most frequently committed, and be sure of telling it.

2. *Have sorrow for our sins.* After examining your conscience and finding out the sins you have committed, the next thing is to be sorry for them. The

sorrow is the most essential part in the whole sacrament of penance. In this sacrament there are, as you know, three parts: contrition, confession, and satisfaction—and contrition is the most important part. When, therefore, we are preparing for confession, we should spend just as much time, and even more, in exciting ourselves to sorrow for our sins as in the examination of our conscience. Some persons forget this and spend all their time examining their conscience. We should pray for sorrow if we think we have none. Remember the act of contrition made at confession is not the sorrow, but only an outward sign by which we make known to the priest that we have the sorrow in our heart, and therefore we must have the sorrow before making the confession, or, at least, before receiving the absolution.

Now what kind of sorrow must we have? Someone might say, "I am not truly sorry because I cannot cry. If some of my friends died, I would be more sorry for that than for my sins." Do not make any such mistake. The true and necessary kind of sorrow for sin is to know that by sin you have offended God, and now feel that it was very wrong, and that you have from this moment the firm determination never to offend him more. If God adds to this a feeling that brings tears to your eyes, it is good, but not necessary.

3. Remember real sorrow for sin supposes and contains *a firm resolution* never to sin again. How can you say to God, "O my God, I am heartily sorry," etc., if you are waiting only for the next opportunity to sin? How can we be sorry for the past if we are going to do the same in the future? Do you think the thief would be sorry for his past thefts if he had his mind made up to steal again as soon as he had the chance? Ah, but you will say, "Nearly all persons sin again after confession." I know that; but when they were making their confession, they thought they never would, and really meant never to sin again; but when temptation came, they forgot the good resolution, did not use God's help, and fell into sin again. I mean, therefore, that at the time you make the act of contrition, you must really mean what you say and promise never to sin, and take every means you can to keep that promise. If you do fall afterward, renew your promise as quickly as possible and make a greater effort than before. Be on your guard against those things that make you break your promise, and then your act of contrition will be a good one. A person may be afraid that he will fall

again, but being afraid does not make his contrition worthless as long as he wishes, hopes, and intends never to sin again. We should always be afraid of falling into sin, and we will fall into it if we depend upon ourselves alone, and not on the help which God gives us in his grace.

4. *Confess our sins.* Having made the necessary preparation, you will next go into the confessional; and while you are waiting for the priest to hear you, you should say the *confiteor*. When the priest turns to you, bless yourself and say: "Bless me, Father, for I have sinned. It is a month or a week (or whatever time it may be) since my last confession, and I have since committed these sins." Then tell your sins as you found them in examining yourself.

In confession, you must tell only such things as are sins. You must not tell all the details and a long story with every sin. For example, if a boy should confess that he went to see a friend, and, after that, met another friend, and, when he came home, he was asked what had kept him, and he told a lie. Now, the going to see the friend and the meeting of the other friend, and all the rest, was not a sin: the sin was telling the lie, and that was all that should have been confessed. Therefore, tell only the sins. Then tell only your own sins, and be very careful not to mention anyone's name—even your own—in confession.

Be brief, and do not say, "I broke the first commandment or the second by doing so-and-so": tell the sin simply as it is, and the priest himself will know what commandment you violated. Again, when you have committed a sin several times a day, do not multiply that by the number of days since your last confession and say to the priest, "I have told lies," for example, "four hundred and forty-two times." Such things only confuse you and make you forget your sins. Simply say, "I am in the habit of telling lies, about so many, three or four—or whatever number it may be—times a day." Never say *sometimes* or *often* when you are telling the number of your sins. *Sometimes* might mean ten or it might mean twenty times. How then can the priest know the number by that expression? Give the number as nearly as you can, and if you do not know the whole number, give the number of times a day, etc.

Never say "*maybe* I did so-and-so"; because maybe you did not, and the priest cannot judge. Tell what you consider your worst sin first, then, if there be any sin you are ashamed to tell or do not know how to tell, say to the priest: "Father, I have a sin I am ashamed to tell, or a sin I do not know how to tell"; and then the priest will ask you some questions and help you to tell it. But never think of going away from the confessional with some sin that you did not tell. The devil sometimes tempts people to do this, because he does not like to see them in a state of grace and friends of God. When you are committing the sin, he makes you believe it is not a great sin, and that you can tell it in confession; but after you have committed it, he makes you believe that it is a most terrible sin, and that if you tell it, the priest will scold you severely. So, it is concealed and the person leaves the confessional with a new sin upon his soul—that of sacrilege. When Judas was tempted to betray our Lord, he thought thirty pieces of silver a great deal of money; and then, after he had committed the sin, he cared nothing for the money, but went and threw it away, and thought his sin so dreadful that he hanged himself, dying in despair.

It is not necessary to tell the priest the exact words you said in cursing or in bad conversation, unless he asks you; but simply say, "Father, I cursed so many times." Do not speak too loud in the confessional, but loud enough for the priest to hear you. If you are deaf, do not go into the confessional while others are near, but wait till all have been heard and go in last, or ask the priest to hear you someplace else.

5. Listen attentively to hear what *penance* the priest gives you, and say the act of contrition when he tells you to say it; and above all, never leave the confessional till the priest closes the little door or tells you to go. If the priest does not say at what particular time you are to say your penance, say it as soon as you can. When he tells you to say anything more than once, he generally means that you are to say it once a day for so many days. If, for example, he tells you to say the Litany of the Blessed Virgin three times, he intends you are to say it once a day for three days.

When you have told all your sins, you will say: "For these and all the sins of my whole life, especially any I have forgotten, I am heartily sorry, and ask pardon and penance." Listen to the priest's advice, and answer simply any question he may ask you. If you should forget a sin in confession and remember it the same day or evening, or while you are still in the church, it will not be necessary to wait and go to confession again. It is forgiven already, because it was included in your forgotten sins; but you must tell it the next time you go to confession, saying before your regular confession: "In my last confession, I forgot this sin." Of course, if you tried to forget your sins, your confession would be invalid. It is only when you examine your conscience with all reasonable care, and then after all forget some sins, that such forgotten sins are forgiven.

Never talk or quarrel for places while waiting for confession, and never cheat another out of his turn in going to confession. It is unjust, it makes the person angry, and lessens his good dispositions for confession. It creates confusion, and annoys the priest who hears the noise. If you are in a hurry, ask the others to allow you to go first; and if they will not be contented and wait, and if you cannot wait, go some other time. Spend your time while waiting in praying for pardon and for sorrow. Never keep the priest waiting for you in the confessional; pass in as soon as he is prepared to hear you.

192. **What is the examination of conscience?**

The examination of conscience is an earnest effort to recall to mind all the sins we have committed since our last worthy confession.

Worthy confession, because, if we made bad confessions, we must tell how often we made them, and whether we received Holy Communion after them or not, and also all the sins we told in the bad confessions, and all others committed since the good confession. If, for example, a boy made a good confession in January, and in confession in February concealed a mortal sin and went to confession after that every month to December, he would have to go back to his last good confession, and repeat all the sins committed since January, and also say that he had gone to confession once a month and made bad confessions all these times.

193. **How can we make a good examination of conscience?**

We can make a good examination of conscience by calling to memory the commandments of God, the precepts of the Church, the seven capital sins, and the particular duties of our state in life, to find out the sins we have committed.

194. **What should we do before beginning the examination of conscience?**
Before beginning the examination of conscience, we should pray to God to give us light to know our sins and grace to detest them.

LESSON EIGHTEENTH

On Contrition

195. **What is contrition or sorrow for sin?**
Contrition or sorrow for sin is a hatred of sin and a true grief of the soul for having offended God, with a firm purpose of sinning no more.

Offended—that is, done something to displease him.

196. **What kind of sorrow should we have for our sins?**
The sorrow we should have for our sins should be interior, supernatural, universal, and sovereign.

197. **What do you mean by saying that our sorrow should be interior?**
When I say that our sorrow should be interior, I mean that it should come from the heart, and not merely from the lips.

Interior—that is, we must really have the sorrow in our hearts. A boy, for example, might cry in the confessional and pretend to the priest to be very sorry, and the priest might be deceived and absolve him; but God, who sees into our hearts, would know that he was not really sorry, but only pretending; that his sorrow was not interior, but exterior; and God therefore would withhold his forgiveness and would not blot out the sins, and the boy would have a new sin of sacrilege upon his soul; because it is a sacrilege to allow the priest to give you absolution if you know you have not the right disposition, and you are not trying to do all that is required for a good confession. So, you understand you might deceive the priest and receive absolution, but God would not allow the absolution to take effect, and the sins would remain; for if the priest knew your dispositions as God did, or as you know them, he would not give you absolution till your dispositions changed.

198. **What do you mean by saying that our sorrow should be supernatural?**
When I say that our sorrow should be supernatural, I mean that it should be prompted by the grace of God, and excited by motives which spring from faith, and not by merely natural motives.

Supernatural—that is, we must be sorry for the sin on account of some reason that God has made known to us. For example, either because our sin is displeasing to God, or because we have lost heaven by it, or because we fear to be punished for it in hell or purgatory. But if we are sorry for our sin only on account of some natural motive, then our sorrow is not of the right kind. If a man was sorry for stealing only because he was caught and had to go to prison for it, his sorrow would only be natural. Or if a boy was sorry for telling lies only because he got a whipping for it, his sorrow would only be natural. Or if a man was sorry for being intoxicated because he lost his situation and injured his health, he would not have the necessary kind of sorrow. These persons must be sorry for stealing, lying, or being intoxicated because all these are sins against God—things forbidden by him and worthy of his punishment. If we are sorry for having offended God, simply on account of his own goodness, and without any thought of what evils might befall us through sin or what benefits we might derive from serving God, our contrition is said to be "perfect." If we are sorry for the sins because by them we are in great danger of being punished by God, or because we have lost heaven by them, and without any regard for God's own goodness, then our contrition is said to be "imperfect." Imperfect contrition is called "attrition."

199. **What do you mean by saying that our sorrow should be universal?**
When I say that our sorrow should be universal, I mean that we should be sorry for all our mortal sins without exception.

Universal. If a person committed ten mortal sins, and was sorry for nine, but not for the tenth, then none of the sins would be forgiven. If you committed a thousand mortal sins, and were sorry for all but one, none would be forgiven. Why? Because you can never have God's grace and mortal sin in the soul at the same time. Now this mortal sin will be on your soul till you are sorry for it, and, while it is on your soul, God's grace will not come to you. Again, you cannot be half sorry for having offended God; either you must be entirely sorry, or not sorry at all. Therefore, you cannot be sorry for only part of your sins.

200. **What do you mean when you say that our sorrow should be sovereign?**
When I say that our sorrow should be sovereign, I mean that we should grieve more for having offended God than for any other evil that can befall us.

201. **Why should we be sorry for our sins?**
We should be sorry for our sins, because sin is the greatest of evils and an offense against God our Creator, Preserver, and Redeemer, and because it shuts us out of heaven and condemns us to the eternal pains of hell.

We consider an evil great in proportion to the length of time we have to bear it. To be blind is certainly a misfortune; but it is a greater misfortune to be blind for our whole life than for one day. Sin, therefore, is the greatest of all evils; because the misfortune it brings upon us lasts not merely for a great many years, but for all eternity. Even slight sufferings would be terrible if they lasted forever, but the sufferings for mortal sin are worse than we can describe or imagine, and they are forever. The greatest evils in this world will not last forever, and are small when compared with sin. Sin makes us ungrateful to God, who gives us our existence.

Our Preserver, because if God ceased to watch over us and provide for us, even for a short time, we would cease to exist.

Our Redeemer, who suffered so much for us.

202. **How many kinds of contrition are there?**
There are two kinds of contrition: perfect contrition and imperfect contrition.

203. **What is perfect contrition?**
Perfect contrition is that which fills us with sorrow and hatred for sin, because it offends God, who is infinitely good in himself and worthy of all love.

It is a very hard thing to have perfect contrition, but we should always try to have it, so that our contrition may be as perfect as possible. This perfect contrition is the kind of contrition we must have if our sins are to be forgiven while we are in danger of death and cannot go to confession. Imperfect contrition with the priest's absolution will blot out our sins.

204. **What is imperfect contrition?**
Imperfect contrition is that by which we hate what offends God, because by it we lose heaven and deserve hell; or because sin is so hateful in itself.

205. **Is imperfect contrition sufficient for a worthy confession?**
Imperfect contrition is sufficient for a worthy confession, but we should endeavor to have perfect contrition.

206. **What do you mean by "a firm purpose of sinning no more"?**
By "a firm purpose of sinning no more," I mean a fixed resolve not only to avoid all mortal sin, but also its near occasions.

Fixed. Not for a certain time, but for all the future.

207. **What do you mean by "the near occasions of sin"?**
By "the near occasions of sin," I mean all the persons, places, and things that may easily lead us into sin.

Occasions. There are many kinds of occasions of sin.

First, we have voluntary and necessary occasions, or those we can avoid and those we cannot avoid. For example: if a companion uses immodest conversation, we can avoid that occasion, because we can keep away from him; but if the one who sins is a member of our own family, always living with us, we cannot so easily avoid that occasion.

Second, near and remote occasions. An occasion is said to be *near* when we always fall into sin by it. For instance, if a man gets intoxicated every time he visits a certain place, then that place is a *near occasion* of sin for him; but if he gets intoxicated only once out of every fifty times or so that he goes there, then it is said to be a *remote occasion*.

Now, it is not enough to avoid the sins: we must also avoid the occasions. If we have a firm purpose of amendment, if we desire to do better, we must be resolved to avoid everything that will lead us to sin. It is not enough to say, "I will go to that place or with that person, but I will never again commit the same sins." No matter what you think now, if you go into the occasion, you will fall again; because our Lord, who cannot speak falsely, says: "He who loves the danger will perish in it."[82] Now the occasion of sin is always "the danger," and if you go into it, our Lord's words will come true, and you will fall miserably.

Take away the cause, take away the occasion, and then the sin will cease of itself. Let us suppose the plaster in your house fell down, and you found that it fell because there was a leak in the water pipe above, and the water coming through wet the plaster and made it fall. What is the first thing your father would do in that case? Why, get a plumber and stop up the leak in the pipe before putting up the plaster again. Would it not be foolish to engage a plasterer to repair the ceiling while the pipe was still leaking? Everyone would say that man must be out of his mind: the plaster will fall down as often as he puts it up, and it matters not either how well he puts it up. If he wants it to stay up, he must first mend the pipe—take away the cause of its falling. Now the occasion of sin is like the leak in the pipe—it will cause you to fall every time. Stop up the leak, take away the occasion, and then you will not fall into sin—at least not so frequently.

The persons are generally bad companions, and though they may not be bad when alone, they are bad when with us, and thus we become also bad companions for them, and occasions of sin.

The places. Liquor-saloons, low theatres, dance halls, and all places where we may see or hear anything against faith or morals.

Things. Bad books, pictures, and the like.

[82] Ecclus 3:27

LESSON NINETEENTH

On Confession

208. **What is confession?**

Confession is the telling of our sins to a duly authorized priest, for the purpose of obtaining forgiveness.

Duly authorized—one sent by the bishop of the diocese in which you are. *Forgiveness.* You might tell a priest all your sins while in ordinary conversation with him, but that would not be confession, because you would not be telling them to have them pardoned. If a person has lost the use of his speech, he can make his confession by writing his sins on a paper and giving it to the priest in the confessional. If the priest returns the paper, the penitent must be careful to destroy it afterward. Also, if you have a poor memory, you may write down the sins you wish to confess, and read them from the paper in the confessional; then you also must be careful to destroy the paper after confession. If a person whose language the priest does not understand is dying, or is obliged to make his yearly confession, he must tell what he can by signs, show that he is sorry for his sins, and thus receive absolution. In a word, the priest would act with him as he would with one who had lost the use of his speech and power to write.

209. **What sins are we bound to confess?**

We are bound to confess all our mortal sins, but it is well also to confess our venial sins.

Bound—obliged in such a way that our confession would be bad if we did not tell them.

Well, because we should tell all the sins we can remember; but if we did not tell a venial sin after we had told a mortal sin, our confession would not be bad. Or if we committed a little venial sin after confession, that should not keep us from Holy Communion; because the Holy Communion itself would blot out that and any other venial sin we might have upon our souls, so that if the priest tells you to go to Holy Communion, you should never let anything keep you away, unless you are certain you have committed a mortal sin after the confession, or have broken your fast. If you have made your first Communion, the priest means that you should go to Communion after the confession in which he gives you absolution, although he may forget to tell you to go. If he wishes you not to go to Holy Communion, he will always tell you not to go. On the other hand, if you have not made your first Communion, and the priest should, after hearing your confession, tell you by mistake to go to Communion, do not go; but if you can, say to him that you have not made your first Communion; and whether you can tell him or not, do not go to Communion after confession unless you have already made your first Communion.

210. **What are the chief qualities of a good confession?**

The chief qualities of a good confession are three: it must be humble, sincere, and entire.

211. **When is our confession humble?**

Our confession is humble when we accuse ourselves of our sins, with a deep sense of shame and sorrow for having offended God.

212. **When is our confession sincere?**

Our confession is sincere when we tell our sins honestly and truthfully, neither exaggerating nor excusing them.

Exaggerating. You must never tell in confession a sin you did not commit, any more than conceal one you did commit. You must tell just the sins committed, and no more or less; and if you are in doubt whether you have committed the sin, or whether the thing done was a sin, then you must tell your doubts to the priest: but do not say you committed such and such sins when you do not know whether you did or not, or only because you think it likely that you did.

213. **When is our confession entire?**

Our confession is entire when we tell the number and kinds of our sins and the circumstances which change their nature.

Number—the exact number, if you know it: as, for example, when we stay from Mass we can generally tell exactly the number of times. But when we tell lies, for instance, we may not know the exact number: then we say how often in the day, or that it is a habit with us, etc.

Kinds—whether they are cursing, or stealing, or lying, etc.

Circumstances which change their nature. In the case of stealing, for example, you need not tell whether it was from a grocery, a bakery, or dry goods store you stole, for that circumstance does not change the nature of the sin: you have simply to tell the amount you took. But if you stole from a church, you would have to tell that, because that is a circumstance that gives the sin of stealing a new character, and makes it sacrilegious stealing. Or if you stole from a poor beggar all he possessed in the world, so that you left him starving, that would be a circumstance making your sin worse, and so you would have to tell it. Therefore, you have to tell any circumstance that really makes your sin much worse or less than it seems; all other circumstances you need not tell: they will only confuse you, and make you forget your sins and waste the priest's time.

214. **What should we do if we cannot remember the number of our sins?**

If we cannot remember the number of our sins, we should tell the number as nearly as possible, and say how often we have sinned in a day, a week, or a month, and how long the habit or practice has lasted.

215. **Is our confession worthy if, without our fault, we forget to confess a mortal sin?**

If without our fault we forget to confess a mortal sin, our confession is worthy, and the sin is forgiven; but it must be told in confession if it again comes to our mind.

216. **Is it a grievous offense willfully to conceal a mortal sin in confession?**

It is a grievous offense willfully to conceal a mortal sin in confession, because we thereby tell a lie to the Holy Ghost, and make our confession worthless.

A lie to the Holy Ghost. God sees every sin we commit, and in his presence, we present ourselves to the priest in the confessional, and declare that we are confessing all. If, then, we willfully conceal a sin that we are bound to confess, God is a witness to our sacrilegious lie. If I see you in some place to which you were forbidden to go, and you, knowing that I saw you, positively deny that you were there, your guilt would be doubly great, for, besides the sin of disobedience committed by going to the forbidden place, you also resist the known truth, and endeavor to prove that I, when I declare I saw you, am telling what is untrue. In a similar manner, concealing a sin in confession is equivalent to denying before God that we are guilty of it. Besides, it is a great folly to conceal a sin, because it must be confessed sooner or later, and, the longer we conceal it, the deeper will be our sense of shame for the sacrileges committed. Again, why should one be ashamed to confess to the priest what he has not been ashamed to do before God, unless he has greater respect for the priest than he has for Almighty God—an absurdity we cannot believe.

Moreover, the shame you experience in telling your sins is a kind of penance for them. Do you not suppose our Lord knew, when he instituted the sacrament of penance, that people would be ashamed to confess? Certainly he did; and that act of humility is pleasing to God, and is a kind of punishment for your sins, and probably takes away some of the punishment you would have to suffer for them. Often, too, the thought of having to confess will keep you from committing the sin.

There is another thought that should encourage us to gladly make a full confession of all our sins, and it is this: it is easier to tell them to the priest alone than to have them exposed, unforgiven, before the whole world on the day of judgment. Do not imagine that your confessor will think less of you on account of your sins. The confessor does not think of your sins after he leaves the confessional. How could he remember all the confessions he hears—often hundreds in a single month? And what is more—he does not even wish to recall the sinful things heard in the confessional, because he wishes to keep his own mind pure, and his soul free from every stain.

The priest is always better pleased to hear the confession of a great sinner or of one who has been a long time from the sacraments, than of one who goes frequently or who has little to tell. He is not glad, of course, that the sinner has committed great sins, but he is glad that since he has had the misfortune to sin so much, he has now the grace and courage to seek forgiveness. Our Lord once said while preaching, that the angels and saints in heaven rejoice more at seeing one sinner doing penance than they do over ninety-nine good persons who did not need to do penance.[83] The greater the danger to which a person has been exposed, the more thankful he and his friends are for escape or recovery from it. If your brother fell into the ocean and was rescued just as he was going down for the last time, you would feel more grateful than if he was rescued from some little pond into which he had slipped, and in which there was scarcely any danger of his being drowned. So, also, the nearer we are to losing our souls and going to hell, the more delighted the angels and saints are when we are saved. One who has escaped great danger will more carefully avoid similar accidents in the future: in like manner, the sinner, after having escaped the danger of eternal death by the pardon of his sins, should never again risk his salvation.

217. **What must he do who has willfully concealed a mortal sin in confession?** He who has willfully concealed a mortal sin in confession must not only confess it, but must also repeat all the sins he has committed since his last worthy confession.

Willfully. Remember, forgetting is not the same as concealing; but if you should willfully neglect to examine your conscience or make any effort to know your sins before going to confession, then forgetting would be equivalent to concealing. Without any preparation, your confession could hardly be a good one. When you are in doubt whether an action is sinful or not, or whether you have confessed it before, you should not leave the confessional with the doubt upon your mind.

It is a foolish practice, however, to be always disturbing your conscience by thinking of past sins, especially of those that occurred very early in your life. Sometimes it is dangerous; because if, while thinking of your past sins, you should take pleasure in them, you would commit a new sin similar to the past sins in which you take delight.

It is best, therefore, not to dwell in thought upon any particular past sin with the time, place, and circumstances of its commission; but simply

[83] Cf. Lk 15:7

to remember in general that you have in the past sinned against this or that commandment or virtue.

The past is no longer under our control, while the future is, and becomes for us, therefore, the all-important portion of our lives. Not unfrequently it may be an artifice of the devil to keep us so occupied with past deeds that we may not attend to the dangers of the future. Do not, then, after your confession spend your time in thinking of the sins you confessed, but of how you will avoid them in the future. When a wound is healed up, nobody thinks of opening it again to see if it has healed properly; so, when the wounds made in our souls by sin are healed up by the absolution, we should not open them again.

This is the rule with regard to our ordinary confessions; but we should sometimes make a general confession. What is a general confession? It is the confession of the sins of our whole life or of a portion—say one, two, or five, etc., years—of our life. A general confession may be necessary, useful, or hurtful.

It is necessary, as you know, when our past confessions were bad. It is useful, though not necessary, on special occasions in our lives: for example, in the time of a retreat or mission; in the time of preparation for first Communion, confirmation, matrimony, etc.; or in preparing for death. It is very useful also for persons about to change their state in life; for such as are about to become priests or religious, etc. It is useful because it gives us a better knowledge of the state of our souls, as we see their condition not merely for a month or two, but for our whole lifetime. We are looking at them as God will look at them in the last judgment, considering all the good and evil we have ever done, and comparing the amount of the one with the amount of the other. We resolve to increase the good and diminish the evil in our future lives. We promise to do penance for the past and to avoid sin for the future; and thus, we are benefited in general confession by this judgment of ourselves, as we may call it.

General confession is hurtful to scrupulous persons. Scrupulous persons are those who think almost everything they do a sin. They are always dissatisfied with their confessions, and fear to approach the sacraments. Their conscience is never at ease, and they are forever unhappy. It is very wrong for them to think and act in this manner, and they must use every means in their power to overcome their scruples.

Our Lord in his goodness never intended to make us unhappy by instituting the sacraments, but, on the contrary, to make us happy, and set our minds and consciences at ease in the reception of his grace. Scrupulous persons must do exactly whatever their confessor advises, no matter what they themselves may think. Such persons, as you can plainly see, should not make general confessions, because their consciences would be more disturbed than pacified by them.

You prepare for general confession as you would for any other, except that you take a longer time for it, and do not pay so much attention to your more trifling sins.

218. **Why does the priest give us a penance after confession?**
The priest gives us a penance after confession that we may satisfy God for the temporal punishment due to our sins.

Penance. The little penance the priest gives may not fully satisfy God, but shows by our accepting it that we are willing to do penance. What, for example, is a penance of five Our Fathers compared with the guilt of one mortal sin, for which we would have to suffer in hell for all eternity? Then think of the penances performed by the Christians many centuries ago, in the early ages of the Church. There were four stages of penance. The churches were divided into four parts by railings and gates. The first railing across the church was at some distance from the altar, the second was a little below the middle of the church, and the third was near the door. Those who committed great sins had to stand clad in coarse garments near the entrance of the church, and beg the prayers of those who entered. After they had done this kind of penance for a certain time, they were allowed to come into the church as far as the second railing. They were allowed to hear the sermon, but were not permitted to be present at the Mass. After doing sufficient penance, they were allowed to remain for Mass, but could not receive Holy Communion. When they had performed all the penance imposed upon them, they were allowed to receive the sacraments and enjoy all the rights and privileges of faithful children of the Church. These penances lasted for many days and sometimes for years, according to the gravity of the sins committed. The sins for which these severe penances wore performed were generally sins that had been committed publicly, and hence the penance, amendment, and reparation had also to be public.

Temporal punishment. Every sin has two punishments attached to it, one called "the eternal" and the other "the temporal." Let me explain by an example. If I, turning highway robber, waylay a man, beat him, and steal his watch, I do him, as you see, a double injury, and deserve a double punishment for the twofold crime of beating and robbing him. He might pardon me for the injuries caused by the beating, but that would not free me from the obligation of restoring to him his watch or its value, for the fact that he forgives me for the act of stealing does not give me the right to keep what justly belongs to him. Now, when we sin against God, we in the first place insult him, and secondly rob him of what is deservedly his due; namely, the worship, respect, obedience, love, etc., that we owe him as our Creator, Preserver, and Redeemer.

In the sacrament of penance, God forgives the insult offered by sinning, but requires us to make restitution for that of which the sin has deprived him. In every sin, there is an act of turning away from God and an act of turning to some creature in his stead. If a soldier pledged to defend his country deserts his army in time of war, he is guilty of a dishonorable, contemptible act; but if, besides deserting his own army, he goes over to aid the enemy, he becomes guilty of another and still greater crime—he becomes a traitor for whom the laws of nations reserve their severest penalties. By sin, we, who in baptism and confirmation have promised to serve God and war against his enemies, desert him and go over to them; for our Blessed Lord has said: "He that is not with me is against me."[84]

We pay the temporal debt due to our sins, that is, make the restitution, by our penances upon earth, or by our sufferings in purgatory, or by both combined.

The penances performed upon earth are very acceptable and pleasing to God; and hence we should be most anxious to do penance here that we may have less to suffer in purgatory. St. Augustine, who had been a great

[84] Mt 12:30

sinner, often prayed that God might send him many tribulations while on earth, that he might have less to endure in purgatory. Therefore, after performing the penance the priest gives you in the confessional, it is wise to impose upon yourself other light penances in keeping with your age and condition, but never undertake severe penances or make religious vows and promises without consulting your confessor. In every case, be careful first of all to perform the penance imposed upon you in the reception of the sacrament. The penance given in confession has a special value, which none of the penances selected by yourself could have.

If you forget to say your penance, your confession is not on that account worthless; but as the penance is one of the parts of the sacrament, namely, the satisfaction, you should say it as soon as possible, and in the manner your confessor directs. If you cannot perform the penance imposed by your confessor, you should inform him of that fact, and ask him to give you another in its stead.

Indulgences also are a means of satisfying for this temporal punishment. Sometimes God inflicts the temporal punishment in this world by sending us misfortunes or sufferings, especially such as are brought on by the sins committed.

219. **Does not the sacrament of penance remit all punishment due to sin?**
The sacrament of penance remits the eternal punishment due to sin, but it does not always remit the temporal punishment which God requires as satisfaction for our sins.

Remember that baptism differs from penance in this respect: that, although they both remit sin, penance does not take away all the temporal punishment, while baptism takes away all the punishment, both eternal and temporal; so that if we died immediately after baptism, we would go directly to heaven, while if we died immediately after penance, we would generally go to purgatory to make satisfaction for the temporal guilt.

220. **Why does God require a temporal punishment as a satisfaction for sin?**
God requires a temporal punishment as a satisfaction for sin to teach us the great evil of sin, and to prevent us from falling again.

221. **Which are the chief means by which we satisfy God for the temporal punishment due to sin?**

The chief means by which we satisfy God for the temporal punishment due to sin are: prayer, fasting, almsgiving, all spiritual and corporal works of mercy, and the patient suffering of the ills of life.

Chief, but not the only means. *Fasting*, especially the fasts imposed by the Church—in Lent for instance. Lent is the forty days before Easter Sunday during which we fast and pray to prepare ourselves for the resurrection of our Lord, and also to remind us of his own fast of forty days before his passion. *Almsgiving*—that is, money or goods given to the poor. *Spiritual* works of mercy are those good works we do for persons' souls. *Corporal* works of mercy are those we do for their bodies. *Ills of life*—sickness or poverty or misfortune, especially when we have not brought them upon ourselves by sin.

222. **Which are the chief spiritual works of mercy?**

The chief spiritual works of mercy are seven: to admonish the sinner, to instruct the ignorant, to counsel the doubtful, to comfort the sorrowful, to bear wrongs patiently, to forgive all injuries, and to pray for the living and the dead.

To admonish the sinner. If we love our neighbor, we should help him in his distress, even when it is an inconvenience to us. We should help him also to correct his faults, we should point them out and warn him of them. We are obliged to do so in the following circumstances: First, when his fault is a mortal sin. Second, when we have some authority or influence over him. Third, when there is reason to believe that our warning will make him better instead of worse. If our advice only makes him worse, then we should not say anything to him about his fault, but keep out of his company ourselves. *Ignorant* especially in their religion. *Doubtful* about something in religion which you can explain and make clear to them. *Comfort*, saying kind words of encouragement to them. *Wrongs*, things not deserved; for example, persons talking ill about us, accusing us falsely, etc.; but if the false accusations, etc., are going to give scandal, then we must defend ourselves against them. If, for instance, lies were told about the father of a family, and it were likely all his children would believe them and lose their respect for his authority, then he must let them know the truth. But when we patiently suffer wrongs that injure only ourselves, and that are known only to God and ourselves, God sees our sufferings and rewards us. What matters it what people think we are if God knows all our doings and is pleased with them? *Living*—especially for the conversion of sinners, or for those who are on their deathbed. *The dead*—those suffering in purgatory, especially if we have ever caused them to sin.

223. **Which are the chief corporal works of mercy?**

The chief corporal works of mercy are seven: to feed the hungry, to give drink to the thirsty, to clothe the naked, to ransom the captive, to harbor the harborless, to visit the sick, and to bury the dead.

Ransom the captive—that is, chiefly those who, while teaching or defending the true religion in pagan lands, are taken prisoners by the enemies of our faith. You have perhaps heard of the Crusades or read about them in your history. Now let me briefly tell you what they were and why they were commenced.

About the year 570, that is, about thirteen hundred years ago, when the Christian religion was spread over nearly the whole world, a man named Mahomet was born in Arabia. He pretended to be a great prophet sent from God, and gathered many followers about him. He told them his religion must be spread by the sword. He plundered cities and towns, and divided the spoils with his followers. He told them that all who died fighting for him would certainly go to heaven. In a short time, his followers became very numerous; for his religion was an easy and profitable one, allowing them to commit sin without fear of punishment, and giving them share of his plunder. Many others not influenced by these motives joined his religion for fear of being put to death. His followers were afterward called by the general name of "Saracens." They took possession of the Holy Land, of the city of Jerusalem, of the tomb of our Lord, and of every spot rendered dear to Christians by our Savior's life and labors there. They persecuted the Christians who went to visit the Holy Land, and put many of them to death.

When the news of these dreadful crimes reached Europe, the Christian kings and princes, at the request of the pope, raised large armies and set out for the East to war against the Saracens and recover the Holy Land. Eight of these expeditions, or Crusades, as they are called, went out during two hundred years, that is, from 1095 to 1272. Those who took part in them are called "Crusaders," from the word *cross*, because every soldier wore a red cross upon his shoulder.

Some of these expeditions were successful, and some were not; but, on the whole, they prevented the Saracens from coming to Europe and taking possession of it. Many of the Christian soldiers and many of the pilgrims who visited the Holy Land were taken prisoners by the Saracens and held, threatened with death, till the Christians in Europe paid large sums of money as a ransom for their liberty. To free these captives was a great act of charity, and is one of the corporal works of mercy. *Ransom* means "to pay money for another's freedom." Even now there are sometimes captives in pagan lands.

A pilgrim is one who goes on a journey to visit some holy place for the purpose of thus honoring God. He would not be a pilgrim if he went merely through curiosity. He must go with the holy intention of making his visit an act of worship. In our time, pilgrimages to the Holy Land, to Rome, and other places are quite frequent. *To harbor*—that is, to give one who has no home a place of rest. A harbor is an inlet of the ocean where ships can rest and be out of danger; so, we can also call the home or place of rest given to the homeless a "harbor." *Sick*, especially the sick poor and those who have no friends. *To bury* those who are strangers and have no friends. All Christians are bound to perform these works of mercy in one way or another.

We have been relieved of doing the work ourselves by the establishment of institutions where these things are attended to by communities of holy men or women called "religious." They take charge of asylums for the orphans, homes for the aged and poor, hospitals for the sick, etc., while many devote themselves to teaching in colleges, academies, and schools. But if these good religious do the work for us, we are obliged on our part to give them the means to carry it on. Therefore, we should contribute, according to our means, to charitable institutions, and indeed to all institutions that promote the glory of God and the good of our religion.

To explain more fully, religious are self-sacrificing men and women who, wishing to follow the evangelical counsels, dedicate their lives to the service of God. They live together in communities approved by the Church, under the rule and guidance of their superiors. Their day is divided between prayer, labor, and good works, more time being given to one or other of these according to the special end or aim of the community. The houses in which they live are called "convents" or "monasteries," and the societies of which they are members are called "religious orders," "communities," or "congregations."

In some of these religious communities of men, all the members are priests; in others, some are priests and some are brothers; and in others still, all are brothers. Priests belonging to the religious orders are called "the regular clergy," to distinguish them from "the secular clergy" or priests who live and labor in the parishes to which they are assigned by their bishops. "Sisters" and "nuns" mean almost the same thing, but we generally call those "nuns" who live under a more severe rule and never leave the boundaries of their convent. In like manner "friars," "monks," and "brothers" lead almost the same kind of life, except that the monks practice greater penances and live under stricter rules. A hermit is a holy man who lives alone in some desert or lonely place, and spends his life in prayer and mortification. In the early ages of the Church, there were many of these hermits, or fathers of the desert, but now religious live together in communities.

The members of religious orders of men or women take three vows, namely of poverty, chastity, and obedience. These orders were founded by holy persons for some special work approved of by the Church. Thus, the Dominicans were founded by St. Dominic, and their special work was to preach the gospel and convert heretics or persons who had fallen away from the faith. The Jesuit fathers were organized by St. Ignatius Loyola, and their work is chiefly teaching in colleges, and giving retreats and missions. So also have the Redemptorists, Franciscans, Passionists, etc., their special works, chiefly the giving of missions. In a word, every community, of either men or women, must perform the particular work for which it was instituted.

"But why," you will ask, "are there different religious orders?" In the first place, all persons are not fitted for the same kind of work: some can teach, others cannot; some can bear the fatigue of nursing the sick, and others cannot. Secondly, when our Lord was on earth, he performed every good work and practiced every virtue perfectly. He fasted, prayed, helped the needy, comforted the sorrowful, healed the sick, taught the ignorant, defended the oppressed, admonished sinners, etc. It would be impossible for any one community to imitate our Lord in all his works: so each community takes one or more particular works of our Lord, and tries to imitate him as perfectly as possible in these at least. Some communities devote their time to prayer; others attend the sick; others teach, etc.; and thus, when all unite their different works, the combined result is a more perfect imitation of our Lord's life upon earth.

LESSON TWENTIETH

On the Manner of Making a Good Confession

224. **What should we do on entering the confessional?**
On entering the confessional, we should kneel, make the sign of the cross, and say to the priest: "Bless me, Father"; then add, "I confess to Almighty God, and to you, Father, that I have sinned."

225. **Which are the first things we should tell the priest in confession?**
The first things we should tell the priest in confession are the time of our last confession and whether we said the penance and went to Holy Communion.

226. **After telling the time of our last confession and Communion, what should we do?**
After telling the time of our last confession and Communion, we should confess all the mortal sins we have since committed, and all the venial sins we may wish to mention.

We may wish. We should tell every real sin we have never confessed. If we have no mortal sin to confess, it is well to tell some kind of mortal sin we have committed in our past life, though confessed before. We should do this because, when we have only very small sins to confess, there is always danger that we may not be truly sorry for them, and without sorrow there is no forgiveness. But when we add to our confession some mortal sin that we know we are sorry for, then our sorrow extends to all our sins, and makes us certain that our confession is a good one. If you should hear the sin of another person while you are waiting to make your own confession, you must keep that sin secret forever. If the person in the confessional is speaking too loud, you should move away so as not to hear; and if you cannot move, hold your hands on your ears so that you may not hear what is being said.

227. **What must we do when the confessor asks us questions?**
When the confessor asks us questions, we must answer them truthfully and clearly.

228. **What should we do after telling our sins?**
After telling our sins, we should listen with attention to the advice which the confessor may think proper to give.

The priest in the confessional acts as judge, father, teacher, and physician. As judge, he listens to your accusations against yourself, and passes sentence according to your guilt or innocence. As a father and teacher, he loves you, and tries to protect you from your enemies by warning you against them, and teaching you the means to overcome them. But above all, he is a physician, who will treat your soul for its ills and restore it to spiritual health. He examines the sins you have committed, discovers their causes, and then prescribes the remedies to be used in overcoming them. When anything goes amiss with our bodily health, we speedily have recourse to the physician, listen anxiously to what he has to say, and use the remedies prescribed. In the very same way, we must follow the priest's advice if we wish our souls to be cured of their maladies. Just as a person who is unwell would not go one day to one physician and the next day to another, so a penitent should not change confessors without a good reason; and if you have any choice to make, let it be made in the beginning, and let it rest on worthy motives. In a short time, your confessor will understand the state of your soul, as the physician who frequently examines you does the state of your body. He will know all the temptations, trials, and difficulties with which you have to contend. He will see whether you are becoming better or worse; whether you are resisting your bad habits or falling more deeply into them; also, whether the remedies given are suited to you, and whether you are using them properly. All this your confessor will know, and it will save you the trouble of always repeating, and him the trouble of always asking. Thus, the better your confessor knows you and all the circumstances of your life, the more will he be able to help you; for, besides the forgiveness of your sins, there are many other benefits derived from the sacrament of penance.

But if at any time there should be danger of you making a bad confession to your own confessor—on account of some feeling of false shame—then go to any confessor you please; for it is a thousand times better to seek another confessor than run the risk of making a sacrilegious confession.

Never be so much attached to any one confessor that you would remain away from the sacraments a long time rather than go to another in his absence.

You should not consider the person in the confessional, but the power he exercises. You should be anxious concerning only this fact: Is there a priest there who was sent by our Lord? Is there a minister of Christ there who has power to pardon my sins? If so, I will humbly go to him, no matter who he is or what his dispositions.

229. **How should we end our confession?**

We should end our confession by saying, "I also accuse myself of all the sins of my past life," telling, if we choose, one or several of our past sins.

230. **What should we do while the priest is giving us absolution?**

While the priest is giving us absolution, we should from our heart renew the act of contrition.

All, especially children, should know this act well before going to confession.

LESSON TWENTY-FIRST

On Indulgences

231. **What is an indulgence?**

An indulgence is the remission, in whole or in part, of the temporal punishment due to sin.

I have explained before what the temporal punishment is; namely, the debt which we owe to God after he has forgiven our sins, and which we must pay in order that satisfaction be made. It is, as I said, the value of the watch we must return after we have been pardoned for the act of stealing. I said this punishment must be blotted out by our penance. Now, the Church gives us an easy means of so doing, by granting us indulgences. She helps us by giving us a share in the merits of the Blessed Virgin and of the saints. All this we have explained when speaking in the Creed of the communion of saints.

232. **Is an indulgence a pardon of sin, or a license to commit sin?**

An indulgence is not a pardon of sin, nor a license to commit sin, and one who is in a state of mortal sin cannot gain an indulgence.

If you are in a state of mortal sin, you lose the merit of any good works you perform. God promises to reward us for good works, and if we are in a state of grace when we do the good works, God will keep his promise and give us the reward; but if we are in mortal sin, we have no right or claim to any reward for good works, because we are enemies of God. For this reason alone, we should never remain even for a short time in mortal sin, since it is important for us to have all the merit we can. Even when we will not repent and return to him, God rewards us for good works done by giving us some temporal blessings or benefits here upon earth. He never allows any good work to go unrewarded any more than he allows an evil deed to go unpunished. Although God is so good to us, we nevertheless lose very much by being in a state of mortal sin; for God's grace is in some respects like the money in a bank: the more grace we receive and the better we use it, the more he will bestow upon us. When you deposit money in a savings bank, you get interest for it; and when you leave the interest also in the bank, it is added to your capital, and thus you get interest for the interest. So, God not only gives us grace to do good, but also grace for doing the good, or, in other words, he gives us grace for using his grace.

233. **How many kinds of indulgences are there?**

There are two kinds of indulgences—plenary and partial.

234. **What is a plenary indulgence?**

A plenary indulgence is the full remission of the temporal punishment due to sin.

Full remission—so that if you gained a plenary indulgence and died immediately afterward, you would go at once to heaven. Persons go to purgatory, as you know, to have the temporal punishment blotted out; but if you have no temporal punishment to make satisfaction for, there is no purgatory for you. It is very hard to gain a plenary indulgence, as you may understand from its very great advantages. To gain it, we must not only hate sin and be heartily sorry even for our venial sins, but we must not have a desire for even venial sin. However, we should always try to gain a plenary indulgence, for in so doing, we always gain part of it or a partial indulgence, greater or less according to our dispositions.

235. **What is a partial indulgence?**

A partial indulgence is the remission of a part of the temporal punishment due to sin.

236. **How does the Church by means of indulgences remit the temporal punishment due to sins?**

The Church by means of indulgences remits the temporal punishment due to sin by applying to us the merits of Jesus Christ, and the superabundant satisfactions of the Blessed Virgin Mary and of the saints, which merits and satisfactions are its spiritual treasury.

Superabundant means "more than was necessary."[85]

[85] See explanation of communion of saints in the Creed, above.

237. **What must we do to gain an indulgence?**

To gain an indulgence, we must be in a state of grace and perform the works enjoined.

Works—to visit certain churches or altars; to give alms; to say certain prayers; etc. For a plenary indulgence, it is required generally to go to confession and Holy Communion, and to pray for the intention of our holy father the pope. When an indulgence may be gained by praying for the intention of our holy father, it will be sufficient to say five Our Fathers and five Hail Marys for his intention. Now, what does praying for the intention of the pope or bishop or anyone else mean? It does not mean that you are to pray for the pope himself, but for whatever he is praying for or wishes you to pray for. For instance, on one day, the holy father may be praying for the success of some missions that he is establishing in pagan lands; on another, he may be praying that the enemies of the Church may not succeed in their plans against it; on another, he may be praying for the conversion of some nation, and so on—whatever he is praying for or wishes you to pray for is called his "intention."

To gain an indulgence, you should also have the intention of gaining it. There are many prayers that we sometimes say to which indulgences are attached, and we do not know it. How can we gain them? By making a general intention every morning while saying our prayers to gain all the indulgences we can during the day, whether we know of them or not. For example, there is an indulgence of fifty days granted us every time we make the sign of the cross, being sorry for our sins; and if we make it with holy water, we can gain one hundred days' indulgence. Many may not know of these indulgences; but if they have the general intention mentioned above, they will gain the indulgence every time they perform the work. In the same way, all those who are in the habit of going to confession and Holy Communion every week can gain all the plenary indulgences for which confession and Holy Communion are required conditions, and even when they do not know that they are gaining indulgences.

You sometimes see printed after a little prayer: "An indulgence of forty days," or, "an indulgence of one hundred days," or, "of a year," etc.

What does that mean? Does it mean that a person who says that prayer will get out of purgatory forty days sooner than he would if he did not say it? No. I told you how the early Christians were obliged to do public penance for their sins; to stand at the door of the church and beg the prayers of those entering. Sometimes their penance lasted for forty days, sometimes for one hundred days, and sometimes for a longer period. By "an indulgence of forty days," the Church grants the remission of as much of the temporal punishment as the early Christians would have received for doing forty days' public penance. Just how much of the temporal punishment God blotted out for forty days' public penance we do not know; but whatever it was, God blots out just the same now for one who gains an indulgence of forty days by saying a little prayer to which the indulgence is attached.

But why, you may wonder, did the early Christians do such penances? Because, in those days, their faith was stronger than ours, and they understood better than we do the malice of sin and the punishment it deserves. Later, the Christians grew more careless about their religion and the service of God. The Church therefore, wishing to save its children, made it easier for them to do penance. If it continued to impose the public penances, many would not perform them, and thus lose their souls.

Besides indulgences granted for saying certain prayers or doing certain good works, there are others granted for certain persons, places, or things. For instance, a pair of beads or a cross may have an indulgence attached which you can gain by using them. A church or altar may have an indulgence attached which you can gain by visiting them on certain days. A certain priest may have the power granted him by the holy father of blessing crosses, medals, etc., with special indulgences attached.

LESSON TWENTY-SECOND

On the Holy Eucharist

238. **What is the Holy Eucharist?**

The Holy Eucharist is the sacrament which contains the body and blood, soul and divinity of our Lord Jesus Christ under the appearances of bread and wine.

When we say *contains*, we mean the sacrament which is the body and blood, etc. The Holy Eucharist is the same living body of our Lord which he had upon earth; but it is in a new form, under the appearances of bread and wine. Therefore, our Lord in the tabernacle can see and hear us.

239. **When did Christ institute the Holy Eucharist?**

Christ instituted the Holy Eucharist at the last supper, the night before he died.

Last supper, on Holy Thursday night.[86]

240. **Who were present when our Lord instituted the Holy Eucharist?**

When our Lord instituted the Holy Eucharist, the twelve apostles were present.

241. **How did our Lord institute the Holy Eucharist?**

Our Lord instituted the Holy Eucharist by taking bread, blessing, breaking, and giving to his apostles, saying: "Take ye and eat. This is my body";[87] and then, by taking the cup of wine, blessing and giving it, saying to them: "Drink ye all of this. This is my blood which shall be shed for the remission of sins. Do this for a commemoration of me."[88]

Eucharist means "thanks." Hence this sacrament is called "Eucharist," because our Lord gave thanks before changing the bread and wine into his body and blood, and because the offering of it to God is the most solemn

[86] See explanation of the passion, Lesson Eighth, Question 78.

[87] Mt 26:26; 1 Cor 11:24

[88] Cf. Mt 26:27-28; 1 Cor 11:25

act of thanksgiving. *Do this*—that is, the same thing I am doing, namely, changing bread and wine into my body and blood. *Commemoration*—that is, to remind you of me, that you may continue to do the same till the end of time.

242. **What happened when our Lord said, "This is my body; this is my blood"?** When our Lord said, "This is my body," the substance of the bread was changed into the substance of his body. When he said, "This is my blood," the substance of the wine was changed into the substance of his blood.

Substance literally means "that which stands underneath." Underneath what? Underneath the outward appearances or qualities—such as color, taste, figure, smell, etc.—that are perceptible to our senses. Therefore, we never see the substance of anything. Of this seat, for instance, I see the color, size, and shape; I feel the hardness, etc.; but I do not see the substance, namely, the wood of which it is made. When the substance of anything is changed, the outward appearances change with it. But not so in the Holy Eucharist; for, by a miracle, the appearances of bread and wine remain the same after the substance has been changed as they were before. As the substance alone is changed in the Holy Eucharist, and as I cannot see the substance, I cannot see the change. I am absolutely certain, however, that the change takes place, because our Lord said so; and I believe him, because he could not deceive me. He is God, and God could not tell a lie, because he is infinite truth. This change is a great miracle, and that is the reason we cannot understand it, though we believe it.

Once at a marriage in Cana of Galilee,[89] our Lord changed water into wine. The people were poor, and our Lord, his Blessed Mother, and the apostles were present at the wedding when the wine ran short; and our Blessed Lady, always so kind to everyone, wishing to spare these poor people from being shamed before their friends, asked our Lord to perform the miracle, and, at her request, he did so, and changed many vessels of water into the best of wine. In that miracle, our Lord changed the substance of the water into the substance of the wine. Why, then, could he not change

[89] Cf. Jn 2

in the same way and by the same power the substance of bread and wine into the substance of his own body and blood? When he changed the water into wine, besides changing the substance, he changed everything else about it; so that it had no longer the appearance of water, but everyone could see that it was wine. But in changing the bread and wine into his body and blood, he changes only the substance, and leaves everything else unchanged, so that it still looks and tastes like bread and wine; even after the change has taken place and you could not tell by looking at it that it was changed. You know it only from your faith in the words of our divine Lord, when he tells you it is changed.

Again, it is much easier to change one thing into another than to make it entirely out of nothing. Anyone who can create out of nothing can surely change one thing into another. Now our Lord, being God, created the world out of nothing; and he could therefore easily change the substance of bread into the substance of flesh. I have said our Lord's body in the Holy Eucharist is a living body, and every living body contains blood; and that is why we receive both the body and the blood of our Lord under the appearance of the bread alone. The priest receives the body and blood of our Lord under the appearance of both bread and wine, while the people receive it only under the appearance of bread. The early Christians used to receive it as the priest does—under the appearance of bread and under the appearance of wine; but the Church had to make a change on account of circumstances. First, all the people had to drink from the same chalice or cup, and some would not like that, and show disrespect for the Blessed Sacrament by refusing it. Then there was great danger of spilling the precious blood, passing it from one to another; and, finally, some said that Christ's blood was not in his body under the appearance of bread. This was false; and to show that it was false, and for the other reasons, the Church after that gave Holy Communion to the people under the appearance of bread alone. The Church always believes and teaches the same truths. It always believed that the Holy Eucharist under the appearance of bread contained also our Lord's blood; but it taught it more clearly when it was denied.

243. **Is Jesus Christ whole and entire both under the form of bread and under the form of wine?**
Jesus Christ is whole and entire both under the form of bread and under the form of wine.

244. **Did anything remain of the bread and wine after their substance had been changed into the substance of the body and blood of our Lord?**
After the substance of the bread and wine had been changed into the substance of the body and blood of our Lord, there remained only the appearances of bread and wine.

245. **What do you mean by "the appearances of bread and wine"?**
By "the appearances of bread and wine," I mean the figure, the color, the taste, and whatever appears to the senses.

Senses—that is, eyes, ears, etc. Thus we have the sense of seeing, the sense of hearing, the sense of tasting, the sense of smelling, the sense of feeling. The Holy Eucharist is the body of our Lord just as long as the appearances of bread and wine remain, and when they go away, our Lord's body goes also. For example, if a church, tabernacle and all, was buried by a great earthquake, and, after many years, the people succeeded in getting at the tabernacle and opening it, and then found in the ciborium—that is, the vessel in which the Blessed Sacrament is kept in the tabernacle—only black dust, our Lord would not be there, although he was there when the church was buried. He would not be there, because there was no longer the appearance of bread there: it had all been changed into ashes by time, and our Lord left it when the change took place. But if the appearance of bread had remained unchanged, he would be there even after so many years.

When we receive Holy Communion, the appearance of bread remains for about fifteen or twenty minutes after we receive, and then it changes or disappears. Therefore, during these fifteen or twenty minutes that the appearance remains, our Lord himself is really with us; and for that reason, we should remain about twenty minutes after Mass on the day we receive, making a thanksgiving, speaking to our Lord, and listening to him speaking to our conscience. What disrespect some people show our Lord by rushing out of the church immediately after Mass on their Communion day, sometimes beginning to talk or look around before making any thanksgiving? When you receive Holy Communion, after returning to your seat, you need not immediately begin to read your prayer book, but may bow your head and speak to our Lord while he is present with you. After the appearances of bread vanish, our Lord's bodily presence goes also, but he remains with us by his grace as long as we do not fall into mortal sin.

246. **What is this change of the bread and wine into the body and blood of our Lord called?**

This change of the bread and wine into the body and blood of our Lord is called "transubstantiation."

Transubstantiation—that is, the changing of one substance into another substance; for example, the changing of the wood in a seat into stone.

247. **How was the substance of the bread and wine changed into the substance of the body and blood of Christ?**

The substance of the bread and wine was changed into the substance of the body and blood of Christ by his almighty power.

248. **Does this change of bread and wine into the body and blood of Christ continue to be made in the Church?**

This change of bread and wine into the body and blood of Christ continues to be made in the Church by Jesus Christ through the ministry of his priests.

249. **When did Christ give his priests the power to change bread and wine into his body and blood?**

Christ gave his priests the power to change bread and wine into his body and blood when he said to his apostles: "Do this in commemoration of me."[90]

[90] Lk 22:19; Cf. 1 Cor 11:24-25

250. **How do the priests exercise this power of changing bread and wine into the body and blood of Christ?**

The priests exercise this power of changing bread and wine into the body and blood of Christ through the words of consecration in the Mass, which are the words of Christ: "This is my body; this is my blood."

Consecration. At what part of the Mass are the words of consecration pronounced? Just before the elevation; that is, just before the priest holds up the host and the chalice, while the altar boy rings the bell.

When the priest is going to say Mass, he prepares everything necessary in the sacristy—the place or room near the altar where the sacred vessels and vestments are kept, and where the priest vests. He takes the chalice—that is, the long silver or gold goblet—out of its case; then he covers it with a long, narrow, white linen cloth called a "purificator." Over this he places a small silver or gold plate called the "paten," on which he places a host—that is, a thin piece of white bread prepared for Mass, perfectly round, and about the size of the bottom of a small drinking glass. He then covers this host with a white card, called a "pall," after which he covers the chalice and all with a square cloth or veil that matches the vestments.

Then he puts on his own vestments as follows: over his shoulders the amice, a square, white cloth. Next the alb, a long white garment reaching down to his feet. He draws it about his waist with the cincture, or white cord. He places on his left arm the maniple, a short, narrow vestment. Around his neck he places the stole, a long, narrow vestment with a cross on each end. Over all he places the chasuble, or large vestment with the cross on the back. Lastly, he puts on his cap or berretta.

Before going further, I must say something about the color and signification of the vestments. There are five colors used, namely, white, red, green, violet, and black. White signifies innocence, and is used on the feasts of our Lord, of the Blessed Virgin, and of some saints. Red signifies love, and is used on the feasts of the Holy Ghost and of the martyrs. Green signifies hope, and is used on Sundays from the Epiphany to Pentecost, unless some feast requiring another color falls on Sunday. Violet signifies penance, and is used in Advent and Lent. Black signifies sorrow, and is used on Good Friday and in Masses for the dead. As regards the vestments themselves:

the amice signifies preparation to resist the attacks of the devil; the alb is the symbol of innocence; the cincture of charity; the maniple of penance; the stole of immortality; and the chasuble of love, by which we are enabled to bear the light burden our Lord is pleased to lay upon us.

Vested as described, when the candles have been lighted on the altar, the priest takes the covered chalice in his hand, and goes to the altar, where, after arranging everything, he begins Mass. After saying many prayers, he uncovers the chalice, and the acolyte or altar boy brings up wine and water, and the priest puts some into the chalice. Then he says a prayer, and offers to God the bread and wine to be consecrated. This is called "the offertory of the Mass," and takes place after the boy presents the wine and water.

Immediately after the *Sanctus*, the priest begins what is called "the Canon of the Mass," and soon after comes to the time of consecration, and has before him on the paten the white bread, or host, and in the chalice wine. Remember, it is only bread and wine as yet. After saying some prayers, the priest bends down over the altar and pronounces the words of consecration, namely, "This is my body," over the bread; and, "This is my blood," over the wine. Then there is no longer the bread the priest brought out and the wine the boy gave upon the altar, but, instead of both, the body and blood of our Lord. After the words of consecration, the priest genuflects or kneels before the altar to adore our Lord, who just came there at the words of consecration; he next holds up the body of our Lord—the host—for the people also to see and adore it; he then replaces it on the altar, and again genuflects. He does just the same with the chalice. This is called "the elevation." The altar boy then rings the bell to call the people's attention to it, for it is the most solemn part of the Mass. After more prayers, the priest takes and consumes, that is, swallows the sacred host and drinks the precious blood from the chalice.

Then the people come up to the altar to receive Holy Communion. But where does the priest get Holy Communion for them if he himself took all he consecrated? He opens the tabernacle, and there, in a large, beautiful vessel, he has small hosts. He consecrates a large number of these small hosts sometimes while he is consecrating the larger one for himself. When they are consecrated, he places them in the tabernacle, where they are kept with the sanctuary lamp burning before them, till at the different Masses they have all been given out to the people. Then he consecrates others at the next Mass, and does as before.

The size of the host does not make the slightest difference, as our Lord is present whole and entire in the smallest particle of the host. A little piece that you could scarcely see would be the body of our Lord. However, the particle that is given to the people is about the size of a twenty-five-cent piece, so that they can swallow it before it melts. In receiving Holy Communion, you must never let it entirely dissolve in your mouth, for if you do not swallow it, you will not receive Holy Communion at all.

Here I might tell you what benediction of the Blessed Sacrament is. The priest sometimes consecrates at the Mass two large hosts; one he consumes himself, as I have told you, and the other he places in the tabernacle in a little gold case. When it is time for benediction, he places this little case—made of glass and gold, about the size of a watch—in the gold or silver monstrance which you see on the altar at benediction. It is made to represent rays of light coming from the Blessed Sacrament. After the choir sings, the priest says the prayer and goes up and blesses the people with the Blessed Sacrament; that is, when he holds up the monstrance over the people, our Lord himself blesses them. Should we not be very anxious, therefore, to go to benediction? If the bishop came to the church, we would all be anxious to receive his blessing; and if our holy father the pope came, everybody would rush to the church. But what are they compared to our Lord himself? And yet when he comes to give his blessing, many seem to care little about it. Because our Lord in his goodness is pleased to give us his blessing often, we are indifferent about it. The holy teachers and fathers of the Church tell us that if we could see the sanctuary at Mass and benediction as it really is, we would see it filled with angels all bowed down, adoring our Lord. These good angels must be very much displeased at those who are so indifferent at Mass or benediction as not to pay any attention; and above all, at those who stay away. The large silk cloak the priest wears at benediction is called the "cope," and the long scarf that is placed over his shoulders the "humeral," or "benediction veil."

At the words of consecration, you must know, the priest does not say, "This is Christ's body," but, "This is my body"; for, at the altar, the priest is there in the place of our Lord himself. It is our Lord who offers up the sacrifice, and the priest is his instrument. That is why the priest wears vestments while saying Mass or performing his sacred duties, to remind him that he is, as it were, another Person; that he is not acting in his own name or right, but in the name and place of our Blessed Lord.

I have given you in a general way a description of the Mass: let me now mention its particular parts by their proper names, and tell you what they are. At the foot of the altar the priest says the *confiteor*, a psalm, and other prayers as a preparation. Then he ascends the altar steps—praying as he goes—and says the introit, which is some portion of the holy scripture suitable to the feast of the day. He next says the *Kyrie, Eleison*, which means: "Lord, have mercy on us." He then says the *Gloria*, or hymn of praise, though not in all Masses. After the *Gloria*, he says the collect, which is a collection of prayers in which the priest prays for the needs of the Church, and of its children. This is followed by the epistle, which is a part of the holy scripture. Then the Mass book is removed to the other side of the altar, and the priest reads the gospel—that is, some portion of the gospel written by the evangelists. After the gospel, the priest, except in some Masses, says the Creed, which is a profession of his faith in the mysteries of our religion.

After this, the priest uncovers the chalice, and offers up the bread and wine which is to be consecrated. This is called "the offertory of the Mass." The offertory is followed by the *lavabo*, or washing of the priest's hands: first, that the priest's hands may be purified to touch the sacred host; and, second, to signify the purity of soul he must have to offer the holy sacrifice. After saying some prayers in secret, he says the preface, which is a solemn hymn of praise and thanksgiving. The preface ends with the *Sanctus*. The *Sanctus* is followed by the Canon of the Mass. *Canon* means "a rule"; so this part of the Mass is called "the Canon," because it never changes. The epistle, gospel, prayers, etc., are different on the different feasts, but the Canon of the Mass is always the same. The Canon is the part of the Mass from the *Sanctus* down to the time the priest again covers the chalice. After the Canon, the priest says the post-communion, or prayer after Communion; then he gives the blessing and goes to the other side of the altar, and ends Mass by saying the last gospel.

During the Mass, the priest frequently makes the sign of the cross, genuflects or bends the knee before the altar, strikes his breast, etc. What do all these ceremonies mean? By the cross, the priest is reminded of the death of our Lord; he genuflects as an act of humility, and he strikes his breast to show his own unworthiness. You will understand all the ceremonies of the altar if you remember that our Lord—the King of kings—is present on it, and the priest acts in his presence as the servants in a king's palace would act when approaching their king or in his presence, showing their respect by bowing, kneeling, etc. You will see this more clearly if you watch the movements of the priest at the altar while the Blessed Sacrament is exposed.

LESSON TWENTY-THIRD

On the End for Which the Holy Eucharist Was Instituted

251. **Why did Christ institute the Holy Eucharist?**

Christ instituted the Holy Eucharist:

1. To unite us to himself and to nourish our souls with his divine life.
2. To increase sanctifying grace and all the virtues in our souls.
3. To lessen our evil inclinations.
4. To be a pledge of everlasting life.
5. To fit our bodies for a glorious resurrection.
6. To continue the sacrifice of the cross in his Church.

To nourish. The Holy Eucharist does to our souls what natural food does to our bodies. It strengthens them and makes up for the losses we have sustained by sin, etc. *A pledge*, because it does not seem probable that a person who all during life had been fed and nourished with the sacred body of our Lord should after death be buried in hell. *To fit our bodies*, because our Lord has promised that if we eat his flesh and drink his blood, that is, receive the Holy Eucharist, he will raise us up on the last day, or day of judgment.[91]

[91] Cf. Jn 6:55

252. **How are we united to Jesus Christ in the Holy Eucharist?**
We are united to Jesus Christ in the Holy Eucharist by means of Holy Communion.

253. **What is Holy Communion?**
Holy Communion is the receiving of the body and blood of Christ.

Holy Communion is therefore the receiving of the Sacrament of Holy Eucharist.

254. **What is necessary to make a good Communion?**
To make a good Communion, it is necessary to be in a state of sanctifying grace and to be fasting from midnight.

Midnight—that is, twelve o'clock at night; but you should not take anything, especially solid food, for a little while before twelve, so as to be sure of the time, and also not to have little particles of food in your mouth after twelve. If you find some little pieces of food in your mouth in the morning, when you are going to Holy Communion, spit them out, and your fast will not be broken. One drop of anything taken even in necessity or by mistake after twelve will prevent you from going to Holy Communion. What, then, are you to do if, without thinking, you break your fast? Do not go to Communion that morning, but fast from twelve the next night, and go the following morning. But never, never, on any account go to Holy Communion when you have broken your fast. Never let fear or shame or anything else make you do such a thing. It is no shame to break your fast by mistake; but it is a great sin to knowingly go to Communion after breaking your fast.

255. **Does he who receives Communion in mortal sin receive the body and blood of Christ?**
He who receives Communion in mortal sin receives the body and blood of Christ, but does not receive his grace, and he commits a great sacrilege.

The body and blood, because the appearance of bread and wine is there after consecration, and he receives it. He who receives the Holy Eucharist in mortal sin receives our Lord into a filthy soul. If a great and highly-esteemed friend was coming to visit your house, would you not take care to have everything clean and neat, and pleasing to him? And the greater the dignity of the person coming, the more careful you would be. But what are all the persons of dignity in the world—kings or popes—compared with our Lord, who leaves the beauties of heaven to come to visit our soul? And the purest we can make it is not pure enough for him. But he is kind to us, and is satisfied with our poor preparation if he sees we are doing our very best. But oh, what a shame to receive him into our soul without any preparation! And more horrible still, to fill it with vile sins, that we know are most disgusting to him! No wonder, therefore, that receiving Holy Communion unworthily is so great a crime, and so deserving of God's punishment. Why should not the heavenly Father punish us for treating his beloved Son with such shameful disrespect and contempt?

256. **Is it enough to be free from mortal sin to receive plentifully the graces of Holy Communion?**

To receive plentifully the graces of Holy Communion, it is not enough to be free from mortal sin, but we should be free from all affection to venial sin, and should make acts of lively faith, of firm hope, and ardent love.

257. **What is the fast necessary for Holy Communion?**

The fast necessary for Holy Communion is the abstaining from midnight from everything which is taken as food or drink.

Food or drink. If you swallowed a button, for example, it would not break your fast, because it is not food or drink.

258. **Is anyone ever allowed to receive Holy Communion when not fasting?**

Anyone in danger of death is allowed to receive Communion when not fasting.

Not fasting. But then the Holy Communion is called by another name; it is called the "viaticum," and the priest uses a different prayer in giving it to the sick person. When a person dies, he goes, as it were, on a journey from this world to the next. Now, when persons are going on a journey, they must have food to strengthen them. Our Lord wished, therefore, that all his children who had to go on this most important of all journeys—from this world to the next—should be first strengthened by this sacred food, his own body and blood. The Latin word for road or way is *via*, and *viaticum* therefore means "food for the way." Not only are persons in danger of death allowed to receive when not fasting, but they are obliged to receive; and the priest is obliged under pain of sin to bring Holy Communion to the dying at any hour of the day or night.

When I speak of a great journey from this world to the next, from earth to heaven, you must not understand me to mean that it is a great many miles from earth to heaven, or that it takes a long time to go to the next world. No. We cannot measure the distance, nor does it take time to get there. The instant we die, no matter where that happens, our soul is in the next world, and judged by God.

259. **When are we bound to receive Holy Communion?**

We are bound to receive Holy Communion, under pain of mortal sin, during the Easter time and when in danger of death.

260. **Is it well to receive Holy Communion often?**

It is well to receive Holy Communion often, as nothing is a greater aid to a holy life than often to receive the author of all graces and the source of all good.

261. **What should we do after Holy Communion?**

After Holy Communion, we should spend some time in adoring our Lord, in thanking him for the graces we have received, and in asking him for the blessings we need.

LESSON TWENTY-FOURTH

On the Sacrifice of the Mass

262. **When and where are the bread and wine changed into the body and blood of Christ?**

The bread and wine are changed into the body and blood of Christ at the consecration in the Mass.

263. **What is the Mass?**

The Mass is the unbloody sacrifice of the body and blood of Christ.

The holy sacrifice is called "Mass" probably from the words the priest says at the end when he turns to the people and says, *Ite Missa est*; that is, when he tells them the holy sacrifice is over.

264. **What is a sacrifice?**

A sacrifice is the offering of an object by a priest to God alone, and the consuming of it to acknowledge that he is the Creator and Lord of all things.

Sacrifice. From the very earliest history of man, we find people—for example, Abel, Noe, etc.—offering up sacrifice to God; that is, taking something and offering it to God, and then destroying it to show that they believed God to be the master of life and death, and the supreme Lord of all things. These offerings were sometimes plants or fruits, but most frequently animals.

When men lost the knowledge of the true God and began to worship idols of wood and stone, they began or continued to offer sacrifice to these false gods. Very often, too, they sacrificed human beings to please, as they imagined, these gods. They believed there was a god for everything—a god for the ocean, a god for thunder, a god for wind, for war, etc.; and when anything happened that frightened or injured the people, they believed that some of these gods were offended, and offered up sacrifice to pacify them. They had a temple in Rome called "the Pantheon," or temple of all the gods, and here they kept the idols of all the gods they could think of or know. At Athens, they were afraid of neglecting any god to whom they might thus give offense, and so they had an altar for the unknown god. When St. Paul came to preach, he saw this altar to the unknown god, and told them that was the God he came to preach about.[92] He preached to them the existence of the true God, and showed them that there is only one God and not many gods.

They did not have these idols of wood and stone in their temples for the same reason that we have images in our churches, because they believed that the idols were really gods, and offered sacrifice to them, whereas we know that our images are the works of men. Near the city of Jerusalem, there was a great idol named Molech, to which parents offered their infants in sacrifice. We know, too, from the history of this country that the Indians used to send a beautiful young girl in a white canoe over the falls of Niagara every year, as a sacrifice offered to the god of the falls. Even yet, human sacrifices are offered up on savage islands. Sometimes certain animals were selected to be heathen gods. The people who worship idols, animals, or other things of that kind as gods are called "pagans," "idolaters," or "heathens."

The Israelites, who worshipped the true God and offered him sacrifice, because he made known to them by revelation that they should do so, had four kinds of sacrifice. They offered one for sin, another in thanksgiving for benefits received, another as an act of worship, and another to beg God's blessing. It is just for these four ends or objects we offer up the one Christian Sacrifice of the Holy Mass. In the beginning, the head of the family offered sacrifice—as Noe did when he came out of the ark—but after God gave his laws to Moses, he appointed priests to offer up the sacrifices. Aaron, the brother of Moses, was the first priest appointed; and after him, his descendants were priests. When our Lord came and instituted a new sacrifice, he established the priesthood of the new law, and appointed his own priests, namely, the apostles, with St. Peter as their chief; and after them, their lawfully appointed successors, the bishops of the world, with the pope as their chief. The sacrifices of the old law were figures of the sacrifice of the new law, and were to cease at its institution; and when the ancient sacrifices ceased, the ancient priesthood was at an end.

[92] Cf. Acts 17

265. **Is the Mass the same sacrifice as that of the cross?**

The Mass is the same sacrifice as that of the cross.

But how is the Mass a sacrifice? It is a sacrifice because, at the Mass, the body and blood of our Lord are offered to his heavenly Father at the consecration, and afterward consumed by the priest. In offering up the body and blood of our Lord, the bread and wine are consecrated separately, and kept separate on the altar at Mass to signify their separation at our Lord's death in the sacrifice of the cross, when his sacred blood flowed from his body. The Holy Eucharist is also a sacrament, because it has the three things necessary to constitute a sacrament, namely: 1) The outward sign, that is, the appearance of bread and wine. 2) The inward grace; for it is Jesus Christ himself, the author and dispenser of all graces. 3) It was instituted by our Lord.

The Holy Eucharist is therefore both a sacrifice and a sacrament. It is a sacrifice when offered at Mass, and a sacrament when we receive it and when it is reserved in the tabernacle.

266. **How is the Mass the same sacrifice as that of the cross?**

The Mass is the same sacrifice as that of the cross because the offering and the priest are the same—Christ our Blessed Lord; and the ends for which the Sacrifice of the Mass is offered are the same as those of the sacrifice of the cross.

On the cross, the offering was the body and blood of our Lord; the one who offered it was our Lord; the reason for which he offered it was that he might atone for sin; the one to whom he offered it was his heavenly Father. Now, at Mass it is the same. The object offered is our Lord's body and blood; the one offering is our Lord himself, through the priest; it is offered for sin; and it is offered to the heavenly Father. All things are the same, except that the blood of our Lord is not shed, and our Lord does not die again.

267. **What are the ends for which the sacrifice of the cross was offered?**

The ends for which the sacrifice of the cross was offered were: first, to honor and glorify God; second, to thank him for all the graces bestowed on the whole world; third, to satisfy God's justice for the sins of men; fourth, to obtain all graces and blessings.

268. **Is there any difference between the sacrifice of the cross and the Sacrifice of the Mass?**

Yes; the manner in which the sacrifice is offered is different. On the cross, Christ really shed his blood and was really slain; in the Mass, there is no real shedding of blood nor real death, because Christ can die no more; but the Sacrifice of the Mass, through the separate consecration of the bread and the wine, represents his death on the cross.

269. **How should we assist at Mass?**

We should assist at Mass with great interior recollection and piety and with every outward mark of respect and devotion.

If you were admitted into the presence of a king or of the holy father, you would be careful not to show any indifference or disrespect in his presence. You would not be guilty of looking around or of talking idly to those near you. Your eyes would be constantly fixed on the great person present. So should you be at Mass, for there you are admitted into the presence of the King of kings, our divine Lord. Your whole attention, therefore, should be reverently given to him, and to no other. How displeasing it must be to him to have some in his presence who care so little for him and who insult him without thought or regard! If we acted in the presence of any prince as we sometimes act in the presence of our Lord on the altar, we should be turned out of his house, with orders not to come again. But our Lord suffers all patiently and meekly, though he will not allow any of this disrespect to go unpunished in this world or in the next. Knowing this, some holy persons offer up their prayers and Holy Communions in reparation for these insults, and try to atone for all the insults offered to our Lord in the Blessed Sacrament. They have united in a holy society for this purpose, called "the Apostleship of Prayer" or "League of the Sacred Heart," now established in many parishes. If you do not belong to such a society, you should make such an offering yourself privately.

In the old law, the people brought to the temple whatever they wished the priests to offer up for them—sometimes a lamb, sometimes a dove, sometimes fruit, etc. The offering or sacrifice was theirs, and they offered it up by the hands of the priests. In the early ages of the Church, the

Christians brought to the priests the bread and wine to be consecrated and offered up at Mass. Now, as the bread and wine used at the Mass must be of a particular kind, namely, wheaten bread and wine of the grape, there was some danger of the people not bringing the proper kind: so instead of the people bringing these things themselves, the priests began to buy them, and the people gave him money for his own support; and thus you have the origin of offering money to the priest for celebrating Mass for your intention. The money is not to pay for the Mass, because you could not buy any sacred thing without committing sin. The priest may use the money also for the candles burned, the vestments and sacred vessels, etc., used at the Mass.

To buy a holy thing for money is the sin of simony—so called after Simon, a magician, who tried to bribe the apostles to give him confirmation when he was unworthy of it. To buy religious articles before they are blessed is not simony, nor even after they are blessed, if you pay only for the material of which they are made; but if you tried to buy the blessing, it would be simony. When the Holy Mass is offered, the fruits or benefits of it are divided into four classes. The first benefit comes to the priest who celebrates the Mass; the second, to the one for whom he offers the Mass; the third benefit to those who are present at it; and the fourth to all the faithful throughout the world.

270. **Which is the best manner of hearing Mass?**

The best manner of hearing Mass is to offer it to God with the priest for the same purpose for which it is said, to meditate on Christ's sufferings and death, and to go to Holy Communion.

That is, to offer it up for whatever intention the priest is offering it—for the dead, for the conversion of sinners, for the good of others, etc.; but especially for the four ends of which I have already spoken—to worship God, thank him, etc. *Christ's death*, of which it reminds us. *Holy Communion*, if we are in a state of grace, and have prepared to receive Communion.

You should go to Holy Communion as often as your confessor will allow you, and you should try every day to make yourself more worthy of that great sacrament. Think of it! To receive your God and Savior into your soul, and to be united with him, as the word *communion* means! The early Christians used to go to Communion very frequently. The Church requires us to go to Holy Communion at least once a year, but we should not be satisfied with doing merely what is necessary to avoid mortal sin. Do we try to keep away from persons we love? Then if we really love our Lord, should we not desire to receive him? All good Catholics should go to Holy Communion at least once a month, if possible. Persons wishing to lead truly holy lives should go to Communion every week, if their confessor thinks them worthy and will allow them to go.

When we cannot go really to Communion, we can merit God's grace by making a spiritual Communion. What is a spiritual Communion? It is an earnest desire to receive Communion. You prepare yourself as if you were really going to Communion; you try to imagine yourself going up, receiving the Blessed Sacrament, and returning to your place. Then you thank God for all his blessings to you as you would have done had you received. This is an act of devotion, and one very pleasing to God, as many holy writers tell us.

I cannot leave this lesson on the Holy Eucharist without telling you something of the devotion to the Sacred Heart of Jesus, now so universally practiced and so closely connected with the devotion to the Blessed Sacrament. The Church grants many indulgences, and our Lord himself promises many rewards to those who honor the Sacred Heart. But what do we mean by "the Sacred Heart"? We mean the real natural heart of our Lord, to which his divinity is united as it is to his whole body. But why do we adore this real, natural heart of our Lord? We adore it because love is said to be in the heart, and we wish to return our Lord love and gratitude for the great love he has shown to us in dying for us, and in instituting the sacraments, especially the Holy Eucharist, by which he can remain with us in his sacred humanity. When our Lord appeared to Blessed Margaret Mary, he said: "Behold this Heart, that has loved men so ardently, and is so little loved in return." The first Friday of every month and the whole month of June are dedicated to the Sacred Heart.

LESSON TWENTY-FIFTH

On Extreme Unction and Holy Orders

Unction means "the anointing or rubbing with oil or ointment." *Extreme* means "last." Therefore, *extreme unction* means "the last anointing." It is called the "last" because other unctions or anointings are received before it. We are anointed at baptism on three parts of the body—on the breast, the back, and the head. We are anointed on the forehead at confirmation; and when priests are ordained, they are anointed on the hands. The last time we are anointed is just before death, and it is therefore very properly called "the last anointing," or "extreme unction."

But if the person should not die after being anointed, would it still be called "extreme unction"? Yes; because at the time it was given, it was thought to be the last. It sometimes happens that persons receive extreme unction several times in their lives, because they could receive it every time they were in danger of death by sickness.

Suppose a person should die immediately after being anointed in baptism or confirmation, would the anointing in baptism or confirmation then become extreme unction? No. Because extreme unction is in itself a separate and distinct sacrament—a special anointing with prayers for the sick.

Oil is used in extreme unction—as in confirmation—as a sign of strength; for as the priest applies the holy oil in the sacrament, the grace of the sacrament is taking effect upon the soul. This sacrament was instituted as much for the body as for the soul, as all the prayers said by the priest while administering it indicate. It is given generally after a person has made his confession and received the viaticum, and when his soul is already in a state of grace; showing that it is in a special way intended for the body.

It must be given only in sickness; for although one might be in danger of death, if the danger did not come from within, but from without, he could not be anointed. A soldier in battle, persons being shipwrecked, firemen working at a great fire, etc., could not be anointed, although they are in very great danger of death; because the danger is not from within themselves, but from without. If, however, these persons were so frightened that there was danger of their dying from the fright, they could then be anointed.

271. **What is the sacrament of extreme unction?**

Extreme unction is the sacrament which, through the anointing and prayer of the priest, gives health and strength to the soul, and sometimes to the body, when we are in danger of death from sickness.

Anointing. In this sacrament, the priest anoints all our senses—the eyes, the ears, the nose, the mouth, the hands, and the feet—and, at the same time, prays God to forgive the poor sick person all the sins he has committed by any of these. The eyes, by looking at bad objects or pictures; the ears, by listening to bad conversation; the nose, by indulging too much in sensual pleasures; the mouth, by cursing, lying, bad conversation, backbiting, etc.; the hands, by stealing, fighting, or doing sinful things; the feet, by carrying us to do wrong or to bad places. I told you already nearly all our sins are committed for our body, and the senses are the chief instruments. *Strength to the body*, if it is for our spiritual welfare. If God foresees, as he foresees all things, that after our sickness we shall lead better lives and do penance for our sins, then he may be pleased to restore us to health, and give us an opportunity of making up for our past faults. But if he foresees that after our sickness we would again lead bad lives, and fall perhaps into greater sins, then he will likely take us when we are prepared, and will not restore us again to health. As he always knows and does what is best for his children, we must in sickness always be resigned to his holy will, and be satisfied with what he sees fit to do with us.

272. **When should we receive extreme unction?**

We should receive extreme unction when we are in danger of death from sickness, or from a wound or accident.

273. **Should we wait until we are in extreme danger before we receive extreme unction?**

We should not wait until we are in extreme danger before we receive extreme unction, but if possible, we should receive it whilst we have the use of our senses.

We should always be glad to receive the grace of the sacraments. When, therefore, we are sufficiently ill to be anointed—when there is any danger of death—we should send for the priest at once. If the sick person has any chance of recovering, the sacrament will help him and hasten the recovery; but if the priest is sent for just when the person is in the last agony of death, the person could not recover except by a miracle, and God does not perform miracles for ordinary reasons. If you are in doubt whether the person is sick enough to receive the last sacraments, do not be the judge yourself: send for the priest and let him judge; and then all the responsibility is removed from you in case the person should die without the sacraments. Very often, persons are near death, and their relatives do not know it. The priest, like the doctor, has experience in these cases, and can judge of the danger.

Again, do not foolishly believe, as some seem to do, that if the priest comes to anoint the sick person, it will frighten him by making him think he is going to die. It has never been known that the priest killed anyone by coming to see him; and if these same persons who are now sick receive the sacraments in the church from the very same priest, why should they be afraid to receive them from him in their house? And if they are so near death that a little fright would kill them, then they are surely sick enough to receive the sacraments.

The sick person who is afraid that extreme unction will kill him or hasten his death shows that he has not the proper faith and confidence in God's grace. They who do not wish to receive Holy Communion or the holy viaticum in their houses do not want our Lord to visit them. How ungrateful they are! When our Lord was on earth, the people carried the sick out into the streets to lay them near him that he might cure them. Now, he does not require us to do that, but comes himself to the sick in the most humble manner, and they refuse to receive him. See how ungrateful, therefore, and how wanting in faith and devotion such persons are! If the sick person is one who has been careless about his religion, and has for some time neglected to receive the sacraments, do not wait for him to ask for the priest or for his consent to send for him.

Few persons ever believe they are so near death as they really are: they are afraid to think of their past lives, and do not like to send for the priest, or at least they put off doing so, frequently till it is too late. The devil tempts them to put off the reception of the sacraments, in hopes that they may die without them, and be his forever. In these cases, speak to the sick man quietly and gently, and ask him if he would not like to have the priest come and say a few prayers for his recovery. Do not say anything about the sacraments if you are afraid he will refuse. Simply bring the priest to the sick man, and he will attend to all the rest. Even if the person should refuse—if he has been baptized in the Catholic religion—send for the priest and explain to him the circumstances and dispositions of the sick man. It would be terrible to let such persons die without the sacraments if there is any possibility of their receiving them. Even when they refuse to see the priest, it generally happens that after he has once visited them, talked to them, and explained the benefits of the sacraments, they are better pleased than anyone else to see him coming again.

Sometimes it is God's goodness that sends sickness to such persons, to bring them back to his worship and the practice of their religion. What does a good father generally do with an unruly child? He advises and warns it, and when words have no effect, punishes it with the rod, not because he wishes to see it suffer, but for its good, that it may give up its evil habits and become an obedient, loving child. In like manner, God warns sinners by their conscience, by sermons they hear, by accidents or deaths around about them, etc.; and when none of these things have any effect on them, he sends them some affliction—he brings them to a bed of sickness. He punishes them, as it were, with a rod. This he does, not that he may see them suffer, but for their good; that they may understand he is their master, the only one who can give them health; that all the doctors and all the friends and money in the world could not save them if he determined that they should die. Then they come to know that the world is not their friend; then they see things as they really are, and begin to think of the next world, of eternity, etc. Thus, they again turn to God and to the practices of religion. Many persons who reform and begin to lead good lives in sickness would never have changed if God had left them always in good health.

But you must not think that all who are sick are so on account of sin. Sometimes very holy persons are in a state of sickness, and then it is sent them that they may bear it patiently, and have great merit before God for their sufferings, and thus become more holy. Again, very small children who have never sinned are sick, and then it is perhaps that their parents may have merit for patiently taking care of them. I say only that God sometimes sends sickness to persons living in sin for the purpose of bringing them back to a better way of living, and, in that case, their sickness is for them a great mercy from God, who might have allowed them to continue in sin till his judgments and condemnation came suddenly upon them.

274. **Which are the effects of the sacrament of extreme unction?**

The effects of extreme unction are: first, to comfort us in the pains of sickness and to strengthen us against temptations; second, to remit venial sins and to cleanse our soul from the remains of sin; third, to restore us to health when God sees fit.

275. **What do you mean by "the remains of sin"?**

By "the remains of sin," I mean the inclination to evil and the weakness of the will, which are the result of our sins and which remain after our sins have been forgiven.

Remains of sin—that is, chiefly the bad habits we have acquired by sin. If a person does a thing very often, he soon begins to do it very easily, and it becomes, as we say, a habit. So, too, a person who sins very much soon begins to sin easily. This sacrament therefore takes away the ease in sinning, and the desire for past sins acquired by frequently committing them.

276. **How should we receive the sacrament of extreme unction?**

We should receive the sacrament of extreme unction in a state of grace, and with lively faith and resignation to the will of God.

277. **Who is the minister of the sacrament of extreme unction?**

The priest is the minister of the sacrament of extreme unction.

The sacraments that the priest administers in the house are the sacraments for the sick; namely, penance, viaticum, or Holy Communion, and extreme unction. The other sacraments may be administered there in special cases of necessity. You should know what things are to be prepared when the priest comes to administer the sacraments in your house. They are as follows: a small table covered with a clean white cloth, and on it a crucifix and one or two lighted candles in candlesticks; some holy water in a small vessel, with a sprinkler which you can make by tying together a few leaves or small pieces of palm; a glass of clean water, a tablespoon, and a napkin for the sick person to hold under the chin while receiving; also, a piece of white cotton wadding, if the priest should ask for it.

Then you may have ready in another place near at hand some water, a towel, and a piece of bread or lemon for purifying the priest's fingers; but these things are not always necessary: still, it would be better to have them ready in case the priest should require them, so as not to keep him waiting. Every good Catholic family should have all these things put away carefully in the house. It would be well, though it is not necessary, to keep a special spoon, napkin, etc., for that purpose alone. Sometimes persons are taken ill very suddenly in the night, and when the priest comes, they have none of the things they should have; and if their neighbors are as careless as themselves, they will not have them either: so the priest is delayed in giving the sacraments, or is obliged to administer them in a way that is almost disrespectful to our Lord. If we would make such preparations for the coming of a friend to our house, why should we be so careless when our Lord comes? If a friend comes when we are not prepared to receive him, we feel very much ashamed, and make a thousand excuses for our want of thought. Therefore, provide the things necessary for the administration of these sacraments in your house, and keep them though they may be seldom if ever required in your family.

When our Lord comes to visit your house, receive him with all possible respect and reverence. Some good Catholics have the very praiseworthy practice of meeting the priest at the door with a lighted candle when he carries the Blessed Sacrament, and of going before him to the sickroom. This can be done where there is only one family living in the house, or at least in the apartment. All who can do this should do it, because it is in keeping with the wish of the Church. In olden times, and even now in Catholic countries, the priest brings the Blessed Sacrament in procession to the sick. He goes vested as for benediction, accompanied by altar boys with lighted candles and bells. The people kneel by the way as our Lord passes. Our Lord is carried in procession always in the church on the feast of Corpus Christi, on Holy Thursday, and during the devotion of Forty Hours. The Church would like to have this solemn procession in honor of our Lord every time the Blessed Sacrament is brought from one place to another. But this cannot always be done in the streets, because there are many persons not Catholics who would insult our Lord while passing along; and in order to prevent this, the priest brings the Blessed Sacrament to the dying without any outward display. But we should always remember the very great respect due to our Lord, and do all we can to show it when possible.

278. **What is the sacrament of holy orders?**

Holy orders is a sacrament by which bishops, priests, and other ministers of the Church are ordained and receive the power and grace to perform their sacred duties.

Other ministers, means deacons and subdeacons, properly so-called. When a young man goes to study for the priesthood—after he has discovered that God has called him to that sacred office—he passes several years in learning what is necessary, and in fitting himself for his sacred duties. After some time, he receives what is called "tonsure"; that is, on the day of ordination, the bishop cuts a little hair from five places on his head, to show that this young man is giving himself up to God. The tonsure is a mark of the clerical state, and, in Catholic countries, it is made manifest by keeping a small circular spot on the crown of the head shaved perfectly clean. It reminds the cleric or priest of having dedicated himself to God, and also of the crown of thorns worn by our Blessed Savior. For this last reason, some of the holy monks shaved all the hair from their head, with the exception of a little ring, which resembles very much a wreath or crown of hair encircling the head. You often see them thus represented in holy pictures.

After the young student has received the tonsure and studied for a longer time, he receives the four minor orders, by which he is permitted to touch the sacred vessels of the altar, and do certain things about the church which laymen have not the right to do, especially to serve Mass. After more preparation, he becomes a subdeacon, and then he may wear vestments and assist the celebrant at Solemn Mass. At a Solemn Mass, there are three priests in vestments. The priest standing on the platform of the altar and celebrating Mass is called the "celebrant"; the one who stands just behind him, generally one step lower, is called the "deacon"; and the one who stands behind the deacon and on the lowest step is called the "subdeacon." The one who directs the whole ceremony, and gives signs to the others when to stand, sit down, or kneel, is called the "master of ceremonies."

When speaking of the Mass, I forgot to tell you something about the different kinds of Masses—that is, different as far as the ceremonies are concerned, for they are all alike in value. First, we have the Low Mass, such as the priest says every day and at the early hours on Sundays. It is called "low," because there is no display in ceremony about it. Next, we have the High Mass—called *Missa Cantata* (Sung)—at which the priest and choir sing in turn. Lastly, we have the Solemn High Mass, at which we have three ministers or priests, and singing by both ministers and choir, as well as all the ceremonies prescribed by the Church. When any of these Masses are said in black vestments, they are called "Requiem Masses," because the priest offers them for the rest or happy repose of the soul of some dead person or persons, and the word *requiem* means "rest." Vespers is a portion of the divine office of the Church. It is sung generally on Sunday afternoon or evening in the church, and is usually followed by benediction of the Blessed Sacrament. It is not a mortal sin to stay from vespers on Sundays, even willfully, because there is no law of the Church obliging you to attend. Nevertheless, all good Catholics will attend vespers when possible.

To continue about the ministers of the Church: when the subdeacon is ordained a deacon, he can wear still more of the priestly vestments, and also baptize solemnly, preach, and give Holy Communion. After a time, the deacon is ordained a priest, and receives power to celebrate Mass and forgive sins. If, afterward, the priest should be selected by the holy father to be a bishop, he is consecrated; and then he has power to administer confirmation and holy orders, ordaining priests and consecrating bishops. Thus you see there are grades through which the ministers of the Church must pass. First the tonsure, then minor orders, then subdeaconship, then deaconship, then priesthood. Nuns, sisters, brothers, etc., are not, as some might think, ministers of the Church, because they have never received any of the holy orders.

The ordained ministers of the Church can perform the duties of any office for which they have ever been ordained, but not the duties of any office above that to which they have been ordained. For example, a subdeacon cannot take the place of a deacon at Mass, nor a deacon the place of a priest; but a priest may take either of their places, because he has, at one time, been ordained to both these offices.

Altar boys should never forget that they are enjoying a very great privilege in being allowed to take the place of an ordained minister of the Church, and serve Mass without being ordained acolytes. In olden times, princes and noblemen used to seek for this wonderful favor, and count themselves happy if they secured it. Think of it! To stand so near our Blessed Lord that they are able to see his sacred body resting upon the altar, and to offer the wine, which a few minutes later is changed into his very blood!

279. **What is necessary to receive holy orders worthily?**

To receive holy orders worthily, it is necessary to be in the state of grace, to have the necessary knowledge, and a divine call to this sacred office.

Knowledge—that is, to be able to learn and to have learned all that a priest should know.

Divine call, explained before in the explanation of vocation, a word that means "call."[93]

280. **How should Christians look upon the priests of the Church?**

Christians should look upon the priests of the Church as the messengers of God and the dispensers of his mysteries.

Messengers. Our Lord said to his apostles: "As the Father sent me, I also send you."[94] That is, as the heavenly Father sent his beloved Son, our Lord, into the world to save men's souls, so our Lord sends his apostles and their successors through the world to save souls. God told the priests of the old law that if they did not warn the people of coming dangers, they would be held responsible for the people; but if they warned the people and the

[93] See Lesson Sixth, Question 51.

[94] Jn 20:21

people did not heed, then the people would be responsible for their own destruction. So, too, in the new law, the priests warn you against sin, and if you do not heed the warning, the loss of your soul will be upon yourself. Therefore, you should take every warning coming from the ministers of God as you would from himself, for it is really God that warns you against sin, and the priests are only his agents or instruments. *Dispensers*—that is, those who administer the sacraments.

281. **Who can confer the sacrament of holy orders?**

Bishops can confer the sacrament of holy orders.

Confer—that is, give or administer. So can a cardinal, if he be a bishop, and so can the holy father, who is always a bishop, and called "bishop of Rome," while pope of the whole Church. It will be well here to give some explanation about cardinals—who they are, and what they do. In the United States, the president has about him seven or eight prominent men selected by himself, and called his "cabinet." They are his advisers; he consults them on all important matters, and assigns to them various duties. The holy father, who is also a ruler—a spiritual ruler—not of one country, but of the whole world, has also a cabinet, but it is not called by that name: it is called the "sacred college of cardinals." There are seventy cardinals, to whom the pope assigns various works in helping him to govern the Church. Some of these cardinals are in different parts of the world; as our own Cardinal Gibbons here in America. There are cardinals in England, France, Germany, Canada, Spain, etc., but a certain number always remain in Rome with the holy father. When a bishop or priest is made cardinal, he is raised in dignity in the Church, but he does not receive any greater spiritual power than he had when only a bishop or priest. The cardinals, owing to their high dignity, have many privileges which bishops have not. Their greatest privilege is to take part in the election of a new pope when the reigning pope dies.

The pope dresses in white, the cardinals in red, the bishops in purple, and the priests and other ministers in black. A "monsignor" is also a title of dignity granted by our holy father to some worthy priests. It gives them certain privileges, and the right to wear purple like a bishop. The "vicar-general" is one who is appointed by the bishop in the diocese, and shares his power. In the bishop's absence, he acts as bishop in all temporal and worldly matters, and also in some spiritual things, concerning the diocese. A diocese is the extent of country over which a bishop is appointed to rule, as a parish is the extent over which a pastor is appointed to administer the sacraments and rule under the direction of the bishop. Pastors are also called "rectors." *Pastor* means "a shepherd," and *rector* means "a ruler"; and as all pastors rule their flocks, *pastor* and *rector* mean about the same.

An archbishop is higher than a bishop, though he has no more spiritual power than a bishop. The district over which an archbishop rules contains several dioceses with their bishops, and is called an "ecclesiastical province." The bishops in the province are called "suffragan bishops," because subject in some things to the authority of the archbishop, who is also called "the metropolitan," because bishop of a metropolis or chief city of the province over which he presides.

The archbishop can wear the pallium, a garment worn by the pope, and sent by him to patriarchs, primates, and archbishops. It is a band of white wool, worn over the shoulders and around the neck after the manner of a stole. It has two strings of the same material and four black or purple crosses worked upon it. It is the symbol of the plenitude of pastoral jurisdiction conferred by the Holy See. Morally speaking, it reminds the wearer how the good shepherd seeks the lost sheep and brings it home upon his shoulders, and how the loving pastor of souls should seek those spiritually lost and bring them back to the Church, the true fold of Christ.

LESSON TWENTY-SIXTH

On Matrimony

282. **What is the sacrament of matrimony?**

The sacrament of matrimony is the sacrament which unites a Christian man and woman in lawful marriage.

Christian, because if they are not Christians, they do not receive the grace of the sacrament.

283. **Can a Christian man and woman be united in lawful marriage in any other way than by the sacrament of matrimony?**
A Christian man and woman cannot be united in lawful marriage in any other way than by the sacrament of matrimony, because Christ raised marriage to the dignity of a sacrament.

Lawful. Persons are lawfully married when they comply with all the laws of God and of the Church relating to marriage. To marry unlawfully is a mortal sin, in which the persons must remain till the sin is forgiven. *Sacrament.* Before the coming of our Lord, persons were married as they are now, and even lawfully according to the laws of the old testament or old religion; but marriage did not give them any grace. Now it does give grace, because it is a sacrament, and has been so since the time of our Lord. Before his coming, it was only a contract, and when he added grace to the contract, it became a sacrament.

284. **Can the bond of Christian marriage be dissolved by any human power?**
The bond of Christian marriage cannot be dissolved by any human power.

Dissolved—that is, can married persons ever—for any cause—separate and marry again; that is, take another husband or wife while the first husband or wife is living? Never, if they were really married. Sometimes, for good reason, the Church permits husband and wife to separate and live in different places; but they are still married. Sometimes it happens, too, that persons are not really married although they have gone through the ceremony and people think they are married, and they may think so themselves. The Church, however, makes them separate, because it finds they are not really married at all—on account of some impeding circumstance that existed at the time they performed the ceremony.

These circumstances or facts that prevent the marriage from being valid are called "impediments to marriage." Some of them render the marriage altogether null, and some only make it unlawful.

When persons make arrangements about getting married, they should tell the priest every circumstance that they think might be an impediment. Here are the chief things they should tell the priest—privately, if possible: whether both are Christians and Catholics; whether either has ever been solemnly engaged to another person; whether they have ever made any vow to God with regard to chastity, the religious life, or the like; whether they are related and in what degree; whether either was ever married to any member of the other's family—say sister, brother, or cousin, etc.; whether either ever was godparent in baptism for the other or for any of the other's children; whether either was married before, and what proof can be given of the death of the first husband or wife; whether they really intend to get married; whether they are of lawful age; whether they are in good health or suffering from some sickness that might prevent their marriage, etc. They should also state whether they live in the parish, and how long they have lived in it. They should give at least three weeks' notice before their marriage, except in special cases of necessity. They should not presume to make final arrangements and invite friends before they have made arrangements with their pastor; because if there should be any delay on account of impediments, it would cause them great inconvenience.

Let me take an example of a fact that would render the marriage invalid or null, though the persons performing the ceremony might not be aware of it. Suppose a woman's husband went to the war, and she heard after a great many years that he had been killed in battle, and she, believing her first husband to be dead, married another man. But the report of the first husband's death turns out to be false, and, after a time, he returns. Then the Church tells the woman—and she knows it now herself—that the second marriage was invalid, that is, no marriage, because it was performed while the first husband was still living. She must leave the second man and go back to her husband. You see in that case the Church was not dissolving or breaking the marriage bond, but only declaring that the woman and second man were not married from the very beginning, although they thought they were, being ignorant of the existing impediment, and the priest, also being deceived, performed the ceremony in the usual manner. If it ever happens, therefore, that you hear of the Church permitting persons, already apparently married, to separate and marry others, it is only when it discovers that their first marriage was invalid; and, by its action, it does not dissolve the bond of marriage, but simply declares that the marriage was null and void from the beginning, as you now easily understand. Thus, persons might unwittingly marry with existing impediments that would render their marriage invalid or illicit. Such things, however, happen very rarely, for the priest would discover the impediments in questioning the persons about to marry.

Protestants and persons outside the Catholic Church teach that the marriage bond can at times be dissolved, but such doctrines bring great evils upon society. When the father and mother separate and marry again, the children of the first marriage are left to take care of themselves, or receive only such care as the law gives them. They are left without Christian instruction and the good influence of home. Then persons who are divorced once may be divorced a second or third time, and thus all society would be thrown into a state of confusion, and there would be scarcely any such thing as a family to be found. It is bad enough at present, on account of divorces granted by the laws and upheld by protestants: and only for the influence and good public opinion created by the teaching and opposition of the Catholic Church, it would be much worse. Again, if husbands and wives could separate for this or that fault, they would not be careful in making their choice of the person they wish to marry, nor would their motives be always holy and worthy of the sacrament.

285. **Which are the effects of the sacrament of matrimony?**

The effects of the sacrament of matrimony are: first, to sanctify the love of husband and wife; second, to give them grace to bear with each other's weaknesses; third, to enable them to bring up their children in the fear and love of God.

The union and love existing between a husband and wife should be like the union and love existing between our Lord and his Church. The grace of the sacrament helps them to have such a love. *Weaknesses*—that is, their faults, bad dispositions, etc. *Bring up their children.* This is their most important duty, and parents receive grace to perform it, and woe be to them if they abuse that grace!

Children should remember that their parents have received this special grace from God to advise, direct, and warn them of sin; and if they refuse to obey their parents or despise their direction, they are despising God's grace. Remember that nothing teaches us so well as experience. Now your parents, even if God gave them no special grace, have experience. They have been children as you are; they have been young persons as you are; they have received advice from their parents and teachers as you do. If your parents are bad, it is because they have not heeded the advice given them. If they are good, it is because they have heeded and followed it. The years of your youth quickly pass, and you will soon be thrown out into the world among strangers to provide for yourselves, and will perhaps have no one to advise you. If you neglect to learn while you have the opportunity, you will be sorry for it in afterlife. If you waste your time in school, you will leave it knowing very little, and an ignorant man can never take any good position in the world; he can seldom be his own master and independent; he must always toil for others as a servant. God gives us our talents and opportunities that we may use them to the best of our ability, and he will hold us accountable for these.

It is good and praiseworthy to raise ourselves and others in the world if we do so by lawful and proper means. You may have the opportunity of getting a good position, and will not be able to take it because you are not sufficiently educated. Many young men live to be sorry for wasting time in school, and try to make up for it by studying at night. You cannot really make up for lost time. Every moment God gives you he gives for some particular work, and he will require an account from you, at the last day, for the use you made of your time. Besides, you can learn with greater ease while you are young.

But what shall I say of neglecting to learn your holy religion? If you neglect your school lessons, you will not be successful in the world as businessmen or professional men; but if you neglect your religious lessons, you will be miserable, not merely in this world, but in the next, and that for all eternity. Again, will you not feel ashamed to say you are a Catholic when persons who are not Catholics ask you the meaning of something you believe or do, and you will not be able to answer? When they tell falsehoods against your religion, you will not, on account of your ignorance, be able to refute them. Almost the only time you have to learn the truths and practices of your holy religion is during the instructions at Sunday school or day school, and, after a few years, you will not have this advantage. When you grow up, you may hear a sermon, and if you attend early Mass, only a short instruction, on Sundays; and if you do not know your catechism, you will be less able to profit by the instructions given. Therefore, the time to learn is while you are young, have sufficient leisure, and good, willing teachers to explain whatever you do not understand.

When you attend Sunday school, bear in mind that your teachers have frequently to sacrifice their time or pleasure for your sake, and that you should not repay them for their kindness by acts of disobedience, disrespect, and stubbornness. By spending your time in idleness, in giving annoyance to your teacher, and in distracting others who are willing to learn, you show a want of appreciation and gratitude for the blessings God has bestowed upon you, and please the devil exceedingly; and as God will hold you accountable for all his gifts, this one—the opportunity of learning your religion—will be no exception.

286. **To receive the sacrament of matrimony worthily, is it necessary to be in the state of grace?**

To receive the sacrament of matrimony worthily, it is necessary to be in the state of grace, and it is necessary also to comply with the laws of the Church.

The laws, laws concerning marriage. Laws forbidding the solemnizing of marriage at certain times, namely, Advent and Lent; laws forbidding marriage with relatives, or with persons of a different religion or of no religion; laws with regard to age, etc.

287. **Who has the right to make laws concerning the sacrament of marriage?**

The Church alone has the right to make laws concerning the sacrament of marriage, though the state also has the right to make laws concerning the civil effects of the marriage contract.

Civil effects—that is, laws with regard to the property of persons marrying, with regard to the inheritance of the children, with regard to the debts of husband and wife, etc.

288. **Does the Church forbid the marriage of Catholics with persons who have a different religion or no religion at all?**

The Church does forbid the marriage of Catholics with persons who have a different religion or no religion at all.

289. **Why does the Church forbid the marriage of Catholics with persons who have a different religion or no religion at all?**

The Church forbids the marriage of Catholics with persons who have a different religion or no religion at all, because such marriages generally lead to indifference, loss of faith, and to the neglect of the religious education of the children.

We know that nothing has so bad an influence upon people as bad company. Now, when a Catholic marries one who is not a Catholic, he or she is continually associated with one who in most cases ignores the true religion, or speaks at least with levity of its devotions and practices. The Catholic party may resist this evil influence for a time, but will, if not very steadfast in the faith, finally yield to it, and, tired of numerous disputes in defense of religious rights, will become more and more indifferent, gradually give up the practice of religion, and probably terminate with complete loss of faith or apostasy from the true religion. We know that the children of Seth were good till they married the children of Cain, and then they also became wicked; for, remember, there is always more likelihood that the bad will pervert the good, than that the good will convert the bad. Besides the disputes occasioned between husband and wife by the diversity of their religion, their families and relatives, being also of different religions, will seldom be at peace or on friendly terms with one another. Then the children can scarcely be brought up in the true religion; for the father may wish them to attend one church, and the mother another, and to settle the dispute, they will attend neither. Besides, if they have before them the evil example of a father or mother speaking disparagingly of the true religion, or perhaps ridiculing all religion, it is not likely they will be imbued with great respect and veneration for holy things.

There is still another reason why Catholics should dread mixed marriages. If the one who is not a Catholic loses regard for his or her obligations, becomes addicted to any vice, and is leading a bad life, the Catholic party has no means of reaching the root of the evil, no hope that the person may take the advice of the priest, or go to confession, or do any of those things that could effect a change in the heart and life of a Catholic. For all these very good reasons and others besides, the Church opposes mixed marriages, as they are called when one of the persons is not a Catholic. Neither does the Church want persons to become converts simply for the sake of marrying a Catholic. Such conversions are, as a rule, not sincere, and do no good, but rather make such converts hypocrites, and guilty of greater sin.

290. **Why do many marriages prove unhappy?**
Many marriages prove unhappy because they are entered into hastily and without worthy motives.

Hastily—without knowing the persons well or considering their character or dispositions; without trying to discover whether they are sober, industrious, virtuous, and the like; whether they know and practice their religion, or whether, on the contrary, they are given to vices forbidden by good morals, and totally forgetful of their religious duties. In a word, those wishing to marry should look for enduring qualities in their lifelong companions, and not for characteristics that please the fancy for the time being. They should, besides, truly love each other. Again, the persons should be nearly equals in education, social standing, etc., for it helps greatly to secure harmony between their families and unity of thought and action between themselves.

Worthy motives. The motives are worthy when persons marry to fulfill the end for which God instituted marriage. It would, for example, be an unworthy motive to marry solely for money, property, or other advantage, without any regard for the holiness and end of the sacrament. There are many motives that may present themselves to the minds of persons wishing to marry, and they will know whether they are worthy or unworthy, good or bad, if by serious consideration they weigh them well and value them by their desire to please God and lead a good life.

Every person's motive in getting married or in entering into any new state of life should be that he may be able to serve God better in that state than in any other.

291. **How should Christians prepare for a holy and happy marriage?**
Christians should prepare for a holy and happy marriage by receiving the sacraments of penance and Holy Eucharist; by begging God to grant them

a pure intention and to direct their choice; and by seeking the advice of their parents and the blessing of their pastors.

They should pray for a long time that they may make a good choice. They would do well to read in the holy scripture, in the book of Tobias,[95] of the happy marriage of Tobias and Sara, and how they spent their time in prayer both before and after their marriage, and how God rewarded them. Advice is very necessary, as marriage is to last for life, and is to make persons either happy or miserable. They should ask advice from prudent persons, and should try to learn something of the former life of the one they wish to marry. They should know something about the family, whether its members are respectable or not, etc. It is an injustice to parents for sons or daughters to marry into families that may have been disgraced, or that may bring disgrace upon them. Sometimes, however, parents are unreasonable in this matter: they are proud or vain, and want to suit themselves rather than their children. Sometimes, too, they force marriage upon their children, or forbid it for purely worldly or selfish motives. In such cases, and indeed in all cases, the best one to consult and ask advice from is your confessor. He has only your spiritual interests at heart, and will set aside all worldly motives. If your parents are unreasonable, he will be a just judge in the matter, and tell you how to act.

I have now explained all the sacraments, but before finishing, I must say a word about the holy oils. We have seen that oil is used in the administration of some sacraments. There are three kinds of oil blessed by the bishop on Holy Thursday, namely, oil for anointing the sick, called "oil of the infirm"; oil to be used in baptism and in the ordination of priests, called "oil of catechumens" (catechumens are those who are being instructed for baptism); the third kind of oil is used also in baptism, in confirmation, and when the bishop blesses the sacred vessels, altars, etc.; it is called "holy chrism." Therefore, the sacraments in which oil is used are: baptism, in which two kinds are used; confirmation, extreme unction, and holy orders.

[95] Cf. Tb 8

LESSON TWENTY-SEVENTH

On the Sacramentals

292. **What is a sacramental?**

A sacramental is anything set apart or blessed by the Church to excite good thoughts and to increase devotion, and, through these movements of the heart, to remit venial sin.

It is not the sacramental itself that gives grace, but the devotion, the love of God, or sorrow for sin that it inspires. For example, a person comes into the church and goes around the stations of the cross. The stations are a sacramental. In looking at one station, he sees our Lord on trial before Pilate; in another, he sees him crowned with thorns; in another, scourged; in another, carrying his cross; in another, crucified; in another, dead and laid in the tomb. Before all these pictures, he reflects on the sufferings of our Savior, and begins to hate sin that caused them. Then he thinks of his own sins, and begins to be sorry for them. This sorrow, caused by going around the stations, brings him grace that remits venial sins. When we receive the sacraments, we always get the grace of the sacraments when we are rightly disposed; but in using the sacramentals, the more devotion we have, the more grace we receive.

Increase devotion. If we knelt down before a plain white wall, we could not pray with the devotion we would have kneeling before a crucifix. We see the representation of the nails in the hands and feet, the blood on the side, the thorns on the head; and all these must make us think of our Lord's terrible sufferings. The picture of a friend hanging before us will often make us think of him when we would otherwise forget him. So also will the pictures of our Lord and of the saints keep them often in our minds.

293. **What is the difference between the sacraments and the sacramentals?**

The difference between the sacraments and the sacramentals is: first, the sacraments were instituted by Jesus Christ, and the sacramentals were instituted by the Church; second, the sacraments give grace of themselves when we place no obstacle in the way; the sacramentals excite in us pious dispositions by means of which we may obtain grace.

The Church can increase or diminish the number of the sacramentals, but not the number of the sacraments.

294. **Which is the chief sacramental used in the Church?**

The chief sacramental used in the Church is the sign of the cross.

295. **How do we make the sign of the cross?**

We make the sign of the cross by putting the right hand to the forehead, then on the breast, and then to the left and right shoulders, saying, "In the name of the Father, and of the Son, and of the Holy Ghost. Amen."

It is important to make an exact cross, and to say all the words distinctly. From carelessness and habit, some persons do not make the sign of the cross, though they often intend to bless themselves. They put the hand only to the forehead and breast, or forehead and chin, or forehead and shoulders, etc. Some do not even touch the forehead. All these, it is true, are some signs and movements of the hand, but they are not the sign of the cross. Therefore, from childhood, form the good habit of blessing yourself correctly, and you will continue to do it properly all your life.

296. **Why do we make the sign of the cross?**

We make the sign of the cross to show that we are Christians and to profess our belief in the chief mysteries of our religion.

The cross is the banner or standard of Christianity, just as the stars and stripes—the flag of the United States—is our civil standard, and shows to what nation we belong.

297. **How is the sign of the cross a profession of faith in the chief mysteries of our religion?**

The sign of the cross is a profession of faith in the chief mysteries of our religion, because it expresses the mysteries of the unity and trinity of God and of the incarnation and death of our Lord.

298. **How does the sign of the cross express the mystery of the unity and trinity of God?**
The words, "In the name," express the unity of God; the words that follow, "of the Father, and of the Son, and of the Holy Ghost," express the mystery of the trinity.

299. **How does the sign of the cross express the mystery of the incarnation and death of our Lord?**
The sign of the cross expresses the mystery of the incarnation by reminding us that the Son of God, having become man, suffered death on the cross.

Besides these chief mysteries, we will find, if we think a little, that the sign of the cross reminds us of many other things. It reminds us of the sin of our first parents, which made the cross necessary; it reminds us of the hatred God bears to sin, when such sufferings were endured to make satisfaction for it; it reminds us of Christ's love, etc.

300. **What other sacramental is in very frequent use?**
Another sacramental in very frequent use is holy water.

301. **What is holy water?**
Holy water is water blessed by the priest with solemn prayer to beg God's blessing on those who use it, and protection from the power of darkness.

The priest prays that those who use this water may not fall into sin; may be free from the power of the devil and from bodily diseases, etc. Therefore, when they do use the water, they get the benefit of all these prayers, because the priest says: "If they use it, God grant them all these things."

302. **Are there any other sacramentals besides the sign of the cross and holy water?**
Besides the sign of the cross and holy water, there are many other sacramentals, such as blessed candles, ashes, palms, crucifixes, images of the Blessed Virgin and of the saints, rosaries, and scapulars.

Candles, blessed on the feast of the Purification of the Blessed Virgin.[96] The Church blesses whatever it uses. Some say beautifully that the wax of the candle gathered by the bees from sweet flowers reminds us of our Lord's pure, human body, and that the flame reminds us of his divinity. Again, candles about the altar remind us of the angels, those bright spirits ever about God's throne; they remind us, too, of the persecution of the Christians in the first ages of the Church, when they had to hear Mass and receive the sacraments in dark places, where lights were necessary that priests and people might see. Again, lights are a beautiful ornament for the altar, and in keeping with holy things. Lights are a sign of joy: hence the very old custom of lighting bonfires to express joy. So, we have lights to express our joy at the celebration of the Holy Mass. Again, if we wish to honor any great person in the Church or state, we illuminate the city for his reception. So, too, we illuminate our altars and churches for the reception of our Lord, that we may honor him when he comes in the Holy Sacrifice of the Mass, and is present at benediction.

Ashes are placed on our heads by the priest on Ash Wednesday, while he says: "Remember, man, thou art but dust, and unto dust thou shalt return." They are a sign of penance, and so we use them at the beginning of Lent.

Palms, to remind us of our Lord's coming in triumph into Jerusalem, when the people out of respect for him threw palms, and even their garments, beneath his feet on the way, singing his praises and wishing to make him king. Yet these same people only one week later were among those who crucified him. Do we not also at times honor our Lord, call him our King, and shortly afterward insult and, as far as we can, injure him by sin? Do we not say in the Our Father, "Hallowed, or praised, be his name," and blaspheme it ourselves?

Crucifix, if it has an image of our Lord upon it; if not, it is simply a cross, because *crucifix* means "fixed to the cross."

Images—that is, statues, pictures, etc.

Rosaries, called also the "beads." The rosary or beads is a very old and very beautiful form of prayer. In the beginning, pious people, we are told, used to say a certain number of prayers, and keep count of them on a string

[96] See Butler's *Lives of the Saints*, Feb. 2nd, feast of the Purification.

with knots or beads. However that may be, the rosary, as we now have it, comes down to us from St. Dominic. He instructed the people by it, and converted many heretics. In the rosary beads, there are fifty-three small beads on which we say the Hail Mary and six large beads on which we say the Our Father. In saying the rosary, before saying the Our Father on the large beads, we think or meditate for a while on some event in the life of our Lord, and these events we call mysteries of the rosary. There are fifteen of these events taken in the order in which they occurred in the life of our Lord; and hence there are fifteen mysteries in the whole rosary.

Joyful mysteries.—First, we have the five joyful mysteries.

1. The annunciation that is, the angel Gabriel coming to tell the Blessed Virgin that she is to be the Mother of God.

2. The visitation, when the Blessed Virgin went to visit her cousin St. Elizabeth—the mother of St. John the Baptist, who was six months older than our Lord. Elizabeth said to her, "Blessed art thou amongst women, and blessed is the fruit of thy womb"; and the Blessed Virgin answered her in the beautiful words of the *Magnificat*, that we sing at vespers while the priest incenses the altar.

3. The nativity, or birth of our Lord, which reminds us how he was born in a stable, in poverty and lowliness.

4. The presentation of the Child Jesus in the Temple. According to the law of Moses, the people were obliged to bring the first boy born in every family to the Temple in Jerusalem and offer him to God. Then they gave some offering to buy him back, as it were, from God. The Blessed Virgin and St. Joseph, who kept all the laws, took our Lord and offered him in the Temple, although he himself was the Lord of the Temple. Nevertheless, others did not know this, and the Blessed Virgin and St. Joseph observed the laws, though not bound to do so, that their neighbors might not be scandalized in seeing them neglect these things. They did not know, as she did, that the little infant was the Son of God, and need not keep the law of Moses or any law, because he was the maker of the laws. We should learn from this never to give scandal; and even when we have good excuse for not observing the law, we should observe it for the sake of good example to others; or at least, when we can, we should explain why we do not observe the law.

5. The fifth joyful mystery is the finding of the Child Jesus in the Temple. All the men and boys, from twelve years of age upward, were obliged, according to the old laws, to go up to Jerusalem and offer sacrifice on the great feasts. On one of these feasts, the Blessed Virgin, St. Joseph, and our Lord went to Jerusalem. When his parents and their friends were returning home, our Lord was missing. He had not accompanied them from the city. Then the Blessed Virgin and St. Joseph went back to Jerusalem and sought him with great sorrow for three days. At the end of that time, they found him in the Temple sitting with the doctors of the law, asking them questions. Our Lord obediently returned with his parents to Nazareth.

At thirty years of age, he was baptized by John the Baptist in the river Jordan. The baptism of John was not a sacrament, did not give grace of itself; but, like a sacramental, it disposed those who received it to be sorry for their sins and to receive the gift of faith and baptism of Christ. The eighteen years from the time our Lord went down to Nazareth after being found in the Temple till his baptism is called his "hidden life," while all that follows his baptism is called his "public life." It is very strange that not a single word should be given in the holy scriptures about our Lord during his youth—the very time young men are most anxious to be seen and heard. Our Lord knew all things and could do all things when a young man, and yet, for the sake of example, he remained silent, living quietly with his parents and doing his daily work for them. Thus you understand what is meant by the five joyful mysteries of the rosary: the annunciation, the visitation, the nativity of our Lord, the presentation of the Child Jesus in the Temple, and the finding of the Child Jesus in the Temple. You meditate on one of these before each decade (ten) of the beads.

Sorrowful mysteries.—Next in order in the life of our Lord come the five events called "the sorrowful mysteries," namely:

1. The agony in the garden, when our Lord went there to pray on Holy Thursday night, before he was taken prisoner. There the blood came out through his body as perspiration does through ours, and he was in dreadful anguish. The reason of his sorrow and anguish has already been given in the explanation of the passion.

2. The scourging of our Lord at the pillar. This also has been explained. What terrible cruelty existed in the world before Christianity! In our times,

the brute beasts have more protection from cruel treatment than the pagan slaves had then. The Church came to their assistance. It taught that all men are God's children, that slaves as well as masters were redeemed by Jesus Christ, and that masters must be kind and just to their slaves. Many converts from paganism, through love for our Lord and this teaching of the Church, granted liberty to their slaves; and thus, as civilization spread with the teaching of Christianity, slavery ceased to exist. It was not in the power of the Church, however, to abolish slavery everywhere, but she did it as soon as she could. Even at present she is fighting hard to protect the poor negroes of Africa against it, or at least to moderate its cruelty.

3. The third sorrowful mystery is the crowning with thorns.

4. The carriage of the cross to Calvary. It was the common practice to make the prisoner at times carry his cross to the place of execution, and over the cross they printed what he was put to death for. That is the reason they placed over our Lord's cross *I. N. R. I.*, which are the first letters of four Latin words meaning, "Jesus of Nazareth, King of the Jews." They pretended by this sign that our Lord was put to death for calling himself "King of the Jews," and was thus a disturber of the public peace, and an enemy of the Roman emperor under whose power they were. Our Lord did say that he was King of the Jews, but he also said that he was not their earthly but their heavenly king. The real cause of their putting our Lord to death was the jealousy of the Jewish priests and Pharisees. He rebuked them for their faults, and showed the good, sincere people what hypocrites these men were.

5. The last of the sorrowful mysteries is the crucifixion. At the foot of the cross, our Blessed Mother stood on the day of crucifixion, and it must have been a very sad sight for our Lord. She was without anyone to take care of her; for St. Joseph was dead, and her Son was soon to die. Our Lord asked St. John, one of his apostles, to take care of her. St. John was dear to Christ, and on that account is called the "beloved disciple." He is known to us as St. John the Evangelist. He was the last of the apostles to die. At one time, he was cast into a cauldron of boiling oil, but was miraculously saved by God.[97] He lived to be over a hundred years old, and, while on the island of

[97] See Butler's *Lives of the Saints*, Dec. 27.

Patmos, wrote the Apocalypse or Revelations—the last book of the new testament—containing prophecies of what will happen at the end of the world.

The Blessed Virgin lived on earth about eleven years after the ascension of our Lord. They buried her in a tomb, and tradition tells us that, after her burial, the angels carried her body to heaven, where she now sits beside her divine Son. This taking of her body to heaven is called "the assumption." This feast was celebrated in the Church from a very early age. A very strong proof of the assumption is that no persons ever claimed to have any part of the body of the Blessed Virgin as a relic. We have the bodies of some of the apostles, especially St. Peter, St. Paul, and St. James transmitted to us; and certainly, if it had been possible, the first Christians would have endeavored to get some portion, at least, of the Blessed Virgin's body. Surely St. John, who knew her so well, would have given to the church he established some part of her body as a relic; but since her entire body was taken to heaven, it was never possible.

Glorious mysteries.—After the sorrowful mysteries come the five glorious mysteries, and they are:

1. The resurrection of our Lord.
2. The ascension of our Lord.
3. The coming of the Holy Ghost upon the apostles.
4. The assumption of the Blessed Virgin.
5. The coronation of the Blessed Virgin in heaven. All but the last have been explained in foregoing parts of the catechism. In this last mystery, we consider our Blessed Lady just after her entrance into heaven, being received by her divine Son, our Blessed Lord, and being crowned Queen of heaven over all the angels and saints.

In saying the rosary, we are, as I have told you before, to stop after mentioning the mystery and think over the lesson it teaches, and thus excite ourselves to love and devotion before saying the Our Father and Hail Marys in honor of it. Generally, what we call the "beads" is only one third of the rosary; that is, we can only say five mysteries on the beads unless we go over them three times. If you say your beads every day, you will say the whole rosary twice a week and have one day to spare.

On Sundays, except the Sundays of Advent and Lent, we should say always the glorious mysteries. You see, the mysteries run in the order in which they happen in our Lord's life. So, on Monday we say the joyful mysteries, on Tuesday the sorrowful, and on Wednesday the glorious. Then we begin again on Thursday the joyful, on Friday the sorrowful, on Saturday the glorious. In Advent we say the joyful, and in Lent the sorrowful mysteries on every day. In Easter time we always say the glorious mysteries.

I have told you what the letters *I. N. R. I.* mean; now let me tell you what *I. H. S.* with a cross over them mean. You often see these letters on altars and on holy things. They are simply an abbreviation for our Lord's name, *Jesus*, as it was first written in Greek letters. Some also take these letters for the first letters of the Latin words that mean: "Jesus, Savior of men." And as the cross is placed over these letters, it can signify that he saved them by his death on the cross.

Scapulars. The scapular is a large broad piece of cloth, worn by the monks and priests of some of the religious orders. It extends from the toes in front to the heels behind, and is wide enough to cover the shoulders. It is worn over the cassock or habit. It is called "scapular" because it rests on the shoulders. The scapular as we wear it is two small pieces of cloth fastened together by two pieces of braid or cord resting on the shoulders. It is made thus in imitation of the large scapular, and is to be worn under our ordinary garments. The brown scapular is called the "scapular of Mount Carmel." It was given, we are told on good authority, to Blessed Simon Stock by the Blessed Virgin herself, with wonderful promises in favor of those who wear it. The Church grants many privileges and indulgences to those who wear the scapular.

We wear the scapular to indicate that we place ourselves under the special protection of the Blessed Virgin. We can tell to what army or nation a soldier belongs by the uniform he wears; so, we can consider the scapular as the particular uniform of those who desire to serve the Blessed Virgin in some special manner. This wearing of the brown scapular is therefore a mark of special devotion to the Blessed Virgin Mary. As it was first introduced among the people by the Carmelite fathers, or priests of the Order of Mount Carmel, this scapular is called the "scapular of Mount Carmel." We have also a red scapular in honor of our Lord's passion; a white one in honor of the Holy Trinity; a blue one in honor of the immaculate conception; and a black one in honor of the seven dolors or sorrows of the Blessed Virgin. When all these are joined together (not in one piece, but at the top only) and worn as one, they are called the "five scapulars."

The seven dolors are seven chief occasions of sorrow in the life of our Blessed Lady. They are: 1) The circumcision of our Lord, when she saw his blood shed for the first time. 2) Her flight into Egypt to save the life of the little infant Jesus, when Herod was seeking to kill him. 3) The three days she lost him in Jerusalem. 4) When she saw Christ carrying his cross. 5) His death. 6) When he was taken down from the cross. 7) When he was laid in the sepulchre. There are beads called "seven dolor beads" constructed with seven medals bearing representations of these sorrows, and seven beads between each medal and the next. At the medals, we meditate on the dolor, and then in its honor say Hail Marys on the beads.

LESSON TWENTY-EIGHTH

On Prayer

303. **Is there any other means of obtaining God's grace than the sacraments?**
There is another means of obtaining God's grace, and it is prayer.

304. **What is prayer?**
Prayer is the lifting up of our minds and hearts to God to adore him, to thank him for his benefits, to ask his forgiveness, and to beg of him all the graces we need whether for soul or body.

Hearts, because the mere lifting up of the mind would not be prayer. One who blasphemes him might also lift up his mind. We lift up the mind to know God and the heart to love him, and in so doing, we serve him—the three things for which we were created. If we do not think of God, we do not pray. A parrot might be taught to say the Our Father, but it could never pray, because it has no mind to lift up. A phonograph can be made to say the prayers, but not to pray, for it has neither mind nor heart. So, praying does not depend upon the words we say, but upon the way in which we say them. Indeed, the best prayer, called "meditation," is made when we do not speak at all, but simply think of God; of his goodness to us; of our sins against him; of hell, purgatory, heaven, death, judgment, of the end for which we were created, etc. This is the kind of prayer that priests and religious use most frequently.

As you might like to meditate—for all who know how may meditate—let me explain to you the method. First you try to remember that you are in the presence of God. Then you take some subject, say the crucifixion, to think about. You try to make a picture of the scene in your own mind. You see our Lord on the cross; two thieves, one on each side of him, the one praying to our Lord and the other cursing him. You see the multitude of his enemies mocking him. Over at some distance you behold our Blessed Mother, standing sorrowful with St. John and Mary Magdalen. Then you ask yourself—for you must imagine yourself there—to which side would you go. Over to our Blessed Mother to try and console her, or over to the enemies to help them to mock? Then you think how sin was the cause of all this suffering, and how often you yourself have sinned; how you have many a time gone over to the crowd and left the Blessed Mother. These thoughts will make you sorry for your sins, and you will form the good resolution never to sin again. You will thank God for these good thoughts and this resolution, and your meditation is ended. You can spend fifteen minutes, or longer if you wish, in such a meditation. The crucifixion is only one of the many subjects you may select for meditation. You could take any part of the Our Father, Hail Mary, or Creed, and even the questions in your catechism.

Mental prayer, therefore, is the best, because in it we must think; we must pay attention to what we are doing, and lift up our minds and hearts to God; while in vocal prayer—that is, the prayer we say aloud—we may repeat the words from pure habit, without any attention or lifting up of the mind or heart.

305. **Is prayer necessary to salvation?**

Prayer is necessary to salvation, and without it no one having the use of reason can be saved.

We mean here those who never pray during their whole lives, and not those who sometimes neglect their prayers through a kind of forgetfulness.

306. **At what particular times should we pray?**

We should pray particularly on Sundays and holy days, every morning and night, in all dangers, temptations, and afflictions.

Sundays and holy days, because these are special days set apart by the Church for the worship of God. In the *morning*, we ask God's grace that we may not sin during the day. At *night*, we thank him for all the benefits received during the day, and also that we may be protected while asleep from every danger and accident. We should never, if possible, go to sleep in mortal sin; and if we have the misfortune to be in that state, we should make as perfect an act of contrition as we can, and promise to go to confession as soon as possible. So many accidents happen that we are never safe, even in good health; fires, earthquakes, floods, lightning, etc., might take us off at any moment. If you saw a man hanging by a very slender thread over a great precipice where he would surely be dashed to pieces if the thread broke, and if you saw him thus risking his life willfully and without necessity, you would pronounce him the greatest fool in the world. One who commits sin is a greater fool. He suspends himself, as I have told you once before, over an abyss of eternal torments on the slender thread of his own life, that may break at any moment. Do we tempt God and do to him what we dare not do to our fellowmen because he is so merciful? Let us be careful. He is as just as he is merciful, and some sin will be our last, and then he will cut the thread of life and allow us to fall into an eternity of sufferings. *Dangers*, whether of soul or body. *Afflictions*, sufferings or misfortunes of any kind; such as loss of health, death in the family, etc.

307. **How should we pray?**

We should pray: first, with attention; second, with a sense of our own helplessness and dependence upon God; third, with a great desire for the graces we beg of God; fourth, with trust in God's goodness; fifth, with perseverance.

Attention, thinking of what we are going to do. Before praying, we should think for a moment what prayer is. In it, we are about to address Almighty God, our Creator, and we are going to ask him for something—and what is the particular thing we need and seek for? No one would think of going to a store without first considering what he wanted to buy. He would make, too, all the necessary preparations for getting it. He would find out how much he wanted, and what it would cost, and bring with him sufficient money. He would never think of going in and telling the storekeeper to give him anything. Now it is the same in prayer. When we have thought of what we want of God, from whom we can obtain it, and of the reasons why we need it and why God might be pleased to grant it, we can then kneel down and pray for it. We should pray to God just as a child begs favors from its parents. We should talk to him in our own simple words, and tell him the reasons why we ask and why we think he should grant our request. We should, however, be humble and patient in all our prayers. God does not owe us anything, and whatever he gives is a free gift. We should not always read prayers at Almighty God. If you wanted anything very badly from a friend, you would know how to ask for it. You would never ask another to write out your request on paper, and then go and read it to your friend. Now, that is just what we do when we read the prayers that somebody else has written in a prayer book. Try, therefore, to pray with your own prayers.

Of course, when the Church gives you certain prayers to say—as it does to its priests in the divine office—or recommends to you such prayers as the Our Father, Hail Mary, and Creed, you should say them in preference to your own, because then the Church adds its petition to yours, and God is more likely to grant such prayers. I mean, therefore, that we should not always pray from prayer books, and hurry through the Our Father that we may give more time to some printed prayer that pleases us. Our prayer should be a conversation with God. We should, after speaking to him, listen to what he has to say to us, by our conscience, good thoughts, etc.

I must warn you against some prayers that have been circulated by impostors for the purpose of making money. They pretend that these prayers were found in some remarkable place or manner; that those who carry them or say them will have most wonderful advantages; they will never meet with accident; they will be warned of their death; they will go directly to heaven after death, etc. If there were any such wonderful prayers, the Church would surely know of them and commend them to its children. When you find any prayers of the kind I mention, bring them to the priest and ask his opinion before you use them yourself or give them to others. Never buy prayers or articles said to be blessed from persons unknown to you. Persons selling such things are frequently impostors, who, by suave manners and pious speeches, unfortunately find Catholics who believe them. These persons—sometimes not Catholics themselves, or at least very bad ones—laugh at the superstition and foolish practices of Catholics who believe everything they hear about pious books, prayers, or articles.

In the early ages of the Church, when the enemies of Christ found that they could not refute his teaching, they began to circulate foolish doctrines, pretending that they were taught by Christ, and thus they hoped to bring ridicule upon Christianity. So also in our time, many things are circulated as the teaching of the Catholic Church by the enemies of the Church, in hopes that by these falsehoods and foolish doctrines, they may bring disgrace and ridicule upon the true religion. Be on your guard against all impostors, remembering it is a safe rule never to buy a religious article from or give money to persons going about from door to door. If you have anything to give in alms, give it to some charitable institution or society connected with the Church, or put it in the poor box, and then you will be sure it will do the good you intend. Remember, too, that all the religious articles carried about for sale do not come from Rome or the Holy Land, and you are deceived if you think so, notwithstanding the assurance of their owners.

A *trust*—with full confidence that God will grant our petitions if we really need or deserve what we pray for. It is a fault with a great many to pray without the belief that their prayers will be answered. We should pray with such faith and confidence that we would really be disappointed if our prayer was not granted. Once when our Lord was going about doing good, a poor woman who had been suffering for twelve years with a disease, and who, wishing to be healed, had uselessly spent all her money in seeking medical aid, came to follow him.[98] She did not ask him to cure her, but said within herself, "If I can but touch the hem of his garment, I know I shall be healed." So she made her way through the throng and followed our Lord till she could touch his garment without being seen. She succeeded in

[98] Cf. Mk 5:25

accomplishing her wishes, touched his garment, and was instantly cured. Our Lord knew her desires and what she had done, and, turning around, told the people, praising her great faith and confidence, on account of which he had healed her. Such also should be our confidence and trust when we pray to God for our needs.

Perseverance. We should continue to pray though God does not grant our request. Have you ever noticed a little child begging favors from its mother? See its persistence! Though often refused, it will return again and again with the same request, till the mother, weary of its importunity, finally grants what it asks. St. Monica prayed seventeen years for the conversion of her son St. Augustine. St. Augustine's father was a pagan, and Monica, his wife, prayed seventeen years for his conversion, and he became a Christian. Just about that time, her son Augustine, who was attending school, fell in with bad companions and became a great sinner. She prayed seventeen years more for him, and he reformed, became a great saint and learned bishop in the Church. See, then, the result of thirty-four years' prayer: Monica herself became a saint, her son became a saint, and her husband died a Christian. If St. Monica had ceased praying after ten years, Augustine might not have reformed. We never know when God is about to grant our petition, and we may cease to pray just when another appeal would obtain the object of our prayer. So, we should continue to pray till God is pleased to grant our request. Some say their prayers are not heard when they mean to say their prayers are not granted; for God always hears us.

But why does he not always grant our request? There are many reasons: 1) We may not pray in the proper manner, namely, with attention, reverence, humility, patience, and perseverance. 2) We may ask for things that God foresees will not be for our spiritual good. This is true even for things that seem good to us, such as the removal of an affliction, temptation, or the like. It often happens that God shows us his greatest mercy in not granting our prayers. Suppose, for example, a father held in his hand a bright and beautiful but very sharp instrument, for which his little child continually asked. Do you believe the father would give it if he loved the child? Certainly not. The child thinks, no doubt, it would be benefited by the possession of the instrument, but the father sees the danger. As God is our loving Father, he acts with us in the same manner. 3) Our prayers are not granted sometimes that we may learn to pray with proper dispositions, and God withholds what he intends finally to give, that we may persevere in prayer and have greater merit. Have you ever observed a mother teaching her child to walk? What does she do? She goes at some distance from the child and holds out an object that she knows will be pleasing to it, and thus tempts it to walk to her. When the child draws near, she moves still farther away, and keeps it walking for some time before giving the object. This she does, not through unwillingness to give the article, but in order to teach the child to walk, for she loves to see its efforts. When it falls, she lifts it up and makes it try again. So, too, God teaches us to pray; and though he loves us, he withholds his gifts, that we may pray the longer, and thereby afford him greater pleasure.

308. **Which are the prayers most recommended to us?**
The prayers most recommended to us are the Lord's Prayer, the Hail Mary, the Apostles' Creed, the *confiteor*, and the acts of faith, hope, love, and contrition.

309. **Are prayers said with distractions of any avail?**
Prayers said with willful distractions are of no avail.

Distraction—that is, when we willingly and knowingly think of something else while saying our prayers. It would be better not to pray than to pray with disrespect. If there is any time at which we cannot pray well, we should postpone our prayer: for God does not require us to say our prayers just at a particular time; but when we do pray, he requires us to pray with reverence and respect. We would pray well always if we reflected on the great privilege we enjoy in being allowed to pray.

LESSON TWENTY-NINTH

On the Commandments of God

310. **Is it enough to belong to God's Church in order to be saved?**
It is not enough to belong to the Church in order to be saved, but we must also keep the commandments of God and of the Church.

We call some commandments, "the commandments of God," and others, "the commandments of the Church." We do so only to distinguish the commandments that God gave to Moses from those that the Church made afterward. They are all the commandments of God, for whatever laws or commandments the Church makes, it makes them under the inspiration of the Holy Ghost, and by God's authority. It would be a mortal sin to break the commandments of the Church, just as it would be to break the commandments of God. You must remember that the ten commandments always existed from the time of Adam, but they were not written till God gave them to Moses. You know that it was always a sin to worship false gods, to blaspheme, to disobey parents, to kill, etc.; for you know Cain was punished by God for the murder of his brother Abel,[99] and that took place while Adam was still alive.

Before the coming of our Lord, the Israelites, or God's chosen people, had three kinds of laws. They had the civil laws for the government of their nation—just as we have our laws for the people of the United States. They had their ceremonial laws for their services in the Temple—as we have our ceremonies for the Church. They had their moral laws—such as the commandments—teaching them what they must do to save their souls. Their civil laws were done away with when they ceased to be a nation having a government of their own. Their ceremonial laws were done away with when our Lord came and established his Church; because their ceremonies were only the figures of ours. Their moral laws remained, and our Lord explained them and made them more perfect. Therefore, we keep the commandments and moral laws as they were always kept by man. Fifty

[99] Cf. Gn 4

days after the Israelites left Egypt, they came to the foot of Mount Sinai.[100] Here God commanded Moses to come up into the mountain, and in the midst of fire and smoke, thunder and lightning, God spoke to him and delivered into his hands the ten commandments written on two tablets of stone.

Every day, while the Israelites were traveling in the desert, God sent them manna—a miraculous food that fell every morning. It was white, and looked something like fine rice. It had any taste they wished it to have. For instance, if they wished it to taste like fruit, it did taste so to them; but its usual taste was like that of flour and honey.[101]

I said there is no difference between the ten commandments of God and the six commandments of the Church; and there is no difference as far as the sin of violating them is concerned. But they differ in this: the Church can change the commandments it made itself, while it cannot change those that God himself gave directly.

311. **Which are the commandments that contain the whole law of God?**
The commandments which contain the whole law of God are these two: first, thou shalt love the Lord thy God with thy whole heart, with thy whole soul, with thy whole strength, and with thy whole mind; second, thou shalt love thy neighbor as thyself.

As thyself—that is, as explained elsewhere, with the same kind, though not necessarily with the same degree, of love. First, we must love ourselves and do what is essential for our own salvation, because without our cooperation, others cannot save us, though they may help us by their prayers and good works. Next to ourselves, nature demands that we love those who are related to us in the order of parents, children, husbands, wives, brothers, etc., and help them in proportion to their needs, and before helping strangers who are in no greater distress.

[100] Cf. Ex 19
[101] Cf. Ex 16

312. **Why do these two commandments of the love of God and of our neighbor contain the whole law of God?**

These two commandments of the love of God and of our neighbor contain the whole law of God because all the other commandments are given either to help us to keep these two, or to direct us how to shun what is opposed to them.

Of the ten commandments, the first three refer to Almighty God, and the other seven to our neighbor. Thus, all the commandments may be reduced to the two of the love of God and of the love of our neighbor. The first commandment says you shall worship only the true God; the second says you shall respect his holy name; and the third says you shall worship him on a certain day. All these are contained therefore in this: love God all you possibly can, for, if you do, you will keep the first three of the commandments. The fourth says honor your father—who in the sense of the commandment can also be called "your neighbor"—that is, respect him, help him in his needs. The fifth says do not kill him; namely, your neighbor. The others say do not rob him of his goods; do not tell lies about him; do not wish unjustly to possess his goods and do not covet his wife. Thus it is clear that the last seven are all contained in this: love your neighbor, for, if you do, you will keep the last seven commandments that refer to him.

313. **Which are the commandments of God?**

The commandments of God are these ten:

1. I am the Lord thy God, who brought thee out of the land of Egypt, out of the house of bondage. Thou shalt not have strange gods before me. Thou shalt not make to thyself a graven thing, nor the likeness of anything that is in heaven above, or in the earth beneath, nor of those things that are in the waters under the earth. Thou shalt not adore them, nor serve them.
2. Thou shalt not take the name of the Lord thy God in vain.
3. Remember thou keep holy the sabbath day.
4. Honor thy father and thy mother.
5. Thou shalt not kill.
6. Thou shalt not commit adultery.

7. Thou shalt not steal.
8. Thou shalt not bear false witness against thy neighbor.
9. Thou shalt not covet thy neighbor's wife.
10. Thou shalt not covet thy neighbor's goods.

314. **Who gave the ten commandments?**

God himself gave the ten commandments to Moses on Mount Sinai, and Christ our Lord confirmed them.

LESSON THIRTIETH

On the First Commandment

315. **What is the first commandment?**

The first commandment is: "I am the Lord thy God, thou shalt not have strange gods before me."

Strange gods. The Israelites were surrounded on all sides by pagan nations who worshipped idols and false gods, and sometimes, by mingling with these people, they fell into sin, and, forgetting the true God, worshipped their idols. Sometimes, too, they were at war with these pagan nations, and, when defeated, were led captive into pagan countries and there fell into the sin of worshipping false gods. It was against this sin that God cautioned his people in the first commandment. From this sin of idolatry among the Israelites we have an example of the evil results of associating with persons not of the true religion. One would think that the Israelites, knowing the true God, might have converted their pagan neighbors to the true religion by the influence of their teaching and example; but, on the contrary, they lost the true faith themselves, as nearly always happens in such cases. How do we sometimes worship false or strange gods? By making dress, money, honor, society, company, or pleasure our god—that is, by giving up the worship of God and sinning for their sake, and thus making them god, at least for the time being, by giving them our heart, mind, and service.

316. **How does the first commandment help us to keep the great commandment of the love of God?**
The first commandment helps us to keep the great commandment of the love of God because it commands us to adore God alone.

317. **How do we adore God?**
We adore God by faith, hope, and charity, by prayer and sacrifice.

318. **How may the first commandment be broken?**
The first commandment may be broken by giving to a creature the honor which belongs to God alone; by false worship; and by attributing to a creature a perfection which belongs to God alone.

Creature—that is, anything created; anything but God himself; for all other persons and things have been created. If one knelt before a king and adored him, he would be giving to a creature the honor due to God alone. *False worship*—that is, worshipping God not as he directs us by his Church, but in some way pleasing to ourselves. For example, to sacrifice animals to God would now be false worship; to offer now any of the sacrifices commanded in the old law would be false worship, because all these were figures of the real sacrifice of the cross and Mass, and were to put the people in mind that one day Christ the promised Redeemer would offer up the one great sacrifice of his own body and blood to blot out all the sins of the world. And now that we have the real sacrifice, it would be sinful to use only figures, and it would be a false worship displeasing to God. So, too, all those who leave the true Church to practice a religion of their own have a false worship, for they worship God not as he wishes, but as they wish.

Heaven is a reward, and when we see how the saints labored to secure it, we must be ashamed of the little we do for God. Take out of a whole year—that is, 365 days or 8,760 hours—the time you give to the service of God, and you will find it very little. Even the time you spent at Mass and prayers was filled with distraction, and little of it entirely given to God. Since this is true for one year, what will it be for all the years of your life? Think of them all and you will perceive that God, who gave you all the time you had, and who on the last day will demand an exact account of it, will find very little of it spent in his honor or in his service. Even the time wasted in school and instructions will all stand against you. Time lost is lost forever, and you can never make it up. Next to grace, time is the most valuable thing God gives us, and we should use it well.

Attributing to a creature a perfection, etc. Persons who go to fortune tellers do this. Fortune tellers are persons who pretend to know what is going to happen in the future. We know from our religion that only God himself knows the future. Neither the angels nor saints, nor even the Blessed Virgin, know the future. Even they could not tell your fortune unless God revealed it to them. So, when you go to a fortune teller, you place the poor sinful person who is doing the devil's work above the Blessed Virgin and all the saints and angels, and make that wretch equal to God himself. Surely this is a sin, even if you do not believe these so-called fortune tellers, but go to them merely through curiosity or with others. Again, we pay these persons for telling us some foolish nonsense, and thus encourage them to continue their sinful business. They doubtless laugh at the foolishness of those who go to them or believe what they say, and pay them generously. You might with as much sense stop a man on the street, ask him to tell your fortune, and hand him your money, for he would know as much about it as so-called fortune tellers do. Rarely these sinful people might tell you something that has happened in your life; but if they do, they merely guess at it or are aided by the devil.

The devil did not lose his intelligence when driven out of heaven, and he uses it now for doing evil. He has vast experience, for he is as old as Adam, or older, and has seen and known all the men that have lived in the world. He can move rapidly through the world and easily know what is visibly taking place, so that, strictly speaking, he could make known to his sinful agents what is present or past, but never the future. Thus, some fortune tellers, clairvoyants, mind readers, mediums, or whatever else they call themselves, who are truly in league with the devil, may by his power tell you the past of your life to make you believe that they know also the future. The past and present in your life you already know, and the future they cannot tell; therefore, it is useless as well as sinful to go to them. I say only it is possible for some fortune tellers to employ the assistance of the devil, for all of them, with very rare exception, are clever impostors who take your money for guessing at what they suspect you will be most pleased to hear.

319. **Do those who make use of spells and charms, or who believe in dreams, in mediums, spiritists, fortune tellers, and the like, sin against the first commandment?**

Those who make use of spells and charms, or who believe in dreams, in mediums, spiritists, fortune tellers, and the like, sin against the first commandment, because they attribute to creatures perfections which belong to God alone.

Spells are certain words, the saying of which persons believe will effect for them something wonderful—a miraculous cure, for instance, or protection from some evil.

Charms are articles worn about the body for the same purpose. They may be little black beans, little stones of a certain shape, the teeth of animals, etc. In uncivilized countries, the inhabitants use many of these charms. But you may ask, "Are not these medals, scapulars, etc., that we wear, also charms?" No. These things are blessed and worn in honor of God, of his Blessed Mother, or of the saints. We do not expect any help from the little piece of brass or cloth we wear, but from those in whose honor we wear it, and from the prayers said in the blessing for those who wear it. But they who wear charms expect the help from the thing itself, which makes their conduct foolish and sinful, since God alone can protect from evil. Again, such things as medals, crosses, and scapulars are blessed by the Church and worn by its consent, and it could never allow all its children to do a sinful thing. It is good and praiseworthy, therefore, to wear the blessed sacramentals in God's honor; but, even with these holy things, we must be careful not to go too far. It is true the Blessed Virgin will protect those who wear her scapular; but it would be sinful willfully to expose ourselves to danger without any necessity, because we wear a scapular. Thus, it would be suicide for a boy who could not swim to plunge into deep water because, having his scapulars on, the Blessed Virgin ought to save him by a miracle. Again, it is wrong to look for miracles from God when natural help will answer. Thus, it would be wrong for a man who broke his leg to refuse to have the doctors set it, because he wanted God alone to heal it.

Dreams are caused by the mind being at work while the body is sleeping or at rest. The mind never sleeps; it is always awake and working. Thus, when we are asleep, the imagination, without the reason to guide it, mixes together a number of things we have seen, heard, or thought of, and gives us strange scenes and pictures. Sometimes what we dream of seems to happen; but that is only because we dream so much that it would be strange if none of the things ever happened. We will generally dream about whatever was on our mind shortly before. We read in the holy scriptures that God at times made known his will to certain persons by dreams; as when the king of Egypt dreamt of the great famine that was to come; or when the angel appeared in sleep to St. Joseph, telling him to take our Lord into Egypt, where Herod the king could not kill him.[102] The dreams mentioned in the holy scripture were more frequently visions than dreams. In a vision, the things we see are really present, whereas in dreams they are not, but we imagine they are. God no longer makes use of dreams as a means of communicating with his creatures, because his Church will make known to us his will. He sometimes, however, makes known certain things to his holy servants on earth in a very special and private manner: as, for example, when our Lord appeared to Blessed Margaret Mary and told her he would like to have the devotion to the Sacred Heart established. We must always believe what the Church tells as God has made known to it; but when holy people tell us that God revealed special things to them, we are not obliged to believe what they say, unless the Church confirms it. I say we are not obliged—that is, we may if we please; but we would not be heretics and commit sin if we did not believe all the revelations and wonderful things we find recorded in the lives of saints, though they may all be true.

Mediums and spiritists are persons who pretend they can talk with the dead in the other world, and learn where they are and what they are doing. They have figures to move and apparently speak, and other contrivances to deceive those who confide in them. Their work is all deception and very

[102] Cf. Mt 2

sinful. If any of these things could be done, or if God wished them to be known, he would give the power to the Church founded by his divine Son, and not to a few sinful men or women here and there. After a soul leaves the body, its fate is hidden from us, and we can say nothing with absolute certainty of its reward or punishment. No one ever came back from the other world to give a minute account of its general appearance or of what takes place there. All that is known about it the Church knows and tells us, and all over and above that is false or doubtful.

By thinking a little, you can see how all these dealings with fortune tellers, etc., are giving to creatures what belongs to God alone.

320. **Are sins against faith, hope, and charity also sins against the first commandment?**
Sins against faith, hope, and charity are also sins against the first commandment.

321. **How does a person sin against faith?**
A person sins against faith: first, by not trying to know what God has taught; second, by refusing to believe all that God has taught; third, by neglecting to profess his belief in what God has taught.

Not trying to know. Thus, children who idle their time at Sunday school or religious instruction, and do not learn their catechism, sin against faith in the first way. In like manner, grown persons who do not sometime or other endeavor to hear sermons or instructions, to attend missions or learn from good books, sin against faith. *Refusing to believe*, as all those do who leave the true religion, or who, knowing it, do not embrace it. *Neglecting to profess.* We may do this by not living up to the practice of our holy religion. We believe, for example, we should hear Mass every Sunday and holy day; we should receive the sacraments at certain times in the year; but if we only believe these things and do not do them, we neglect to profess our faith; neglect to show others that we really believe all the Church teaches, and are anxious to practice it. Many know and believe what they should do, but never practice it. Such persons do great injury to the Church, for persons who do not live up to their holy religion but act contrary to its teaching give scandal to their neighbor. How many persons at present not Catholics would be induced to enter the true Church if they saw all Catholics virtuous, truthful, sober, honest, upright, and industrious! But when they see Catholics—be they ever so few—cursing, quarreling, backbiting, drinking, lying, stealing, cheating, etc.—in a word, indulging in the same vices as those who claim to have no religion—what must they think of the moral influence of Catholic faith? Thus they do great injustice to the Church and the cause of religion, and are working against our Blessed Lord when they should be working for him.

The Christian religion spread very rapidly through the world in the first ages of its existence; and one of the chief reasons was the good example given by the Christians; for pagans seeing the holy lives, the kindness and charity of their Christian neighbors, could not help admiring and loving them, and wishing to be members of the Church that made them so good and amiable. How many pagans do you think would be converted nowadays by the lives of some who call themselves Catholics? Not many, I think. Besides this, the early Christians really labored to instruct others in the Christian religion, and to make them converts. Often, we find servants—even slaves—by their instructions converting their pagan masters and mistresses. They all felt that they were missionaries working for Jesus Christ, and their influence reached where the priest's influence could not reach, because they came in contact with persons the priests never had an opportunity of seeing. If all Catholics had the same spirit, what good they could do! Their business or duty may often bring them into daily intercourse with persons not of their faith, and who never knew or perhaps heard any of the beautiful truths of our holy religion. Yes, Catholics could do much good if they had only the good will and knew their religion well. I do not mean that they should be always discussing religion with everyone they meet. Let them preach chiefly by the example of their own good lives, and, when questioned, explain modestly and sincerely the truths they believe.

If you should be asked, for instance: "Why do you not eat flesh meat on Friday?" You should be able to answer: "Because I am a Christian and wish to keep always before my mind how our Blessed Lord suffered for me in his holy flesh on that day; and anyone who claims to be a Christian, ought, I think, to be glad to do what reminds him so regularly and well of our Lord's passion." Such an answer, if given kindly and mildly, would silence and instruct your adversary; it might make him reflect, and might, in time, bring him to the true religion. Sometimes a few words make a great impression and bring about conversion. St. Francis Xavier was a worldly young man, learned and ambitious, and he heard from St. Ignatius these words of our Lord: "What doth it profit a man if he gain the whole world and suffer the loss of his own soul?" He went home and kept thinking of them till they impressed him so strongly that he gave up the world, became a priest, and, by his labors and preaching in India, converted to the true religion many thousand pagans. In the Lives of the Saints, there are many examples of a few words, by God's grace, bringing men from a life of sin to a life of great holiness.

322. **How do we fail to try to know what God has taught?**
We fail to try to know what God has taught by neglecting to learn the Christian doctrine.

323. **Who are they who do not believe all that God has taught?**
They who do not believe all that God has taught are the heretics and infidels.

There are many kinds of unbelievers: atheists, deists, infidels, heretics, apostates, and schismatics. An atheist is one who denies the existence of God, saying there is no God. A deist is one who says he believes that God exists, but denies that God ever revealed any religion. These are also called "freethinkers." An infidel properly means "one who has never been baptized," "one who is not of the number of the faithful"; that is, those believing in Christ. Sometimes atheists are called "infidels."

Heretics are those who were baptized and who claim to be Christians, but do not believe all the truths that our Lord has taught. They accept only a portion of the doctrine of Christ and reject the remainder, and hence they become rebellious children of the Church. They belong to the true Church by being baptized, but do not submit to its teaching and are therefore outcast children, disinherited till they return to the true faith. A schismatic is one who believes everything the Church teaches, but will not submit to the authority of its head—the holy father. Such persons do not long remain only schismatics; for once they rise up against the authority of the Church, they soon reject some of its doctrines and thus become heretics; and indeed, since the Vatican Council, all schismatics are heretics.

324. **Who are they who neglect to profess their belief in what God has taught?** They who neglect to profess their belief in what God has taught are all those who fail to acknowledge the true Church in which they really believe.

There are some outside the Church who feel and believe that the Catholic Church is the true Church, and yet they do not become Catholics, because there are so many difficulties in the way. For example, they have been brought up in another religion, and all their friends, relatives, or associates are opposed to the Catholic religion. Their business, their social life, their worldly interests will all suffer if they become Catholics. So, although they feel they should at once embrace the true religion, they keep putting off till death comes and finds them outside the Church—and most probably guilty of other mortal sins. Such persons cannot be saved, for they reject all the graces God bestows upon them.

A very common fault with such people is to excuse this conduct by saying: "Oh! I was brought up in the protestant religion, and everyone ought to live in the religion in which he was brought up." Let me ask: If persons were brought up with some bodily deformity that their parents neglected to have remedied while they were young, would they not use every means themselves to have the deformity removed as soon as they became old enough to see and understand their misfortune? In like manner, if, unfortunately, parents bring up their children in a false religion, that is, with spiritual deformities, it is the duty of the children to embrace the true religion as soon as they know it. Again, persons will say: "Oh, I believe one religion as good as another; we are all Christians, and all trying to serve God." If one religion is as good as another, why did not our Lord allow the old religions—false or true—to remain? If one man says a thing is black and another says it is white, they cannot both be right, for a thing cannot be black and white at the same time. Only one can be right; and, if we are anxious about the color of the object, we must try to find which one is right.

Just in the same way, all the religions that claim to be Christian contradict one another; one says a thing is false, and another says it is true; one says our Lord taught so-and-so, and another says he did not. Now since it is very important for us to know which is right, we must find out which is really the Church our Lord established; and when we have found it, we will know that all the other pretended Christian religions must be false. Our Lord has given us marks by which we can know his Church, as we saw while speaking of the marks of the Church; and the Roman Catholic Church is the only Church that has all these marks. We say that we are Roman Catholics to show that we are in communion with the Church of Rome, established by St. Peter, the chief of the apostles.

325. **Can they who fail to profess their faith in the true Church in which they believe expect to be saved while in that state?**

They who fail to profess their faith in the true Church in which they believe cannot expect to be saved while in that state, for Christ has said: "Whoever shall deny me before men, I will also deny him before my Father who is in heaven."[103]

326. **Are we obliged to make open profession of our faith?**

We are obliged to make open profession of our faith as often as God's honor, our neighbor's spiritual good, or our own requires it. "Whosoever," says Christ, "shall confess me before men, I will also confess him before my Father who is in heaven."[104]

It is not necessary for us to proclaim in the streets that we are Catholics; neither need we tell our religion to impudent people that may ask us only to insult us; but when a real need of professing our faith presents itself, then we must profess it. Suppose you are stopping in a hotel in which you are the

[103] Mt 10:33
[104] Mt 10:32

only Catholic. If flesh meat is placed before you on Friday, you must quietly push it aside and ask for fish or other food; although by so doing, you will show that you are a Catholic and make a silent profession of your faith. God's honor and your own good require it, for you must keep the laws of God and of his Church on every possible occasion. Suppose again there were in the same hotel some indifferent Catholics, socially your equals or inferiors, who through human respect were ashamed to go to Mass on Sunday; then you should publicly go to Mass and even declare that you must go, for by so doing you would encourage these indifferent Catholics to follow your example. In that case, your neighbor's good requires that you profess your faith. In a word, you must keep up the practice of your religion even if by so doing you have to make an open profession of your faith and suffer for it. But suppose it is something that God or the Church does not command you to do, but only recommends, such as blessing yourself before meals or some pious practice: you could in public omit such an action if you pleased, without any sin or denial of faith, because you violate no law.

327. **Which are the sins against hope?**
The sins against hope are presumption and despair.

328. **What is presumption?**
Presumption is a rash expectation of salvation without making proper use of the necessary means to obtain it.

A person who goes on leading a bad life, and says, when warned of his danger, that he is in no hurry to reform, that he will repent some day before he dies, is always living in and committing the sin of presumption. It is a great sin, for it is living in open defiance of Almighty God. Such persons are very seldom given the opportunity to repent at the last moment, and are, in most cases, called to judgment when they least expect it.

We are all presumptuous sometimes. Do we not often, when we have fallen into a certain sin, easily repeat the act, saying to ourselves, now that we will have to confess the sin committed, the mention of the number of times will not make much difference for it will not increase our shame and confusion? This is presumption; for we do not know whether God will ever give us the opportunity of making a confession. Again, one mortal sin is sufficient to keep our souls in hell for all eternity; what then will be our punishment for many mortal sins?

Then there is another thing you should remember: God has fixed a certain number of sins that he will suffer you to commit before he sends his punishment. You do not know which sin will complete the number and be the last. The very sin you are now about to commit may be that one, and the moment you have committed it, God will call you to judgment, whether it be night or day, whether you are at home or in the streets—though perhaps not immediately, but before you commit another sin. Such a thought alone should keep you from sinning.

Moreover, after confession, you strongly resist the first temptation to mortal sin, but after you have yielded to the first, you scarcely make any more resistance, but easily yield again and again. You should therefore, to prevent this, go to confession just as soon as you possibly can after falling into mortal sin. It is bad enough to commit mortal sin, but it is terrible to be living in that state day and night—always an enemy of God—losing the merit of all the works you do, and yet you must stay in that state of sin till you go to confession and receive absolution. Peter the apostle committed the sin of presumption.[105] Our Lord told him to watch and pray, for he would be tempted and yield that night, but Peter said: "No Lord, I will never deny thee." Instead of begging our Lord's help and grace, he trusted to himself and fell miserably into sin. He went into dangerous company, and that was another cause of his fall. But afterward, he saw his sin and folly and never ceased to repent of it.

329. **What is despair?**

Despair is the loss of hope in God's mercy.

Despair is a sin, because, by it, you deny that God is infinitely merciful—that he is merciful enough to forgive even your many and great sins if you are truly sorry for them. Judas committed the sin of despair. After he had betrayed our Lord, he went and hanged himself, thus committing,

[105] Cf. Mt 26

besides the sin of betraying his divine master, two other great sins, namely: despair in God's mercy and suicide. If he had gone to our Lord and confessed his sin, and implored pardon and promised penance, can we doubt that he would have forgiven even Judas, as he forgave Peter, and those that crucified him, praying that his Father might not punish them for their sins? Therefore, no matter what sins you have committed, never lose confidence in God's mercy. See how our Lord pardoned the thief on the cross and Mary Magdalen and other sinners. Be sorry for your sins, and God will hear your prayers. Call upon the Blessed Virgin, your patron saint, and guardian angel to help you, and ask others, especially good persons, to pray for you.

330. **How do we sin against the love of God?**
We sin against the love of God by all sin, but particularly by mortal sin.

LESSON THIRTY-FIRST

The First Commandment—On the Honor and Invocation of Saints

331. **Does the first commandment forbid the honoring of the saints?**
The first commandment does not forbid the honoring of the saints, but rather approves of it; because, by honoring the saints, who are the chosen friends of God, we honor God himself.

Think of the many helps God gives us to save our souls: an angel to be always with us upon earth; a saint always praying for us in heaven, and, besides these, all the graces, the sacraments, the Masses, the prayers, etc. If then we lose our souls, surely we cannot say, "God did not give us sufficient help." *Invocation* means "calling upon them to help us." Everyone is pleased when his friends are honored. Who is not glad to hear his parents praised or see them respected? By praying to the saints, instead of dishonoring God as protestants say we do, we really honor him more than by praying directly to himself. We show that we believe in his great dignity, his awful majesty and our own nothingness. If a poor person wanted to obtain a favor from the president of the United States, would he go directly to the president himself? No. He would find someone who had influence with the president, and ask him to obtain the favor. Why, the very persons that say we should not use the influence of saints do themselves use the influence of others to obtain favors. They never go to an enemy of the one from whom they desire the favor, but to some of his friends, knowing that a person will often grant a favor for a friend's sake that he would not grant for the sake of others. Now we do exactly the same when we pray to the saints. They are the special friends of God. They fasted, prayed, preached, labored, or suffered death for his honor and glory. He showed them great favors while they were upon earth. He performed miracles at their request. Will he deny them now, when they are always present with him in heaven—where they could not possibly sin? He loves to grant them favors; and, as they do not need any for themselves, he grants them for others through their intercession.

Again, men are honored by the praises of their fellow men. A great general is honored by having all his countrymen praise him; so, too, God wants his saints honored, for their great spiritual deeds, by the praise of the children of the Church. God is not annoyed by being asked for favors. Nothing can trouble him, for all is done by an act of his will. He loses nothing by giving, for he is infinite. By praying to the saints for help, we confess that we are too unworthy to present ourselves to God and address him—to come before his awful Majesty, and that we will wait here in the humble attitude of prayer while you, holy saints, his dearest friends, go into his presence and ask for us the favors and graces we require.

332. **Does the first commandment forbid us to pray to the saints?**

The first commandment does not forbid us to pray to the saints.

We do not pray to them as to God. We never say to them, "Give us this or that," but always, "Obtain it for us." In all the litanies, you cannot find one petition where we say, even to the Blessed Virgin, "Have mercy on us," but, "Pray for us," or, "Intercede for us."

333. **What do we mean by "praying to the saints"?**

By "praying to the saints," we mean the asking of their help and prayers.

334. **How do we know that the saints hear us?**
We know that the saints hear us because they are with God, who makes our prayers known to them.

335. **Why do we believe that the saints will help us?**
We believe that the saints will help us because both they and we are members of the same Church, and they love us as their brethren.

336. **How are the saints and we members of the same Church?**
The saints and we are members of the same Church, because the Church in heaven and the Church on earth are one and the same Church, and all its members are in communion with one another.

337. **What is the communion of the members of the Church called?**
The communion of the members of the Church is called "the communion of saints."

338. **What does "the communion of saints" mean?**
"The communion of saints" means the union which exists between the members of the Church on earth with one another and with the blessed in heaven and with the suffering souls in purgatory.

339. **What benefits are derived from the communion of saints?**
The following benefits are derived from the communion of saints: the faithful on earth assist one another by their prayers and good works, and they are aided by the intercession of the saints in heaven, while both the saints in heaven and the faithful on earth help the souls in purgatory.

340. **Does the first commandment forbid us to honor relics?**
The first commandment does not forbid us to honor relics, because relics are the bodies of the saints or objects directly connected with them or with our Lord.

Relic means "a thing left." Relics are pieces of the body—bones, etc. Pieces of saints' clothing, writing, etc., are also called "relics." Pieces of the true cross, the nails that pierced Christ's hands, etc., are relics of our Lord's passion. We have no relic of our Lord's body, because he took it into heaven with him when he ascended. All relics of the saints must be examined at Rome, by those whom the holy father has appointed for that work. They must be marked and accompanied by the testimony of the cardinals, or others who examined them, to show that they are true relics. It would be superstitious to use anything as a relic unless we were sure of its being genuine.

341. **Does the first commandment forbid the making of images?**
The first commandment does forbid the making of images if they are made to be adored as gods, but it does not forbid the making of them to put us in mind of Jesus Christ, his Blessed Mother, and the saints.

Protestants and others say that Catholics break the first commandment by having images in their churches, because the first commandment says: "Thou shalt not make graven images or the likeness of anything upon the earth," etc. Now, if that is exactly what the commandment means, then they break it also, because they make the images of generals, statesmen, writers, etc., and place them in their parks. They also take photographs of their relatives and friends and hang them on the walls of their homes. They do this, they say, and we believe them, to show their respect and veneration for the persons represented, and not to worship their images. Now we do no more. We simply place in our churches the images of saints to show our respect and veneration for the persons they represent, and not to worship the images themselves. So, if we break the first commandment, they who make any picture or statue break it also.

Can our accusers not see that they and every citizen do the very thing for which they reproach us? On Decoration Day, they place flowers around the statue of Washington and other great men. Does anyone believe that they are trying to honor the piece of metal or stone, or that the metal or stone statue knows that it is being honored? Certainly not. They do so to honor Washington or whomsoever the statue represents; and for the same reason, Catholics place flowers and lights around the statues and images of saints. Every child knows that the wood in the statue might as well have been a pillar in the Church, and that its selection for a statue was merely accidental, and hence he knows that the statue cannot hear or see him, and so he prays not to the statue but to the person it represents. Again, if you can offer a person insult by dishonoring his image, may we not honor him by treating it with respect? What greater insult, for instance, could be offered to your deceased father and yourself than to burn him in effigy, or contemptuously trample his picture underfoot in your presence? Thus, they who treat the images of Christ or his saints with disrespect dishonor Christ and his saints.

Again, we may learn our religion by our sight as well as by our hearing, and may be led by these visible objects to a knowledge of the invisible things they represent. Let us take an example. A poor ignorant man enters a Catholic church, and sees hanging there a picture of St. Vincent de Paul. He can learn the life of the saint from that picture almost as well as if he read it in a book. He sees the saint dressed in a cassock, and that tells him St. Vincent was a priest. He sees him surrounded by little ragged children and holding some of them in his arms; that tells him the saint took care of poor children and orphans, and founded homes and asylums for them. He sees on the saint's table a human skull, and that tells him St. Vincent frequently meditated upon death and what follows it. He sees beside the skull a little lash or whip, and that tells him the saint was a man who practiced penance and mortification. Thus, you have another reason why the true Church is very properly called "Catholic"; because its teaching suits all classes of persons. The ignorant can know what it teaches as well as the learned; for if they cannot read, they can listen to its priests, watch its ceremonies, and study its pictures, by all of which it teaches.

The protestant religion, on the contrary, is not adapted to the needs of every class, for it teaches that all must find their doctrines in the Bible, and understand them according to their lights, giving their own interpretation to the passages of the sacred text; and thus we come to have a variety of protestant denominations, all claiming the Bible for their guide, though following different paths. If every protestant has the right to take his own meaning out of the holy scripture, what right have protestant ministers to preach the meaning they have found, and compel others to accept it?

The Bible alone is not sufficient. It must be explained by the Church that teaches us also the traditions that have come down to us from the apostles. If the Bible alone were the rule of our faith, what would become of all those who could not read the Bible? What would become of those who lived before the apostles wrote the new testament? for they did not write in the first years of their ministry, neither did they commit to writing all the truths they taught, because our Lord did not command them to write, but to preach, and he himself never wrote any of his doctrines. Again, Catholics are accused of superstition for keeping the relics of saints. Yet, when General Grant died and was buried in New York, many citizens of every denomination, anxious to have a relic of the great man they loved and admired, secured, even at a cost, small pieces of wood from his house, of cloth from his funeral car, a few leaves or a little sand from his tomb. Now, if it was not superstition to keep these relics, why should it be superstition to keep the relics of the saints?

Even God himself honored the relics of saints, for he has often performed or granted miracles through their use. We read in the Bible[106]—and it is the word of God—that once some persons who were burying a dead man, seeing their enemies coming upon them, hastily cast the body into a tomb and fled. It was the tomb of the holy prophet Eliseus, and when the dead body touched the bones of this great servant of God, the dead man came to life and stood erect. Here is at least one miracle that God performed through the relics of a saint.

God does not forbid the mere making of images, but only the making of them as gods. He gave the commandments to Moses and afterward told him to make images; namely, angels of gold for the Temple.[107] Now, God does not change his mind or contradict himself as men do. Whatever he does is done forever. Therefore, if he commanded Moses by the first commandment not to make any images, he could not tell him later to make some. It is not the mere making, therefore, that God forbids, but the adoring. What he insists upon is: "You shall not adore or serve the images

[106] Cf. 4 Kgs 13:21

[107] Cf. Ex 25:18

you make." This is very clear if we consider the history of the Israelites, to whom God first gave the law. They were the only nation in the whole world that knew and worshipped the true God, and often, as I told you, they fell into idolatry and really worshipped images. When Moses delayed on the mountain with God, and they thought he was not coming back, they made a golden calf and adored it as a god.[108]

The Israelites fell into idolatry chiefly by associating with persons not of the true religion. Let us learn from their sins never to run the risk of weakening or losing our faith by making bosom friends and steady companions of those not of the true religion or of no religion at all. You are not, however, to treat any person with contempt or to despise anyone, but to look upon all as the children of God, and pray for those not of the true religion, that they may be converted and saved.

342. **Is it right to show respect to the pictures and images of Christ and his saints?**
It is right to show respect to the pictures and images of Christ and his saints, because they are the representations and memorials of them.

343. **Is it allowed to pray to the crucifix or to the images and relics of the saints?**
It is not allowed to pray to the crucifix or images and relics of the saints, for they have no life, nor power to help us, nor sense to hear us.

344. **Why do we pray before the crucifix and the images and relics of the saints?**
We pray before the crucifix and the images and relics of the saints because they enliven our devotion by exciting pious affections and desires, and by reminding us of Christ and of the saints, that we may imitate their virtues.

[108] Cf. Ex 32

LESSON THIRTY-SECOND

On the Second and Third Commandments

345. **What is the second commandment?**

The second commandment is: "Thou shalt not take the name of the Lord thy God in vain."

In vain—that is, without necessity.

346. **What are we commanded by the second commandment?**

We are commanded by the second commandment to speak with reverence of God and of the saints, and of all holy things, and to keep our lawful oaths and vows.

A very common sin against this commandment is to use the words and sayings of holy scripture in a worldly or bad sense. The Church forbids us to use the words and sayings of holy scripture to convey any meaning but the one God intended them to convey, or at least to use them in any but a sacred sense.

347. **What is an oath?**

An oath is the calling upon God to witness the truth of what we say.

We declare a thing to be so or not, and call God to be our witness that we are speaking truly. This is one of the most solemn acts that men can perform in the presence of their fellow men. All the nations of the earth regard an oath as a most sacred thing, and one who swears falsely is the vilest of men—a perjurer. God is infinite truth and hates lies. What a frightful thing then to call him to sanction a lie!

348. **When may we take an oath?**

We may take an oath when it is ordered by lawful authority or required for God's honor or for our own or our neighbor's good.

An oath is generally taken in a court of law when the judge wishes to find out the truth of the case. We may be a witness against one who is guilty, or in defense of an innocent person, and, in such cases, a lie would have most evil consequences. The judge has a right, therefore, to make us take an oath that we will testify truly. Officers of the law, magistrates, judges, etc., take an oath when entering upon their duties that they will perform them faithfully.

349. **What is necessary to make an oath lawful?**

To make an oath lawful, it is necessary that what we swear be true, and that there be a sufficient cause for taking an oath.

350. **What is a vow?**

A vow is a deliberate promise made to God to do something that is pleasing to him.

Deliberate—that is, with full consent and freedom. If we are forced to make it, it is not valid. *To God*, not to another; though we may vow to God that we will do something in honor of the Blessed Virgin, or of the saints, or for another. *Something pleasing*, because if we promise something that is forbidden by God or displeasing to him, it is not a vow. A solemn promise, for instance, to kill your neighbor or steal his goods could not be a vow. You would commit a sin by making such a vow, and another by keeping it; for if you promise something you cannot do without committing sin, then you must not keep that promise.

We have an example in the life of St. John the Baptist. King Herod was leading a sinful life; and St. John rebuked him for it. The wife of the king's brother—Herodias was her name—hated St. John for this, and she sought to have him killed. Once, when the king had a great feast and all his nobles were assembled, this woman's daughter danced before them, and the king was so pleased with her that he vowed to give her whatever she asked. He should have said, "if it is something pleasing to God," but he did not. Her mother made her ask for the head of John the Baptist. The king was sad, but because he had made the vow or promise, he thought he had to keep it, and ordered St. John to be beheaded and his head brought to her.[109] He was not bound to keep any such vow, and sinned by doing so.

Again, they also commit sin who become members of such secret societies as the Freemasons or similar organizations, promising to do whatever

[109] Cf. Mt 14

they are ordered without knowing what may be ordered; for they sin not only by obeying sinful commands, but by the very fact of being in a society in which they are exposed to the danger of being forced to sin. Such secret societies are forbidden by the Church because they strive to undermine its authority, and make their rules superior to its teaching. They also influence those in authority to persecute the Church and its ministers, and do not hesitate to recommend even assassination at times for the accomplishment of their ends. Therefore, the Church forbids Catholics to join societies of which 1) the objects are unlawful, 2) where the means used are sinful, 3) where the rights of our conscience and liberty are violated by rash or dangerous oaths.

The Church does not oppose associations founded on law and justice; but on the contrary, has always encouraged and still encourages every organization that tends to benefit its members spiritually and temporarily, and opposes only societies that have not a legitimate end. Therefore, you may understand that labor unions and benefit societies in which persons are leagued together for their own protection or the protection of their interests are not secret societies, though they may conduct their meetings in secret.

351. **Is it a sin not to fulfill our vows?**

Not to fulfill our vows is a sin, mortal or venial, according to the nature of the vow and the intention we had in making it.

Vows—that is, lawful vows. When a man, who is in the habit of getting intoxicated, vows not to take liquor for a certain time, he generally intends to bind himself only under venial sin; that is, if he breaks that pledge or promise it will be a venial and not a mortal sin; but he can make it a mortal sin by intending, when he takes the pledge, that if he breaks it he will be guilty of mortal sin.

352. **What is forbidden by the second commandment?**

The second commandment forbids all false, rash, unjust, and unnecessary oaths, blasphemy, cursing, and profane words.

Rash—swearing a thing is true or false without knowing for certain whether it is or not. *Blasphemy* is not the same as cursing or taking God's name in vain. It is worse. It is to say or do something very disrespectful to

God. To say that he is unjust, cruel or the like, is to blaspheme. We can blaspheme also by actions. To defy God by a sign or action, to dare him to strike us dead, etc., would be blasphemy.

We have a terrible example of blasphemy related in the life of Julian the Apostate. An apostate is one who renounces and gives up his religion, not one who merely neglects it. Julian was a Roman emperor and had been a Catholic, but apostatized. Then, in his great hatred for our Lord, he wished to falsify his prophecies and prove them untrue. Our Lord had said that of the Temple of Jerusalem there would not be left a stone upon a stone. To make this false, Julian began to rebuild the Temple. In making the preparation, he cleared away the ruins of the old building, not leaving a single stone upon a stone, and thus was instrumental himself in verifying the words of our Lord; for while the ruins remained, there were stones upon stones. He wished to defy God, but, when he began to build, fire came forth from the earth and drove back the workmen, and a strong wind scattered the materials. Afterward, Julian was wounded in battle, an arrow having pierced his breast. He drew it out, and, throwing a handful of his blood toward heaven, said: "Thou hast conquered, O Galilean," meaning our Lord. This was a horrible blasphemy—throwing his blood in defiance, and calling the Son of God a name which he thought would be insulting.[110] Therefore, we can blaspheme by actions or words, doing or saying things intended to insult Almighty God.

Profane words—that is, bad, but especially irreverent and irreligious words.

353. **What is the third commandment?**

The third commandment is: "Remember thou keep holy the sabbath day."

354. **What are we commanded by the third commandment?**

By the third commandment, we are commanded to keep holy the Lord's day and the holy days of obligation, on which we are to give our time to the service and worship of God.

[110] See Fredet's *Modern History*, "Life of Julian."

Holy days we are bound to keep holy just in the same manner we do Sundays—that is, by hearing Mass and refraining from servile works. Those who after hearing Mass must attend to business or work on those days should make this known to their confessor, that he may judge if they have a sufficient excuse for engaging in servile works, and thus they will avoid the danger of sinfully violating an important law. There must always be a good reason for working on a holy day. Those who are so situated that they can readily refrain from servile work on holy days must do so. And, where it is possible, the same opportunity must be afforded to their servants.

Of obligation, because there are some holy days not of obligation. We celebrate them, but we are not bound under pain of mortal sin to hear Mass or keep from servile works on such days. For example, St. Patrick's day is not a holy day of obligation. The great feast of Corpus Christi is not a holy day of obligation. Not satisfied with doing only what the Church obliges us to do on Sundays and holy days, those who really love God will endeavor to do more than the bare works commanded. Sunday is a day of rest and prayer. While we may take innocent and useful amusement, we should not join any public or noisy entertainments. We may rest and recreate ourselves, but we should avoid every place where vulgar and sometimes sinful amusements, scenes, or plays are presented. Even in taking lawful recreation, we may serve God and please him if we take it to strengthen our bodies that we may be enabled to do the work he has assigned to us in this world.

Sunday is well spent by those who, after hearing Mass, devote some part of the day to good works, such as pious reading, teaching in Sunday school, bringing relief to the poor and sick, visiting the Blessed Sacrament, attending vespers, rosary, etc. Not that I mean they should do nothing but pray on Sundays; but that they should not give the whole day to useless enjoyment or idleness, and forget God. Some begrudge God even the half hour they are obliged to give to Mass on Sundays: they stand near the door, ready to be the first out, and perhaps were the last in; or they come late, and do not give the full time necessary to hear the entire Mass. Others spend the whole day in reading newspapers, magazines, or useless—I will not say sinful—books. It is not a sin to read daily newspapers, etc., on Sunday;

but to give the whole time to them, and never to read anything good and instructive, is a willful waste of time—and waste of time is sinful.

There should be in every family, according to its means, one or more good Catholic newspapers or magazines. Not all papers that bear the name of Catholic are worthy of it. A truly Catholic paper is one that teaches or defends Catholic truth, and warns us against its enemies, their snares, deceptions, etc.; one, too, that tells us what is being done in the interests of religion, education, etc. Besides such a paper, there should be a few standard good books in every family; such as the new testament, the *Imitation of Christ*, a large and full catechism of Christian doctrine, etc. On the other hand, all the books in your house need not be books treating of religion or piety. Any book that is not against faith or morals may be kept and read. A book may not be bad in itself, but it may be bad for you, either because it is suggestive of evil, or you misunderstand it, and take evil out of it. In such a case, you should not read it. At the present time, there are so many bad books that persons should be very careful as to what they read.

Not only should we keep Sunday well ourselves, but we should endeavor to have it so kept by others. We must be careful, however, not to fall into the mistake of some who wish the Sunday to be kept as the Pharisees of old kept the sabbath, telling us we must not walk, ride, sail, or take any exercise or enjoyment on that day. This is not true, for our Lord rebuked the Pharisees for such excessive rigor; God made the Sunday for our benefit, and if we had to keep it as they say we must, it would be more of a punishment than a benefit.

355. **How are we to worship God on Sundays and holy days of obligation?**
We are to worship God on Sundays and holy days of obligation by hearing Mass, by prayer, and by other good works.

356. **Are the sabbath day and the Sunday the same?**
The sabbath day and the Sunday are not the same. The sabbath is the seventh day of the week, and is the day which was kept holy in the old law; the Sunday is the first day of the week, and is the day which is kept holy in the new law.

Old law means the law that God gave to the Jews; the *new law*, the law that our Lord gave to Christians.

357. **Why does the Church command us to keep the Sunday holy instead of the sabbath?**
The Church commands us to keep the Sunday holy instead of the sabbath because on Sunday Christ rose from the dead, and on Sunday he sent the Holy Ghost upon the apostles.

We keep Sunday instead of Saturday also to teach that the old law is not now binding upon us, but that we must keep the new law, which takes its place.

358. **What is forbidden by the third commandment?**
The third commandment forbids all unnecessary servile work and whatever else may hinder the due observance of the Lord's day.

359. **What are servile works?**
Servile works are those which require labor rather of body than of mind.

Servile—that is, work which was formerly done by the slaves. Therefore, writing, reading, studying, etc., are not servile, because they were not the works of slaves.

360. **Are servile works on Sunday ever lawful?**
Servile works are lawful on Sunday when the honor of God, the good of our neighbor, or necessity requires them.

Honor of God—for example, erecting an altar that could not be erected at another time, so that the people may hear Mass on that day.

Good of our neighbor—such as reconstructing a broken bridge that must be used every day; or clearing away obstacles after a railroad accident, that trains may not be delayed.

Necessity—firemen endeavoring to extinguish a fire, sailors working on a ship at sea, etc.

LESSON THIRTY-THIRD

On the Fourth, Fifth, and Sixth Commandments

361. **What is the fourth commandment?**
The fourth commandment is: "Honor thy father and thy mother."

362. **What are we commanded by the fourth commandment?**
We are commanded by the fourth commandment to honor, love, and obey our parents in all that is not sin.

In all that is not sin, because if our parents or superiors, being wicked, bid us do things that we know to be certainly sinful, then we must not obey them under any circumstances. God will not excuse us for doing wrong because we were commanded. But if, on the contrary, we are forced in spite of our resistance to do the sinful act, then not we but they have to answer for the sin. If, however, you simply doubt about the sinfulness of the act, then you must obey; because you must always suppose that your superiors know better than you the things that concern their duty. Even if they should be mistaken in the exercise of their authority, God will reward your obedience.

Besides obeying them, you must also help and support your parents if they need your assistance. You must not scoff at or despise them for their want of learning or refinement, because they perhaps have made many sacrifices to give you the advantages of which they in their youth were deprived. Do we not sometimes find persons of pretended culture ignorantly slighting their plain-mannered parents, or showing that they are ashamed of them or unwilling to recognize them before others, ungratefully forgetting that whatever wealth or learning they themselves have came through the love and kindness of these same parents? Again, is it not sinful for the children, especially of such parents, to waste their time in school, knowing that they are being supported in idleness by the hard toil and many sacrifices of a poor father? Never, then, be guilty of an unkind or ungrateful act. No matter who they are or what their condition, never forget those who have helped you and been your temporal or spiritual benefactors.

If you cannot return the kindness to the one who helped you, at least be as ready as he was to do good to another. It is told of a great man that, wishing always to do good, he made it a rule never to stand looking at the effects of a disturbance, disaster, or accident unless he could do some good by being there. Wherever you are, ask yourselves now and then, "Why am I in this particular place; what good am I doing here?" etc. St. Aloysius, when about to perform any action, used to ask himself, it is said, "What has this action to do with my eternal salvation?" And St. Alphonsus de Liguori made a vow never to waste a moment of his time. These were some of the great heroes of the Church, and this is one of the reasons why they could accomplish so much for God.

363. **Are we bound to honor and obey others than our parents?**
We are also bound to honor and obey our bishops, pastors, magistrates, teachers, and other lawful superiors.

Magistrates—that is, civil rulers, like the president, governor, mayor, judges, etc.

364. **Have parents and superiors any duties toward those who are under their charge?**
It is the duty of parents and superiors to take good care of all under their charge and give them proper direction and example.

It is so much their duty that God will hold them responsible for it, and punish them for neglecting it; so that your parents are not free to give you your own way. They have to do God's work, and, as his agents, punish you when you deserve it. You should take their punishment as coming from God himself. They do not punish you because they wish to see you suffer, but for your good. Think of the terrible responsibility of parents. Let us suppose that the parents of a family give bad example; their children follow their example, and, when they become heads of families, their children also will grow up in wickedness: and thus we can go on for generations, and all those sins will be traced back to the first bad parents. What is true for bad example is true also for good example; that is, the good done by the children will all be traced back to the parents.

Sometimes you may be punished when you are not guilty; then think of the times you were guilty and were not punished. Remember also how our Lord was falsely accused before Herod and Pilate, and yet he never opened his lips to defend himself, but suffered patiently. God sees your innocence and will reward you if you bear your trial patiently.

Indeed, we are foolish not to bear all our sufferings patiently, for we have to bear them anyway, and we might just as well have the reward that patient suffering will bring us. Those who suffer should find comfort in this: by suffering they are made more like our Lord and his Blessed Mother. She lived on earth over sixty years, and during all that time she seems never to have had any of those things that bring worldly pleasure and happiness. She was left an orphan when quite young, and spent her early life in the Temple, which was for her a kind of school; then she was married to a poor old carpenter, and must have found it very hard at times to get a living. Our Lord was born while she was away from home in a strange place. After she had returned and had just settled down in her little dwelling, she had to fly with St. Joseph into Egypt to save the life of the little infant Jesus, whom the king's officers were seeking to kill. In Egypt, they were strangers, among people not of their own nationality or religion, and St. Joseph must have found great difficulty in providing for them; yet they had to remain there for some time.

Then when our divine Lord was grown to manhood and could be a great comfort to his Mother, he was seized and put to death in her presence. Her most beloved and innocent Son put to death publicly as a criminal before all her neighbors! The same persons who insulted our Lord would not hesitate to insult and cruelly treat his Blessed Mother also. At his death, he left her no money or property for her support, but asked a friend, St. John, to receive her into his house and do him the favor of taking care of her. She must have often felt that she was a burden in that man's house; that she had no home of her own, but was living like a poor woman on the charity of kind friends, for St. Joseph died before our Lord's public life began. The Blessed Mother was, however, obliged to remain upon earth for about eleven years after our Lord's ascension. Thus, we see her whole life was one of trials and sorrows.

Now, certainly our Lord loved his Mother more than any other son could; and certainly also he, being God, could have made his Blessed Mother a queen upon the earth, rich and powerful among men, and free from every suffering or inconvenience. If, then, he sent her sorrows and trials, it must have been because these were best for her, and because he knew that, for this suffering here upon earth, her happiness and glory in heaven would be much increased; and as he wished her to have all the happiness and glory she was capable of possessing, he permitted her to suffer. If, then, suffering was good for our Lord's Mother, it is good also for us; and when it comes, we ought not to complain, but bear it patiently, as she did, and ask our Lord to give us that grace.

365. **What is forbidden by the fourth commandment?**

The fourth commandment forbids all disobedience, contempt, and stubbornness toward our parents or lawful superiors.

Contempt. Showing by our words or actions that we disregard or despise those placed over us. A man who is summoned to appear in court and does not come is punished for "contempt of court," because he shows that he disregards the authority of the judge. A thing not very bad in itself may become very bad if done out of contempt. For example, there would be a great difference between eating a little more than the Church allows on a fast day, simply because you were hungry, and eating it because you wanted to show that you despised the law of fasting and the authority of the Church. The first would be only a venial sin, but the latter mortal. So, for all your actions. An act which in itself might be a venial sin could easily become a mortal sin if you did it through contempt.

Stubbornness—that is, unwillingness to give in, even when you know you are wrong and should yield. Those who obey slowly and do what they are ordered in a sulky manner are also guilty of stubbornness.

366. **What is the fifth commandment?**

The fifth commandment is: "Thou shalt not kill."

367. **What are we commanded by the fifth commandment?**

We are commanded by the fifth commandment to live in peace and union with our neighbor, to respect his rights, to seek his spiritual and bodily welfare, and to take proper care of our own life and health.

Proper care of our own life. It is not our property, but God's. He lends it to us and leaves it with us as long as he pleases: nor does he tell us how long he will let us have the use of it. Thus suicide, or the taking of one's own life, is a mortal sin, for by it we resist the will of God. One who in sound mind and full possession of reason causes his own death is guilty of suicide. But it is sometimes very difficult to determine whether the person was really sane at the time he committed the act; hence, when there is any reasonable doubt on that point, the unfortunate suicide is usually given the benefit of it.

It is also a sin to risk our lives uselessly or to continue in any habit that we are sure is injuring our health and shortening our lives. Thus a habitual drunkard is guilty of sin against the fifth commandment, for, besides his sin of drunkenness, he is hastening his own death. So, too, boys or girls who indulge in habits which their parents forbid are guilty of sin. For example, a boy is forbidden to smoke, and he does smoke. Now to smoke is not in itself a sin, but it becomes a sin for that boy, because in the first place he is disobedient, and secondly is injuring his health. Thus, persons who indulge in sinful habits may commit more than one kind of sin, for besides the sins committed by the habits themselves, these vices may injure their health and bring sickness and disease upon their bodies.

368. **What is forbidden by the fifth commandment?**

The fifth commandment forbids all willful murder, fighting, anger, hatred, revenge, and bad example.

Therefore, it forbids all that might lead to murder. So, we can violate any of the commandments by doing anything that leads to breaking them. *Revenge* is a desire to injure others because they injured you.

369. **What is the sixth commandment?**

The sixth commandment is: "Thou shalt not commit adultery."

370. **What are we commanded by the sixth commandment?**

We are commanded by the sixth commandment to be pure in thought and modest in all our looks, words, and actions.

We should be most careful about this commandment, because almost every violation of it is a mortal sin. For example, if you steal only a little, it is a venial sin; for in stealing, the greatness of the sin will depend upon the amount you steal; but if you do a real bad action, or think a real bad thought against the sixth commandment, it will be a mortal sin, no matter how short the time. Again, we have more temptations against this commandment, for we are tempted by our own bodies and we cannot avoid them: hence the necessity of being always guarded against this sin. It enters into our soul through our senses; they are, as it were, the doors of our soul. It enters by our eyes, looking at bad objects or pictures; by our ears, listening to bad conversation; by our tongue, saying and repeating immodest words, etc. If, then, we guard all the doors of our soul, sin cannot enter. It would be foolish to lock all the doors in your house but one, for one will suffice to admit a thief, and we might as well leave them all open as one. So, too, we must guard all the senses; for sin can enter by one only as well as by all.

371. **What is forbidden by the sixth commandment?**
The sixth commandment forbids all unchaste freedom with another's wife or husband; also all immodesty with ourselves or others in looks, dress, words, or actions.

372. **Does the sixth commandment forbid the reading of bad and immodest books and newspapers?**
The sixth commandment does forbid the reading of bad and immodest books and newspapers.

Reading brings us into the company of those who wrote the book. Now, we should be just as careful to avoid a bad book as a bad man, and even more so; for while we read we can stop to think, and read over again, so that bad words read will often make more impression upon us than bad words spoken to us. You should avoid not only bad, but useless books. You could not waste all your time with an idle man without becoming like him—an idler. So, if you waste your time on useless books, your knowledge will be just like the books—useless. Many authors write only for the sake of money, and care little whether their book is good or bad, provided it sells well. How many young people have been ruined by bad books, and how many more by foolish books! Boys, for example, read in some worthless book of desperate deeds of highway robbery or piracy, and are at once filled with the desire to imitate the hero of the tale. Young girls, on the other hand, are equally infatuated by the wonderful fortunes and adventures of some young woman whose life has been so vividly described in a trashy novel. As the result of such reading, young persons lose the true idea of virtue and valor, of true, noble manhood and womanhood, and, with their hearts and minds corrupted, set up vice for their model.

Again, these books are filled with such terrible lies and unlikely things that any sensible boy or girl should see their foolishness at once. Think, for example, of a book relating how two boys defeated and killed or captured several hundred Indians! Is that likely? The truth is, if two Indians shook their tomahawks at as many boys as you could crowd into this building, every single one of them would run for his life.

Let me give you still another reason for not reading trashy books. Your minds can hold just so much good or evil information, and, if you fill them full of lies and nonsense, you leave no room for true knowledge.

Do not, therefore, get into the habit of reading foolish story-papers and cheap novels. Read good books in which you can find information that will be useful to you all through your life.

If now and then you read storybooks for amusement or rest from study, let them be good storybooks, written by good authors. Ask someone's advice about the books you read—someone who is capable of giving such advice: your pastor, your teachers, and frequently your parents and friends. Learn all through your life to ask advice on every important matter. How many mistakes in life would have been prevented if those making them had only asked advice from the proper persons and followed it. Your parents have traveled the road of life before you. Now it is known to them and they can point out its dangers. To you the road is entirely new, and it will be only after you have traveled it and arrived nearly at its end in the latter days of your life that you also will be able to advise others how to pass through it in safety. This road can be traveled only once, so be advised by those who have learned its many dangers by their own experience. You should be very glad that those of experience are willing to teach you; and if you neglect their warnings, you will be very sorry for it some day.

LESSON THIRTY-FOURTH

On the Seventh, Eighth, Ninth, and Tenth Commandments

373. **What is the seventh commandment?**

The seventh commandment is: "Thou shalt not steal."

Stealing is one of those vices of which you have to be most careful. Children should learn to have honest hearts, and never to take unjustly even the smallest thing; for some begin a life of dishonesty by stealing little things from their own house or from stores to which they are sent for goods. A nut, a cake, an apple, a cent, etc., do not seem much, but nevertheless to take any of them dishonestly is stealing. Children who indulge in this trifling thievery seldom correct the habit in afterlife and grow up to be dishonest men and women. How do you suppose all the thieves now spending their miserable lives in prison began? Do you believe they were very honest—never having stolen even the slightest thing—up to a certain day, and at once became thieves by committing a highway robbery? No; they began by stealing little things, then greater, and kept on till they made stealing their business and thus became professional thieves. Again, the little you steal each day does not seem much at the time, but if you put all the "littles" together you may soon have something big, and almost before you know it—if you intend to continue stealing—you may have taken enough to make you guilty of mortal sin. If you intended to steal, for instance, only a few cents every day for the whole year, you would at the end have stolen many dollars and committed a mortal sin.

There are many ways of violating the seventh commandment. Workmen who do not do a just day's work, or employers who cheat their workmen out of wages earned; merchants who charge unjust prices and seek unjust profits; dealers who give light weight or short measure or who misrepresent goods; those who speculate rashly or gamble with the money of others, and those who borrow with no intention or only slight hope of being able to pay back, all violate this commandment. You violate it also by not paying your just debts or by purchasing goods that you know you will never be able to pay for. Moreover, besides the injustice, it is base ingratitude not to pay your debts when in your power to do so. The one who trusted or lent you helped you in your need and did you a great favor, and yet, when you can, you will not pay, and what is worse, frequently abuse and insult him for asking his own. Though such dishonest and ungrateful persons may escape in this world, they will not escape in the next, for Almighty God will make them suffer for the smallest debt they owe.

Again, others often suffer for the dishonesty of those I have mentioned, for when some good person who really intends to pay is in great need and wishes to borrow or be trusted, he is refused because others have been dishonest. Everyone should pay his debts, and even keep from buying things that are not really necessary till he is thus enabled to pay what he owes. You must pay your just debts even before you can give anything in charity.

374. **What are we commanded by the seventh commandment?**

By the seventh commandment, we are commanded to give to all men what belongs to them and to respect their property.

Respect their property—that is, acknowledge and respect their rights to their property and do nothing to violate these rights.

375. **What is forbidden by the seventh commandment?**

The seventh commandment forbids all unjust taking or keeping what belongs to another.

Taking, either with your own hands or from the hands of another; for the one who willingly and knowingly receives from a thief the whole or part of anything stolen becomes as bad as the thief. Even if you only help another to steal, and receive none of the stolen goods, you are guilty. There are several ways of sharing in the sin of another, namely: by ordering or advising him to do wrong; by praising him for doing wrong and thus encouraging him; by consenting to wrong when you should oppose it—for instance, a member of a society allowing an evil act to be done by the society when his vote would prevent it; again, by affording wrongdoers protection and means of escape from punishment for their evil deeds. This does not mean that we should not defend the guilty. We should defend them, but should not encourage them to do wrong by offering them a means of escape from just punishment.

We share in another's sin also by neglecting to prevent his bad action when it is our duty to do so. For example, if a police officer paid for guarding your property should see a thief stealing it and not prevent him, he would be as guilty as the thief. Your neighbor indeed might warn you that the thief was stealing your goods, but he would not be bound in justice to do so, as the officer is, but only in charity, because it is not his duty to guard your property. Parents who know that their children steal and do not prevent them or compel them to bring back what they stole, but rather encourage them by being indifferent, are guilty of dishonesty as well as the children, and share in their sins of theft.

But suppose you did not know the thing was stolen when you received it, but learned afterward that it was, must you then return it to the proper owner? Yes; just as soon as you know to whom it belongs you begin to sin by keeping it. But suppose you bought it not knowing that it was stolen, would you still have to restore it? Yes, when the owner asks for it, because it belongs to him till he sells it or gives it away. If you have bought from a thief, you have been cheated and must suffer the loss. Your mistake will make you more careful on the next occasion. Suppose you find a thing, what must you do? Try to find its owner, and if you find him, give him what is his, and that without any reward for restoring it, unless he pleases to give you something, or unless you have been put to an expense by keeping it. If you cannot find the owner after sincerely seeking for him, then you may keep the thing found. But suppose you kept the article so long before looking for the owner that it became impossible for you to restore it to him, either because he had died or removed to parts unknown during your delay—what then? Then you must give the article or its value to his children or others who have a right to his goods; and if no one who has such a right can be found, you must give it to the poor, for you have it unjustly—since you did not look for the owner when it was possible to find him—and therefore cannot keep it.

376. **Are we bound to restore ill-gotten goods?**

We are bound to restore ill-gotten goods, or the value of them, as far as we are able; otherwise, we cannot be forgiven.

Ill-gotten—that is, unjustly gotten. *Value*. It sometimes happens that persons lose or destroy the article stolen, and therefore cannot return it. What must be done in such cases? They must give the owner the value of it. However, when you have stolen anything and have to restore it, you need not go to the owner and say, "Here is what I stole from you." It is only necessary that he gets what is his own or its value. He need not even know that it is being restored to him, unless he knows you stole it; and then it would be better for your own good name to let him know that you are making amends for the injustice done. Therefore, no one need have any excuse for not restoring what he has unjustly, because he has only to see that it is returned in some way to its owner, or to those who have the next right to it, or to the poor.

But you must remember you cannot make restitution by giving to the poor if you can restore to the proper owner. You must restore by giving to the poor only when the owner cannot be found or reached. Some persons do not like the duty of restoring to the proper owner, and think they satisfy their obligation by giving the ill-gotten goods to the poor; but they do not. You cannot give even in charity the goods of another without being guilty of dishonesty. If you wish to be charitable, give from your own goods.

It is a sin to delay making restitution after you are able to restore. You must restore just as soon as you can, because the longer you keep the owner out of his property and its benefits, the greater the injury you do him and the greater the sin. One who, after being told by his confessor to make restitution, and promising to do so, still delays or keeps putting off, runs the risk of being guilty of sacrilege by receiving the sacraments without proper dispositions.

But suppose a person cannot restore; suppose he lost the thing stolen and has not the value of it. What must he do? He must have the firm resolution of restoring as soon as he possibly can; and, without this good resolution, he could not be absolved from his sins—even if he had not the real means of restoring. The good intention and resolution will suffice till he has really the means; but this intention must be serious, otherwise there will be no forgiveness.

377. **Are we obliged to repair the damage we have unjustly caused?**

We are bound to repair the damage we have unjustly caused.

378. **What is the eighth commandment?**

The eighth commandment is: "Thou shalt not bear false witness against thy neighbor."

Either in a court, while we are acting as witnesses, or by telling lies about him at any other time.

379. **What are we commanded by the eighth commandment?**

We are commanded by the eighth commandment to speak the truth in all things, and to be careful of the honor and reputation of everyone.

Reputation. If it be a sin to steal a man's money, which we can restore to him, it is certainly a much greater sin to steal his good name, which we can never restore, and especially as we have nothing to gain from injuring his character. It is a sin to tell evil things about another—his sins, vices, etc.—even when they are true. The only thing that will excuse us from telling another's fault is the necessity to do so in which we are placed, or the good we can do to the person himself or others by exposing his faults.

How shall you know when you have injured the character of another? You have injured another's character if you made others think less of him than they did before. If you have exposed some crime that he really committed, your sin is called detraction; if you accuse him of one he did not commit, your sin is calumny; and if you maliciously circulate these reports, to injure his character, your sin is slander.

But how shall you make reparation for injuring the character of another? If you have told lies about him, you must acknowledge to those with whom you have talked that you have told what was untrue about him, and you must even compensate him for whatever loss he has suffered by your lies: for example, the loss of his situation by your accusing him of dishonesty. But if what you said of him was true, how are you to act? At every opportunity, say whatever good you can of him in the presence of those before whom you have spoken the evil.

380. **What is forbidden by the eighth commandment?**

The eighth commandment forbids all rash judgments, backbiting, slanders, and lies.

Rash judgment—that is, having in your mind and really believing that a person is guilty of a certain sin when you have no reason for thinking so, and no evidence that he is guilty. *Backbiting*—that is, talking evil of persons behind their backs. You would not like your neighbor to backbite you, and you have no right to do to him what you would not wish him to do to you. Besides, everyone hates and fears a backbiter; because, as he brings to you a bad story about another, he will in the same manner bring to someone else a bad story about you. It is certainly an honor to be able to say of a person, "He never has a bad word of anyone"; while, on the other hand, he must be a despicable creature who never speaks of others except to censure or revile them. Never listen to a backbiter, detractor, or slanderer—it is sinful.

Another way of injuring your neighbor is revealing the secrets he has confided to you. You will tell one friend perhaps and caution him not to repeat it to another; but if you cannot keep the secret yourself, how can you expect others to keep it? Again, you may injure your neighbor by reading his letters without his consent, when you have no authority to do so. This is considered a crime in the eyes even of the civil law, and anyone who opens and reads the letters of another can be punished by imprisonment. It is a kind of theft, for it is stealing secrets and information that you have no right to know. It is dishonorable to read another's letter without his consent, even when you find it open.

To carry to persons the evil things said about them by others so as to bring about disputes between them is very sinful. The holy scripture[111] calls this class of sinners "whisperers," and says that they will not enter into heaven—that is, as long as they continue in the habit. If ever, then, you hear one person saying anything bad about another, never go and tell it to the person of whom it was said. If you do, you will be the cause of all the sin that follows from it—of the anger, hatred, revenge, and probably murder itself, as sometimes happens.

[111] Cf. Rom 1:29

381. **What must they do who have lied about their neighbor and seriously injured his character?**

They who have lied about their neighbor and seriously injured his character must repair the injury done as far as they are able, otherwise they will not be forgiven.

382. **What is the ninth commandment?**

The ninth commandment is: "Thou shalt not covet thy neighbor's wife."

383. **What are we commanded by the ninth commandment?**

We are commanded by the ninth commandment to keep ourselves pure in thought and desire.

384. **What is forbidden by the ninth commandment?**

The ninth commandment forbids unchaste thoughts, desires of another's wife or husband, and all other unlawful impure thoughts and desires.

385. **Are impure thoughts and desires always sins?**

Impure thoughts and desires are always sins, unless they displease us and we try to banish them.

386. **What is the tenth commandment?**

The tenth commandment is: "Thou shalt not covet thy neighbor's goods."

Covet means to long for or desire inordinately or unlawfully. If I should desire, for example, my friend to be killed by an accident, in order that I might become the owner of his gold watch, I would be coveting it. But if I desired to have it justly—that is, to be able to purchase it, or another similar to it—that would not be covetousness.

387. **What are we commanded by the tenth commandment?**

By the tenth commandment, we are commanded to be content with what we have, and to rejoice in our neighbor's welfare.

388. **What is forbidden by the tenth commandment?**
The tenth commandment forbids all desires to take or keep wrongfully what belongs to another.

LESSON THIRTY-FIFTH

On the First and Second Commandments of the Church

389. **Which are the chief commandments of the Church?**
The chief commandments of the Church are six:

1. To hear Mass on Sundays and holy days of obligation.
2. To fast and abstain on the days appointed.
3. To confess at least once a year.
4. To receive the Holy Eucharist during the Easter time.
5. To contribute to the support of our pastors.
6. Not to marry persons who are not Catholics, or who are related to us within the fourth degree of kindred, nor privately without witnesses, nor to solemnize marriage at forbidden times.

390. **Is it a mortal sin not to hear Mass on a Sunday or a holy day of obligation?**
It is a mortal sin not to hear Mass on a Sunday or a holy day of obligation, unless we are excused for a serious reason. They also commit a mortal sin, who, having others under their charge, hinder them from hearing Mass without a sufficient reason.

Serious reason—that is, a very good reason, such as sickness, necessity of taking care of the sick, great danger of death, etc. Some persons when they go to the country in the summer believe themselves excused from hearing Mass because the church is a little further from them, or the Mass at more inconvenient times than in the city. When they are in the country, they are bound by the same obligations as the Catholics who live in that parish the whole year round, and they must go to Mass as these do, even if it is more inconvenient than in the city. Persons who have it in their power to select their own summer resort should not, without great necessity, select a place where there is no Catholic church, and where they will be deprived of Mass and the sacraments for several months, and where there is danger of their dying without the sacraments.

Some excuse themselves from going to Mass because they are too tired to rise in the morning. They should be ashamed to give such an excuse. Was our Blessed Lord not tired when he carried his cross? He was tired, for he fell under it several times. And where was he going? To Calvary, to offer up the bloody sacrifice of the cross for you. Will you plead fatigue as an excuse when you come to be judged by him?

Others again have a great habit of coming late for Mass. No matter at what hour the Mass may be, they will always be late; and I am afraid these persons will also be too late to enter heaven. By coming late, they show disrespect to our Lord and distract others; and to avoid doing so, they should, when late, take a place in the rear of the church. When you are very late for one Mass, you should wait for the next—at least, for as much of the next as you did not hear in the first. You should not, however, begrudge a little extra time to God.

To hear Mass properly, you should be in your place a few minutes before the priest comes out, and make up your mind what blessing you will ask, or for what intention you desire to hear the Mass.

Having others under their charge. Some parents are very careless about their children attending Mass, especially on holy days. Now, they must remember that in such neglect, the sin will be theirs as well as the children's. Again, masters and mistresses do not at times give their workmen and servants sufficient opportunity to hear Mass, above all on holy days. All masters and mistresses must remember that they are bound not only to give their servants an opportunity to hear Mass, but they are bound as far as they conveniently can to see that they embrace the opportunity, just as they should see to their children in such matters. Catholics having in their employ others, such as engineers, drivers, conductors, etc., must make some arrangement between their men by which they will be able to attend Mass on Sundays and holy days. The same holds good for companies and corporations having under their charge a large force of men who are obliged by circumstances to work on Sundays.

391. **Why were holy days instituted by the Church?**

Holy days were instituted by the Church to recall to our minds the great mysteries of religion and the virtues and rewards of the saints.

For just the same reason that the government has legal holidays. What would the people of this country know or think at the present time about the Declaration of Independence and all connected with it, if they did not celebrate from childhood every year, on the fourth of July, the great day on which their forefathers claimed to be free and independent from the nation that was persecuting them? The fourth of July keeps alive in our memory the struggles of our ancestors of one hundred years or more ago—their great battles, their sufferings and triumph, the blessings they secured for us, and for which we praise them. In like manner, the feast of the Resurrection of our Lord keeps us in mind of the sad condition in which we were before our Lord redeemed us, and how he liberated us from the slavery of the devil and secured for us so many wonderful blessings. Again, what would we remember about George Washington if we did not celebrate his birthday? That holiday keeps before our minds the life and actions of that great man and all he did for our benefit. So, too, when we celebrate every year the feast of a saint in the Church, it keeps before our minds his works and all that he did for God and the Church, and makes us anxious to imitate his virtues. On every day in the year, the Church honors some mystery of our holy faith or some saint by saying Mass all over the world in honor of the feast, and by obliging the priests and bishops to say the divine office for the same purpose. The feast day of a saint is generally the day on which he died; because that is considered the day on which he entered into heaven—the day on which he was born into the new world.

The *divine office* is a collection of prayers, hymns, lessons, and psalms which every priest and bishop must read every day of his life. As it is said each day in honor of some particular mystery or saint, the greater part of it differs for each day. The prayers are to God, asking some grace or blessing in honor of the saint—generally such graces as were granted to the saint. The hymns are in the saint's honor; the lessons are parts of the holy scripture, or an account of the saint's life; and the psalms are those beautiful poems that King David composed and sung to God. The divine office is the prayer of the universal Church for its children, and if a priest neglects to say it, he commits a mortal sin. It takes about an hour to say the whole divine office, but it is not intended to be said all at once. It is so divided that it is said at three times in the day. The part called "matins" and "lauds" is said very early in the morning and before Mass. The part called "little hours" is said later in the day; and the part called "vespers" and "compline" is said in the afternoon. See, therefore, how anxious the Church is for the good of its children, when it makes its bishops, priests, and religious pray daily for all the faithful, and send up in one voice the same prayer to the throne of God.

392. **How should we keep the holy days of obligation?**

We should keep the holy days of obligation as we should keep the Sunday.

393. **What do you mean by "fast days"?**

By "fast days," I mean days on which we are allowed but one full meal.

One full meal, with a collation, or very light meal (eight ounces), in the evening. Tea, coffee, water, or liquids taken at this collation are not included in the eight ounces. We are also allowed, in the morning, a small piece of bread (weighing not more than two ounces) and a cup of tea, coffee, or chocolate. They, therefore, who follow the above regulations obey the precept of fasting. If it is more convenient to take the full meal in the evening and the collation at noon, the order may be inverted; but flesh meat should not be eaten by those who are obliged to fast before twelve o'clock as a general rule, even on days on which by dispensation it is allowed at the principal meal. I say "those who are obliged to fast," because they who are excused can, where the dispensation is granted, use flesh meat more than once a day and at any hour on days when it is allowed to all at the principal meal. Fish and flesh must not be used at the same meal on fast days, nor even on the Sundays of Lent.

Those who, for sufficient reasons, are excused from the obligation of fasting, are not on that account freed from the law of abstinence, for all who have come to the use of reason are bound to abstain from flesh meat on days when it is forbidden. In general, the following persons are excused from fasting: 1) those who are not yet twenty-one or over sixty years of age; 2) those whose infirmity, condition, or occupation renders it impossible or dangerous for them to fast. If you think you should be excused from fasting or abstaining, state your reasons to your confessor and ask his advice. Any day on which the Church forbids the use of flesh meat becomes the same as Friday. On a fast day, therefore, you have to look both to the quantity and the kind of food, while on a day of abstinence—as Friday—you have to look only to the kind, and may take as much as you please of anything but flesh meat. Every fast day is a day of abstinence, but every day of abstinence is not a fast day.

394. **What do you mean by "days of abstinence"?**
By "days of abstinence," I mean days on which we are forbidden to eat flesh meat, but are allowed the usual number of meals.

395. **Why does the Church command us to fast and abstain?**
The Church commands us to fast and abstain in order that we may mortify our passions and satisfy for our sins.

Mortify our passions, keep our bodies under control, do bodily penance. Remember it is our bodies that generally lead us into sin; if, therefore, we punish the body by fasting and mortification, we atone for the sin, and thus God wipes out a part of the temporal punishment due to it.

396. **Why does the Church command us to abstain from flesh meat on Fridays?**
The Church commands us to abstain from flesh meat on Fridays in honor of the day on which our Savior died.

LESSON THIRTY-SIXTH

On the Third, Fourth, Fifth, and Sixth Commandments of the Church

397. **What is meant by the command of confessing at least once a year?**

By the command of confessing at least once a year is meant that we are obliged, under pain of mortal sin, to go to confession within the year.

Within the year—that is, the time between your confessions must never be longer than a year, or at least not longer than the period between the beginning of one Easter time and the end of the next. All persons who have attained the age of reason are bound to comply with this precept, and parents should remind their children of it.

398. **Should we confess only once a year?**

We should confess frequently, if we wish to lead a good life.

Some seem to think that they need not go to confession if they have not committed sin since their last confession. Two graces are given in penance, as you already know: one, to take away the sins confessed; and the other, to strengthen us against temptation and enable us to keep our good resolutions. Now, as we are always tempted, we should go frequently to confession to get the grace to resist. The saints used to go to confession very frequently, sometimes every day. They used to go when tempted, to obtain the grace to resist and to expose their temptations to their confessor and ask his advice.

Again, the holy scripture tells us that "the just man falls seven times";[112] and "just man" in holy scripture means a very good man, that is, one doing for God, his neighbor, and himself what he ought to do. St. Joseph is called in the scripture a "just man,"[113] and he was the foster-father of our Lord. Now, if the good man falls seven times, he must arise after each fall; for if he did not get up after the first fall, he could not fall the second time. This

[112] Prv 24:16
[113] Mt 1:19

teaches us that we all commit some kind of sin, at least, and have always something to confess if we only examine our conscience closely. It teaches us also that when we have the misfortune to fall into sin, we should rise as quickly as possible.

399. **Should children go to confession?**
Children should go to confession when they are old enough to commit sin, which is commonly about the age of seven years.

To commit sin—that is, when they know the difference between good and evil.

400. **What sin does he commit who neglects to receive Communion during the Easter time?**
He who neglects to receive Communion during the Easter time commits a mortal sin.

401. **What is the Easter time?**
The Easter time is, in this country, the time between the First Sunday of Lent and Trinity Sunday.

Trinity Sunday is the Eighth Sunday after Easter. Therefore, the whole Easter time is from the First Sunday of Lent—that is, seven weeks before Easter—to Trinity Sunday, eight weeks after it, or fifteen weeks in all; and anyone who does not go to Holy Communion sometime within these fifteen weeks commits mortal sin.

402. **Are we obliged to contribute to the support of our pastors?**
We are obliged to contribute to the support of our pastors, and to bear our share in the expenses of the Church and school.

And any charitable institution connected with the Church. The Holy Land was divided among the tribes of Israel, who were the descendants of the twelve sons of Jacob. Now, one of these twelve tribes was made up entirely of priests and persons who served in the Temple of God, called "Levites." They received none of the land, but were to be supported by the other eleven tribes. All the people were obliged by the law to give what they called "firstfruits" and "tithes"—that is, one tenth of their income in goods or money each year to the Temple for its support and the support of those who served it. In the new law, no definite amount is assigned, but every Christian is left free to give what he can to God's Church according to his generosity. But if God left you free, should you therefore be stingy with him? Moreover, all that we have comes from God, and should we return him the least and the worst? For every alms you give for God's sake, he can send you a hundred blessings; and what you refuse to give to his Church or poor, he can take from you in a thousand ways, by sending misfortunes.

We read in the Bible[114] that Adam's sons, Cain and Abel, both offered sacrifice to God. Abel's sacrifice was pleasing, but Cain's was not. Why? Because, as we are told, Cain did not offer to God the best he had, but likely the worst; or at least, he offered his sacrifice with a bad disposition. Then, when he saw that his brother's sacrifice was pleasing to God, being filled with jealousy, he killed him; and in punishment, God marked him and condemned him to be a wanderer on the face of the earth. We are told he was always afraid of being killed by everyone he saw. See, then, what comes of being unwilling to be generous with God.

What we give him he does not need, but, by giving, we worship and thank him. Do not people in the world often give presents to those who have done them a favor, that they may thus show their gratitude? Now, God is always doing us favors, and why should we not show our gratitude to him by giving generously in his honor? When we give to the orphans, etc., we give to him; for he says: "Whatsoever you give to these little ones you give to me."[115] Again, when our Lord tells what will happen on the day of judgment,[116] he says the judge will divide all the people of the world into two bodies; the good he will place on his right hand and the wicked on his left. Then he will praise the good for what they did and welcome them to heaven; but to the wicked he will say, "Depart from me, because when I was hungry you gave me not to eat; when I was thirsty you gave me not to drink; you clothed me not," etc. And then the wicked shall ask,

[114] Cf. Gn 4
[115] Cf. Mt 10:42
[116] Cf. Mt 25:31ff

"When did we see you in want and not relieve you?" He will tell them that he considered the poor just the same as himself; and as they did nothing for his poor, they did nothing for him.

403. **What is the meaning of the commandment not to marry within the fourth degree of kindred?**

The meaning of the commandment not to marry within the fourth degree of kindred is that no one is allowed to marry another within the fourth degree of blood relationship.

Fourth degree. What relatives are in the fourth degree? Brother and sister are in the first degree; first cousins are in the second degree; second cousins are in the third degree; and third cousins are in the fourth degree. Therefore, all who are third cousins or in nearer relationship cannot be married without a dispensation from the Church allowing them to do so. A dispensation granted by the Church is a permission to do something which its law forbids. Since it made the law, it can also dispense from the observance of it. The Church could not give permission to do anything that God's law forbids. It could not, for example, give permission to a brother and sister to marry, because it is not alone the law of the Church but God's law also that forbids that. But God's law does not forbid first, second, or third cousins to get married; but the Church's law forbids it, and thus it can in special cases dispense from such laws. God's law is called also the "natural law."

You must be very careful not to confound the marriage laws that the Church makes with the marriage laws that the state makes. When the state makes laws contrary to the laws of God or of the Church, you cannot obey such laws without committing grievous sin. For instance, the state allows divorce; it allows persons to marry again if the husband or wife has been sentenced to imprisonment for life; it does not recognize all the impediments to marriage laid down by the Church. Such laws as these Catholics cannot comply with; but when the state makes laws which regard only the civil effects of marriage, such as refer to the property of the husband or wife, the inheritance of the children, etc., laws, in a word, which are not opposed either to the laws of God or of his Church, then you may and must obey them; for the authorities of the government are our lawful superiors, and must be obeyed in all that is not sin.

What we have said with regard to the marriage laws is true for all the rest. Thus, the civil court might, on account of some technicality, free you legally from the payment of a debt; but that would not free you in conscience from paying what you justly owe. Again, the court might legally decide in your favor in an unjust suit; but that would not give you the right in conscience to keep what you have thus fraudulently or unjustly obtained.

404. **What is the meaning of the command not to marry privately?**
The command not to marry privately means that none should marry without the blessing of God's priests or without witnesses.

If persons wishing to be married suspect that there is any impediment existing between them, they should express their doubts and the reasons for them to the priest.

Here it is well for you to know that if any Catholic goes to be married before a protestant minister, he is, by the laws of the Church in the United States, excommunicated. You must know *excommunication* means "cut off from the communion of the Church and the body of the faithful; cut off from the sacraments and from a share in all the Holy Masses and public prayers offered by the Church throughout the world." It is a punishment the Church inflicts upon its disobedient children who will not repent but persist in wrongdoing. If they die willfully excommunicated, they die in mortal sin, and no Mass or funeral prayers can be publicly offered for them; nor can they be buried in consecrated ground.

Besides the excommunicated, there are others who cannot be buried in consecrated ground: namely, infants or others who have not been baptized; those who deliberately committed suicide; those who have publicly lived sinful lives and evidently died in that public sin; and all persons who are not Catholics. If a Catholic who is not publicly a sinner dies suddenly, we cannot judge that he is in mortal sin; and hence such a one may be buried in consecrated ground. It is the desire of the Church that all its faithful children should be buried in the ground which it has blessed for their remains; and wherever it is possible, Catholics must have their own burying ground.

405. **What is the meaning of the precept not to solemnize marriage at forbidden times?**

The meaning of the precept not to solemnize marriage at forbidden times is that, during Lent and Advent, the marriage ceremony should not be performed with pomp or a nuptial Mass.

Persons may be married at these times quietly, wherever it is not positively forbidden by the laws of the diocese.

406. **What is the nuptial Mass?**

The nuptial Mass is a Mass appointed by the Church to invoke a special blessing upon the married couple.

It is a Mass especially for them and cannot be said for anyone else. At the most solemn parts of the Mass, the priest turns to them and prays that God may bless their union.

407. **Should Catholics be married at a nuptial Mass?**

Catholics should be married at a nuptial Mass, because they thereby show greater reverence for the holy sacrament and bring richer blessings upon their wedded life.

The Church wishes to give to the marriage of its children observing its laws all the solemnity possible, and to impress its dignity and sanctity so deeply upon their minds that they may never forget the solemn promises made at the altar of God. The thought of that day will keep them from sin. On the other hand, the Church shows its great displeasure when Catholics do not keep its laws, but marry persons not of their own religion. At a mixed marriage, the couple cannot be married in the church, nor even in the sacristy; the priest cannot wear a surplice or stole or any of the sacred vestments of the Church; he cannot use holy water, or the sign of the cross; he cannot bless the ring or even use the Church's language—Latin. Everything is done in the coldest manner, to remind Catholics that they are doing what is displeasing to their mother the Church.

Again, the Church wishes its children to prepare for the sacrament of matrimony just as they would prepare for any other sacrament—penance, Holy Eucharist, holy orders, etc. Imagine a boy going up for first Communion laughing, talking, or gazing about him, without any thought of the great sacrament he is about to receive; thinking only of how he appears in his new clothing, of those who are present, etc., and spending all his time of preparation not in purifying his soul, but in adorning his body! Think of him returning from Holy Communion and immediately forgetting our Lord! Now, matrimony is deserving of all the respect due to a sacrament, and hence the Church wishes all its children to be married at Mass; or at least in the morning. It does not like them to marry in the evening, and go to the reception of the sacrament as they would to a place of vain amusement. For on such occasions, they cannot show the proper respect in the church, and possibly turn the ceremony into an occasion of sin for all who attend; for they often seem to forget the holiness of the place and the respect due to the presence of our Lord upon the altar. Indeed, it should be remembered, at whatever time the marriage takes place, that conduct, dress, and all else must be in keeping with the dignity of the place and the holiness of the sacrament, and that women should not come into the church with uncovered heads.

LESSON THIRTY-SEVENTH

On the Last Judgment and the Resurrection, Hell, Purgatory, and Heaven

408. **When will Christ judge us?**

Christ will judge us immediately after our death, and on the last day.

Immediately. In the very room and on the very spot where we die, we shall be judged in an instant, and even before those around us are sure that we are really dead. When we have a trial or judgment in one of our courts, we see the judge listening, the lawyers defending or trying to condemn, and the witnesses for or against the person accused. We are in the habit of imagining something of the same kind to take place in the judgment of God. We see Almighty God seated on his throne; our angel and patron saint giving their testimony about us—good or bad—and then we hear the judge pronounce sentence. This takes place, but not in the way we imagine, for God needs no witnesses: he knows all.

An example will probably make you understand better what really takes place. If you are walking over a very muddy road on a dark night, you cannot see the spattered condition of your clothing; but if you come suddenly into a strong light, you will see at a glance the state in which you are. In the same way, the soul during our earthly life does not see its own condition; but when it comes into the bright light of God's presence, it sees in an instant its own state and knows what its sentence will be. It goes immediately to its reward or punishment. This judgment, at the moment of our death, will settle our fate forever. The general judgment will not change, but only repeat the sentence before the whole world.

Oh, how we should prepare for that awful moment! See that poor sick man slowly breathing away his life. All his friends are kneeling around him, praying; now he becomes unconscious; now the death rattle sounds in his throat; now the eyes are fixed and glassy. A few minutes more and that poor soul will stand in the awful presence of God, to give an account of that man's whole life—of every thought, word, and deed. All he has done on earth will be spread out before him like a great picture. He will, toward the end of his life, have altogether forgotten perhaps what he thought, said, or did on a certain day and hour—the place he was in and the sin committed, etc.; but at that moment of judgment, he will remember all. How he will wish he had been good! How, then, can we be so careless now about a matter of such importance, when we are absolutely certain that we too shall be judged, and how soon we know not.

When you are about to be examined on what you have learned in school or instructions in six months or a year, how anxious you are in making the necessary preparation, and how you fear you might not pass, but be kept back for a while! How delighted you would be to hear that a very dear friend, and one who knew you well, was to be your examiner! Prepare in the same way for the examination you have to stand at the end of your life. Every day you can make a preparation by examining your conscience on the sins you have committed; by making an act of contrition for them, and resolving to avoid them for the future. You should never go to sleep without some preparation for judgment. But above all, try to become better acquainted with your examiner—our Lord Jesus Christ; try by your prayers and good works to become his special friend, and, when your judgment comes, you will be pleased rather than afraid to meet him.

409. **What is the judgment called which we have to undergo immediately after death?**
The judgment we have to undergo immediately after death is called "the particular judgment."

Particular, because one particular person is judged.

410. **What is the judgment called which all men have to undergo on the last day?**
The judgment which all men have to undergo on the last day is called "the general judgment."

General, because every creature gifted with intelligence will be judged on that day—the angels of heaven, the devils of hell, and all men, women, and children that have ever lived upon the earth. The holy scripture gives us a terrible account of that awful day.[117] On some day—we know not when, it might be tomorrow for all we know—the world will be going on as usual, some going to school, others to business; some seeking pleasure, others suffering pain; some in health, others in sickness, etc. Suddenly they will feel the earth beginning to quake and tremble; they will see the ocean in great fury, and will be terrified at its roar as, surging and foaming, it throws its mighty waves high in air. Then the sun will grow red and begin to darken; a horrid glare will spread over the earth, beginning to burn up. Then, says the holy scripture, men will wither away for fear of what is coming; they will call upon the mountains to fall and hide them; they will be rushing here and there, not knowing what to do. Money will be of no value then; dress, wealth, fame, power, learning, and all else will be useless, for at that moment all men will be equal.

Then shall be heard the sound of the angel's great trumpet calling all to judgment. The dead shall come forth from their graves, and the demons

[117] Cf. Mt 24-25

rush from hell. Then all shall see our Blessed Lord coming in the clouds of heaven in great power and majesty, surrounded by countless angels bearing his shining cross before him. He will separate the good from the wicked; he will welcome the good to heaven and condemn the wicked to hell. The sins committed shall be made public before all present. Imagine your feelings while you are standing in that great multitude, waiting for the separation of the good from the bad. To which side will you be sent? Our Lord is coming, not with the mild countenance of a savior, but with the severe look of a judge. As he draws nearer and nearer to you, you see some of your dear friends, whom you thought good enough upon earth, sent over to the side of the wicked; you see others that you deemed foolish sent with the good, and you become more anxious every instant about the uncertainty of your own fate. You see fathers and mothers sent to opposite sides, brothers and sisters, parents and children, separated forever. Oh, what a terrible moment of suspense! How you will wish you had been better and always lived a friend of God!

The side you will be on depends upon what you do now, and you can be on the better side if you wish. Do, then, in your life, what you would wish to have done at that terrible moment. Learn to judge yourself frequently. Say this, or something similar, to yourself: "Now I have lived twelve, fifteen, twenty, or more years; if that judgment came today, on which side should I be?" Probably on the side of the wicked. If then I spend the rest of my life as I have lived in the past, on the last day I shall surely be with the wicked. If my good deeds and bad deeds were counted today, which would be more numerous? What, then, must I do? It will not be enough for me simply to be better for the future—I must try also to make amends for the past. If a man wishing to complete a journey on a certain time, by walking a fixed number of miles each day, falls behind a great deal on one day, he must not only walk the usual number of miles the next, but must make up for the distance lost on the previous day. So, in our journey through this life, we must do our duty each day for the future, and, as far as we can, make up for what we have neglected in the past.

411. **Why does Christ judge men immediately after death?**

Christ judges men immediately after death to reward or punish them according to their deeds.

412. **What are the rewards or punishments appointed for men's souls after the particular judgment?**

The rewards or punishments appointed for men's souls after the particular judgment are heaven, purgatory, and hell.

413. **What is hell?**

Hell is a state to which the wicked are condemned, and in which they are deprived of the sight of God for all eternity, and are in dreadful torments.

Deprived of the sight of God. This is called the "pain of loss," while the other sufferings the damned endure are called the "pain of sense"—that is, of the senses. The pain of loss causes the unfortunate souls more torment than all their other sufferings; for as we are created for God alone, the loss of him—our last end—is the most dreadful evil that can befall us. This the damned realize, and know that their souls will be tortured by a perpetual yearning never to be satisfied. This is aggravated by the thought of how easily they might have been saved, and how foolishly they threw away their happiness and lost all for some miserable pleasure or gratification, so quickly ended.

Besides this remorse, they suffer most frightful torments in all their senses. The worst sufferings you could imagine would not be as bad as the sufferings of the damned really are; for hell must be the opposite of heaven, and since we cannot, as St. Paul says, imagine the happiness of heaven, neither can we imagine the misery of hell. Sometimes you will find frightful descriptions of hell in religious books that tell of the horrible sights, awful sounds, disgusting stenches, and excruciating pains the lost souls endure. Now, all these descriptions are given rather to make people think of the torments of hell than as an accurate account of them. No matter how terrible the description may be, it is never as bad as the reality.

We know that the damned are continually tormented in all their senses, but just in what way we do not know. We know that there is fire in hell, but it is entirely different from our fire; it neither gives light nor consumes what it burns, and it causes greater pain than the fire of earth, for it affects both body and soul. We know that the damned will never see God, and there will never be an end to their torments.

Now, all this is contained in the following: hell is the absence of everything good and the presence of everything evil, and it will last forever. Now, a priest coming out to preach on hell would not say to the people: "Hell is the absence of everything good and the presence of everything evil, and it will last forever," and then step down from the altar and say no more. He must give a fuller explanation to those who are unable to think for themselves. He must point out some of the evils present in hell and some of the good things absent, and thus teach the people how to meditate on these dreadful truths. If, then, you bear in mind that there is nothing good in hell and it will last forever, and often think of these two points, you will have a holy fear of the woeful place and a deep sorrow for your sins, which expose you to the danger of suffering its torments.

It should be enough, therefore, for you to remember: there is nothing good in hell, and it will last forever. Think of anything good you please and it cannot be found in hell. Is light good? Yes. Then it is not in hell. Is hope good? Yes. Then it is not in hell. Is true friendship good? Yes. Then it is not in hell. There the damned hate one another. There the poor sufferers curse forever those who led them into sin. Hence, persons should try to bring back to a good life every one they may have led into sin or scandalized by bad example.

414. **What is purgatory?**

Purgatory is the state in which those suffer for a time who die guilty of venial sins, or without having satisfied for the punishment due to their sins.

Punishment—that is, temporal punishment, already explained to you. After the general judgment, there will be heaven and hell, but no purgatory, for there will be no men living or dying upon the earth in its present condition to go there. All will be dead and judged and sent to their final abodes. Those in purgatory are the friends of God; and knowing him as they do now, they would not go into his holy presence with the slightest stain upon their souls; still they are anxious for their purgatory to be ended that they may be with God. They suffer, we are told, the same pains of sense as the damned; but they suffer willingly, for they know that it is making them more pleasing to God, and that one day it will all be over and he will receive them into heaven. Their salvation is sure, and that thought makes them happy. If, therefore, you believe any of your friends are in purgatory, you should help them all you can, and try by your prayers and good works to shorten their time of suffering. They will help you—though they cannot help themselves—by their prayers. And oh, when they are admitted into heaven, how they will pray for those that have helped them out of purgatory! If you do this great charity, God will, when you die, put it in some good person's heart to pray for you while you suffer in purgatory. There must be a purgatory, for one who dies with the slightest stain of sin upon his soul cannot enter heaven, and yet God would not send him to hell for so small a sin. But why does God punish those he loves? Why does he not forgive everything? He punishes because he is infinitely just and true. He warned them that if they did certain things they would be punished; and they did them, and God must keep his promise. Moreover, he is just, and must give to every one exactly what he deserves.

415. **Can the faithful on earth help the souls in purgatory?**
The faithful on earth can help the souls in purgatory by their prayers, fasts, almsdeeds; by indulgences, and by having Masses said for them.

416. **If everyone is judged immediately after death, what need is there of a general judgment?**
There is need of a general judgment, though everyone is judged immediately after death, that the providence of God, which on earth often permits the good to suffer and the wicked to prosper, may in the end appear just before all men.

Providence of God. Sometimes here on earth we see a good man always in want, out of employment, sickly, unsuccessful in all his undertakings, while his neighbor, who is a very bad man, is wealthy and prosperous, and seems to have every pleasure. Why this is so we cannot understand now, but God's reason for it will be made known to us on the day of judgment. Sometimes the wicked do good actions here on earth—help the poor, or contribute to some charity, for instance; and as God on account of their wickedness cannot reward them in the next world, he rewards them chiefly in this world by temporal goods and pleasures. For all their good deeds they get their reward in this world, and for the evil their punishment in the next. The good man who suffers gets all his reward in the next world, and even his sufferings here atone partly for the evil he has done.

A second reason for a general judgment is to show the crimes of sinners and the justice of their punishment; also, that the saints may have all their good works made known before the world and receive the glory they deserve. On earth, these saints were sometimes considered fools and treated as criminals, falsely accused, etc.; and now, the whole truth will stand out before the world. But above all, the general judgment is for the honor and glory of our Lord. At his first coming into the world, he was poor and weak; many would not believe him the Son of God, and insulted him as an impostor. He was falsely accused, treated shamefully, and was put to death, many believing him guilty of some crime. Now he will appear before all as he really is—their Lord and master, their Creator and judge. How they will tremble to look upon him whom they have crucified! How all those who have denied him, blasphemed him, persecuted his Church, and the like, will fear when they see him there as judge! How they will realize the terrible mistake worldlings made!

417. **Will our bodies share in the reward or punishment of our souls?**
Our bodies will share in the reward or punishment of our souls, because, through the resurrection, they will again be united to them.

418. **In what state will the bodies of the just rise?**
The bodies of the just will rise glorious and immortal.

We honor the dead body and treat it with great respect because it was the dwelling place of the soul and was often nourished with the sacraments; also, because it will rise in glory and be united with the soul in the presence of God forever. For these reasons, we use incense and holy water when the body is to be buried, and even bless the ground in which it is laid. *Faithful departed* means "all those who died in a state of grace and who are in heaven or purgatory." They may be in purgatory, and so we pray for them. We pray that they may "rest in peace"—that is, be in heaven, where they will have no sufferings.

419. **Will the bodies of the damned also rise?**

The bodies of the damned will also rise, but they will be condemned to eternal punishment.

420. **What is heaven?**

Heaven is the state of everlasting life in which we see God face-to-face, are made like unto him in glory, and enjoy eternal happiness.

The most delightful place we could possibly imagine as heaven would not be near what it really is. Everything that is good is there and forever, and we shall never tire of its joys. All the pleasures and beauties of earth are as nothing compared with heaven; and though we think we can imagine its beauty and happiness now, we shall see how far we have been from the real truth if ever we reach this heavenly home. *God face-to-face*—that is, as he is. We shall not see him with the eyes of the body, but of the soul. That we may see with our natural eyes, two things are necessary: first, an object to look at, and secondly, light to see it. Now, to see God in heaven, we need a special light, which is called the "light of glory." God himself gives us this light and thus enables us to see him as he is. This beautiful vision of God in heaven is called the "beatific vision," and thus our whole life in heaven—our joy and happiness—consists in the enjoyment of the beatific vision.

421. **What words should we bear always in mind?**

We should bear always in mind these words of our Lord and Savior Jesus Christ: "What doth it profit a man if he gain the whole world and suffer the loss of his own soul, or what exchange shall a man give for his soul? For the Son of Man shall come in the glory of his Father with his angels: and then will he render to every man according to his works."[118]

What does it benefit the poor creatures in hell to have been rich, or beautiful, or learned, or powerful? If they had been good, it was all that was necessary to escape all their sufferings. Is there anything on earth that they would not give to be released? Why, then, did they sell their souls for

[118] Cf. Mk 8:36-38; Rom 2:6

so little while on earth? The present is the only time you have to merit heaven and escape hell. The past you cannot recall, and of the future you are not sure. Then use the present well and decide daily whether you wish to be in heaven or in hell.

Questions on the Explanations

The Lord's Prayer

1. Who made the Lord's Prayer?
2. Why do we say *our* and not *my* Father?
3. Why do we call God "Father"?
4. What Person of the Blessed Trinity is meant by *Father* in the Lord's Prayer?
5. Was God called "Father" before the time of our Lord? Why?
6. Why do we say, "Who art in heaven," if God is everywhere?
7. What does *hallowed* mean?
8. What do we ask for by "Thy kingdom come"?
9. What does "Thy kingdom" mean here?
10. Who do God's will in heaven?
11. What do we ask for by "our daily bread"?
12. Why do we say *daily*?
13. What do *trespasses* mean?
14. What do we mean by "as we forgive those who trespass against us"?
15. What example did our Lord give?
16. What is temptation?
17. Does God tempt us to sin?
18. Is it a sin to be tempted?
19. Are there any tempters besides the devil?
20. Should we seek temptation?

21. What does *Amen* mean?
22. What does *Christian* mean?
23. What makes us Christians?
24. What does *doctrine* mean?

The Angelical Salutation

25. How many parts in the Hail Mary?
26. What part did the angel Gabriel make?
27. When did he make it?
28. How did Mary know what the angel's words meant?
29. What part of the Hail Mary did St. Elizabeth make?
30. Who was St. Elizabeth's son?
31. Why is Mary called "blessed amongst women"?
32. What part of the Hail Mary did the Church make?
33. What does *hail* mean?
34. Why do we say, "full of grace"?
35. Why is Mary called "holy"?
36. Why do we need Mary's prayers at the hour of death?
37. What is the *Angelus*?
38. What does "the Word" mean?
39. What does "made flesh" mean in the third part of the *Angelus*?
40. What is the Litany of the Blessed Virgin?
41. Are there other litanies besides the Litany of the Blessed Virgin?

The Apostles' Creed

42. What is a creed?
43. Who were the apostles?
44. Were the apostles bishops or priests?
45. How do you know?
46. Who were the disciples of our Lord?
47. Why did the apostles make the Creed?
48. How many articles or parts in the Apostles' Creed?

49. What does *Creator* mean?
50. By what names is our Lord called?
51. How many sons had God the Father?
52. Why do we say, "died," instead of, "was killed"?
53. Why do we say, "He was buried"?
54. Is limbo the same as purgatory? Why?
55. Who were in limbo at the time our Lord was crucified?
56. Name some good men who lived before Christ.
57. Did our Lord's body descend into limbo?
58. Was our Lord three full days in the holy sepulchre?
59. How can you prove they could not put our Lord to death unless he permitted it?
60. Why do we say, "right hand of God," when God has no hands?
61. What do you mean by "judge the living and the dead"?
62. Who are "the living"?
63. Who are "the dead" mentioned here?
64. What are ghosts?
65. Are there any?
66. What do you mean by the "Church militant"?
67. Who are its members?
68. Who are the enemies of our salvation?
69. Why does the devil wish to keep us out of heaven?
70. What do we mean when we say "the world" is one of our spiritual enemies?
71. Have all the saints their bodies in heaven?
72. Who are in heaven in their bodies at present?
73. What is meant by our *concupiscence*?
74. Which tempts us most to sin, our soul or our body? Why?
75. Why did God leave concupiscence in us?
76. What do we mean by the "Church suffering"?
77. Who are its members?
78. Why are souls in purgatory?
79. What do you mean by the "Church triumphant"?
80. Who are its members?
81. Are there any saints in heaven whose names we do not know?

82. Who are saints?
83. What is the difference between a saint and an angel?
84. Why does the Church canonize holy persons?
85. Does canonization make the person a saint?
86. How does the Church canonize a saint?
87. Explain the "communion of saints."
88. What is the difference between beatification and canonization?
89. How is the resurrection of the body possible?
90. What is death?
91. What does "life everlasting" mean?
92. How many fathers had our Lord? Who were they?
93. How many mothers had he?
94. Of what religion was Pontius Pilate?
95. Are all in heaven saints?

The Confiteor and Acts

96. In how many ways can we sin?
97. What should we think of when we say the *confiteor*?
98. What is the substance of the "act of faith"?
99. Why do we find different acts of faith?
100. What is the substance of the "act of hope"?
101. What is the substance of the "act of love"?
102. Do an "act of love" and an "act of charity" mean the same?
103. How do you show that they are the same?
104. What makes us help others?
105. How may we be charitable to our neighbor?
106. What is the substance of the "act of contrition"?
107. What does *grace* at meals mean?
108. Why should we say grace at meals?
109. Why should we be content with our food?
110. Is the Apostles' Creed an act of faith?
111. Did John the Baptist institute the sacrament of baptism?
112. In giving baptism, can one pour the water and another say the words?

CATECHISM

Lesson First

113. What is a catechism?
114. What does our catechism contain?
115. Why should we learn the catechism?
116. What do we mean by the "end of man"?
117. For what end was man created?
118. In what respect are all men equal?
119. What is woman?
120. In the first question, what does *world* mean?
121. What is a creature?
122. Is every invisible thing a spirit?
123. Of what use is reason to us?
124. What makes man different from all other animals?
125. Have any brute animals reason?
126. How do you know brute animals have not reason?
127. Can we learn all truths by our reason alone?
128. What is revelation?
129. What is "free will" in man?
130. Have brute animals free will?
131. Why is it necessary for us to know God?
132. What does *worship* mean?
133. How do we know when we love God above all?
134. Does the Apostles' Creed contain all the truths we must believe?
135. Name some truths not mentioned in it.
136. Is a tree a creature?

Lesson Second

137. What is a spirit?
138. What does *infinite* mean?
139. Why does God watch over us?

140. Why is it necessary for God to watch over us?
141. Why must God be just as well as merciful?

Lesson Third

142. What does *supreme* mean?
143. When are two persons said to be equal?
144. From whom does authority come?
145. Is there any difference in the ages of God the Father and God the Son?
146. Do *first*, *second*, and *third* in the Blessed Trinity mean that one Person was before the other?
147. Why must we believe mysteries?
148. Must we understand everything we believe?

Lesson Fourth

149. How may the things God created be classed?
150. Why did God create angels?
151. If angels have no bodies, how can they appear?
152. Are the angels all equal in dignity?
153. How many classes of angels are there?
154. What did the archangel Michael do?
155. What did the archangel Gabriel do?
156. Who gave the angels their names?
157. What are the duties of the angels?
158. What does our angel guardian do for us?
159. How do you know that the angels offer our prayers and good works to God?
160. Give a short history of Tobias.
161. What do we mean by "Jacob's ladder"?
162. Are there other guardian angels besides the guardian angels of persons?
163. Name some persons to whom angels appeared.
164. Were angels ever sent to punish men?
165. If God watches over us, why should angels guard us?

166. What was the devil's name before he was cast out of heaven?
167. Why was he cast out?
168. Is the Blessed Virgin only a creature? Why?

Lesson Fifth

169. How did God create Eve?
170. What relation was Eve to Adam?
171. Were Adam and Eve created at the same time?
172. What was the "garden of paradise"?
173. How did Adam commit his first sin?
174. How was Eve tempted to disobey God?
175. In what way do we sometimes imitate Eve's conduct?
176. Why does the devil tempt us?
177. What were the effects of Adam's sin?
178. Why do we suffer for the sin of our first parents?
179. What did Adam lose by his sin?
180. What do you mean when you say Adam's will was *weakened* by sin?
181. Can we always overcome temptation if we wish?
182. Why was the Blessed Virgin preserved from original sin?

Lesson Sixth

183. How is sin divided?
184. In what ways can we commit actual sin?
185. What is a sin of omission? Give an example.
186. How is heaven a reward?
187. How can we merit it?
188. Are all religions equally good? Why?
189. What do you mean by a person's *vocation*?
190. How are we to know our vocation?
191. How should parents act with regard to their children's vocation?
192. When is a soul said to be dead?
193. How can we judge whether a thing is sinful or not?

194. What is a material sin?
195. Why is it wrong to judge others guilty of sin?
196. Why does venial sin lessen the love of God in our hearts?
197. Why are pride, covetousness, etc., called "capital sins"?
198. What is meant by our *predominant* or *ruling* sin?
199. What is pride?
200. Why should we take care of our bodies?
201. What sins follow pride?
202. What is covetousness?
203. What sins follow covetousness?
204. What is lust?
205. What sins follow lust?
206. What is gluttony?
207. What kind of sin is drunkenness?
208. How can we commit gluttony by eating?
209. How can we commit gluttony by drinking?
210. What sins does the drunkard commit?
211. What three great sins should you always guard against?
212. Why are drunkenness, dishonesty, and impurity so dangerous?
213. What is envy?
214. How do we commit the sin of sloth?
215. How can we best destroy sin in our souls?
216. Should we cease striving to be good, if we seem to be making no improvement? Why?

Lesson Seventh

217. What does *incarnation* mean?
218. What does *redemption* mean?
219. Who are slaves?
220. How were we in slavery by the sin of Adam?
221. What price did our Lord pay to redeem us?
222. Did our Lord leave us any means of being redeemed more than once?
223. What does *abandon* mean?

224. Has heaven really gates?
225. What are the "gates of heaven"?
226. Is our Lord now in heaven as God or as man?
227. Who was our Lord's foster-father?
228. What is a foster-father?
229. How many years from the time Adam sinned till the Redeemer came?
230. Why did God allow so long a time to pass before redeeming us?
231. What was the deluge?
232. When and why did God send it?
233. Who were saved from the deluge? How?
234. What animals did Noe have in the ark?
235. What were the "clean animals"? Name some.
236. Why did he have more *clean* than *unclean* animals?
237. How long did Noe spend in making the ark?
238. How old was Adam when he died?
239. Who was the oldest man?
240. What was his age?
241. How did the deluge come upon the earth?
242. How long did the ark float upon the waters?
243. How did Noe learn that the waters were going down?
244. What was the condition of men before the coming of our Lord?
245. When and to whom did God promise the Redeemer?
246. What did the prophets foretell about Christ?
247. Why was the Redeemer not welcomed by all when he came?
248. What day of the year is Annunciation day?
249. How could the good people of the old law be saved by the merits of Christ, when Christ was not yet born?
250. In what kind of a stable was our Lord born?
251. Why did the Blessed Virgin and St. Joseph go to Bethlehem before the birth of our Lord?
252. Who were the Magi?
253. What brought them to Bethlehem?
254. Why did King Herod wish to find the infant Jesus?
255. On what feast do we commemorate the adoration of the Magi?

256. At what time of the year is the Epiphany?
257. What is the feast of Holy Innocents?
258. When does it come?
259. Give a short history of our Lord's life.
260. What do we mean by his "hidden life"?
261. What do we mean by his "public life"?
262. How old was our Lord when he began his public life?
263. What do we know of our Lord's hidden life?
264. Why did he lead a hidden life for so many years?
265. Does *mankind* mean men or women?
266. Had our Lord any brothers or sisters?
267. What did the angel Gabriel say at the annunciation?

Lesson Eighth

268. What do you mean by our Lord's *passion*?
269. When did it begin and when did it end?
270. Give an account of our Lord's passion.
271. Where was Gethsemani or the Garden of Olives?
272. Who went into it with our Lord?
273. What did our Lord do in this garden?
274. What else happened there?
275. What caused our Lord's sufferings in the garden?
276. Why could Christ's body suffer greater pain than ours?
277. What do we mean by the "agony in the garden"?
278. Who betrayed our Lord?
279. How did the Jews act unjustly in the trial of our Lord?
280. What was the "scourging at the pillar"?
281. What was the "crowning with thorns"?
282. What happened at the death of our Lord?
283. Where was Calvary?
284. Why were no criminals put to death in Jerusalem?
285. How was the Temple of Jerusalem divided?
286. What was the "holy of holies"?

287. What was the "ark of the covenant," and what did it contain?
288. Of what were the ark and its contents figures?
289. What was the veil of the Temple?
290. Why was this veil rent asunder at the death of our Lord?
291. What does *Calvary* mean?
292. Why was our Lord crucified between thieves?
293. Why do we call one of these the "penitent thief"?
294. Why did Christ suffer more than was necessary?
295. What is a sepulchre?
296. How was our Lord buried?
297. What did the Jews count the beginning and the end of their day?
298. Was the Jewish religion ever the true religion?
299. What is a miracle?
300. What does a miracle prove?
301. What miracles did our Lord perform?
302. What was his greatest?
303. What are the qualities of a glorified body?
304. Show that our Lord's body had all these qualities.
305. What was the "transfiguration of our Lord"? Describe it.
306. Who were present at it?
307. What happened on the way to Emmaus?
308. What benefit is derived from Thomas the apostle doubting the resurrection of our Lord?
309. Will all who rise on the last day have glorified bodies?
310. What does the "stigmata of our Lord" mean?
311. Did anyone ever have it?
312. Was our Lord visible to everyone during the forty days after his resurrection?
313. About how many times and to whom did he appear during the forty days?
314. Describe our Lord's ascension.
315. Did Christ live always at Bethlehem?

Lesson Ninth

316. Did the Holy Ghost ever appear?
317. When and under what forms?
318. What does *Whitsunday* mean?
319. What does *Pentecost* mean?
320. What effect did the coming of the Holy Ghost have upon the apostles?
321. How many temples had the Jews?
322. What was a *synagogue?*
323. What was done in the synagogues?
324. How did the synagogues differ from the Temple?
325. What did the feast of the Pasch or Passover commemorate?
326. Give a short history of Moses?
327. How did the Israelites come to be in Egypt?
328. Give an account of their sufferings in Egypt?
329. How were they delivered or liberated?
330. Give a short account of Joseph and his family?
331. Why did Joseph's brothers wish to put him to death?
332. What did they do to hide their crime?
333. What did the king of Egypt dream?
334. What did his dream mean?
335. What do we learn from the life of Joseph in Egypt?
336. How was Moses saved on the bank of the Nile?
337. What was the "burning bush" that Moses saw?
338. Why did God command Moses to remove his shoes before coming to the burning bush?
339. Who went with Moses to deliver the Israelites?
340. What signs did God give Moses to show King Pharao?
341. What did the king's magicians do?
342. What were the "ten plagues of Egypt"?
343. Describe each plague.
344. Why did God send them?
345. What was the "paschal lamb"?
346. Of what was it a figure?

347. What happened to the Israelites and Egyptians at the Red Sea?
348. How long were the Israelites in the desert?
349. What was the *manna*?
350. Why were the Israelites so long in the desert?
351. What do you mean by the "gift of tongues"?
352. Why did God perform more miracles in the first ages of the Church than now?
353. How and where was St. Peter put to death?
354. How did the other apostles die?
355. St. Paul?
356. What did the apostles prove by suffering death for their faith?

Lesson Tenth

357. What do we mean by an *effect*?
358. What does *supernatural* mean?
359. What is merit?
360. What is a virtue?
361. What is a vice?
362. Does habit excuse us for the sins committed through it?
363. When will habit excuse us for the sin?
364. Why do we believe revealed truths?
365. Who is our neighbor?
366. What example did our Lord give to explain this?
367. How do we love our neighbor as ourselves?
368. Why should we love our neighbor?
369. Can we merit the grace of perseverance?

Lesson Eleventh

370. When did men begin to speak different languages?
371. Who were the prophets?
372. Give a short history of religion before the time of Christ.
373. What are the chief works of the Church?

374. Why are our churches holy?
375. What are the catacombs, and why were they made?
376. What are altar stones?
377. Why are relics placed in them?
378. How many general persecutions of the Church were there?
379. Tell what you know of these persecutions?
380. What lessons do we learn from the sufferings of the early Christians?
381. Who are "lawful pastors"?
382. Could anyone be pope without being bishop of Rome?
383. What does *vicar* mean?
384. Why are Catholics called "Roman"?
385. What do we mean by the "soul of the Church"?

Lesson Twelfth

386. What is an attribute?
387. What is authority?
388. Why is it sinful to resist lawful authority?
389. What does *cathedra* mean?
390. Why is the bishop's church called "cathedral"?
391. How do we know when the pope speaks *ex cathedra?*
392. What is required that the pope may so speak?
393. Is the pope infallible in everything he says?
394. What do you mean by "faith and morals"?
395. How many popes from St. Peter to Leo XIII?
396. Why should we have the greatest respect for the opinions of the holy father on any subject?
397. Why must the pope sometimes speak on political matters?
398. Can the pope commit sin?
399. What do we mean by the "temporal power" of the pope?
400. How did he acquire it, and how did he lose it?
401. Why has he need of it?
402. How is the temporal power useful to the Church?
403. What is "Peter's pence"?

404. Does the Church change its doctrines?
405. How can you show that the Church is one in government and doctrine?
406. What is the hierarchy of the Church?
407. Could a person be a Catholic and not believe all the Church teaches?
408. Why are protestants so called?
409. Why does the Church use Latin as its language?
410. Why does the Church define some truths?
411. Does the Church, by defining truths, make new doctrines?
412. Give a short history of Luther.
413. Why was he cut off from the true Church?
414. Why did many follow him?
415. How did the first protestants act toward the Church?
416. What foolish excuses do some give for not becoming Catholics?
417. Why must the true Church be visible?
418. Who are heathens?
419. Who were the *publicans* mentioned by our Lord?

Lesson Thirteenth

420. What three things are necessary to make a sacrament?
421. What is the outward sign in baptism?
422. Why is water used in baptism?
423. What is the outward sign in confirmation?
424. Why is oil used in confirmation?
425. What is the use of the outward sign in the sacraments?
426. In what ways does the life of the soul resemble the life of the body?
427. What does a "sacrament of the dead" mean?
428. In what ways can we commit sacrilege?
429. What is the sacramental grace given in penance?
430. What are the "right dispositions" for penance, for Holy Eucharist?
431. What is conditional baptism, and when is it given?
432. Can all the sacraments be given conditionally?
433. What is the outward sign in matrimony?
434. Can a bishop give all the sacraments?

435. Can a priest?
436. Can a person receive all the sacraments?
437. Can any of the sacraments be given to the dead?

Lesson Fourteenth

438. What is an heir?
439. Why is the Bible called "the old and new testament"?
440. What does the old testament contain?
441. What does the new testament show?
442. What is the difference between baptism and penance in the remission of the guilt and punishment?
443. Could a person gain an indulgence immediately after baptism? Why?
444. What does the "temporal punishment" for sin mean?
445. Where will persons go who have never sinned and who die without baptism?
446. What do we mean by "the ordinary minister" of a sacrament?
447. Can you baptize an infant when its parents are unwilling?
448. What is private baptism?
449. How is it given?
450. What ceremonies are used in solemn baptism?
451. What do they signify?
452. What is the baptistery?
453. What do we mean by the *pomps* of the devil?
454. What is martyrdom?
455. Who are catechumens?
456. What is necessary that persons may be really martyrs?
457. What is meant by "patron saint"?
458. On what day is a saint's feast kept by the Church?
459. What does *sponsors* mean? Who are sponsors by proxy?
460. With whom do godparents contract relationship?
461. What names should be given in baptism?

Lesson Fifteenth

462. What does balm in the chrism signify?
463. Why should we be proud of the Catholic religion?
464. When are we required to profess our religion?

Lesson Sixteenth

465. Why is the devil wiser than we are?
466. Who made the beatitudes?
467. Where did our Lord generally preach?
468. What do the beatitudes teach?
469. How is a person "poor in spirit"?
470. How can the rich be poor in spirit?
471. Explain the other beatitudes.

Lesson Seventeenth

472. How does the institution of penance show the goodness of our Lord?
473. What is absolution?
474. How do you know our Lord could forgive sins?
475. How does the power to forgive sins imply the obligation of going to confession?
476. How do we prepare for confession?
477. What is the best method of examining our conscience?
478. What is the most important part of the sacrament of penance?
479. What kind of sorrow should we have for our sins?
480. When should you say the penance given in confession?

Lesson Eighteenth

481. When is our contrition perfect?
482. What is attrition?
483. How many kinds of occasions of sin are there?

484. Why must we avoid occasions of sin?

Lesson Nineteenth

485. Who is a "duly authorized" priest?
486. How can a dumb man make his confession?
487. What can one do who cannot remember his sins in confession?
488. How can persons whose language the priest cannot understand confess if they are in danger of death?
489. Is it wrong to accuse ourselves of sins we have not committed?
490. Why is it foolish to conceal sins in confession?
491. How were the ancient Christian churches divided?
492. How did the early Christians do penance?
493. Explain the temporal and eternal punishment for sin.
494. Is your confession worthless if you forget to say your penance?
495. What is Lent?
496. What is almsgiving?
497. How can we distinguish between spiritual and corporal works of mercy?
498. When are we obliged to admonish the sinner?
499. What were the Crusades?
500. Why were they commenced?
501. How many Crusades were there?
502. How long did they last?
503. Why were those who took part in these expeditions called "Crusaders"?
504. What is a pilgrim?
505. How have we been relieved from doing many of the works of mercy ourselves?
506. Who are religious?
507. What is a hermit?
508. What is a general confession?
509. When and why should we make it?
510. Who are scrupulous persons?

Lesson Twentieth

511. When is it well to add to our confession a sin of our past life?
512. What duties does the priest perform in the confessional?
513. Show how he is judge, father, teacher, and physician.
514. Why is it well to confess always to the same priest?
515. Can you have half your sins forgiven?
516. When will perfect contrition blot out mortal sin?

Lesson Twenty-First

517. How does God reward us for good works done in a state of mortal sin?
518. Is it easy to gain a plenary indulgence? Why?
519. What works are generally enjoined for indulgences?
520. What does praying for a "person's intention" mean?
521. How can we have the intention of gaining an indulgence?
522. What does "an indulgence of forty days," etc., mean?
523. Why did the early Christians do more severe penance than we do?
524. Are indulgences attached to anything but prayers?

Lesson Twenty-Second

525. What does *Eucharist* mean?
526. What is the difference between Holy Eucharist and Holy Communion?
527. What did our Lord do at the marriage in Cana?
528. Is our Lord's body in the Holy Eucharist living or dead?
529. How do you know you receive both the body and the blood of our Lord under the appearance of bread alone?
530. Why does the Church not give the Holy Eucharist to the people under the appearance of wine also?
531. Could it do so? Did it ever do it?
532. How long does our Lord remain in the Holy Communion?
533. What is the ciborium?
534. At what part of the Mass are the words of consecration said?

535. What are the parts of the Mass?
536. What is the sacristy?
537. What does the priest prepare for Mass?
538. What is the chalice?
539. What is the paten?
540. What is the purificator?
541. What is the pall?
542. What is the host?
543. Where does the priest get the host?
544. What are the different vestments used at Mass called?
545. What do they signify?
546. What is the *offertory* in the Mass?
547. When does the *Canon* of the Mass begin?
548. What is the *elevation* in the Mass?
549. Where does the priest get the Blessed Sacrament he gives to the people?
550. What is the tabernacle?
551. What is benediction of the Blessed Sacrament?
552. What is the monstrance used at benediction?
553. Why should we be anxious to attend benediction?
554. What is the cope?
555. What is the humeral, or benediction veil?
556. Why does the priest wear vestments?
557. What do their colors signify?
558. Can Holy Communion be given in the afternoon?
559. What is the Holy Eucharist called when received by a person who is not fasting?
560. Can the priest say Mass in the evening? Why?
561. Why does the priest genuflect, etc., during Mass?

Lesson Twenty-Third

562. What should we do if we break our fast before Holy Communion?
563. When is Holy Communion called the "viaticum"?
564. Who offered the first Sacrifice of the Holy Mass?

Lesson Twenty-Fourth

565. When is the Holy Eucharist a sacrifice?
566. When a sacrament?
567. What was the temple of the Pantheon in Rome?
568. Who are pagans, idolaters, heathens?
569. How many kinds of sacrifice had the Israelites?
570. How is the Mass a sacrifice?
571. What is the League of the Sacred Heart?
572. Why was it established?
573. What was the origin of offering the priest money for celebrating Mass for your intention?
574. What is the sin of simony?
575. Why is it so called?
576. How are the fruits of the Mass divided?
577. What is a spiritual Communion?
578. How is it made?

Lesson Twenty-Fifth

579. What does *unction* mean?
580. How often in their lives are Catholics anointed?
581. Is it called "extreme unction" even when the person recovers after receiving it?
582. What parts of the body are anointed in extreme unction?
583. When should the priest be sent for in cases of sickness?
584. What should you do if the sick Catholic does not wish or refuses to see the priest?
585. How is sickness a benefit to some?
586. What sacraments are never given in the church?
587. What things should you prepare when the priest is coming to give the viaticum or extreme unction in your house?
588. How is the Blessed Sacrament carried to the sick in Catholic countries?

589. Who are the "other ministers of the Church," besides bishops and priests?
590. What is the tonsure?
591. Of what does the tonsure remind the priest?
592. What are the duties and privileges of these other ministers of the Church?
593. How many kinds of Masses are there?
594. Do they differ in value, one being better than another?
595. Who is meant by the *celebrant* of the Mass?
596. What does the "master of ceremonies" do?
597. What is a Requiem Mass?
598. Why is it so called?
599. What is vespers?
600. Is it a mortal sin to be willingly absent from vespers?
601. Will vespers take the place of Mass on Sundays for those who do not attend Mass?
602. Who are cardinals?
603. What are their duties?
604. Who is a monsignor?
605. Who is a vicar-general?
606. What is a diocese?
607. What is a parish?
608. Does *rector* and *pastor* mean the same?
609. What do we mean by "suffragan bishops"?
610. What is the pallium?
611. Who can wear it?

Lesson Twenty-Sixth

612. When are persons lawfully married?
613. When was marriage first instituted?
614. What sin is it to marry unlawfully?
615. What are "impediments to marriage"?

616. What things should persons tell the priest when they are making arrangements for marriage?
617. Can persons marry invalidly without knowing it?
618. What evils follow divorce?
619. Why should children study?
620. What is meant by the "civil effects of marriage"?
621. Which are the chief evils of "mixed marriage"?
622. What is a mixed marriage?
623. When are motives for marriage *worthy*?
624. How should persons make a choice for marriage?
625. How are parents sometimes guilty of injustice to their children in case of marriage?
626. What is holy oil?
627. When is it blessed?
628. Can a priest bless it in case of necessity?
629. How many kinds of holy oil are there?
630. For what are they used?
631. In the administration of what sacraments is oil used?
632. Can persons receive the sacrament of matrimony more than once?
633. Where and at what time of the day should Catholics be married?
634. What is balm?
635. Was there any sacrament of matrimony before the time of our Lord?
636. Were the people of the old law validly married?
637. How did their marriage differ from Christian marriage?

Lesson Twenty-Seventh

638. Can the Church change the number of sacramentals? Why?
639. Why is it necessary to bless yourself properly?
640. When are candles blessed in the Church?
641. Of what do candles on the altar remind us?
642. When are ashes blessed in the Church?
643. Of what do they remind us?
644. Of what do palms remind us?

645. What is the difference between a cross and a crucifix?
646. What is the rosary?
647. How do we say the beads?
648. What is meant by "mysteries of the rosary"?
649. How many mysteries of the rosary are there?
650. How are they divided?
651. Name the different mysteries of the rosary.
652. What is the *Magnificat*?
653. Who baptized our Lord?
654. Was the baptism by John the Baptist a sacrament? Why?
655. To whom did our Lord give an example by his hidden or private life?
656. What did the Church do for slaves?
657. What do the letters *I. N. R. I.* over the cross mean?
658. Did our Lord claim to be king of the Jews?
659. Why was our Lord put to death?
660. With whom did the Blessed Virgin live after the death of our Lord?
661. Who was St. John the Evangelist?
662. What is the Apocalypse?
663. About how long did the Blessed Virgin live on earth after the ascension of our Lord?
664. What is meant by the *assumption* of the Blessed Virgin?
665. What proof have we of it?
666. On what days are the different mysteries of the rosary said?
667. What does *I. H. S.* with a cross over it mean?
668. What is the scapular, and why do we wear it?
669. What is the brown scapular called?
670. How many kinds of scapulars are there?
671. What are the "seven dolors" of the Blessed Virgin? Name them.
672. What are seven-dolor beads?
673. What are "religious orders"?
674. What vows do the members of religious orders take?
675. Why were religious orders founded?
676. Why are there different kinds of religious orders?

Lesson Twenty-Eighth

677. How many kinds of prayer are there?
678. What is *meditation*?
679. What should we do before praying?
680. What do you know of St. Monica?
681. Of St. Augustine?
682. Why does God not always grant our prayers?
683. If prayer is necessary for salvation, how can infants be saved who die without having prayed?

Lesson Twenty-Ninth

684. Were people obliged to keep the commandments before the time of Moses?
685. How many kinds of laws had the Israelites?
686. When were these laws abolished?
687. How were the commandments given to Moses?
688. What was manna?
689. What is the difference between the commandments of God and the commandments of the Church?
690. What does "love thy neighbor as thyself" mean?

Lesson Thirtieth

691. How did the Israelites come to worship false gods?
692. How do we sometimes worship strange gods?
693. What are "fortune tellers"?
694. Why is going to fortune tellers a sin?
695. What are spells, charms?
696. Are medals, scapulars, etc., worn about us charms?
697. What are dreams?
698. Did God ever use them to make known his will?
699. Why does he not use them now?
700. What are mediums and spiritists?
701. How do bad Catholics do injury to the Church?

702. Why did the Christian religion spread so rapidly?
703. Who are atheists, deists, infidels, heretics, apostates, schismatics?
704. Are all religions equally true?
705. Why is presumption a great sin?
706. How are we frequently presumptuous?
707. Are heretics Christians?

Lesson Thirty-First

708. What help does God give us to save our souls?
709. How do we honor God by praying to the saints?
710. What is a relic?
711. Have we any relics of our Lord's body? Why?
712. Why does the Catholic religion suit all classes of persons?
713. Why are there so many kinds of protestants?
714. Does the Bible contain all the truths of our religion?
715. How did God honor the relics of saints? Give an example.
716. When did the Jewish religion cease to be the true religion?

Lesson Thirty-Second

717. Is it a sin to use the words of scripture in a bad sense?
718. What is a perjurer?
719. Why was John the Baptist put to death?
720. Why is it sinful to be a member of a secret society?
721. When is an oath rash?
722. What is the difference between blasphemy and cursing?
723. Can we blaspheme by action?
724. Tell what happened to Julian the Apostate.
725. Are there any holy days not of obligation?
726. How is the Sunday well kept?
727. What is a real Catholic newspaper?
728. What books should be found in every Catholic family?
729. What is meant by "the old law"?

730. What by "the new"?
731. Are we bound to keep an unlawful oath?

Lesson Thirty-Third

732. What do we mean by *magistrates*?
733. What should we remember when we are unjustly punished?
734. How does suffering make us more like to our Lord and his Blessed Mother?
735. Why did the Blessed Virgin suffer so many trials upon earth?
736. What is contempt?
737. What is stubbornness?
738. Why is suicide a mortal sin?
739. What is revenge?
740. Why should we be most careful about the sixth commandment?
741. Why should we guard against bad reading?
742. Why should we seek advice?

Lesson Thirty-Fourth

743. In how many ways may we violate the seventh commandment?
744. Why is it unkind and ungrateful not to pay our debts?
745. Is the receiver of stolen goods as bad as the thief?
746. In how many ways may we share in the sin of another?
747. If you bought an article not knowing that it was stolen, would you be obliged to give it up to its owner?
748. What must you do with anything you find?
749. What must you do if you have lost or destroyed the article you stole?
750. Can we always make restitution by giving to the poor?
751. Is it a sin to delay making restitution?
752. What must a person do who cannot restore?
753. What will excuse us for telling another's faults?
754. How can you know when you have injured the character of another?
755. What is detraction?
756. What is calumny?

757. What is slander?
758. How can you make reparation for injuring another's character?
759. Are you bound to do so?
760. What is "rash judgment"?
761. What is backbiting?
762. Is it sinful to listen to backbiting, slander, etc.?
763. Why is it wrong to tell another's secrets or read another's letters?
764. What does *covet* mean?

Lesson Thirty-Fifth

765. What is meant by a "serious reason" for missing Mass?
766. What excuse do some give for not hearing Mass?
767. Why is it wrong to come late for Mass?
768. On what day do we keep a saint's feast?
769. What is the "divine office"?
770. How is it divided?
771. Who are excused from fasting?
772. Who are obliged to abstain from flesh meat on fast days and days of abstinence?
773. Is every fast day a day of abstinence?

Lesson Thirty-Sixth

774. Why should we go to confession even when we have not committed sin since our last confession?
775. When is Trinity Sunday?
776. How was the Holy Land divided?
777. Who were the *Levites* in the old law?
778. What were *firstfruits* and *tithes* in the old law?
779. Why was Cain's sacrifice displeasing to God?
780. What relations are within the fourth degree of kindred?
781. What is a *dispensation* granted by the Church?
782. What is meant by the "natural law"?

783. When can we obey the laws that the state makes with regard to marriage?
784. What is *excommunication*?
785. What effect has it?
786. Who are excluded from Christian burial?
787. How does the Church show its displeasure when Catholics marry persons not Catholics?
788. How should persons prepare for marriage?
789. Are women ever allowed in the Church with their heads uncovered?
790. Can the priest say a "nuptial Mass" for a husband or wife after their death?

Lesson Thirty-Seventh

791. Where will the particular judgment be held?
792. How will it take place?
793. Will the sentence given at the particular judgment be changed at the general judgment?
794. How can we daily prepare for judgment?
795. Who will be judged at the general judgment?
796. How will the general judgment take place?
797. What do we mean by the "pain of loss"?
798. What is meant by the "pain of sense" that the damned suffer?
799. Why can we not imagine the sufferings of hell?
800. How does the fire of hell differ from our fire?
801. Will there be a purgatory after the general judgment?
802. Why must there be a purgatory now?
803. If God loves those in purgatory, why does he punish them?
804. Why do we show respect to the bodies of the dead?
805. What does "faithful departed" mean?
806. What does "rest in peace" mean?
807. What does "seeing God face-to-face" mean, if God has no face?
808. What is the beatific vision?
809. Of what does our happiness in heaven consist?
810. How long will purgatory last?

ABOUT THIS SERIES

Tradivox was first conceived as an international research endeavor to recover lost and otherwise little-known Catholic catechetical texts. As the research progressed over several years, the vision began to grow, along with the number of project contributors and a general desire to share these works with a broader audience.

Legally incorporated in 2019, Tradivox has begun the work of carefully remastering and republishing dozens of these catechisms which were once in common and official use in the Church around the world. That effort is embodied in this *Tradivox Catholic Catechism Index*, a multi-volume series restoring artifacts of traditional faith and praxis for a contemporary readership. More about this series and the work of Tradivox can be learned at www.Tradivox.com.

SOPHIA INSTITUTE

Sophia Institute is a nonprofit institution that seeks to nurture the spiritual, moral, and cultural life of souls and to spread the Gospel of Christ in conformity with the authentic teachings of the Roman Catholic Church.

Sophia Institute Press fulfills this mission by offering translations, reprints, and new publications that afford readers a rich source of the enduring wisdom of mankind.

Sophia Institute also operates the popular online resource Catholic Exchange.com. *Catholic Exchange* provides world news from a Catholic perspective as well as daily devotionals and articles that will help readers to grow in holiness and live a life consistent with the teachings of the Church.

In 2013, Sophia Institute launched Sophia Institute for Teachers to renew and rebuild Catholic culture through service to Catholic education. With the goal of nurturing the spiritual, moral, and cultural life of souls, and an abiding respect for the role and work of teachers, we strive to provide materials and programs that are at once enlightening to the mind and ennobling to the heart; faithful and complete, as well as useful and practical.

Sophia Institute gratefully recognizes the Solidarity Association for preserving and encouraging the growth of our apostolate over the course of many years. Without their generous and timely support, this book would not be in your hands.

www.SophiaInstitute.com
www.CatholicExchange.com
www.SophiaInstituteforTeachers.org

Sophia Institute Press® is a registered trademark of Sophia Institute.
Sophia Institute is a tax-exempt institution as defined by the
Internal Revenue Code, Section 501(c)(3). Tax ID 22-2548708.